Psychology in the World Today

THE AUTHOR

Robert V. Guthrie is a Professor of Psychology in the Behavioral Sciences Department at San Diego Mesa College. Professor Guthrie is a member of the Western Psychological Association and has taught at San Diego City College. He has also served as a supervising psychologist for San Diego County's Office of Economic Opportunity.

Psychology in the World Today

AN INTERDISCIPLINARY APPROACH

Edited by **ROBERT V. GUTHRIE**
San Diego Mesa College

ADDISON-WESLEY PUBLISHING COMPANY
Reading, Massachusetts · Menlo Park, California · London · Don Mills, Ontario

Printed in the United States of America. Published simultaneously in Canada. Library of Congress Catalog Card No. 68–25924.

Preface

Psychology In The World Today: An Interdisciplinary Approach has been compiled to meet the need of the college student for a well-integrated and modern book of readings which will contribute to his understanding of the behavioral sciences. This volume contains readings and discussions of how the behavioral sciences are in use today. Each of the fourteen units is introduced by a discussion designed to establish the relevancy of the unit and to aid the student in understanding the significance of the selections.

The absence of so-called classical studies and experimental reports is intentional. Though they give a scholarly appearance, they are likely to be confusing to students who, for the most part, will never become professional psychologists. Therefore, this is not just another traditional book of readings; rather, the emphasis is on the student.

These readings have been carefully selected from sources which, although scientifically accurate, are of primary interest to the layman rather than to psychologists or advanced psychology students. The selections, written by either behavioral scientists or outstanding science writers, are not ends in themselves. I have attempted to present different and opposing viewpoints within many of the units in order to provoke thought and discussion. In this way, the student becomes intellectually involved in his study of psychology.

The book is flexible in that it can be used as a text, when supplemented by classroom lectures and/or discussions, or it can be used as a helpful adjunct to a basic text.

To the many authors, editors, and publishers who directly or indirectly contributed suggestions and permission to use copyrighted materials I gratefully acknowledge my indebtedness and appreciation.

R. V. G.

San Diego, California
March 1968

Contents

Unit One **Introduction** 1

1 What Is Psychology? 1
ROBERT V. GUTHRIE, *San Diego Mesa College*

2 Significant Contributions in Psychology 3
ROBERT V. GUTHRIE, *San Diego Mesa College*

Unit Two **The Science of Behavior** 5

3 How Accurate Are Your Beliefs? 6
GREGORY A. KIMBLE, *Duke University,* and NORMAN GARMEZY, *University of Minnesota*

4 Undermining the Student's Faith in the Validity of "Common Sense" 7
RANCE HILL, *Kent State University*

5 Goals in Understanding Science 10
GLENN T. SEABORG, *U.S. Atomic Energy Commission*

6 Methodology in Behavioral Research 14
BERNARD BERELSON, *The Population Council,* and GARY A. STEINER, *University of Chicago*

7 Privacy and Behavioral Research 23
Panel on Privacy and Behavioral Research

Unit Three **The Psychobiological Determinants of Behavior** 31

8 DNA's Code: Key to All Life 32
ALICIA HILLS and ALBERT ROSENFELD, *Life Magazine*

9 That Odd Chemical Complex, the Human Mind 38
ISAAC ASIMOV, *Boston University Medical School*

10 How the Machine Called the Brain Feels and Thinks . . 47
DEAN E. WOOLDRIDGE, *California Institute of Technology*

11 The Interpretive Cortex 54
WILDER PENFIELD, *Montreal Neurological Institute*

Unit Four **Maturation and Learning** 69

12 What Do We Know About Learning? 70
GOODWIN WATSON, *Teachers College, Columbia University*

13 Formulas for Learning 74
Staff, Science News

14 Sex and the Nature of Things 77
N. J. BERRILL, M.D.

15 The Sex Ratio 81
ELIZABETH B. HURLOCK, *University of Pennsylvania*

16 Middle-Class Delinquency 83
DAVID ELKIND, *Rochester University*

17 Golden Years? 88
Staff, Ford Foundation

Unit Five **Individual Differences** 95

18 How Different Are They? 96
STANLEY F. YOLLES, *National Institute of Mental Health*

19 Individual Differences in Behavior and Autonomic Activity in Newborn Infants 100
WAGNER H. BRIDGER, *Albert Einstein College of Medicine*

20 Biological and Environmental Interchange in the Development of Children 102
JOHN B. REINHART, M.D. and ELIZABETH ELMER, M.S.S.

21 Environment Important 109
Staff, Science News

Unit Six **Evaluating and Measuring Behavior** 112

22 What Can We Predict? 113
RUBY YOSHIOKA, *Science News*

23 Methods of Expressing Test Scores 116
Psychological Corporation

24 The I.Q. Is an Intelligent Test 121
DAVID WECHSLER, *New York University School of Medicine*

25 Psychometric Scientism 128
BANISH HOFFMANN, *Queens College, City University of New York*

26 How to Cheat on Personality Tests 136
WILLIAM H. WHYTE, JR., *Fortune Magazine*

Unit Seven **Extrasensory and Subliminal Perception, Dreams, and Hypnosis** 144

27 The Uncomfortable Facts About Extrasensory Perception 145
IAN STEVENSON, *University of Virginia Medical School*

28 A Sixth Sense? 154
Staff, Soviet Life Magazine

29 Subliminal Perception 159
ANN ANASTASI, *Fordham University*

30 The Reality of Dreams 163
EDITH LEDERER, *Science News Letter*

31 Regarding Hypnosis 166
American Psychiatric Association

Unit Eight **Evaluating Abnormal Behavior** 169

32 One of the Great Mystery Stories of Medicine 170
LAWRENCE GALTON

33 Mental Illness Is a Myth 179
THOMAS S. SZASZ, *College of Medicine, State University of New York*

34 Psychiatrists Use Dangerous Words 188
KARL MENNINGER, *The Menninger Foundation*

35 The Defense of Insanity: A Survey of Legal and Psychiatric Opinion 192
RITA JAMES SIMON, *University of Illinois,* and WENDELL SHACKELFORD, *University of Pennsylvania*

Unit Nine **LSD, Alcohol, and Narcotic Addiction** 206

36 Ours Is the Addicted Society 208
LESLIE H. FARBER, M.D.

37 Deviance and Deviates 216
HOWARD S. BECKER, *Northwestern University*

38 Marijuana: Millions of Turned-on Users 224
ALBERT ROSENFELD, *Life Magazine*

39 LSD: A Remarkable Mind Drug Suddenly Spells Danger . 229
Staff, Life Magazine

40 Bright Light on the Alcoholic 236
GERARD LITTMAN, *Lakeview-Uptown Mental Center*

Unit Ten **Preventive Measures and Psychotherapy** 242

41 Prevention in Psychiatry 243
PAUL V. LEMKAU, *Johns Hopkins University*

42 Revolutionary Treatment of the Mentally Ill 250
CHANDLER BROSSARD, *Look Magazine*

43 Dr. Berne Plays the Celebrity Game 259
JACK LANGGUTH

44 Tracking Down the Causes of Birth Defects 267
RICHARD L. MASLAND, *National Institute of Neurological Disease and Blindness*

45 Children in Conflict 274
BARBARA CULLITON, *Science News*

Unit Eleven **Self-Understanding and Social Feeling** 279

46 The Will to Meaning 280
VIKTOR E. FRANKL, *University of Vienna Medical School*

47 Learning To Be Free 284
CARL R. ROGERS, *Western Behavioral Sciences Institute*

48 A Humanistic Psychology Is Born 289
HENRY WINTHROP, *University of South Florida*

49 Self-Understanding and Social Feeling 299
JAMES F. BRENNAN, *Western State School and Hospital*

Unit Twelve **College and Occupational Success** 305

50 Tomorrow's Jobs—Where the Best Will Be 306
Staff, Changing Times, The Kiplinger Magazine

51 Time to Kill: Automation, Leisure and Jobs 312
ERIC LARRABEE, *The Nation*

52 What People Think About College 318
Staff, American Education

53 Dear Freshman . . . If You Want Our Advice About . . . 323
The Intercollegian Magazine

54 College Students Change Majors 327
M. OLIN COOK, *Commission of Higher Educational Finance*

Unit Thirteen **Courtship and Marriage** 332

55 Marriage Is Not a Personal Matter 333
JOHN FINLEY SCOTT, *University of Washington*

56 Initial Adjustment Processes in Young Married Couples . 341
BEVERLY R. CUTLER and WILLIAM G. DYER, *Brigham Young University*

57 The Unsolved Mystery of Marriage 351
Staff, Changing Times, The Kiplinger Magazine

58 Eight Myths About Divorce 356
HUGH CARTER

Unit Fourteen **Applied Behavioral Sciences** 360

59 Psychology and the Space Frontier 361
WALTER F. GRETHER, *U.S.A.F. Aerospace Medical Research Laboratory*

60 The Impact of Television Advertising: Learning Without Involvement 370
HERBERT E. KRUGMAN, *Vice-President, MARPLAN*

61 Mind and Language 377
ROBERT T. OLIVER, *Pennsylvania State University*

Unit One Introduction

1 | What Is Psychology?

Psychology, a relatively new science, has grown from a varied foundation. Not until 1879 was the first laboratory established with behavior as its principal subject. When Wilhelm Wundt established his laboratory in Leipzig, Germany, he ushered in a new era in the study of behavior. Prior to this point, man's attempt to understand himself, his fellow man, and his environment was based primarily on speculations. Earlier views of behavior can be found in the writings of ancient civilizations and outstanding religious figures. Philosophers of other centuries introduced many ideas that today serve as a foundation for modern psychology. For example, the Greek philosophers Plato and Aristotle wrote concerning the "psyche" or "soul" as the basis of behavior. Between 1600 and 1800, Descartes, Hobbes, Locke, Hume, Leibnitz, and others contributed much to the understanding of human behavior.

Today's psychology is the scientific study of behavior; it attempts to understand life as it is lived. The student of psychology finds himself involved in a most interesting, interwoven kind of investigation. He finds himself concerned with struggles, pleasures, interests, desires, habits, aims, drives, motivations, feelings, actions, wants—all those bits of behavior that mold man into a complex, unique living being. Psychology not only attempts to understand behavior, it strives to predict and control behavior.

Psychology finds itself akin to various fields: psychiatry, sociology, linguistics, biology, anthropology, and political science. In emphasizing the fusion of our discipline with others, one psychologist recently stated that psychology thrives on polygamy with her kindred disciplines and that the marriage between psychology, anthropology, sociology, and the biological sciences has produced significant knowledge. This interdisciplinary involvement creates psychology as a behavioral science.

The behavioral sciences are those areas of academic inquiry which study the behavior of man. *Sociology* is the study of group life and social organization. *Anthropology* is the comparative study of man and his works, including physical characteristics, social habits, and customs. *Biology* is the study of living things. *Psychiatry* is the branch of medicine which studies and treats behavioral disorders. *Linguistics* is the study of languages which are expressive of man. *Political Science* is the study of human relationships that involve, to a significant extent, power and authority.

At the present time there are more than 25,000 American psychologists involved in a myriad of activities. The fact that the American Psychological Association is subdivided into twenty-six divisions testifies to the diversity of the field.

Divisions of the American Psychological Association

1. Division of General Psychology
2. Division on the Teaching of Psychology
3. Division of Experimental Psychology
5. Division of Evaluation and Measurement
6. Division of Physiological and Comparative Psychology
7. Division on Developmental Psychology
8. Division of Personality and Social Psychology
9. The Society for the Psychological Study of Social Issues
10. Division of Esthetics
12. Division of Clinical Psychology
13. Division of Consulting Psychology
14. Division of Industrial and Business Psychology
15. Division of Educational Psychology
16. Division of School Psychologists
17. Division of Counseling Psychologists
18. Division of Psychologists in Public Service
19. Division of Military Psychologists
20. Division on Maturity and Old Age
21. The Society of Engineering Psychologists
22. National Council on Psychological Aspects of Disability
23. Division of Consumer Psychology
24. Division of Philosophical Psychology
25. Division for the Experimental Analysis of Behavior
26. Division of the History of Psychology
27. Division on Community Psychology
28. Division of Behavioral Pharmacology

The purpose of the APA is to advance psychology as a science, as a profession, and as a means of promoting human welfare. It attempts to further these objectives by holding annual meetings, publishing psychological journals, and working toward improved standards for psychological training and service.

Approximately 35% of these psychologists work in colleges and universities. About 25% work in hospitals, penal institutions, research laboratories, and the armed forces. Others are employed by industry, public schools, businesses, and private practices. These figures, however, do not include the vast numbers of men and women who are working as aides and assistants in jobs of a psychological nature.

Frequently, a confusion exists in distinguishing between a *psychiatrist,* a *clinical psychologist,* and a *psychoanalyst.* The psychiatrist has a doctor of medicine (M.D.) degree in addition to specialized training in psychiatry. He diagnoses, prescribes treatment of either medicines or psychotherapies. The clinical psychologist usually has a doctor of philosophy (Ph.D.) degree and has received specialized training in psychology. He is primarily involved in administering psychological tests, research, and psychotherapy. He does not prescribe medicines. The psychoanalyst utilizes the basic methods and theories of psychoanalysis in the treatment of the mentally ill. He is usually a medical doctor.

RECOMMENDED READINGS

BERELSON, B. (Ed.), *The Behavioral Sciences Today*. New York: Harper & Row, 1964.

FINCHER, C., *A Preface to Psychology*. New York: Harper & Row, 1964.

HEIDBREDER, EDNA, *Seven Psychologies*. New York: Appleton-Century-Crofts, 1963.

MANDLER, G. and W. KESSEN, *The Language of Psychology*. New York: Wiley & Sons, Science Editions, 1959.

---

2 | Significant Contributions in Psychology

Approximate Date	*Contributions*
1879	Wilhelm Wundt established the first laboratory for the study of psychology.
1879	"Structuralist" viewpoint of psychology following the teachings of Wundt. (The emphasis was on the physiological bases of conscious experience through introspection.)
1884	G. Stanley Hall established the first psychological laboratory in America at Johns Hopkins University.
1890	William James published *The Principles of Psychology*.
1892	The American Psychological Association was formed.
1900	"Functionalist" viewpoint of psychology led by John Dewey. (The emphasis was on the value of mental experience in adjusting to the environment. Interested in behavior as well as conscious experience.)
1900	"Psychoanalysis" viewpoint of personality was established by Sigmund Freud. (Emphasis was on the unconscious mental processes.)
1908	First mental-age scale intelligence test created by Binet and Simon.
1909	National Committee for Mental Hygiene established in America largely through the efforts of Clifford Beers.
1912	"Gestalt" viewpoint in psychology introduced by Max Wertheimer. (Emphasis was on whole patterns of behavior rather than units.)
1914	"Behaviorist" viewpoint in psychology led by Pavlov and Watson. (Emphasis was on overt behavior.)
1916	Stanford Revision of the Binet-Simon intelligence test scale by Louis Terman, Stanford University.

1917	First mass use of group intelligence tests. The Army Alpha administered to 2,000,000 soldiers.
1921	Hermann Rorschach constructed ink-blot test.
1925	First teaching machine created by Sidney L. Pressey. (Concept of programed learning later expanded by B. F. Skinner.)
1926	Ivan Pavlov reported his work in "classical conditioning."
1929	Wechsler-Bellevue Intelligence scale created by David Wechsler.
1938	Instrumental/Operant conditioning postulated by B. F. Skinner.
1948	Concept of "client-centered" approach introduced by Carl Rogers.
1949	Wechsler Intelligence Scale for Children (WISC) developed.
1955	Wechsler Adult Intelligence Scale (WAIS) developed.
1960	Third revision of Stanford-Binet Intelligence Scale.

Unit One | DISCUSSION QUESTIONS

1. *What Is Psychology?*
   What similarities exist between psychology and other behavioral sciences?
   In what ways are the goals of the American Psychological Association similar to those of other professional organizations?
   How does this concept of psychology differ from what you expected it to be?
2. *Significant Contributions in Psychology*
   Why do you think so few significant contributions are listed for the years 1950 to the present?
   In what ways are the various *viewpoints* in psychology alike?

Unit Two *The Science of Behavior*

To define a science as "any body of organized knowledge which has been gathered through the use of systematic methods of investigation" (English and English)* introduces the foundation of psychological study. The goals of science are description, prediction, and control. Present scientific knowledge has been the result of conclusions reached by scientists all over the world. These conclusions have been the outgrowth of objective and critical observations. Objectivity, therefore, is a basic requirement for scientific observation. Observations are performed under carefully controlled conditions which are recorded by a predetermined method. Two well-defined methods are: (1) introspection and (2) observation. Introspection involves the contemplation and reporting of one's own experiences and behavior. As a result, introspection is subjective by its very nature, hence clinical objectivity is lost. Not all behavior is empirically verifiable by the scientist; some is implicit and requires the use of introspection. Objectivity, on the other hand, may be of two types: (1) scientific or critical, and (2) uncritical observation. Scientific observation involves accurate laboratory methods with suitable instruments of precision. It is performed by way of experimentation. Uncritical observation is that casual bit of notice given to that which, for some reason or another, catches the eye or interest. Noticing the behavior of others while you are walking on the campus, riding in an automobile, or waiting for the bus is an example of uncritical observation. This kind of observation, like introspection, is generally unreliable. Critical observation, on the other hand, is largely responsible for the accumulation of authentic knowledge now available concerning human behavior. Such knowledge is accurate whenever the observations are accurate. The preferred method of learning about behavior is through critical observation.

In the first task of this unit, you will be asked to decide, on the basis of prior knowledge, whether certain "common-sense" statements are true or false. Many students have voiced difficulty in substantiating their answers. Opinions which have been part of an individual's thoughts and ideas for many years are difficult to dispel; and, as a result, many are based on unsound and uncritical observations. Many have been reached by prejudiced or wishful thinking. The first reading by Rance Hill, *Undermining the Student's Faith in the Validity of "Common Sense,"* shows how a sociologist views the major source of these common-sense views. Hill offers insight into the preconceptions that block the acquisition of new knowledge to correct these views.

* Horace B. English and Ava Champney English, *A Comprehensive Dictionary of Psychological and Psychoanalytic Terms.* David McKay, Inc., New York, 1958.

Glenn T. Seaborg's *Goals in Understanding Science* recognizes two major interrelated objectives: (1) the utilization of man's capacity in increasing knowledge, and (2) the continuation of scientific freedom during social change. In addition, the author discusses gaps that need to be filled in our society in order to improve the public's understanding of the scientist.

In the third reading, *Methodology in Behavioral Research,* Bernard Berelson and Gary Steiner discuss three designs frequently used by the behavioral sciences: (1) the experiment, (2) the sample survey, and (3) the case study.

Occasionally the collection of research data has led to discussions concerning the propriety of certain procedures in gathering data. Research into the social behavior of humans has often been done without the knowledge of the individuals involved. As a result, individuals have frequently questioned whether this constitutes an invasion of privacy. The behavioral scientist, therefore, finds himself faced with a moral issue growing out of the attempt to understand behavior without sacrificing validity. *Privacy and Behavioral Research* is a condensation of a recent report made on this pressing subject.

---

3 | How Accurate Are Your Beliefs?

Below are a number of statements. Some of them you may consider true, some of them false.

1. A low forehead means a low level of intelligence.
2. People probably never learn anything while they are deeply asleep.
3. Genius and insanity have little or no relationship to each other.
4. Better college students make less money after graduation than average students.
5. Frequent masturbation leads to feeblemindedness.
6. A person who learns rapidly remembers longer than a person who learns slowly.
7. All people in America are born equal in capacity for achievement.
8. Animals lower than man are able to reason.
9. Teaching a child to roller skate very early in life will give him a permanent advantage in this skill.
10. People are definitely introverted or extroverted.

---

11. After you learn something you forget more of it in the next few hours than in the next several days.
12. Famous men tend to be born of poor but hard-working parents.
13. The intelligence of the average Negro is inferior to that of the dullest white.
14. Lessons learned just before going to sleep are remembered better than those learned early in the morning.
15. A moron is a person of perverted character.
16. On the average men of forty-five are more intelligent than those of twenty.
17. If one must punish a child, it is best to do it immediately after the misdeed.
18. Infants learn nothing until they are about a year old.
19. The tendency to imitate is probably learned.
20. There is a law of compensation in nature; e.g., blind persons are born with a highly developed sense of touch.
21. Child prodigies tend to maintain their superiority in later life.
22. To see a dim object at night, it is best to look slightly to one side of it.
23. An especially favorable environment can probably raise the IQ a few points.
24. If a person born blind were to have his sight restored as an adult, he would perceive the world as we see it almost immediately.

---

4 | Undermining the Student's Faith in the Validity of "Common Sense"

Rance Hill

The thesis of this article stems from a remark attributed to Einstein: "Common sense is the layer of prejudice laid down in our minds before we are 18." He was speaking of prejudice not in the racial or ethnic sense (though this would certainly apply), but of prejudice in the broader form of preconceptions adopted unquestioningly from the culture. In this form, "common sense" is a block to the student's learning because it is an inadequate mode of thought and presents a faulty frame of reference. If left

---

From *Mental Health,* January 1967, p. 69. Reprinted by permission of the author and publisher.

undisturbed, it tends either to stop learning, because of unrelieved tension between known and new material, or to lead to compartmentalized thinking, in which known and new material are kept separate.

These tendencies are especially unfortunate in the student of sociology, leading, as they do, to the allegation that sociology is only "common sense" and therefore obvious. Sociology is subject to this claim since it deals with the commonplace—man's interactions—the same subject matter that is the content of "common sense."

COMPONENTS OF "COMMON SENSE"

"Common sense" stems from two major sources, personal experience and the criterion of "obviousness," and from two processes, the substitution of correlation for cause and the organization of this material into a "folk knowledge." Since the first three of these components have been admirably delineated by Toby[1], Lazarsfeld[2], and Cameron[3], this article emphasizes folk knowledge.

Folk knowledge consists of the accretions and precipitates of the society's experiences over its history, which become embodied in the culture. It is marked by a duality of content and by a self-fulfilling process. The duality of content comes from two sources: (1) the nature of primary process thought [4], in which representation by allusion or analogy is frequent and in which mutually contradictory ideas may coexist peacefully, and (2) the dualistic nature of the value system of the culture[5]. The self-fulfilling process results from two sources, the first, the ex post facto application of the dictates of "common sense" and the second, reinforcement of this application through perceived consensuality.

Folk knowledge shares with the other components of "common sense" the characteristics of selective abstraction of data, the application of the preconceived frame of reference, and the development and acceptance of untested hypotheses. This becomes a circular process, reinforced by its own feedback, thus influencing the manner in which the student brings order to his own personal experiences and to any new subject matter.

THE EXPERIMENT

Since it is a reordering of the frame of reference that is being asked of the student and it is this frame that is blocking the acquisition of new knowledge, material from these preconceptions had to be used. The manner of such use needed to expose the duality of the mode of thought and of the value systems.

The students were asked to prepare a paper listing opposing maxims, aphorisms, homilies, epigrams, or proverbs. The possibilities are enormous, so only a few examples are given from the student papers.

> Man is Heaven's masterpiece.—Frances Quarles
> Man is Nature's sole mistake.—W. S. Gilbert

> It is better to know useless things than to know nothing.—Seneca
> 'Tis better not to know than knowing err.—Ben Franklin

The cheerful loser is a winner.—Elbert Hubbard
Losers are always in the wrong.—H. G. Bond

People are more fun than anybody.—Dorothy Parker
The only real people are the people who never existed.—Oscar Wilde

REACTIONS FROM THE EXPERIMENT

Student comments give some insight into the usefulness of the experiment.

> Man is plagued throughout his life with many opposing sayings which cause his life to be more trying. Rarely can he make a decision in which he cannot apply a saying and then find one which contradicts it. Now man can't even look to the past for "words of wisdom."

> Though these and many other sayings are commonly, and often loosely, used, the sociologist should beware of them when trying to find basis for fact. Probably every folk saying or adage has an opposite which directly negates it. We, of course, accept these sayings as a part of our everyday life and American culture. For a sociologist to form a valid hypothesis based on any of them would be dangerous indeed.

Since the purpose of the experiment was not explained, the comments serve to point toward the validity of the approach used.

DISCUSSION

When the student is asked to examine the concept of "common sense" and to judge by inference whether it is the same as, or preferable to, a sociological view, he is faced with the understanding that the imposition of an a priori form of logic masks rather than exposes what actual order may be present. He begins to recognize that "common sense" and a scientific sense are of two different orders of logic, that the first is an attempt to impose order whereas the second is a search for existing order. If the student is freed of the dictum of "common sense" that holds that "what ought to be, is," he is prepared for the sociological admonition of "what is, not what ought to be."

REFERENCES

1. Toby, J., *American Sociological Review,* **20**:717 (December), 1955.
2. Lazarsfeld, P. E., "Sociology and Common Sense," in Barron, M. L. (ed.), *Contemporary Sociology*. New York, Dodd, Mead and Company, 1964, pp. 27–28.
3. Cameron, W. B., *Informal Sociology*. New York, Random House, 1963, pp. 7–11.
4. Brenner, C., *An Elementary Textbook of Psychoanalysis.* Garden City, N.Y., Doubleday, 1955, p. 53.
5. Lynd, R. S., *Middletown in Transition.* New York, Harcourt, Brace and Company, 1937.

5 | Goals in Understanding Science

Glenn T. Seaborg

Why should it be so important that our people understand something about science? Why should people know what a scientist does, what motivates him, and the implications of scientific results? What are our goals?

In my opinion, there are two major, interrelated goals. The first is philosophical, involving the quality and the dignity of human life and the fullest use by man of his capacities; in sum, the increase in man's significance. The evolution of cultures from the primitive to the sophisticated, from intellectual poverty to intellectual riches, from needless fears and superstitions to the relative security of relative understanding; these forward movements have been paced by the painstaking ascent of the mountain of knowledge.

Our lives are better for knowing the sources of lightning and earthquakes, and for understanding that the earth, far from being the center of the universe, is but a tiny speck in a pageant of immense grandeur.

KNOWLEDGE ENRICHES

We are enriched by knowing why a tree is green and how it captures and stores the energy of the sun, and thereby grows.

To know that we inherit our individual characteristics from a lovely, orderly strand of molecules and to comprehend the arrangement of those molecules seems to me to be a triumph for the human spirit, entirely apart from the future practical nature of this knowledge.

All of this knowledge, it seems to me, increases and in no way diminishes man. For me, the beauty of a starry night or a forest or a rainbow is enhanced by an understanding of them. Nor does scientific knowledge, in my opinion, reduce appreciation of a poet's sonnet, a musician's theme or a painter's canvas.

A second major goal, not unrelated to the first, is concerned with the continuation of freedom and of the most effective functioning of democratic government in a period of revolutionary social change. This revolution is well-named "The Scientific Revolution," since the engines that drive it are science and technology. In the last three decades, science, once a peripheral preoccupation of a few intellectuals, has emerged as a central force in domestic and world affairs. . . .

Excerpts of remarks by Dr. Glenn T. Seaborg, Chairman, U.S. Atomic Energy Commission at the Arches of Science Award Banquet, Pacific Science Center, Seattle, Oct. 19. From *Science News,* **90**, 292, 1966. Reprinted by permission of *Science News,* weekly summary of current science, © 1966 by Science Service, Inc.

Today, flourishing industries, employing thousands of people, are based on knowledge that did not exist a decade ago. We use science and technology as instruments for improving the material quality of human life, both in our own country and abroad.

Moreover, we are dependent upon science and an aggressively exploitative technology for the continuation of the kind of society in which we now live. And we must redouble these efforts if we are to realize present, and perhaps better, living conditions for immensely larger populations in the world of the future.

All of this means, of course, that some of the most important decisions affecting our lives and those of millions of people around the world revolve around science and technology. Our form of government is flexible enough so that we have, I believe, an excellent cross section of representation in making these decisions in the executive and legislative branches of the government. This representation is similar in kind to that employed in technical decisions in finance, foreign affairs, agriculture, and other fields.

Yet, the heart of freedom and its agency, democracy, is widespread, informed participation in the processes of government. I fear that the central forces of change in today's world—science and technology—are but dimly understood, or not understood at all, by the majority of the electorate.

We cannot hope that now, or perhaps ever, the majority of people will be able to explain the quantum theory or the third law of thermodynamics. Nor is this necessary. But I believe there are minimum levels of understanding that can be conveyed to all citizens and there is more sophisticated knowledge that can be conveyed to a large percentage of our people.

Such understanding can, I believe, help our society to react more intelligently and quickly, and in a democratic way, to challenge and opportunity as we travel farther along the road of the Scientific Revolution.

We may learn, for example, to better adapt to swift social changes like those forced by automation, more readily accept necessary technologies such as automation and nuclear power, and perhaps even support science for the right reasons. . . .

There are certain fundamental ideas that, I believe, virtually every citizen can grasp and that represent minimum attainable levels in public understanding. The minimum level that can be achieved almost universally, I believe, is an understanding of what science is, what technology is, and the difference between the two.

SEARCH FOR KNOWLEDGE

As we all know, science is a search for an understanding of new knowledge about nature. Generally, it does not have an immediately practical goal, although sometimes applications may be easy to foresee. The essence of basic research is freedom of the scientist to pursue his curiosity where it leads him.

New knowledge is hard to acquire; nevertheless, it is necessary in order to synthesize the bits and pieces into general laws representing major progress.

On the other hand, technology, or more correctly engineering development, involves the transformation of the knowledge we gain from basic science into useful things. Our radios, television sets, automobiles, synthetic fibers and plastics, nuclear reactors and moon rockets are all engineering developments rising from towering edifices of basic knowledge erected by chemists and physicists. . . .

Confusion over what science is and is not can do considerable mischief. Not uncommonly, men are hostile to what they do not understand. Many people, among them some otherwise well informed individuals, are critical of government support of science.

Not infrequently this criticism is based on two mistaken notions: first, that the $15 billion annual Federal budget for research and development is all for "science," and second, that "science" may not be "producing" enough "gadgets" to justify the outlay. Actually, only about $1.5 billion, or about 10 per cent of this sum, is allocated for basic science, with the remainder being allocated for applications of knowledge.

Lack of understanding causes still other mischief. Science receives much credit for its accomplishments, of course, but it also is the whipping boy for those who would like to find a simple explanation for man's destructive weapons.

It is true, for example, that nuclear weapons were an outgrowth of new scientific knowledge. But so is the nuclear reactor, which promises to perpetuate a technological civilization that is dependent upon the production of huge quantities of energy.

In other words, knowledge is born without moral properties. It is man who applies knowledge, and he applies it according to his acquired patterns of behavior. The point is that misunderstanding on this can mislead us about causality. Man, not knowledge, is the cause of violence. . . .

A great deal of dedicated work toward public understanding of science has been done for many years, and is being expanded. A commendable contribution is being made by newspapers, magazines, television, radio and through educational films to give the public a sense of the significance and scope of scientific discovery.

Considerable credit belongs to the National Association of Science Writers and the Council for the Advancement of Science Writing for improving and increasing the nation's corps of professional writers on science for the mass media.

Private foundations and the Government have supported these and other efforts at popularization. Science Service, of which I have the honor to be president, has done yeoman's service for over 40 years in popularizing science through its news services and Science News Letter, now Science News.

The scientific societies have also established helpful programs, among them the American Association for the Advancement of Science, the American Institute of Physics and the American Chemical Society. Government agencies, including the National Science Foundation and the Atomic Energy Commission, have made significant efforts to explain science to the public.

Occupying the middle ground is the unique Scientific American, serving highly motivated, intelligent laymen as well as scientists, engineers and other technical people. I had the privilege of being among the company of those who encouraged Gerard Piel and Dennis Flanagan in launching this valuable publication in 1948.

SOME GAPS

I wonder if there are not some gaps in the popularization of science in the mass media for communication that might be filled to the profit of media management and the public. For example, some surveys indicate that the public is interested in reading more science than they are getting in the newspapers.

Is there a place, for example, for more regular column or feature material that would make good reading and that, being free of the restriction of the news lead, would provide a larger opportunity for revealing more about the rather interesting processes and personalities of science? Is there a place for a national science newspaper?

Might it not be profitable to publish a high quality popular science magazine that would interest a mass audience? In connection with these thoughts, I believe it is germane to remember that the technically oriented community is growing larger every day, and will inevitably grow larger in the future.

While the mass media are the primary instruments for informing the present generation on science, I have always believed that there should be intensive concentration on developing a future electorate well versed in the principles and processes of science.

I believe we can all take heart in the significant programs that have been developing in recent years to make science a real part of the education of the young. These include experimental programs to develop materials and techniques for teaching science to elementary school children.

The curricula of high school science have been immensely improved by the work in physics of the Physical Sciences Study Committee and Educational Services, Inc.; by the work in chemistry of the Chemical Educational Material (CHEM) Study and the Chemical Bond Approach Project; and by the work in biology of the Biological Sciences Study Committee.

Science Service's extensive program with its local science fairs and its International Science Fair, and with its more than 25,000 youth science clubs having over three-quarters of a million members, is making an important impression on a national and international basis.

NEW CENTERS RISING

New centers, with dynamic concepts for imparting knowledge of science, are beginning to rise. The Pacific Science Center is an outstanding example. The Lawrence Hall of Science, in Berkeley, holds great promise, being in part a national research institute on the teaching of science at all levels. The new Hall of Science of the City of New York is also incorporating programs to assist the schools in the improvement of science teaching. All of these fine centers also provide science learning opportunities for the public at all age levels. . . .

I should like to touch on one other subject that is pertinent to the matter of public understanding of science, and it involves the scientists themselves. Science long since has departed the ivory tower, as any researcher can testify who has been called to a Congressional hearing. I believe there is wide appreciation among scientists of the value of public understanding of what the scientist is doing.

Scientists have been among those who have taken the lead in many efforts to improve public understanding. The ethical code and the culture of science, however, often inhibit the efforts of scientists in this field. I would hope that senior scientists might help to break down needless inhibitions among their students and junior colleagues. I would hope that senior scientists would encourage those among their juniors who have a talent for popularization to cultivate that talent in acceptable ways.

In conclusion, I offer my congratulations to this community for contributing, through the Arches of Science Award and the Pacific Science Center Foundation, to one of the most important educational problems of our time. I believe that we are only at the beginning of the Scientific Revolution.

As this Revolution accelerates, so will our dependence on the processes of science and technology. We can expect change to be swifter and more profound. The decisions we must make will increasingly involve science and applications of new knowledge. Wisdom in self-government requires that we as a people know more and still more about those processes of the Scientific Revolution that deeply affect our lives.

Let our learning, however, not be only a duty. For in the learning, I am sure, larger numbers of us will come to enjoy the rich experience of seeing the wonders of our environment through the revealing eyes of science.

---

6 | Methodology in Behavioral Research

Bernard Berelson and Gary A. Steiner

DESIGN

In the broadest terms, there are three designs used in the behavioral sciences: the experiment, the sample survey, and the case study.

The Experiment

By *experiment* is meant any investigation that includes two elements: manipulation or control of some variable by the investigator and systematic

From *Human Behavior: An Inventory of Scientific Findings* by Bernard Berelson and Gary A. Steiner, © 1964, by Harcourt, Brace & World, Inc., and reprinted with their permission.

observation or measurement* of the result. In short, it means active intervention on the phenomena of interest to see what, if any, effects are produced by the intervention.

The experiment has had a central place in the history of science. The importance of experimentation depends not so much on its precision, its objectivity, or its instruments as on the inherent efficiency of intervention in disentangling cause-and-effect relationships. Whenever its use is feasible, intentional intervention is the method that most readily exposes cause and effect; and if the behavioral sciences were able to experiment more widely on their materials they would be better equipped today with important findings. For example, we would know much more about the effects on personality of different ways of rearing children if experimentation were not precluded on moral and humanitarian grounds. And the field is currently making some progress on such basic problems as mental disease and emotional disturbance by means of physiological intervention in the nervous system accompanied by controlled observation of the behavioral results. The implantation of tiny electrodes in the brain has been used to induce fear, rage, joy, even "pleasure"; and ultimately such mapping of the brain centers that mediate emotions may have far-reaching clinical implications. Similarly, in human beings, chemical intervention has produced behavior that closely resembles certain manifestations of schizophrenia; and, in animals, certain parts of the brain have been systematically removed to see what effect that has on learned problem-solving.

The Classical Experiment

The prototype of scientific experimentation, and in many ways its most foolproof form, is the classical experiment. The general question it answers is whether, and to what extent, one variable (called the experimental or independent variable) affects another variable (the dependent variable).

The logic is simple. Two groups are matched at the outset; one is given the experimental intervention (a piece of propaganda, a new drug that affects behavior, a French lesson taught in a new way, a special procedure that can introduce changes in working procedures in a factory); the result of the intervention is subsequently measured (i.e., its effect on attitudes, on personality, on the amount of French learned, on morale and productivity). The essentials of the classical experiment can be schematized as follows:

Experimental group, but not control group, exposed to intervention (the experimental or independent variable)

	Before	*After*
Experimental group or subject	B_e	A_e
Control group or subject	B_c	A_{cc}

* By *measurement* the behavioral scientist typically means something broader than what the term means to the layman. The behavioral scientist considers that an attitude has been measured if it can simply be distinguished as "for" or "against," "more" or "less." Finer quantitative distinctions, of course, are also measurements, but so are dichotomies or classificatory categories in general.

The figures represent measurements of the dependent variable, and the effect of the experimental variable is $(A_e - A_c) - (B_e - B_c)$.

Here is an illustration of a classical experiment concerned with the effects of a new tranquilizer pill on psychotic behavior:

1. Define the population of subjects and draw a sample—e.g., a random sample of all the patients with a given diagnosis at a certain institution.

2. Divide the sample at random into two groups. By definition the two groups will now be similar, within limits of sampling error, on *any* measurement. Thus there is no reason to expect one group to behave any differently in the future than the other. Flip a coin to decide which will be "experimental" and which "control."

3. Define the dependent variable ("psychotic behavior"): How will it be measured or rated? Take a "before" measurement on each group.

4. Define the experimental variable precisely—What doses of the tranquilizer over what period of time?—and administer it to the experimental group only. The control group will probably get a placebo—a pill that looks the same but has no active ingredients—to control for the effects of autosuggestion, and even for the effect of participating in the experiment at all (since that will involve some special attention, at the least. In some cases of this kind, for extra precaution, the experiment is "double blind": not only does the subject not know which pill he gets but, in order to control the expression of his own (conscious or unconscious) wishes in the matter, the experimenter does not know at the time either.

5. Take "after" measurements of the dependent variable on each group.

6. The difference between the two groups after the experiment, beyond any difference that may have existed before, is the effect of the experimental variable. In this case, it is the effect of the tranquilizer upon psychotic behavior.

The glory of the classical experiment is that its logic has no loophole. When all the conditions of the classical experiment have been met, and all four cells have been filled in, the final difference between control and experimental group *must* be due to the effect of the experimental or independent variable: both groups reflect the effects of any other variables not directly manipulated by the experimenter (such as time itself, atmospheric conditions, or the effects of having been selected to participate in the study). Thus the control group protects the experimenter against many of the common fallacies that plague less rigorous studies. Before-and-after observation of an experimental group alone is particularly vulnerable to the fallacy of *post hoc, ergo propter hoc.* Without a control group there is a temptation to attribute any subsequent change in the observed subjects to the experimental variable, whereas the change may have occurred without the experimenter's intervention.

Although there is a logical model for the classical experiment, in actual experiments the design is frequently modified for various reasons: costs, practical difficulties, and so on. In some cases, statistical approximations will do. For example, if the experimental and control groups are truly divided at random, the before-measurement may be omitted in the knowledge that the two groups will vary only within known limits of sampling error. The experiment simply consists of the administration of the experimental condition to one group and the subsequent after-measurements of both. If this after-measurement records a difference between the two groups that cannot be attributed to chance variation, it is taken to be the result of the experimental variable.*

Similarly, many experiments add onto the basic four-fold model. Some measure the effect of the experimental variable over time: propaganda may be effective right after its administration, but how long does it last? Others assess the effects of several experimental variables within a single investigation. The simplest form of this involves two or more experimental groups, each of which is measured against a single control group. For example, the patients can be divided into three or more groups: one is the control, one gets tranquilizer A, one gets tranquilizer B, etc.

Moreover, modern statistical designs make it possible to evaluate the relative effects of a number of independent variables acting simultaneously and in combination. An investigation of classroom learning might vary the method of instruction, the sex of the teacher, the room lighting, and student motivation, all at one stage of observations; and then conclude which of these factors is the most important influence on learning, and how they act in combination.

So much for the general logic of experimental design: the principal point, worth repeating, is that the fundamental advantage of experimentation is not its precision or its instrumentation but its inherent logical rigor. Now let us apply the method to the settings and subjects of behavioral science experimentation. In our field, we can distinguish experiments in the laboratory and in natural settings.

The Laboratory Experiment—Animal. Behavioral scientists, notably psychologists, conduct intensive studies on animals in the laboratory: historically, the animals have usually been rats, pigeons, or apes. Why study lower animals when the objective is to understand people? The reasons are both practical and theoretical.

On the practical side, many experiments cannot be conducted on human subjects for legal and moral reasons—e.g., the behavioral effect of systematic destruction of various parts of the nervous system. In general, any experimental variable that involves bodily harm or undue pain, discomfort, embarrassment, or psychological or social damage is naturally excluded from

---

* It is sometimes hard to believe, but it is still true, that when a group has been divided at random into two groups, the groups will differ by no more than chance on *any* characteristic whatsoever. The proportion of blue-eyed people in the two groups, of redheads, of people over and under 5′7″, of Catholics, of those who skipped breakfast this morning, of those opposed to capital punishment or in favor of a stronger United Nations—all will be roughly equivalent. There are statistical procedures that determine the probability of a given difference having arisen simply by such random division. Therefore, when a difference is greater than that which could reasonably be expected on the basis of random division, and the groups have in fact been randomly divided, the conclusion is that the difference is not due to their division but to something that happened to them afterward.

experimental intervention with human subjects. In addition, animals are cheap, they cannot resist captivity, they are almost always available, and they do not have to be paid for their services.

On the theoretical side, the environment of animals, unlike that of human beings, can be completely and systematically controlled twenty-four hours a day. The lower animals reproduce more quickly and in greater numbers than human beings, and their mating can be controlled, thus making possible longitudinal studies of hereditary effects. With animals, far greater homogeneity of subjects can be attained by inbreeding, thus reducing sources of behavioral variation that are irrelevant and bothersome for some purposes. Animals are presumably simpler and thus more easily understood than people, hence some scientists argue that the study of human behavior must begin with the simpler forms (in the sense that arithmetic has to be mastered before the calculus). Finally, the acceptance of evolution as a biological fact leads to the assumption that, in principle, the processes underlying human behavior are an outgrowth of those represented in lower forms, and therefore the study of animals cannot be irrelevant. Findings from animal studies are not expected to be directly replicated in human behavior, but they may well provide the foundations on which the elaborations introduced at the human level must be built.

The Laboratory Experiment—Human. Human beings are also studied intensively in laboratory situations, both individually and in groups. Given the practicalities of the matter, the human beings involved are usually college students, and many of the practical advantages of using lower animals apply as well with students as subjects: they do not have to be paid, they are readily accessible, and they often cannot effectively resist the experimentation.*

We have reviewed the theoretical justification for studying rats and pigeons. What is the justification for using college sophomores or, more generally, representatives of any selected type of human subject for laboratory investigation?

The answer depends largely upon the expected variation of the phenomenon under study. There is little reason to suspect, for example, that the visual or auditory processes of college students vary considerably from those of other types of people; or that their eye movements, which signal dreams, are unique. Accordingly, the tendency to generalize to people at large on such issues is frequently supported by further studies, and college students turn out to be a reasonably good sample of human beings on such limited topics as those closely tied to physiological processes.

However, when the question deals with political attitudes, feelings toward the family, reactions to stress, life values, or such complicated or culturally determined matters, it is safest to assume, until proved otherwise, that there *are* important differences between college students and other cate-

* In this connection, it is worth recalling an observation of the late Edward Tolman, a distinguished psychologist. He once noted how much of American psychology was based on two sets of subjects, rats and college sophomores, and enjoined his colleagues to remember that the former certainly are not people and the latter may not be!

gories of citizens. Hence, a priori generalizations of findings of this character must be avoided.

Another general problem of much experimental work done in the laboratory is that of "translation." Some laboratory experiments deal with phenomena that can be reproduced directly in the laboratory, such as depth perception, small-group problems, or the learning of certain skills. In these cases, the experimenter simply brings the behavior of interest into the laboratory for more careful scrutiny under experimental conditions. Many phenomena, however, cannot be transplanted to a laboratory either in principle or for such practical considerations as time, money, cooperation of subjects, and so on; or the phenomenon that interests the experimenter is a general one (motivation, love, hostility) that must be delineated to one specific instance for a given investigation. Such conditions require acts of "translation": before the experiment, translation of the phenomena of interest to the experimenter into the specific laboratory operations that will "tap" them; after the experiment, translation of the results of the specific operations performed back into the original concepts and phenomena.

An illustration will, we hope, make the point. The psychoanalytic notion of "repression" states that under certain circumstances individuals will force out of their awareness the memories of certain traumatic or psychologically damaging events. In addition, some impulses or desires that are unacceptable (e.g., killing or having sexual relations with one's father) may be repressed, that is, not be consciously acknowledged although they are actively present in the personality. When experimentally inclined psychologists wanted to test some of these notions in the laboratory, one design used was to show subjects a series of pictures—some pleasant, some unpleasant or gruesome—and at a later sitting ask them to describe the pictures seen. So the hypothesis that traumatic events get repressed is translated into the test: "Gruesome pictures will be accurately recalled less frequently than non-gruesome pictures."

Evaluation of such experimental results demands critical consideration of the translation involved and its validity. Students of repression might reject the experiment (as many of them did) not because it was poorly designed or failed to produce conclusive results but simply because they considered it irrelevant to their views of the concept of repression.

Note how this example illustrates the scientific requirement that results be reported operationally (what was done) as well as conceptually or theoretically (what they mean). When the experimenter reports that gruesome pictures were not described accurately with the same frequency as non-gruesome pictures, behavioral scientists can decide for themselves what relevance, if any, the finding has for issues in which they are interested.

The Natural Experiment

Frequently the major elements of an experiment occur or are produced in the natural habitat of the behavior under study. Such experimentation avoids many of the problems of the laboratory situation discussed above, e.g., oversimplification and artificiality. In the natural experiment the subjects ordinarily do not know they are under investigation and hence do not modify their behavior as a result of being watched. On the other hand, natural experimentation is usually less precise, because the pertinent events are less fully under the experimenter's control.

The Planned Natural Experiment. In this type, as in the laboratory, the investigator intentionally manipulates the independent variable and then makes systematic measurements of the result. The tranquilizer study is an example; so is the illustrative study mentioned above dealing with classroom learning. A planned natural experiment often used in advertising research is the "split-run" technique: metropolitan newspapers frequently offer advertisers the opportunity to run two versions of an advertisement in the same issue, with coupons or other coded devices enabling "returns" from the two versions to be compared.

The Spontaneous Natural Experiment. Sometimes behavioral scientists are fortunate enough to come on a situation that happened by itself yet has most or all of the elements of a successful experiment. In such cases, an approximation of experimental results may be obtained.

For example, when television was being introduced, there was a period during which technical considerations were the principal determinants of which towns and cities would have stations. Thus it was possible to find a number of cities without TV and to know about when the medium would be introduced in them. This provided an opportunity to study "what television does" on a before-and-after basis, as compared with matched towns without TV (the controls). Similarly, studying the culture of a primitive community during and after the advent of technological developments provides an attenuated natural experiment under spontaneous conditions. Since, as noted above, the absence of a proper control is the technical failing of such studies, the investigator must often decide between naturalness and control, or compromise on some of each.

The Sample Survey

The sample survey, as a type of research design, does not refer simply to a public opinion poll, though a properly designed poll is certainly one example of a sample survey, and probably the most familiar one. In our sense, a sample survey is properly named in that it contains the indicated two elements:

1. *A sample.* The investigator first decides what group or "population" he is interested in (American adults, voters, women of childbearing age, college students, etc.) and then selects a sample in the statistical sense. It may be "random," "representative," "quota," "weighted," or any of a number of technical types. The main point is that the sample is so chosen as to enable the experimenter to draw conclusions regarding the entire "population" and not simply those members of the population who happen to turn up in the sample.

2. *A survey.* The investigator then collects some measures on the appropriate characteristics of the population being studied (number of television sets or children in the household; how the members feel about Russia or religion; what they know about India or space; and so on).

Obviously there are certain questions that can be answered only by a sample survey. The question, "To what extent do American psychologists today believe that extrasensory perception exists?" can be answered by specifying a population and then asking a selected sample. No experiment will answer the question once and for all and neither will a case study. In general, whenever the investigator is interested in assessing or estimating the present state of affairs with regard to some variable that changes over time for a large group of subjects, a sample survey is the only practical way to get the answer. If the variable did not change over time, we could probably learn the answer once and for all by experiment; or if there were interest in only one or a few instances, case studies could provide the answer. These are certainly not the only conditions under which the sample survey is useful, but these are the conditions under which it is the imperative form of design.

In addition to simple measures of magnitude (How many people will vote?), sample surveys provide clues to relations between variables (and thus ultimately to cause and effect) by correlation of the various measures obtained. For example, a survey of number of children per family can provide a series of tables showing how fertility varies by families of differing class, race, rural-urban residence, religion, etc. This example, incidentally, illustrates another advantage of the sample survey in the study of relationships: many times the variables of interest are difficult or impossible to manipulate by experiment (years of schooling, race), so the only approach is to compare people who already differ on the characteristic in question and see how their behavior differs.

Such correlations are difficult to disentangle causally, because the direction of the influence is uncertain (and it is often reciprocal, which makes the matter more difficult still). To take a simple example, a correlation between reading an advertisement for a given make of car and buying the car could go either way—reading influenced purchase, purchase influenced reading. Even when the direction is clear, when one characteristic (e.g., race) antedates and is not affected by another (e.g., fertility), the nature of the causal relationship is quite complex, with several other factors usually involved (e.g., income, social position, religion, place of residence, age at marriage).

To handle change over time in certain investigations, a variant of the sample survey has been developed that is called the panel. This requires repeated measures of the appropriate characteristics on the same people, so that the investigation can study how changes were brought about over time. This method is particularly useful in campaigns that bring a variety of stimuli to the subjects' attention, and it is no accident that the method is used mainly in studies of marketing and voting. A major limitation of the panel technique is that, as the same people are queried repeatedly, they may change their behavior simply as a result of panel membership. As a control, panel responses are often checked against samples of "fresh" respondents.

The Case Study

The case study is complementary to the sample survey. The sample survey measures many people on few characteristics, usually at one point in time.

The case study intensively examines many characteristics of one "unit" (person, work group, company, community, culture), usually over a long period of time. The goal of such investigations is to learn "all" about the area of interest for the one case involved. Typical case studies in the behavioral sciences might include: the life history of a psychotic; an intensive analysis of a patient's psychological disturbance;* an anthropological monograph describing in detail the technology and customs of a primitive culture; a detailed description and analysis of the socioeconomic classes existing in a small Southern town.

As the examples suggest, the detail and the depth of information over time that the case study provides makes this design particularly relevant for questions involving etiology and development: How does a particular neurotic manifestation emerge and change over time? What are the critical incidents that lead up to an industrial strike? How does the industrialization of a traditional society affect the family?

The chief limitation of this method is that the results are based on a sample of one, so that the degree of their generality is not known. Would another individual, another company, another community, another culture respond in the same way? In addition, the case study is often subject to the *post hoc, ergo propter hoc* fallacy, since neither a "control group" nor intervention by the investigator is provided as a safeguard.

Hence, case studies rarely *prove* anything, although they are frequently rich in clues and insights for further investigation. In many areas the case study is the idea-getting investigation par excellence. But since in this book we limit ourselves to what is more or less proved about human behavior, we shall bring in the results of case studies only when they have been verified in some way.

RECOMMENDED READINGS

R. G. Barker and H. F. Wright, *One Boy's Day: A Specimen Record of Behavior.* Harper, 1951.

W. G. Cochran and Gertrude M. Cox, *Experimental Designs,* 2nd Ed. Wiley, 1950.

John Dollard, *Criteria for the Life History.* Yale University Press, 1935.

A. L. Edwards, *Experimental Design in Psychological Research,* Rev. Ed. Holt, Rinehart & Winston, 1960.

R. A. Fisher, *The Design of Experiments.* 4th Ed. Oliver & Boyd, 1947.

Herbert Hyman, *Survey Design and Analysis.* Free Press, 1955.

Herbert Hyman *et al., Interviewing in Social Research.* University of Chicago Press, 1954.

---

* In fact, case studies are one of the principal sources of data on many questions in clinical psychology, since the practicing clinician is interested in specific individuals and collects intensive data on his patients. The most important questions in this area revolve around such time-bound issues as how and when the various syndromes arise, develop, and change. Thus, clinical histories have practical significance for the therapist and stimulate many hypotheses in personality theory.

HENRY MURRAY, ed., *Explorations in Personality: A Clinical and Experimental Study of Fifty Men of College Age*. Oxford University Press, 1938.

SAMUEL A. STOUFFER *et al., Measurement and Prediction*. Princeton University Press, 1950.

---

7 | Privacy and Behavioral Research

Preliminary Summary of the Report of the Panel on Privacy and Behavioral Research

In recent years there have been growing threats to the privacy of individuals. Wiretapping, electronic eavesdropping, the use of personality tests in employment, the use of the lie detector in security or criminal investigations, and the detailed scrutiny of the private lives of people receiving public welfare funds all involve invasions of privacy. Although the social purpose is usually clear, the impact on the persons involved may be damaging. Our society has become more and more sensitive to the need to avoid such damage.

This concern has led to extensive discussion about the propriety of certain procedures in behavioral research, by the Congress, by officials in the various agencies of the Government, by university officials, by the scientific community generally, and by leaders in professional societies in the behavorial sciences. The Office of Science and Technology appointed a panel, in January 1966, to examine these issues and to propose guidelines for those who are engaged in behavioral research or associated with its support and management.

The panel has restricted its attention to issues of privacy arising in connection with programs of data collection and study which are intimately associated with behavioral research. For example, it has not reviewed a number of the programs for data collection which are sponsored by the Federal Government, such as the various censuses, health and welfare statistics, and financial information secured from business and industry. These programs may also encroach upon the privacy of individuals, either through the burden of disclosure which they impose on respondents or through their availability for unintended purposes.

It is our opinion that the principles described in this report for protection of privacy in behavioral research should apply equally to such inquiries. When response is mandatory, as in the case of information that must be furnished to the Government, there is an even greater burden on the sponsoring agency to protect the individual against disclosure unless disclosure is specifically sanctioned by statute.

The panel has not reviewed in detail the wide variety of mechanical or electronic devices which make it possible to intrude into private lives. We have become acquainted with a few of the problems in that field, however, and are dismayed to observe the disregard for human values indicated by the advocacy or actual practice of eavesdropping, the use of lie detection without clear justification, and the frequent willingness to institute surveillance procedures to handle the problems of a small proportion of our population at the risk of eroding the rights and the quality of life for the majority.

Likewise, the panel has not reviewed in detail the propriety of procedures involved in employment or social welfare activities. Enough examples have been brought to our attention, however, to make us feel that examination of procedures in these spheres is needed also.

The attitudes of various segments of our society about proper procedures for the protection of privacy and the right to self-determination have been explored by the panel. It has reviewed relevant research in the behavioral sciences and the administrative practices of universities and Government agencies. It has also consulted with the scientific community through its professional organizations.

THREATS TO PRIVACY

The right to privacy is the right of the individual to decide for himself how much he will share with others his thoughts, his feelings, and the facts of his personal life. It is a right that is essential to insure dignity and freedom of self-determination. In recent years there has been a severe erosion of this right by the widespread and often callous use of various devices for eavesdropping, lie detection, and secret observation in politics, in business, and in law enforcement. Indeed, modern electronic instruments for wiretapping and bugging have opened any human activity to the threat of illicit invasion of privacy. This unwholesome state of affairs has led to wide public concern over the methods of inquiry used by agencies of public employment, social welfare, and law enforcement.

Behavioral research, devoted as it is to the discovery of facts and principles underlying human activity of all types, comes naturally under scrutiny in any examination of possible threats to privacy. All of the social sciences, including economics, political science, anthropology, sociology, and psychology, take as a major object of study the behavior of individuals, communities, or other groups. In one context or another, investigators in all of these disciplines frequently need to seek information that is private to the men, women, and children who are the subjects of their study. In most instances this information is freely given by those who consent to cooperate in the scientific process. But the very nature of behavioral research is such that there is a risk of invasion of privacy if unusual care is not taken to secure the consent of research subjects, or if the data obtained are not given full confidentiality.

While the privacy problem in scientific research is small in comparison to that which exists in employment interviewing, social welfare screening, and law enforcement investigations, the opportunity for improper invasion is not negligible. About 35,000 behavioral scientists are engaged in research in the United States, 2,100 new PhDs are graduated each year, and the total number of students enrolled for advanced degrees in the behavioral sciences exceeds 40,000 at the present time.

It is probable that relatively few of the studies undertaken by these scientists raise serious questions of propriety in relation to privacy and human dignity. From a survey of articles published in professional journals and of research grant applications submitted to Government agencies, we have concluded that most scientists who conduct research in privacy-sensitive areas are aware of the ethical implications of their experimental designs and arrange to secure the consent of subjects and to protect the confidentiality of the data obtained from them.

It cannot be denied, however, that, in a limited number of instances, behavioral scientists have not followed appropriate procedures to protect the rights of their subjects, and that in other cases recognition of the importance of privacy-invading considerations has not been as sophisticated, or the considerations as affirmatively implemented, as good practice demands. Because of this failure there has been pressure from some quarters, both within the Government and outside of it, to place arbitrary limits on the research methods which may be used. Behavioral scientists as a group do not question the importance of the right to privacy and are understandably concerned when suggestions are made that the detailed processes of science should be subjected to control by legislation or arbitrary administrative ruling. All scientists are opposed to restrictions which may curtail important research. At the same time they have an obligation to insure that all possible steps are taken to assure respect for the privacy and dignity of their subjects.

CONFLICTING RIGHTS

It is clear that there exists an important conflict between two values, both of which are strongly held in American society.

The individual has an inalienable right to dignity, self-respect, and freedom to determine his own thoughts and actions within the broad limits set by the requirements of society. The essential element in privacy and self-determination is the privilege of making one's own decision as to the extent to which one will reveal thoughts, feelings, and actions. When a person consents freely and fully to share himself with others—with a scientist, an employer, or a credit investigator—there is no invasion of privacy, regardless of the quality or nature of the information revealed.

Behavioral science is representative of another value vigorously championed by most American citizens, the right to know anything that may be known or discovered about any part of the universe. Man is part of this universe, and the extent of the Federal Government's financial support of human behavioral research (on the order of $300 million in 1966) testifies to the importance placed on the study of human behavior by the American people. In the past there have been conflicts between theological beliefs and the theoretical analyses of the physical sciences. These conflicts have largely subsided, but the behavioral sciences seem to have inherited the basic conflict that arises when strongly held beliefs or moral attitudes—whether theologically, economically, or politically based—are subjected to the free ranging process of scientific inquiry. If society is to exercise its right to know, it must free its behavioral scientists as much as possible from unnecessary restraints. Behavioral scientists in turn must accept the constructive restraints that society imposes in order to establish that level of dignity, freedom, and personal fulfillment that men treasure virtually above all else in life.

The root of the conflict between the individual's right to privacy and society's right of discovery is the research process. Behavioral science seeks to assess and to measure many qualities of men's minds, feelings, and actions. In the absence of informed consent on the part of the subject, these measurements represent invasion of privacy. The scientist must therefore obtain the consent of his subject.

To obtain truly informed consent is often difficult. In the first place, the nature of the inquiry sometimes cannot be explained adequately because it involves complex variables that the nonscientist does not understand. Examples are the personality variables measured by questionnaires, and the qualities of cognitive processes measured by creativity tests. Second, the validity of an experiment is sometimes destroyed if the subject knows all the details of its conduct. Examples include drug testing, in which the effect of suggestion (placebo effect) must be avoided, and studies of persuasibility, in which the subjects remain ignorant of the influences that are being presented experimentally. Clearly, then, if behavioral research is to be effective, some modification of the traditional concept of informed consent is needed.

Such a change in no sense voids the more general proposition that the performance of human behavioral research is the product of a partnership between the scientist and his subject. Consent to participate in a study must be the norm before any subject embarks on the enterprise. Since consent must sometimes be given despite an admittedly inadequate understanding of the scientific purposes of the research procedures, the right to discontinue participation at any point must be stipulated in clear terms. In the meantime, when full information is not available to the subject and when no alternative procedures to minimize the privacy problem are available, the relationship between the subject and the scientist (and between the subject and the institution sponsoring the scientist) must be based upon trust. This places the scientist and the sponsoring institution under a fiduciary obligation to protect the privacy and dignity of the subject who entrusts himself to them. The scientist must agree to treat the subject fairly and with dignity, to cause him no inconvenience or discomfort unless the extent of the inconvenience and discomfort has been accepted by the subject in advance, to inform the subject as fully as possible of the purposes of the inquiry or experiment, and to put into effect all procedures which will assure the confidentiality of whatever information is obtained.

Occasionally, even this degree of consent cannot be obtained. Naturalistic observations of group behavior must sometimes be made unbeknownst to the subjects. In such cases, as well as in all others, the scientist has the obligation to insure full confidentiality of the research records. Only by doing so, and by making certain that published reports contain no identifying reference to a given subject, can the invasion of privacy be minimized.

Basically, then, the protection of privacy in research is assured first by securing the informed consent of the subject. When the subject cannot be completely informed, the consent must be based on trust in the scientist and in the institution sponsoring him. In any case the scientist and his sponsoring institution must insure privacy by the maintenance of confidentiality.

In the end, the fact must be accepted that human behavioral research will at times produce discomfort to some subjects, and will entail a partial invasion of their privacy. Neither the principle of privacy nor the need to discover new knowledge can supervene universally. As with other conflicting values in our society, there must be constant adjustment and compromise, with the decision as to which value is to govern in a given instance to be determined by a weighing of the costs and the gains—the cost in privacy, the gain in knowledge. The decision cannot be made by the investigator alone, because he has a vested interest in his own research program, but must be a positive concern of his scientific peers and the institution which sponsors his work. Our society has grown strong on the principle of minimizing costs and maximizing gains, and, when warmly held values are in conflict, there must be a thoughtful evaluation of the specific case. In particular we do not believe that detailed Governmental controls of research methods or instruments can substitute for the more effective procedures which are available and carry less risk of damage to the scientific enterprise.

ETHICAL ASPECTS OF HUMAN RESEARCH

Greater attention must be given to the ethical aspects of human research. The increase in scientists and in volume of research provides more chance for carelessness or recklessness and, in the hurried search for useful findings, can lead to abuses. Furthermore, if standards are not carefully maintained, there could develop an atmosphere of disregard for privacy that would be altogether alien to the spirit of American society. The increased potentials for damage and for fruitful outcomes from new knowledge are in no small part results of increased Federal support of behavioral science. While no one would suggest that ethical standards should be different for scientists supported by public funds and for those supported by private funds, the Government has an especially strong obligation to support research only under conditions that give fullest protection to individual human dignity. Government must avow and maintain the highest standards for the guidance of all.

To summarize, three parties—the investigator, his institution, and the sponsoring agency—have the responsibility for maintaining proper ethical standards with respect to Government-sponsored research. The investigator designs the research and is in the best position to evaluate the propriety of his procedures. He has, therefore, the ultimate responsibility for insuring that his research is both effective and ethical. The formalization of our ethics concerning privacy in connection with research is too recent, and perhaps too incomplete, to permit the assumption that all investigators have a full understanding of the proper methods for protecting the rights of subjects. Furthermore, the investigator is first and foremost a scientist in search of new knowledge, and it would not be in accord with our understanding of human motivation to expect him always to be as vigilant for his subject's welfare as he is for the productiveness of his own research.

We conclude, therefore, that responsibility must also be borne by the institution which employs the investigator. The employing institution is often a university or a Government laboratory in which there are other scientists capable of reviewing the research plan. Such persons, drawn in part from disciplines other than the behavioral sciences, can present views that are colored neither by self-interest nor by the blind spots that may characterize the specific discipline of the investigator.

Finally, the sponsoring agency is obligated to make certain that both the investigator and his institution are fully aware of the importance of the ethical aspects of the research and that they have taken the necessary steps to discharge their responsibility to the human subjects involved. We believe that, in the majority of instances, it is neither necessary nor desirable for an agency to exceed this level of responsibility.

CONCLUSIONS

From our examination of the relation of behavioral science research to the right to privacy, we have been led to the following conclusions.

1. While most current practices in the field pose no significant threat to the privacy of research subjects, a sufficient number of exceptions have been noted to warrant a sharp increase in attention to procedures that will assure protection of this right. The increasing scale of behavioral research is itself an additional reason for focusing attention in this area.

2. Participation by subjects must be voluntary and based on informed consent to the extent that this is consistent with the objectives of the research. It is fully consistent with the protection of privacy that, in the absence of full information, consent be based on trust in the qualified investigator and the integrity of his institution.

3. The scientist has an obligation to insure that no permanent physical or psychological harm will ensue from the research procedures, and that temporary discomfort or loss of privacy will be remedied in an appropriate way during the course of the research or at its completion. To merit trust, the scientist must design his research with a view to protecting, to the fullest extent possible, the privacy of the subjects. If intrusion on privacy proves essential to the research, he should not proceed with his proposed experiment until he and his colleagues have considered all of the relevant facts and he has determined, with support from them, that the benefits outweigh the costs.

4. The scientist has the same responsibility to protect the privacy of the individual in published reports and in research records that he has in the conduct of the research itself.

5. The primary responsibility for the use of ethical procedures must rest with the individual investigator, but Government agencies that support behavioral research should satisfy themselves that the institution which

employs the investigator has effectively accepted its responsibility to require that he meet proper ethical standards.

6. Legislation to assure appropriate recognition of the rights of human subjects is neither necessary nor desirable if the scientists and sponsoring institutions fully discharge their responsibilities in accommodating to the claim of privacy. Because of its relative inflexibility, legislation cannot meet the challenge of the subtle and sensitive conflict of values under consideration, nor can it aid in the wise decision making by individuals which is required to assure optimum protection of subjects, together with the fullest effectiveness of research.

RECOMMENDATIONS

These conclusions lead us to make the following recommendations.

1. That Government agencies supporting research in their own laboratories or in outside institutions require those institutions to agree to accept responsibility for the ethical propriety of human research performed with the aid of Government funds.

2. That the methods used for institutional review be determined by the institutions themselves. The greatest possible flexibility of methods should be encouraged in order to build effective support for the principle of institutional responsibility within universities or other organizations. Institutions differ in their internal structures and operating procedures, and no single, rigid formula will work for all.

3. That investigators and institutions be notified of the importance of consent and confidentiality as ethical requirements in research design, and that when either condition cannot be met, an explanation of the reasons be made in the application for funds.

4. That when research is undertaken directly by, or purchased on specification by, a Government agency, responsibility for protection of privacy lies with the agency. When independent research is funded by the Government, however, responsibility lies primarily with the scientist and his institution, and research instruments or design should not be subject to detailed review by Government agencies with respect to protection of privacy.

5. That universities and professional associations be encouraged to emphasize the ethical aspects of behavioral research. When a training grant is made, a university should be requested to indicate its understanding that support of education on the ethics of research is one of the purposes of the grant.

Unit Two | DISCUSSION QUESTIONS

3. *How Accurate Are Your Beliefs?*
   Discuss the sources of two common-sense viewpoints held by many college students.
   Why do many individuals believe their analysis of human behavior correct when it has been shown to be false?

4. *Undermining the Student's Faith in the Validity of "Common Sense"*
   Distinguish between common-sense knowledge and scientific knowledge.
   What does the author mean by "reordering the frame of reference"?
5. *Goals in Understanding Science*
   What is meant by "the scientific revolution"?
   Discuss the popularization of science in mass media.
6. *Methodology in Behavioral Science*
   Why do behavioral scientists study lower animals when the objective of behavioral science is to understand people?
   List and discuss three designs used in the behavioral sciences.
7. *Privacy and Behavioral Research*
   What are the recommendations presented by the panel?
   Discuss how the protection of privacy can be assured during research.

Unit Three *The Psychobiological Determinants of Behavior*

Life in its never-ending ability of the species to reproduce, to develop, and to pass on to its progeny the qualities of individuality is the object of the study of psychobiology. The uniqueness and complexity of human behavior is the result of certain inherited factors interacting with its environment via maturation. It is this combination of factors that illustrate the need for studying and understanding the physiological and psychological bases of behavior.

The human being, developing from a single cell zygote, grows into an adult with about twenty-five billion cells. Each one of these cells is capable of reproducing itself in a like manner. What is the key to this phenomenon? What are the biological determinants that distinguish the difference between you and another? To answer these questions we must first acknowledge the contributions of the Austrian monk Gregor Mendel who, in 1866, formed the basis for our understanding of psychobiology. His inquiry into the physical differences of garden peas led to the establishment of the science of genetics, the branch of biology concerned with heredity and the transmission of hereditary characteristics. Mendel's discovery was of major importance because it showed that genetic data come to the individual in *units* rather than a blending of qualities from one's ancestors. He called these units of life, *genes.* In recent years, this construct was further spelled out to be a polynucleotide called deoxyribonucleic acid, DNA. Although DNA itself has been known for quite some time, it was the discovery of the *function* of the DNA by Britisher Francis H. C. Crick and American James D. Watson, who, for their efforts were awarded the Nobel Prize in medicine in 1962.

In the first reading of Unit 3, Alicia Hills and Albert Rosenfeld cite new advances made in molecular biology in *DNA's Code: Key to All Life.* In addition to the discussion of DNA, the authors relate the importance of RNA, ribonucleic acid, which serves as a kind of chemical messenger for DNA. Finally, the authors question what man's knowledge of the code will ultimately reveal concerning the behavior of man.

Behavioral processes are affected by the organism's responses to stimulation; behavioral activity is experienced through the functioning of the central nervous system as it is affected internally and/or externally by a stimulus that brings about a response. The nervous system serves as a connecting branch between the receptor and the brain. Not only is the brain a relayer of messages to and from other parts of the body; it also serves as an evaluator and analyzer of sensations. In the second reading, *That Odd Chemical Complex,* Isaac Asimov presents a lucid description of the parts and function of the brain. Asimov explores the possibility that "mental disorders" may simply be changes in the chemical workings of the brain.

The third article, *How the Machine Called the Brain Feels and Thinks* by Dean E. Wooldridge concerns itself with the sensory aspect of the interpretation of emotions and drives. Wooldridge discusses how experiments involving lower animals have helped to explain the higher level mental functions of man.

Finally in the last selection, *The Interpretive Cortex,* Wilder Penfield discusses the structure and functions of the human brain. This article tells how "the stream of consciousness" in the brain can be electrically reactivated.

---

8 | DNA's Code: Key to All Life

Alicia Hills and Albert Rosenfeld

The unveiling of the DNA molecule, the delineation of its architecture, and the growing comprehension of how it performs its genetic wonders, together constitute the most exciting frontier in all of science today. The frontier is expanding rapidly and the pioneers are pushing their explorations into the new country with impatient vigor.

This new country is called "molecular biology," and it promises to yield unprecedented power for man—power to manipulate nature in ways that he cannot now even imagine. The pioneers are a new breed called "molecular biologists." Many began as mathematicians, physicists and chemists, then turned their attention, their ingenious techniques and their precision instruments to the study of living organisms. Their forays into the new country have resulted in a series of seven-league-boot advances in man's knowledge that have already won them a hatful of Nobel Prizes. In fact, their collective research will certainly go down as one of the grandest intellectual adventures in human history.

What really distinguishes molecular biology from all biology before it is that it penetrates down to individual molecules—molecules like DNA and RNA. Biologists were once limited to studying gross organisms, or pieces of them. Later they refined their techniques so that they could deal with individual cells. But getting down to the manipulation of individual molecules represents a revolutionary advance.

To appreciate what this means, imagine a Martian scientist who has been studying life on earth. He has done the best he can do from way out there, observing us through the best instruments at his command—just as the biologist has done the best he can do, looking through his microscopes. All the Martian could observe were the mass activities of entire populations.

He had no idea that a Napoleon or an Einstein might exist or how his deeds might affect the destinies of millions. What he knows about human behavior is understandably limited.

But suddenly, through some remarkable new techniques and instruments, he finds out about individual people. He learns that they communicate and order their lives with the help of a language. More than that, he figures out all the letters of their alphabet. Now, if he can only learn to spell with the letters. . . . You can imagine his excitement. You can see how rapidly his knowledge of life on earth will begin to proliferate.

Biologists have arrived at exactly this stage. Heretofore they could only observe cells. A cell is not an individual, but a community—a highly organized community in which a vast and diverse population of molecules go about their business. When Dr. James Watson of Harvard and Dr. Francis Crick of Cambridge worked out the spiral-ladder structure of DNA, biologists found out what individual molecules look like. Since then they have learned the four-letter alphabet of the molecular language—the genetic code. They are much more excited than the imaginary Martian scientist, for what they are studying is not life on another planet but the life pulsing in their own bodies. "We must now learn to spell with the genetic code," says Dr. Marshall Nirenberg of the National Institutes of Health. "Only then can we hope to write genetic messages of our own."

Nirenberg is the brilliant young biochemist who took the first great stride toward cracking the genetic code. His experiment has already become historic though it was performed only two years ago. Before 1961 the genetic code was as indecipherable as Egyptian hieroglyphics before the discovery of the Rosetta Stone. Nirenberg provided the biological Rosetta Stone, the crucial key to translating the hieroglyphics of life's code.

When they began their work, Nirenberg and his associates were of course familiar with the knowledge about DNA and RNA. In all this complexity, the most promising place to look for clues to the code seemed to be in the making of proteins. They knew that RNA, using a code of only four letters, makes proteins out of 20 amino acids. They also knew that each of the 20 amino acids had a specific RNA code word for it; otherwise, how would the RNA know which amino acid to select? The amino-acid words had to contain more than two letters because there would not be enough two-letter words to go around for all 20 amino acids. Three-letter words however, ought to work just fine. But which three-letter words, out of 64 possible combinations, would select which amino acids?

It was as if there were a pack of 20 dogs whose names you had to learn. Though you don't know their names, you do know that all the names are different, and that each dog will answer to his own name and to no other. All you can do, then, is start thinking of possible dogs' names and calling them out. If you holler "Rover" and nothing happens, you try again. If you holler "Fido" and one comes running, then there are only 19 names left to learn.

This is the same sort of technique Nirenberg used. First, he mixed up a batch of chemicals prepared from living cells, including all the amino acids. He made sure that his precise recipe contained no messenger-RNA of its own to foul up the experiment. Then he manufactured an artificial messenger-RNA, made up entirely of only one of its four code chemicals—uracil, which can be thought of as the letter U. The only three-letter word that can possibly be made out of U's is UUU, and the order doesn't matter since, whichever way you scramble it, it still comes out UUU.

Adding his artificial RNA, made of nothing but U's, to the amino-acid soup, Nirenberg got a protein made entirely of a single amino acid, phenylalanine. There could be no mistake—he had talked to the amino acid in its own language. Instead of "Fido," he had hollered "UUU," and phenylalanine had come running. It was clear that UUU meant phenylalanine. In the new molecular dictionary, phenylalanine was the first word to be translated from the genetic.

Other scientists quickly joined Nirenberg, hollering "Rover" and "Sport" and all the other names they could think of. Their hollering, of course, consisted of delicate and painstaking chemical operations, often using radioactive tracers to signal the whereabouts of specific substances. In their work they had to deal with complications which did not concern Nirenberg in his pioneer undertaking. For one thing, they had to make their artificial RNA out of more letters than merely U. For another, in words with more than one letter, the order begins to matter—cta does *not* spell cat.

Despite these disadvantages, scientists have gradually come to know the code words—or, at least, the letters in the code words—for all 20 amino acids. They have also learned that sometimes there is more than one word for the same amino acid—just as "car" and "auto" can convey the same message in English. This gives the organism a better chance to survive. If one of the key code chemicals were knocked out, or in short supply for any reason, the amino acid would have an alternate choice, and protein manufacture would not necessarily come to a stop.

Still another recent discovery is genetic punctuation. It turns out that the DNA molecule is not a single, uninterrupted chain full of nothing but the code chemicals. Every so often the genetic messages are interrupted by punctuation marks. Instructions for how to make a specific protein may take up, say, a thousand rungs in the DNA ladder. At the end of this set of instructions there is a bit of protein which acts as the period at the end of the sentence.

To an earlier generation of biologists, the word "gene" was a vague abstraction to specify whatever-it-was in the cell that governed a specific hereditary trait. Molecular biologists now believe they can pinpoint the gene physically as that uninterrupted stretch of DNA code rungs—the sentence of instructions between the two punctuation marks.

Apart from their all-out assault on the problem of deciphering the code, scientists have been working intensively at solving other DNA mysteries. One of the most perplexing of these was posed by the discovery of DNA—or, rather, by the discovery of DNA's function (DNA itself was actually discovered way back in 1870). DNA is present in every cell of the body, and the DNA in every cell contains all the same information as the original fertilized egg contained. How then does DNA manage to employ only the information it wants—and only when it wants it? How does the DNA in a liver cell suppress all its voluminous instructions except those that the liver cell needs to keep going?

Fascinating partial answers have already been found in a series of substances which cover up those portions of the DNA molecule not in use, thus stopping the flow of information. Providing this protection for itself is one more job for DNA to do—since it, after all, is the source of all the cell's instructions. Added to the burden of information which DNA must carry, then, are the directions for making these cover-up substances, informing them which parts of itself to cover up and when—and then arranging to have the covered-up parts uncovered at the right times.

It has been speculated that the breaking down of this cover-up mechanism might be a cause of cancer. If the entire molecule—or even substantial parts of it—suddenly became exposed, the DNA would go haywire. It might begin multiplying again, cells would begin to divide, and the result would be an abnormal growth, perhaps a malignant one.

Every new advance in molecular biology opens up new territories to be explored. Today there is hardly an area of research in biology or medicine that is not eagerly investigating DNA and RNA—and hardly an area of human life that will not be touched by these investigations.

One of the most puzzling facets of the human mind, for example, is memory. This phenomenon may soon be a little less puzzling, thanks to a startling series of recent experiments in animals. The surprising results make it appear that RNA plays a key role in memory. It might be the very stuff that memory is made of.

Memory is really stored learning. When an animal is trained to do something, the training represents stored memories. Scientists do not know precisely how the storage is achieved, but, suspecting that the nucleic acids had something to do with it, they set out to pursue their hunch.

They have been using a variety of animals to carry out their experiments. One is a lowly flatworm called the planarian. The planarian can be taught, by means of electrical shocks, to cringe whenever a light is turned on or to avoid parts of a maze. When well-trained planarians are cut up and fed to untrained planarians, the cannibalistic worms learn much faster than those on a less educated diet.

When scientists first observed this, they wondered if the memory of the trained worms—or at least part of it—had in some way been passed on to the untrained ones. They had reason to believe that RNA might be the transmitting substance. To test this belief, another experiment was carried out.

A planarian, when cut in half, regenerates itself into two new flatworms. Scientists had already confirmed that when a trained planarian is cut in half, each of the new flatworms gets some of the benefit of the training. Knowing this, they cut a trained planarian in half. The top half developed, as expected, into a new planarian, partly trained. But the lower half was treated with a substance that destroys RNA, and this half became a worm with no training—hence no memory—at all.

There have been intriguing experiments with rats, too. In some of these, it was ascertained that rats learn faster when their RNA production is increased, and slower if their RNA production is lowered. Rats trained to walk a tightwire have more RNA in their brain cells after training than untrained rats. Moreover, their RNA contains proportions of the four code chemicals which vary considerably from the RNA in untrained rats, indicating that the training has changed the nature of the RNA code molecules.

The changes caused in the RNA by training appear to be permanent changes. The new information is retained in the nerve cells, which somehow get copies of the new RNA. Exactly how this can help us remember a telephone number is yet to be determined, but some evidence of RNA's influence on human memory has already been offered. Old people with failing memories were dosed with RNA prepared from yeast, and their memories did seem to improve.

The aging process itself seems to be tied up in some way with the nucleic acids. Scientists now theorize that, with the passing years, the DNA and RNA in human cells are subjected to all sorts of disturbing influences, from chemical action to random radiation. Thus, in steadily increasing numbers of cells, the code message is garbled, making the organism correspondingly less efficient.

Long before senility has set in, though, the body is subject to a host of ills. Some of these are directly traceable to defects in the genes. As one example, sickle-cell anemia—a debilitating and often fatal blood disease known to be hereditary—has been traced to a single amino acid in a single protein molecule—hence probably to a single fault on the DNA chain. Aside from those ailments known to be hereditary, there are a number of others—illnesses as diverse as diabetes, muscular dystrophy, feeblemindedness and cancer—which may prove to be tied in directly with faulty information in the DNA molecule. When enough is learned about DNA and RNA, might such defects be corrected and the diseases wiped out? Can the human memory be substantially improved by biochemical means? Can the clock of aging be turned back, or even slowed down? Scientists are cautious about making predictions. But in view of what has already been achieved, they see no reason to set any limits to the possibilities.

No one is quite clear exactly how man will put DNA and RNA to practical use after he learns how to read and write messages in the genetic code. Unlike the planarian, whose primitive digestive tract can absorb and use molecules virtually in the same form they are eaten, man must break down all his food and process it in quite a complicated manner before his body can use it. So merely eating genetic materials is not the answer.

However, one possible answer which scientists are giving close scrutiny is the making of artificial viruses. A virus is simply a packet of DNA or RNA, wrapped in a protective protein overcoat. Some forms of artificial DNA, RNA and protein have already been made in the laboratory. There seems to be no technical barrier to the ultimate manufacture of viruses—beneficial viruses rather than infective ones—containing nucleic acids and proteins built according to specifications. Assuming that man can turn out made-to-order viruses, how can he use them?

We have already described—at the end of the color section of this article—how a virus's nucleic acid sneaks in, takes over a cell and begins ordering the manufacture of its own materials. This does not always happen right away. A virus's DNA or RNA can quietly integrate itself with the cell's and lie dormant for years before being triggered into subversive activity. The virus's genetic material may even be passed on for several generations before it acts up. There is no telling what strange maladies may suddenly and inexplicably turn up in this fashion—including cancer, which has been more and more linked with viruses.

Here again, no one is sure what happens. But it is speculated that one way in which a virus might cause cancer, apart from taking over the cell, is to dictate the manufacture of substances alien to the cell and perhaps damaging to it. In man's war against the virus, the virus has so far won most of the battles. But when he really cracks the virus's secret code, man will win the war. When he does, he will put the tamed virus to work for his own purposes.

If artificial viruses were available, they might be injected into the body. Their synthetic protein overcoats would keep them from acting up—just as with natural viruses—until their nucleic acids entered cells. If the DNA or RNA in the virus was a wholesome, friendly type designed to help the cell rather than destroy it, it is quite possible that memory-bearing RNA might be carried to the nerve and brain cells to improve people's memories, that efficient new supplies of DNA might hold back the ravages of old age, that the cells could be better armed against all sorts of invading enemy viruses.

There is simply no calculating at this point the amount of benefit man might gain medically through his mastery of the genetic code. This mastery will not only permit him to improve the lot of individuals. By manipulating the DNA in human eggs and sperm cells, he may be able to correct genetic defects and thus save countless future generations from illness and premature death. Most scientists regard this potential as a mixed blessing, however, for if man can manipulate the genes of all humankind in this fashion, it means he can decide what characteristics he deems desirable in future generations and simply write the genetic messages into the DNA.

Evolution up to now has apparently been carried out largely by means of chance mutations—that is, through changes in the genetic material caused by, say, random impact of cosmic radiation or by chemical action. But in the future most mutations may not be left to chance. Nobel Prizes have already been awarded to Dr. Arthur Kornberg of Stanford and Dr. Severo Ochoa of New York University for making DNA and RNA artificially in their laboratories. By tampering with DNA other scientists have been able to produce new hereditary traits in bacteria and insects. There seems to be no insurmountable obstacle to eventually doing this with human genes.

The DNA molecule has been called "the atom of life." When man succeeds in harnessing *this* atom, the problems raised by the harnessing of the uranium atom will look simple indeed. As they contemplate the golden opportunities the new powers will give man, scientists also stop to think about the opportunities for the abuse of these powers—and, when they do, their thoughts sometimes make them shudder.

RECOMMENDED READINGS

Bonner, D. and S. Mills, *Heredity* (2nd Ed.). Englewood Cliffs, N.J.: Prentice-Hall, 1964, $1.75.

Dobzhansky, T., *Evolution, Genetics, and Man.* New York: Wiley & Sons, Science Editions, 1955, $2.45.

Galton, F., *Hereditary Genius.* Cleveland, Ohio: World Publishing, Meridian Books, $1.95.

GOLDSTEIN, P., *Genetics is Easy*. New York: Viking, 1961, $1.45.

McKUSICK, V. A., *Human Genetics*. Englewood Cliffs, N.J.: Prentice-Hall, 1964.

MOORE, J. A., *Heredity and Development*. New York: Oxford University Press, 1963, $1.95.

(All books listed above are inexpensive paperbacks.)

---

9 | That Odd Chemical Complex, the Human Mind

Isaac Asimov

What is mind? No matter!
What is matter? Never mind!

This ancient witticism testifies to man's firm conviction through the ages that the human mind transcends the material, that it is not bound by the ordinary rules that govern gross matter.

The physical structure of the living organism is accepted as a thing of atoms and molecules, governed by the same laws that govern the rocks underfoot and the stars overhead. That is as true for Man the Proud as for Worm the Lowly. But man's mind? Can one analyze the creative genius that gives rise to a masterpiece? Can one weigh, count, and measure emotion and imagination, love and hate, passion, thought, and a sense of good and evil?

There has always been a strong impulse to place mind over matter and to apply different and more subtle rules to the former. It seems natural, then, that doctor's medicine should prove unable to work on the mind. Shakespeare has Macbeth ask cynically of the doctor treating his nightmare-ridden wife:

Canst thou not minister to a mind diseased,
Pluck from the memory a rooted sorrow,
Raze out the written troubles of the brain,
And with some sweet oblivious antidote
Cleanse the stuffed bosom of that perilous stuff
Which weighs upon the heart?

To which the doctor can only reply humbly:

Therein the patient
Must minister to himself.

Three centuries after Shakespeare, when doctors began to "minister to a mind diseased," they did it without any "sweet oblivious antidote," without any potion, nostrum, or material device. To reach the mind the laws of matter were insufficient; the mind itself had to be the tool. Doctors began to talk to patients and, more important, to listen while patients talked. In place of the physician's stethoscope and the clinician's test tube we had the psychiatrist's couch.

Physical scientists have been strongly tempted to leave it at that and to make no move toward the mentally disturbed person upon the psychiatrist's couch. To approach the vast complexities of the mind with the cold, material instruments of science required a kind of heroism. There was a grim promise of inevitable failure about the fire-breathing dragon of mind-chemistry that tended to daunt the would-be St. George of the microscope and the slide rule.

And yet the brain is made up of atoms and molecules—as is the rest of the body. The molecules in the cells of the body, and in those of the brain in particular, are so many and so various and so versatile that they interact and change in a dazzling pattern that we do not, as yet, understand well. But the very dazzle of this chemical complexity is hopeful, for it is, quite conceivably, complex enough to account for all the nearly infinite subtlety of what we call the mind.

This complexity is now being tackled by new techniques that are making top news out of advances in brain chemistry and physiology. Computers are being used to analyze brain-wave data with a completeness never before possible. Greater understanding of nucleic acids in connection with the machinery of heredity is producing exciting hints concerning the mechanics of memory.

Most of all, new drugs are being used that affect the workings of the brain, sometimes drastically, and by that very fact are giving us possible insights into these workings. It is this last technique that has been creating the most stir, for it involves, among other things, the compound called LSD, which offers mankind a new dimension in drug use and drug consequence.

The new advances, striking as they do at the most subtle manifestations of the brain—memory, perception, reason—do not come from nowhere. There is a century of advance in connection with the less complex aspects of brain action. Although the nervous system is an intricately interlaced whole on almost every level of its activity, it shows, in some respects, a sort of gradually increasing complexity of function from the bottom upward. This has helped scientists move onward by easy stages until now they can reasonably try to cope with the mental machinery that knits together all levels of the nervous system.

Below the brain is the spinal cord, a narrow 18-inch-long mass of nerve tissue that runs down the center of the bones making up the spinal column. The spinal cord is a switching center for many of our common reflexes. Touch something hot and the sensation sparks its way to the cord and is converted into an outward-surging nerve impulse calling for a quick withdrawal. Your finger moves away even before your conscious mind has a chance to say, "It's hot."

(Mind you, this is not to say that this is *all* the spinal cord does. It is knit by nerve tracts to the various centers of the brain and it forms part of a unified whole. However, it is this reflex action that was first understood, and I am deliberately oversimplifying to get across the historical perspective.)

At its upper end the spinal cord widens into the medulla oblongata, or "brain stem," upon which the brain itself sits like a swollen piece of wrinkled fruit. The brain stem handles matters that are more complicated than the simple reflexes. It is an important center for the control of the manner in which we stand, for instance.

In standing, we are actively using muscles to keep our back and legs stiff against the pull of gravity. To do this efficiently, there must be a constant, delicately adjusted interplay. No one set of muscles is allowed to overbalance us to one side or another without a countering set being quickly thrown in to readjust the balance accurately. We are not ordinarily aware of this activity, but if we have been standing a long time, weariness makes itself unpleasantly evident, and if we lose consciousness while standing, the muscles relax and we crumple to the ground at once.

If it were our conscious mind that were continually concerned with the muscles involved in standing, we would have little time for anything else. It is the brain stem that is in charge, however, with scarcely any conscious interference. We remain standing, balancing ourselves accurately, no matter how distracted we are, no matter how lost in thought, provided only that we are not actually asleep or unconscious.

Above the brain stem are two swollen bodies with wrinkled surfaces, each divided nearly in half. The larger is the cerebrum (the Latin word for brain); the smaller, in the rear, is the cerebellum (little brain).

The cerebellum goes one step beyond the brain stem. It does more than keep us balanced while motionless; it keeps us balanced in motion. While we walk, we lift one leg, throw ourselves off balance temporarily and then move the leg forward and bring it to a halt upon the ground in just the manner calculated to retrieve that balance. If we move our hand toward a pencil, that hand must begin to slow before it reaches the pencil and must come to a halt just as it reaches it.

There must be "feedback." We must see (or otherwise sense) the motion of a portion of our body, estimate its distance from its goal and adjust its speed and direction constantly on the basis of the changing situation. It is the cerebellum that is in charge of this. It takes care of the matter automatically, so that if we reach for a pencil we seize it with perfect efficiency, without any awareness of the delicacy of the task. But watch someone with cerebral palsy who cannot manage this feedback. He is unable to perform the slightest task without a pathetic overshooting and undershooting of the mark.

In accomplishing all this, incoming sensations must produce chemical changes in the brain cells which, in turn, give rise to nerve impulses that produce specific muscle responses. What the details of these chemical changes might be we don't know.

As we come to the cerebrum we find ourselves more directly involved with chemistry. At the bottom of the cerebrum, for instance, is a section called the hypothalamus, one of the functions of which is to act as a thermostat. The body's heat is produced through a constant gentle vibration of the muscles at a rate of from seven to thirteen times per second, a fact reported in 1962. The hypothalamus senses the temperature of the blood passing through it. If that temperature is too low, it sparks an increase in the vibration rate, producing additional heat. If the temperature is too high, the vibration rate is lowered. This is one way in which body heat is maintained at an almost constant level despite changes in outside temperature.

The hypothalamus also detects the water concentration in the blood and acts through a nearby gland, the pituitary, to adjust the workings of the kidney accordingly. More water is eliminated if the blood is getting too thin; less water, if it is too thick. The hypothalamus is also constantly measuring the sugar concentration in the blood. When that concentration falls too low, the hypothalamus acts to set up hunger sensations.

Here we have clearer examples of actual chemical involvement. Small (as yet harmless) chemical changes in the blood call forth alterations in the body's mechanism to prevent any further (and increasingly harmful) changes in that direction. The body's chemistry is thus kept in accurate balance.

The details must be extraordinarily complex, however. The body's mechanism is intricately interconnected, and the hypothalamus must bring about desirable changes in one part of that supercomplicated network without bringing about undesirable changes elsewhere. The difficulty here is exemplified by the manner in which almost every man-applied drug, despite the most careful use, has always the possibility of bringing on unpleasant "side effects." The hypothalamus must work with the kind of incredible sure-footedness that avoids side effects.

But what about the upper parts of the cerebrum—the parts particularly concerned with conscious motion and sensations, with thought and reason, memory and imagination? If we are stumped by the chemistry of such things as reflexes and water balance, surely we must be completely, hopelessly, and helplessly at sea in connection with the chemistry of memory, for instance?

In fact, we are not. We are actually making progress, or seem to be, in the understanding of memory, and the most exciting prospects may be looming on the far horizon.

And it is not only the reasonably healthy mind that is in question. What we call mental disorders may simply be shifts in the chemical workings of the brain. If mental disease is a material malfunction, then through the study of brain chemistry we may well find the cures that have steadily eluded the psychiatrists.

Consider schizophrenia, for instance—the most common of the serious mental illnesses. The name was coined in 1911 by a Swiss psychiatrist, Paul E. Bleuler, from the Greek words meaning "split mind" because it was frequently noted that persons suffering from this disease seemed to be dominated by one set of ideas (or "complex") to the exclusion of others, as though the mind's harmonious workings had been disrupted and split, with one portion of that split mind seizing control of the rest. An older name for the disease was dementia praecox ("early ripening madness"), a term intended to differentiate it from senile dementia, mental illness affecting the old through the deterioration of the brain with age. Schizophrenia shows itself at a comparatively early age, generally between 18 and 28.

Schizophrenia may exist in several varieties, depending on which complex predominates. It may be hebephrenic ("childish mind"), where one prominent symptom is childish or silly behavior. It may be catatonic ("toning down"), in which behavior is indeed toned down and the patient seems to withdraw from participation in the objective world, becoming mute and rigid. It may also be paranoid ("madness"), characterized by extreme hostility and suspicion, with feelings of persecution.

At least half of all patients in mental hospitals are schizophrenics of these or other types, and it is estimated that one percent of mankind is affected. This means that there are at least 30 million schizophrenics in the world, a figure equal to the total population of a nation like Spain.

Can this most common variety of the mind diseased be treated by "some sweet oblivious antidote"?

There are precedents that give us ground for hope. Some mental illnesses have already been cured, and the mind has shown itself amenable to physical treatment—in certain cases at least.

One example is pellagra, a disease once very common in Mediterranean lands and in our own South. It was characterized by what were called the three D's: diarrhea, dermatitis, and dementia. As it turned out, pellagra was caused by a vitamin deficiency, the lack of niacin in the diet. Once niacin was supplied to patients in the necessary quantities the disease cleared up. Not only did the diarrhea stop, not only was the red, inflamed, roughened skin restored to normal, but the mental disorders ceased. The same chemical that healed the body healed the mind. In this instance, at least, it was a case of matter over mind.

Pellagra is caused by a failure of supplies from outside. But what about malfunctions caused by inadequacies in the body's own chemical machinery? Every chemical reaction in the body is controlled by complex substances known as enzymes; each reaction has its own particular enzyme. What, then, if a person is born without the ability to manufacture some particular enzyme?

This is the situation in cases of a disease called phenylpyruvic oligophrenia, which is characterized by serious mental deficiency. This disease (not common, fortunately) is present at birth. A child is born without the ability to make a certain enzyme that brings about the conversion of a substance called phenylalanine into another called tyrosine. The phenylalanine, unable to follow its normal course, changes into other, abnormal substances. These abnormal substances accumulate and interfere with brain chemistry.

Here, unfortunately, the situation cannot be corrected as simply as in the case of pellegra. Although it is easy to supply a missing vitamin, it is as yet impossible to supply a missing enzyme. However, some improvement in mental condition has been reported among patients with the disease who have been kept on a diet low in phenylalanine.

Is it possible, then, that schizophrenia is also the result of a chemical failure, either from without or within? Dr. A. Hoffer at the University Hospital in Saskatoon, Canada, has been treating schizophrenia for years by the administration of large doses of niacin and has been reporting considerable success. Apparently at least some forms of schizophrenia are a vitamin-deficiency disease rather like a more serious pellagra.

It takes more niacin to handle schizophrenia than pellagra, and Hoffer suggests a reason for this. Niacin is converted in the body into a more complex substance called NAD, which is what really does the work. The normal body can form NAD out of niacin easily and quickly if the latter is present in the diet. (Hence pellagra is cured as soon as small quantities of niacin are added to the otherwise deficient diet.) But the schizophrenic may have a disordered chemistry, characterized in part by the inability to form NAD easily. Therefore, a great deal of niacin must be supplied as a means of seeing to it that the inefficient chemical machinery produces at least a little NAD.

Hoffer reports that in the first half of 1966 he tried administration of NAD, ready-made, with very hopeful results. Smaller doses produced more rapid improvement. (As is usual in the case of experimental treatments on the border of the known, there have also been reports from other laboratories that NAD treatment has proven disappointing.)

The chemical failure in the case of the schizophrenic (whether it is the inability to make NAD out of niacin, or something else altogether) is apparently something that is inherited; for certainly the tendency to develop the disease is inherited. The chance of a particular individual in the general population developing schizophrenia is about 1 in 100. If, however, a person has a brother or sister who is schizophrenic, he has a one in seven chance of becoming schizophrenic himself. If he has an identical twin who is schizophrenic, his own chances rise to three in four.

People aren't usually born with schizophrenic symptoms to be sure; it is not inborn in the sense that phenylpyruvic oligophrenia is. We might put it this way: The schizophrenic is born not with a part of his chemical machinery missing but rather with a part that is fragile and wears out relatively early in life. It is the fragility of the part that is inherited.

But what is it that NAD (if it is NAD) does that keeps the body normal? What goes wrong in the body if NAD is missing?

Suspicion has fallen upon a portion of the chemical scheme that begins with a substance called adrenalin. In very tiny quantities, adrenalin stimulates certain nerves controlling the heart beat, blood pressure, breathing rate and so on. The adrenal gland (a small bit of tissue over each kidney) has, as one of its functions, the secretion of adrenalin into the blood stream in times of stress. When we are angry or afraid, adrenalin is produced at once so that our blood pressure rises, our heart beats faster, our lungs pump more rapidly. We are placed on an emergency footing that fits us to fight or run.

Naturally, it is important that, once the emergency is over, the body be returned to normal. For that reason the body has chemical devices for the rapid destruction of adrenalin. This destruction is supervised by an enzyme called amine oxidase, which combines with adrenalin and holds it still, so to speak, while it is altered into harmlessness.

But suppose the enzyme is occupied in some other direction? Ordinarily, enzymes are quite specific; that is, they will deal only with certain molecules possessing one particular shape and will not work with any others. This is the "lock-and-key" view of enzyme-workings. A particular key will open a particular lock, and other keys will not do.

Enzyme specificity is not perfect, however. An enzyme may combine with a molecule that is nearly but not quite the shape of the right one. The wrong molecule then competes with the right one for union with the enzyme, and if the enzyme is busy with the wrong molecule it cannot work with the right one, so that its action is inhibited. This phenomenon is called "competitive inhibition" and it can be serious indeed.

When the enzyme unites with the right molecule, it performs a task upon it and lets go; but when it unites with the wrong one it may find itself more or less permanently stuck, like a wrong key jammed into a lock and broken off there. When that happens, even a tiny quantity of a wrong molecule can bring about a long-continued chemical disorder that may do permanent damage or even bring about death. Poisons generally work in this way.

Perhaps, then, some enzyme, amine oxidase or some other, is subjected to competitive inhibition by something that is formed in the absence of NAD but not in its presence.

The possibility that competitive inhibition is indeed involved is pointed up dramatically by the case of a cactus, native to the American Southwest, that contains the compound called mescaline. The mescaline molecule bears a certain general resemblance to adrenalin—apparently close enough to allow mescaline to interfere with amine oxidase. This kind of interference, even with a single enzyme, can have a widespread effect upon brain function. The chemical workings of the brain can be likened to a vast three-dimensional lacework, intricately interconnected. A jab or yank at any one portion is going to move and shift every other portion to one extent or another. Consequently, when the portions of the cactus containing mescaline are chewed, the adrenalin-destroying enzyme is occupied with the mescaline and the adrenalin accumulates, producing all sorts of effects. A person experiences sense perceptions that have no objective existence. Ordinary objects take on strange and bizarre overtones. In short, the mescaline produces hallucinations and is therefore a "hallucinogen."

Furthermore, the reactions of the mescaline eater are inappropriate to the real universe. They depend on his distorted sense perceptions—and sometimes don't even match those. His behavior becomes peculiar and unpredictable. The Indians of the Southwest, experiencing all this when they ate the cactus, made the rather natural assumption that they were opening a door into a world beyond the common one of the ordinary senses. They made use of mescaline, therefore, in religious rites.

Mescaline-induced behavior resembles that of schizophrenics, and it is natural to wonder if perhaps a chemical may be formed within the body which produces effects similar to those of mescaline. Perhaps the chemical is formed more easily in the case of NAD deficiency, so that people born with a tendency to develop inefficiencies in the NAD-manufacturing reactions will therefore be subjected to the effect of these chemicals.

In the test tube, adrenalin can be easily altered to a slightly changed compound called adrenochrome. Adrenochrome, if injected into the blood stream, will also produce temporary bouts of schizophrenic-like behavior.

To be sure, adrenochrome isn't formed in the normal body, but it might be in the schizophrenic.

It became a matter of interest, then, to study and analyze in detail those portions of the schizophrenic body which could be easily obtained and tested —the blood, for instance, or the urine. Any substance that could be found in all, or almost all, schizophrenics and was not found in all, or almost all, nonschizophrenics would be instantly suspect.

One way of testing body fluids is to use a technique called paper chromatography. Different kinds of molecules in the fluids are made to spread out and occupy separate spots on pieces of porous paper. These spots can then be made visible by allowing the molecules occupying them to undergo a chemical reaction that produces a colored material.

In 1962, Arnold J. Friedhoff of New York University found that with a certain course of treatment a pink spot could be obtained from the urine of 15 out of 19 schizophrenics, but from not one of 14 nonschizophrenics.

Similar tests have since been conducted on larger numbers of people. In one series of experiments, conducted by C. A. Clarke at the University of Liverpool, not one pink spot was found in tests on 265 healthy people—or on 126 people who were sick with diseases other than schizophrenia. Pink spots *were* found, however, with 46 out of 84 schizophrenics. Most of the schizophrenics who did not show the pink spot were of the paranoid variety. Among the nonparanoids, four out of every five showed it.

And what was the pink spot? It turned out to be a chemical called dimethoxyphenylethylamine (DMPE), and its structure lies somewhere between adrenalin and mescaline!

In other words, certain schizophrenics (whether for lack of NAD or some other cause) *form their own hallucinogens* and are, in effect, on a permanent mescaline kick.

This is only a bare beginning in the physical-chemical attack on schizophrenia, but it is a hopeful beginning. The pink spot (and any other chemical giveaways that may turn up) can help doctors spot the oncoming of schizophrenia earlier than might otherwise be possible and at a time when therapy might be easier. By studying the chemical processes that give rise to the pink spot, the abnormal section of the chemical mechanism in a schizophrenic may be detected and treatment might then be sharpened.

But adrenalin is not the only chemical that seems to be intimately concerned with the workings of the brain. There is also a substance called serotonin.

Serotonin's importance was brought out most dramatically in connection with lysergic acid diethylamide, the now-famous LSD. LSD has a structure somewhat more complicated than serotonin, but chemists can easily trace out a serotonin "backbone" in the LSD molecule. It is not surprising, then, that LSD may compete with serotonin for a particular enzyme as DMPE competes with adrenalin—and with the same results. In other words, the ingestion of LSD may lead to the accumulation of serotonin in the brain and the appearance of schizophrenic-like symptoms.

This fact was discovered accidentally in 1943, when a chemist, Dr. Albert Hofmann, was working on LSD with some perfectly ordinary chemical purpose in mind. He must have gotten a few crystals on his fingertips and transferred them to his lips, for he fell into a dreamlike state that left him unable to work. He returned home and experienced a kind of drunken fantasy of hallucination. He suspected it was the LSD and the next day (with remarkable courage) he swallowed about a hundred-thousandth of an ounce of it, risking only what he thought was a small test dose. It was actually a large dose, as it happened, for a tenth that quantity would have been sufficient. The fantasies and hallucinations returned and the rest is history.

Hofmann was completely normal after 24 hours, and he did no harm to himself or to others while he was under its influence. Unfortunately, this is not something we can rely on as a general rule. Each individual has a chemical machinery of his own, so that the effect of LSD will vary from one person to another. One will experience a mild case of fantasy, others a severe one; some will recover quickly, others much more slowly.

The chemical machinery is, in some individuals, more fragile at particular key points than in others in the sense that it may be more prone to snap at those points. If the point in question is one which would produce schizophrenia if broken, taking LSD is certainly not an advisable experiment.

Ordinarily, the fragile point in the chemical scheme might hold up quite well through a long lifetime of ordinary stress so that a person might be schizophrenia-prone, without ever developing schizophrenia. Yet under the powerful jab of LSD, the point gives, and what might be merely an unusual and temporary experience for someone else becomes a permanent and serious change in the man in question.

Since none of us know just how firm some crucial part of our chemical fabric might be, using LSD without the greatest of professional care is a kind of mental Russian roulette. It is an invitation to temporary insanity for all—and possibly permanent insanity for some.

LSD is an important tool for research into mental illness. It is by studying the causes of illness that we may work out the cure. We can see that from the medical researchers who, a century ago, were led to study dangerous bacteria in order to work out a cure for infectious disease. By and large they succeeded and it is to be hoped that the second half of the 20th century will be to mental disease what the second half of the 19th was to infectious disease.

But there is one important difference. College students in the late 19th century didn't think it was exciting fun to inject themselves with cholera bacilli.

10 | How the Machine Called the Brain Feels and Thinks

Dean E. Wooldridge

In a provocative series of experiments, a team of scientists at Western Reserve University in Cleveland has developed techniques to remove the brain of a monkey from its body and keep it alive for many hours. Bare except for two small bits of bone to help support it, the nerves and blood vessels that once connected it to the monkey's body severed, the brain is

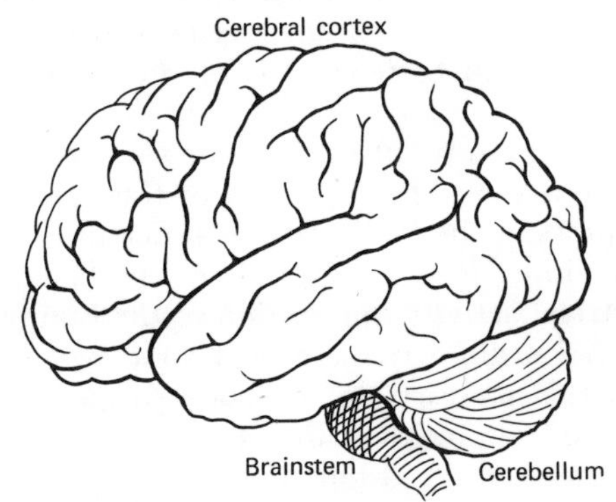

Control Center. The human brain is a mass of 10 billion nerve cells weighing about three pounds. By means of electro-chemical impulses traveling along the nerves at speeds of 2 to 200 miles an hour, it receives and transmits messages from and to every part of the body. The human brain (above) consists of three main parts:

The brainstem. This is the core of the brain, essentially an extension of the spinal cord (through which all nerve impulses are channeled). The brainstem controls such involuntary but vital functions as breathing and the heart beat, and generates such primitive drives as feelings of hunger, anger and pleasure. Sometimes called the "old brain," it existed in much the same form in the dinosaurs.

The cerebellum. This bulbous structure, part way up the brainstem and protruding toward the back of the head, coordinates muscular activity. It has been called the "private secretary" of the brain.

The cerebrum, or cerebral cortex. This convoluted mantle covers the other parts of the brain and fills the rest of the skull. It is divided, left and right, into two equal hemispheres. Sometimes called the "new brain," it is the seat of mental activity, voluntary action and the senses.

From *The New York Times Magazine,* October 1964.

suspended above a laboratory table. Attached to it are the tubes of a mechanical heart to maintain its blood supply; from it run wires to recording instruments. Their measurements of its electrical activity not only show that it remains alive but even suggest that sometimes this isolated brain is conscious.

While the immediate goal of the team, headed by Dr. Robert J. White, is the development of methods for obtaining answers to basic questions related to the physiology of the brain, one cannot help being fascinated by less specifically scientific, but perhaps more profoundly philosophic, considerations. Can the truly "detached minds" of the Cleveland monkeys really be conscious? If so, conscious of what?

Sensation, for example, is an important ingredient of the conscious state. Does biological science give us any clues as to what sensations, if any, the conscious incorporated brains of the Western Reserve monkeys could have felt? After all, the nerves that normally carry to the brain indications of touch, taste, odor, light and sound were all cut, and the associated sensory organs were far removed. Does this mean that, during its conscious periods, the isolated monkey brain floated in a sensory void, with no flashes of touch, pain, sight or sound to remind it of the kind of existence it once knew?

No one can know for sure, of course, but the answer is: Probably not. We know that the conscious, "feeling" part of the brain does not reach out to the sensory receptors of the finger tips in order to find out what the outside environment is doing to the periphery of the body. Instead, "feeling" is the result of electrical activity in a section of the brain's surface called the "sensory strip," which ordinarily serves as a "receiving station" for signals coming in through the nerves from the body surface. It is the activity in this "receiving station," rather than in the "wires" leading to it, that actually produces the conscious sensation that, say, a toe is cold.

Severing or otherwise mistreating the nerves leading to the sensory strip can result in patterns of electrical activity that "fool" the conscious part of the brain. This is why an amputee can feel the specific sensation of the fingers of his hand being twisted in an uncomfortable position for months after the arm carrying that hand has been cut off.

Similarly, while useful vision requires functioning eyes, and meaningful hearing requires operating ears, the sensations of sight and sound, involving uncoordinated but nonetheless vivid flashes of light or bursts of sound, can be experienced by an eyeless or earless individual. All that is necessary is that the conditions at the extremities of his severed nerves be such as to produce the rather simple kinds of electrochemical impulses that, upon arrival at the visual or auditory areas of the brain, are interpreted as sight or sound.

The detached monkey brain could even have felt hungry or thirsty. Such sensations are determined by local electric currents and related chemical activity in specific small regions, or "centers," in the brainstem—the "primitive" lower part of the brain that is really an extension of the spinal cord. When stimulating electric impulses are injected into the appropriate part of an animal's "appetite center," for example, by means of a surgically implanted wire, the animal will exhibit the only kind of appetite that truly deserves the adjective "insatiable": It will continue to eat any food provided to it, even though it is so stuffed that it must regurgitate what it has already swallowed. If the stimulating electrode is placed in another part of the appetite center, only a fraction of an inch away, the animal will be unable to eat—even to the extent of starving to death while surrounded by its favorite food.

Hunger of another sort would also have been possible for the isolated monkey brain. There are small regions of nerve tissue in the brainstem that control activities related to reproduction and care of the young. While electric stimulation in these centers is effective, some of the most interesting recent work has been with hormones. By implanting the right chemicals in the right spots in rats' brains, Dr. Alan E. Fisher, psychologist at the University of Pittsburgh, found that he could cause a male rat to exhibit typically female behavior, and vice versa. Thus, males were observed building nests and gently carrying to shelter the baby rats they would ordinarily have eaten.

We can even speculate on the state of mind of the detached monkey brain, during its periods of consciousness. If it at all understood what was happening to it, it may well have been angry and afraid. Perhaps it felt like biting with the teeth it once possessed, or like scratching or running with the legs it formerly controlled. If so, it is not unlikely that the brain did in fact generate such commands and send them in the form of electrochemical impulses to the severed ends of the nerves which formerly went to the muscles.

But it is also possible that the brain felt relaxed and comfortable. It could even have felt happy. For there appear to be "pleasure" and "punishment" centers in the brain. The feelings of anger, fright, horror, ease, relaxation, pleasure and ecstasy, just like those of hunger and thirst, are now known to be turned on or off selectively by local patterns of electrochemical activity in the brainstem. Whether you are a rat, cat, monkey or human being, sites deep in the brain have been located where electric stimulation will produce a sense of horror; other sites are known where stimulation will result in feelings of euphoria or ecstasy.

(Experimenters do not enjoy subjecting their animals to fright and pain, and do so as little as is consistent with obtaining the important information they seek. The justification for all such work is, of course, that the knowledge gained may ultimately make it possible to relieve human suffering.)

The Western Reserve experiments on isolated monkey brains constitute only one example of the progress that is being made toward clarifying some of the mysteries of the conscious state. For example, a "consciousness switch" has been located in the brain. Dr. H. W. Magoun, now at the University of California at Los Angeles, was able to show that an arrangement of interconnected nerve cells in the brainstem—the "reticular activating system" he called it—is the source of a special pattern of electrochemical nerve impulses that must be received by the brain if we are to be aware of what is going on.

During a surgical operation under general anesthesia, measurements have shown that the nerve impulses caused by the manipulation of the surgeon's scalpel arrive at the major brain centers with at least as great strength as though the patient were conscious. He does not feel them only because the chemical anesthetic has suppressed the reticular activating system. Without its steady flow of impulses to the higher portions of the brain, our sense of awareness is "turned off."

But this consciousness control need not be an "all or nothing" matter. The "switch" can regulate degrees of awareness as well.

For example, if a cat in a cage is exposed to a monotonous sequence of musical tones, measuring equipment will detect a corresponding sequence of electric impulses in the nerve leading from ear to brain. If then, with no change in the tone sequence or intensity, an object of great feline interest is displayed to the cat—a beaker containing mice, let us say—the measurements will show a great decrease or perhaps complete disappearance of the tone-generated nerve impulses.

It is the same reticular activating system in the brainstem—the "consciousness switch"—that is at work. The appearance of an object of overriding interest generates a new electric signal that serves to turn down the "volume control" of the nerve system registering the object of lesser interest. In this way we are permitted to "focus" our attention—to enhance our consciousness of events of interest by freeing our minds from unimportant distractions.

One of the most interesting and puzzling phenomena related to consciousness was first observed nearly 30 years ago by Dr. Wilder Penfield, at that time head of the Montreal Neurological Institute.

In connection with operations to remove tumors or epileptically defective brain tissue, Penfield had developed a new kind of electric-probe technique. After removal of the section of skull covering the area where defective tissue was believed to be, the patient would be restored to consciousness in the operating room, and asked to describe his sensations as needles were stuck into various parts of his brain and electricity injected. (The brain contains no nerve endings that can sense pain; a patient suffers no discomfort in such tests). By the nature of the responses, it was frequently possible to determine the boundaries of defective tissue more accurately than by visual observation alone.

In 1936, several years after the first use of this new technique, Penfield was preparing to operate on a woman whose lesion was on the side of the cortex (the outer surface of the brain) just above the ear—a region that later work was to implicate with the memory mechanisms. When the needle electrode was inserted and the electric current turned on, the patient suddenly reported that she felt transported back to her early childhood. In the operating room, she essentially relived an episode out of her remote past, even feeling again the same fear that had accompanied the original event.

In the succeeding years, Penfield and many other brain surgeons have observed, in many patients, this kind of triggering of memory by cortical stimulation. The phenomenon possesses a number of fascinating features, which the developing understanding of brain function must some day explain. For example: The electrically elicited experiences always appear to be real although the patient usually has not been consciously carrying them in his memory. The induced recollection can be stopped abruptly by turning off the stimulating current, and often restarted by turning it on again. But, when restarted, the recalled episode never continues where it left off—instead, it starts again from the beginning, as though it were stored on a film or tape which automatically rewinds each time it is interrupted.

Perhaps most startling is the vividness of the elicited experience. Instead of being a remembering, according to Penfield, "it is a hearing-again and seeing-again—a living-through-moments-of-past-time."

Nevertheless, the patient does not lose contact with the present. He seems to have concurrent existences—one in the operating room, and one in the part of the past that he is reliving. The term "double-consciousness" is employed by brain surgeons to describe these peculiar sensations of their patients.

Penfield's discovery no longer stands as the sole example of the successful tampering with the unity of consciousness by brain surgeons and research scientists. In the biology laboratories of the California Institute of Technology, Dr. R. W. Sperry has had under way for several years a series of experiments on cats and monkeys that in some ways are even more spectacular.

Sperry's methods are based on the left-right symmetry that characterizes higher animals, including cats, monkeys and men. In particular, in such animals the brain consists of two similar hemispheres.

They are interconnected by a vast system of nerve fibers numbering several hundred million in a human brain.

In concept, Sperry's idea was simple: Break these connections and see what happens. The trouble was that when he tried it on laboratory animals (usually cats) nothing much did happen. Even after most of the connections between the brain hemispheres had been cut, the animal appeared substantially unchanged. It behaved about as before; it achieved about the same scores on intelligence tests; it remembered its old tricks and could learn new ones.

The experiment had to be refined. This was done by adding to the brain-splitting surgery an operation on the visual system of the animal, as a result of which the left eye was connected only with the left half of the brain, and the right eye with the right half (ordinarily there are also crossing connections; these were cut).

Cats prepared in this way were then subjected to special training procedures. They were taught to choose between two swinging doors that they could easily open, one carrying a conspicuous circular design, the other a cross.

The cat under training would learn that choice of the door with a circle, say, would lead to a reward, choice of the door with a cross would lead to punishment. This was routine animal training; the distinguishing feature of the experiment was that the cat was provided with an eyepatch, so that all of its trials involved the use of, say, the left eye only, which in turn was connected to the isolated left half of the brain.

The animals learned their lessons about as fast as cats that had not had their brains split. Everything seemed normal—up to a point. This point was reached when the cat had been trained to near perfection using its left eye, and then was reintroduced into the training cage with the eyepatch shifted, so that the untrained eye—and the associated half of the brain—came into play.

The result was spectacular. Changing the eyepatch was exactly equivalent to changing cats. When employing the eye connected to the untrained half of its brain, the animal appeared to have not the slightest recollection of ever having been in the problem box. It could be trained again, using the new eye and hemisphere, to perform the desired discrimination, but its rate of learning was exactly the same as that of an entirely fresh, untrained cat.

In the new condition, it could even be taught, equally easily, a discrimination opposite to that learned originally. Using its right eye and right hemisphere, it could learn to open the door with the cross despite its earlier acquisition, when using its left eye and left hemisphere, of the habit of opening the door with the circle. Such a doubly trained animal would shift its performance automatically, without confusion, when the eyepatch was shifted.

By severing the connections between the two halves of the brain, Sperry had apparently split into two distinct parts what had previously been a single sense of consciousness.

In some respects, the split-consciousness implications of the work on cats was demonstrated even more vividly by later experiments on monkeys. In this work the two halves of the brain were provided with different properties, not by training, but by surgical modification. On one side of the monkey's brain the nerve fibers running from the brainstem to a forward part of the brain were severed. This operation—a frontal lobotomy—has for years been known to produce significant personality changes if performed on both sides of the brain. Specifically, it produces under these circumstances a relaxed, "I-don't-care" person or animal. Before the development of tranquilizing drugs, it was sometimes employed to ease the unbearable tensions of psychotic mental patients.

In addition to the frontal lobotomy on one side of the brain, the monkeys were subjected to the split-brain operation, including modification of their optic connections, just as in the cat experiments. After the surgery, they were fitted with an arrangement of contact lenses similar to the cat's eyepatches.

A monkey employing the eye that was connected to the unmodified half of its brain would then be shown a snake. Monkeys are normally deathly afraid of snakes and the split-brain monkey was no exception. It showed the usual fright and escape reactions.

Then the conditions were changed so that the monkey had to employ the eye connected with the hemisphere that had had the lobotomy. Again the snake was displayed. This time, the monkey could not have cared less; the snake held no terrors for it. It was as though two different animal personalities now inhabited the body that had formerly been occupied by one.

The existence of pleasure and punishment centers in the brain, the discovery of the consciousness switch, the peculiar "double-consciousness" of Penfield's patients, the split-personality of Sperry's split-brain animals—

all are variations on a single theme: the operation of the principle of cause and effect in the content and quality of the conscious state.

We feel horror or ecstasy, are conscious or unconscious, *because* of the electrochemical activity in specific brainstem tissue; we appear to have concurrent existences in past and present *because* of the disturbance of our brain mechanisms produced by Penfield's electric probe; we have two separate states of consciousness *because* Sperry has cut the connections between the two halves of our brain.

Is consciousness, then, finally to become an early and predictable physical quantity like gravity, electric charge or magnetism? Is it to be only another property of matter, to be dealt with by the impersonal and objective techniques of the mathematician and physicist? To be sure, consciousness seems to be connected with intelligence, but are we to learn that it is automatically and inevitably associated with the complex organizations and states of matter required for intelligence, much as gravity is associated with mass?

Must we even come to speculate that, among the wires and transistors of our electronic computers, there already stirs a dim glimmering of the same kind of sense of awareness that has become, for man, his most personal and precious possession? Fantastic? Perhaps.

The immediate human reaction—that consciousness is by its very nature a mysterious and unexplainable phenomenon—is really not very pertinent. All the laws and properties of nature are fundamentally mysterious; science can no more explain gravitational attraction or electric charge than it can the sense of consciousness. The scientist delineates the orderly and predictable interactions among his quantities; he never explains the quantities themselves.

If future investigation continues to disclose consistent interrelationships between the physical conditions of the brain and the qualities of consciousness, it is hard to see how consciousness can escape ultimate acceptance as a property of certain organizations and states of matter. Then consciousness would be no longer a question of metaphysics but part of the realm described by the physical laws of nature.

It would be hard to imagine a development of more far-reaching importance to science and philosophy. Yet it could come as a consequence of the exciting work now under way in the laboratories of the brain research scientists.

11 | The Interpretive Cortex

Wilder Penfield

There is an area of the surface of the human brain where local electrical stimulation can call back a sequence of past experience. An epileptic irritation in this area may do the same. It is as though a wire recorder, or a strip of cinematographic film with sound track, had been set in motion within the brain. The sights and sounds, and the thoughts, of a former day pass through the man's mind again.

The purpose of this article is to describe, for readers from various disciplines of science, the area of the cerebral cortex from which this neuron record of the past can be activated and to suggest what normal contribution it may make to cerebral function.

The human brain is the master organ of the human race. It differs from the brains of other mammals particularly in the greater extent of its cerebral cortex. The gray matter, or cortex, that covers the two cerebral hemispheres of the brain of man is so vast in nerve cell population that it could never have been contained within the human skull if it were not folded upon itself, and refolded, so as to form a very large number of fissures and convolutions (Fig. 1). The fissures are so deep and so devious that by far the greater portion of this ganglionic carpet (about 65 percent) is hidden in them, below the surface (Fig. 2).

The portion that is labeled "interpretive" in Figs. 1 and 3 covers a part of both temporal lobes. It is from these two homologous areas, and from nowhere else, that electrical stimulation has occasionally produced physical responses which may be divided into (i) experiential responses and (ii) interpretive responses.

EXPERIENTIAL RESPONSES

Occasionally during the course of a neurosurgical operation under local anesthesia, gentle electrical stimulation in this temporal area, right or left, has caused the conscious patient to be aware of some previous experience [1]. The experience seems to be picked out at random from his own past. But it comes back to him in great detail. He is suddenly aware again of those things to which he paid attention in that distant interval of time. This recollection of an experiential sequence stops suddenly when the electrical current is switched off or when the electrode is removed from contact with the cortex. This phenomenon we have chosen to call an experiential response to stimulation.

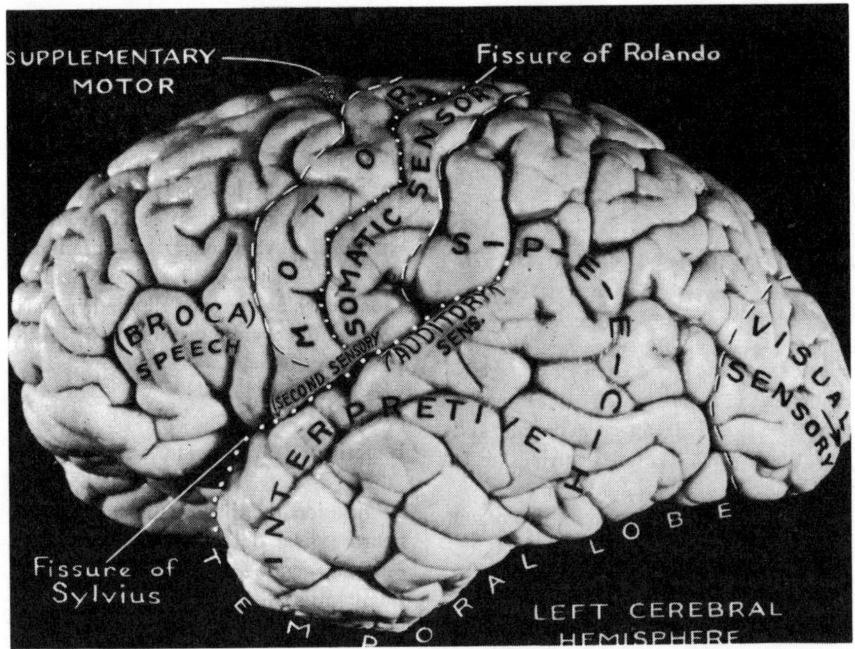

Fig. 1. Photograph of the left hemisphere of a human brain. The frontal lobe is on the left, the occipital lobe on the right. The major motor and sensory areas are indicated, as well as the speech areas and the interpretive area. [Penfield and Roberts (18)]

Case Examples [2]

The patient S.Be. observed, when the electrode touched the temporal lobe (right superior temporal convolution), "There was a piano over there and someone playing. I could hear the song you know." When the cortex was stimulated again without warning, at approximately the same point, the patient had a different experience. He said: "Someone speaking to another, and he mentioned a name but I could not understand it. . . It was like a dream." Again the point was restimulated without his knowledge. He said quietly: "Yes, 'Oh Marie, Oh Marie'! Someone is singing it." When the point was stimulated a fourth time he heard the same song again and said it was the "theme song of a radio program."

The electrode was then applied to a point 4 centimeters farther forward on the first temporal convolution. While the electrode was still in place, S.Be. said: "Something brings back a memory. I can see Seven-Up Bottling Company—Harrison Bakery." He was evidently seeing two of Montreal's large illuminated advertisements.

The surgeon then warned him that he was about to apply the electrode again. Then, after a pause, the surgeon said "Now," but he did not stimulate. (The patient has no means of knowing when the electrode is applied, unless he is told, since the cortex itself is without sensation.) The patient replied promptly, "Nothing."

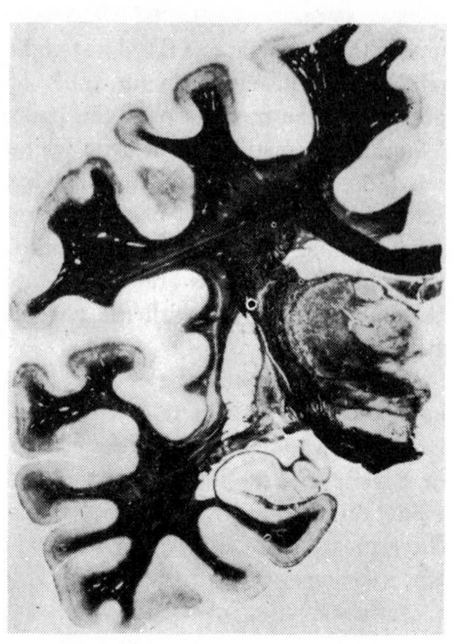

Fig. 2. (Right) Photograph of a cross section of the left cerebral hemisphere [Jelgersma (19)]. The white matter is stained black and the gray matter is unstained. The major convolutions of the cerebral cortex and the subcortical masses of gray matter can be identified by reference to the diagram below. (Bottom) Drawing of the cross section shown at right, above, with additions. The surfaces and convolutions of the temporal lobe are identified, and the relationship of one hemisphere to the other and the relationship of the hemispheres to the brain stem and cerebellum are shown.

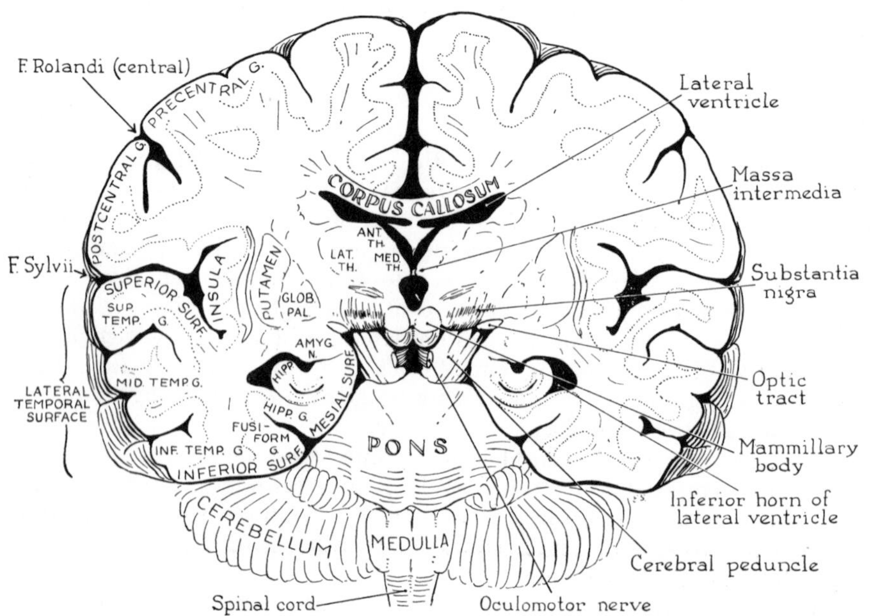

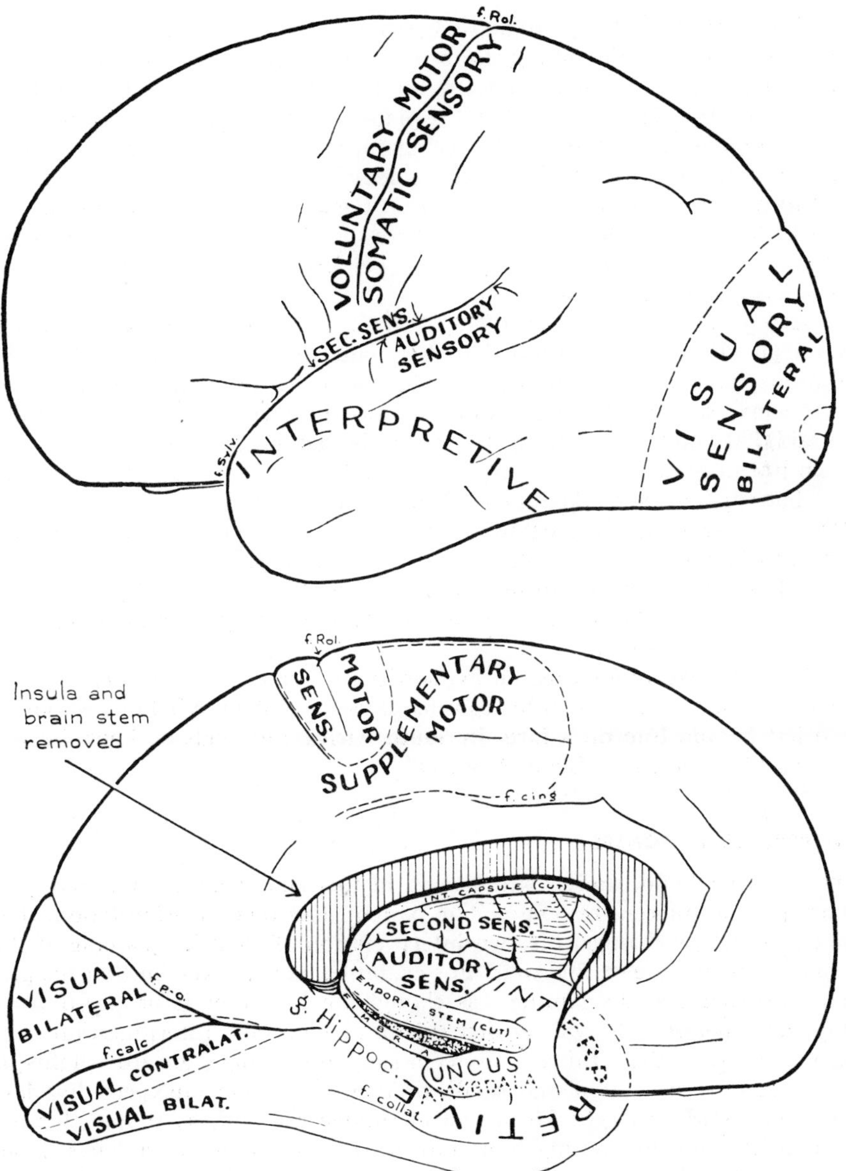

Fig. 3. The left cerebral hemisphere; the lateral surface is shown above and the mesial surface below. In the lower drawing the brain stem with the island of Reil has been removed to show the inner banks of the fissure of Sylvius and the superior surface of the temporal lobe. The interpretive cortex extends from the lateral to the superior surface of the temporal lobe. [Penfield and Roberts (18)]

A woman (D.F.) [3] heard an orchestra playing an air while the electrode was held in place. The music stopped when the electrode was removed. It came again when the electrode was reapplied. On request, she hummed the tune, while the electrode was held in place, accompanying the orchestra. It was a popular song. Over and over again, restimulation at the same spot produced the same song. The music seemed always to begin at the same place and to progress at the normally expected tempo. All efforts to mislead her failed. She believed that a gramaphone was being turned on in the operating room on each occasion, and she asserted her belief stoutly in a conversation some days after the operation.

A boy (R.W.) heard his mother talking to someone on the telephone when an electrode was applied to his right temporal cortex. When the stimulus was repeated without warning, he heard his mother again in the same conversation. When the stimulus was repeated after a lapse of time, he said, "My mother is telling my brother he has got his coat on backwards. I can just hear them."

The surgeon then asked the boy whether he remembered this happening. "Oh yes," he said, "just before I came here." Asked again whether this seemed like a dream, he replied: "No, it is like I go into a daze."

J.T. cried out in astonishment when the electrode was applied to the temporal cortex; "Yes doctor, yes doctor. Now I hear people laughing—my friends in South Africa!"

When asked about this, he explained the reason for his surprise. He seemed to be laughing with his cousins, Bessie and Ann Wheliow, whom he had left behind him on a farm in South Africa, although he knew he was now on the operating table in Montreal.

INTERPRETIVE RESPONSES

On the other hand, similar stimulation in this same general area may produce quite a different response. The patient discovers, on stimulation, that he has somehow changed his own interpretation of what he is seeing at the moment, or hearing or thinking. For example, he may exclaim that his present experience seems familiar, as though he had seen it or heard it or thought it before. He realizes that this must be a false interpretation. Or, on the contrary, these things may seem suddenly strange, absurd. Sights or sounds may seem distant and small, or they may come unexpectedly close and seem loud or large. He may feel suddenly afraid, as though his environment were threatening him, and he is possessed by a nameless dread or panic. Another patient may say he feels lonely or aloof, or as though he were observing himself at a distance.

Under normal circumstances anyone may make such interpretations of the present, and these interpretations serve him as guides to action or reaction. If the interpretations are accurate guides, they must be based upon previous comparable experience. It is conceivable, therefore, that the recall mechanism which is activated by the electrode during an experiential response and the mechanism activated in an interpretive response may be parts of a common inclusive mechanism of reflex recognition or interpretation.

No special function had been previously assigned by neurologists to the area in each temporal lobe that is marked "interpretive" in Figs. 1 and 3, though some clinicians have suggested it might have to do with the recall of music. The term *interpretive cortex,* therefore, is no more than slang to be employed for the purposes of discussion. The terms *motor cortex, sensory cortex,* and *speech cortex* began as slang phrases and have served such a purpose. But such phrases must not be understood to signify independence of action of separated units in the case of any of these areas. Localization of function in the cerebral cortex means no more than specialization of function as compared with other cortical regions, not separation from the integrated action of the brain.

Before considering the interpretive cortex further, we may turn briefly to the motor and sensory areas and the speech areas of the cortex. After considering the effects of electrical stimulation there, we should be better able to understand the results of stimulation in the temporal lobes.

SPECIALIZATION OF FUNCTION IN THE CORTEX

Evidence for some degree of localization within the brain was recognized early in the 19th century by Flourens. He concluded from experiment that functional subdivision of "the organ of the mind" was possible. The forebrain [4], he said [cerebral hemispheres and higher brain stem (Fig. 4)] had to do with thought and will power, while the cerebellum was involved in the coordination of movement.

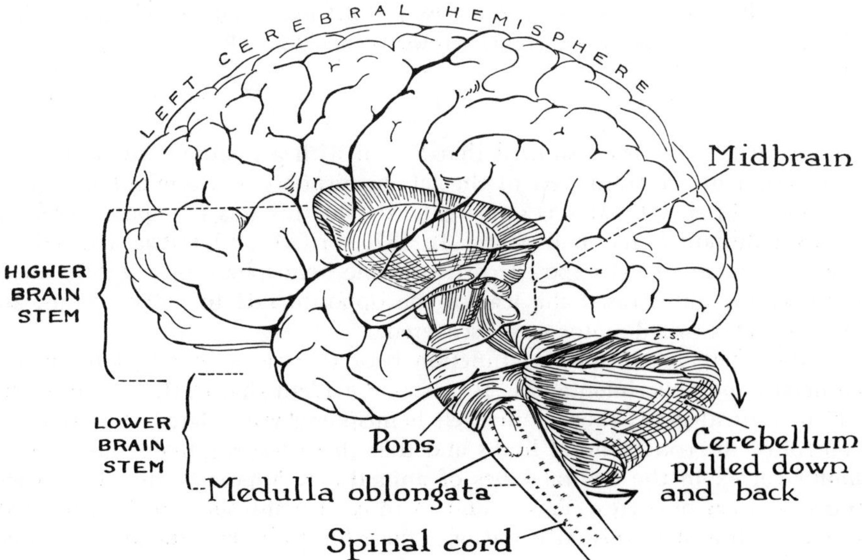

Fig. 4. Drawing of the left cerebral hemisphere, showing the higher brain stem, including the thalamus, within and the lower brain stem and spinal cord emerging below. The cerebellum is shown, attached to the lower brain stem. [Penfield and Roberts (18)]

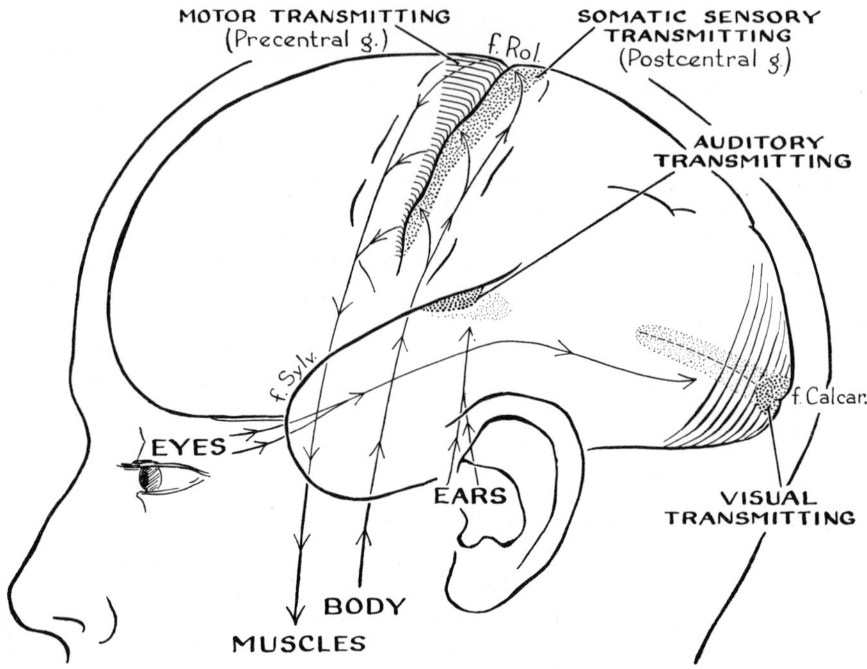

Fig. 5. Sensory and motor projection areas. The sensory areas are stippled, and the afferent pathways to them from eyes, ears, and body are indicated by entering arrows. The motor cortex is indicated by parallel lines, and the efferent cortico-spinal tract is indicated by emerging arrows. [Penfield and Roberts (18)]

In 1861, Paul Broca showed that a man with a relatively small area of destruction in a certain part of the left hemisphere alone might lose only the power of speech. It was soon realized that this was the speech area of man's dominant (left) hemisphere. In 1870, Fritsch and Hitzig applied an electric current to the exposed cortex of one hemisphere of a lightly anesthetized dog and caused the legs of the opposite side to move. Thus, an area of cortex called motor was discovered.

After that, localization of function became a research target for many clinicians and experimentalists. It was soon evident that in the case of man, the precentral gyrus (Fig. 5) in each hemisphere was related to voluntary control of the contralateral limbs and that there was an analogous area of motor cortex in the frontal lobes of animals. It appeared also that other separate areas of cortex (Figs. 1 and 5) in each hemisphere were dedicated to sensation (one for visual sensation, others for auditory, olfactory, and discriminative somatic sensation, respectively).

It was demonstrated, too, that from the "motor cortex" there was an efferent bundle of nerve fibers (the pyramidal tract) that ran down through the lower brain stem and the spinal cord to be relayed on out to the muscles. Through this efferent pathway, voluntary control of these muscles was actually carried out. It was evident, too, that there were separate sensory tracts carrying nerve impulses in the other direction, from the principal organs of special sense (eye, ear, nose, and skin and muscle) into separate sensory areas of the cortex.

These areas, motor and sensory, have been called "projection areas." They play a role in the projection of nerve currents to the cortex from the periphery of the body, and from the cortex to the periphery. This makes possible (sensory) awareness of environment and provides the individual with a means of outward (motor) expression. The motor cortex has a specialized use during voluntary action, and each of the several sensory areas has a specialized use, when the individual is seeing, hearing, smelling, or feeling.

TRAVELING POTENTIALS

The action of the living brain depends upon the movement, within it, of "transient electrical potentials traveling the fibers of the nervous system." This was Sherrington's phrase. Within the vast circuits of this master organ, potentials travel, here and there and yonder, like meteors that streak across the sky at night and line the firmament with trails of light. When the meteors pass, the paths of luminescence still glow a little while, then fade and are gone. The changing patterns of these paths of passing energy make possible the changing content of the mind. The patterns are never quite the same, and so it is with the content of the mind.

Specialized areas in the cortex are at times active and again relatively quiet. But, when a man is awake, there is always some central integration and coordination of the traveling potentials. There must be activity within the brain stem and some areas of the cortex. This is centrencephalic integration [5].

SENSORY, MOTOR, AND PHYSICAL RESPONSES TO CORTICAL STIMULATION

My purpose in writing this article is to discuss in simple words (free of technical terms) the meaning of the "psychical" responses which appear only on stimulation of the so-called interpretive cortex. But before considering these responses let us consider the motor and sensory activity of the cortex for a moment.

When the streams of electrical potentials that pass normally through the various areas of sensory cortex are examined electrically, they do not seem to differ from each other except in pattern and timing. The essential difference is to be found in the fact that the visual stream passes to the visual cortex and then to one subcortical target and the auditory stream passes through the auditory cortex and then on to another subcortical target.

When the surgeon stimulates the intact sensory cortex he must be sending a current along the next "piece of road" to a subcortical destination. This electrode (delivering, for example, 60 "waves" per second of 2-millisecond duration and 1-volt intensity) produces no more than elementary sight when applied to visual cortex. The patient reports colors, lights, and shadows that move and take on crude outlines. The same electrode, applied to auditory cortex, causes him to hear a ringing or hissing or thumping sound. When applied to postcentral gyrus it produces tingling or a false sense of movement.

Thus, sensation is produced by the passage inward of electrical potentials. And when the electrode is applied to the motor cortex, movement is produced by passage of potentials outward to the muscles. In each case positive response is produced by conduction in the direction of normal physiological flow—that is, by dromic conduction [6].

Responses to electrical stimulation that may be called "psychical," as distinguished from sensory or motor, have been elicited from certain areas of the human cortex (Fig. 6). But they have never been produced by stimulation in other areas. There are, of course, other large areas of cortex which are neither sensory nor motor in function. They seem to be employed in other neuron mechanisms that are also associated with psychical processes. But the function of these other areas cannot, it seems, be activated by so simple a stimulus as an electric current applied to the cortex.

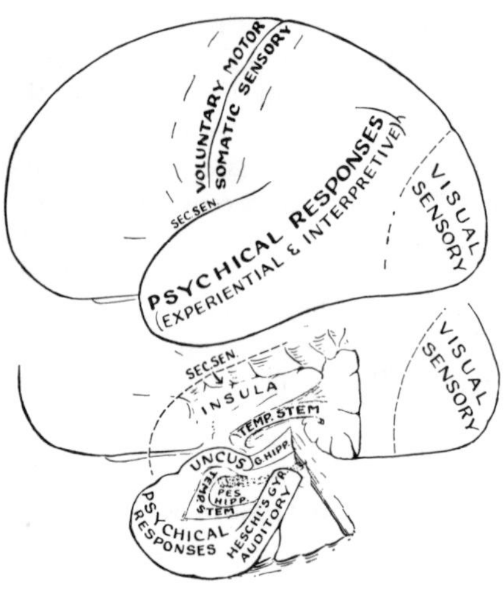

Fig. 6. The left cerebral hemisphere is shown with the temporal lobe cut across and turned down. The areas of cortex from which psychical responses have been elicited are indicated. [Penfield (1)]

DREAMY STATES OF EPILEPSY

"Epilepsy" may be defined, in Jackson's words, as "the name for occasional, sudden, excessive, rapid and local discharges of grey matter." Our aim in the operations under discussion was to remove the gray matter responsible for epileptic attacks if that gray matter could be spared. When the stimulating electrode reproduced the psychical phenomenon that initiated the fit, it provided the guidance sought [7].

During the 19th century clinicians had recognized these phenomena as epileptic. They applied the term *intellectual aura* to such attacks. Jackson substituted the expression *dreamy states* [see 8]. These were, he said, "psychical states during the onset of certain epileptic seizures, states which are much more elaborate than crude sensations." And again, he wrote, "These are all voluminous mental states and yet of different kinds; no doubt they ought to be classified, but for my present purpose they may be considered together."

"The state," he said, "is often like that occasionally experienced by healthy people as a feeling of 'reminiscence.' " Or the patient has "dreamy feelings," "dreams mixing up with present thoughts," "double consciousness," a "feeling of being somewhere else," a feeling "as if I went back to all that occurred in my childhood," "silly thoughts."

Jackson never did classify these states, but he did something more important. He localized the area of cortex from which epileptic discharge would produce dreamy states. His localization was in the anterior and deep portions of the temporal lobes, the same area that is labeled "interpretative" cortex in Fig. 3.

Case Example

Brief reference may be made to a specific case. The patient had seizures, and stimulation produced responses which were first recognized as psychical.

In 1936, a girl of 16 (J.V.) was admitted to the Montreal Neurological Institute complaining of epileptic attacks, each of which was ushered in by the same hallucination. It was a little dream, she said, in which an experience from early childhood was reenacted, always the same train of events. She would then cry out with fear and run to her mother. Occasionally this was followed immediately by a major convulsive seizure.

At operation, under local anesthesia, we tried to set off the dream by a gentle electrical stimulus in the right temporal lobe. The attempt was successful. The dream was produced by the electrode. Stimulation at other points on the temporal cortex produced sudden fear without the dream. At still other points, stimulation caused her to say that she saw "someone coming toward me." At another point, stimulation caused her to say she heard the voices of her mother and her brothers [9].

This suggested a new order of cortical response to electrical stimulation. When the neighboring visual sensory area of the cortex is stimulated, any patient may report seeing stars of light or moving colors or black outlines but never "someone coming toward me." Stimulation of the auditory sensory cortex may cause any patient to report that he hears ringing, buzzing, blowing, or thumping sounds, perhaps, but never voices that speak. Stimulation in the areas of sensory cortex can call forth nothing more than the elements of visual or auditory or tactile sensation, never happenings that might have been previously experienced.

During the 23 years that have followed, although practically all areas of the cerebral cortex have been stimulated and studied in more than 1000 craniotomies, performed under local anesthesia, psychical responses of the experiential or interpretive variety have been produced only from the temporal cortex in the general areas that are marked "psychical responses" in Fig. 3 [10, 11].

CLASSIFICATION

It seems reasonable to subdivide psychical responses and psychical seizures (epileptic dreamy states) in the same way, classifying them as "interpretive" or "experiential." Interpretive psychical responses are those involving interpretations of the present experience, or emotions related to it;

experiential psychical responses are reenactments of past experiences. Interpretive seizures are those accompanied by auras and illusions; experiential seizures are those accompanied by auras and hallucinations.

The interpretive responses and seizures may be divided into groups [11] of which the commonest are as follows: (i) recognition, the illusion that things seen and heard and thought are familiar (*déjà vu* phenomenon); (ii) visual illusion, the illusion that things seen are changing—for example, coming nearer, growing larger (macropsia); (iii) auditory illusion, the illusion that things heard are changing—for example, coming near, going away, changing tempo; (iv) illusional emotion, the emotion of fear or, less often, loneliness, sorrow, or disgust.

Experiential phenomena (hallucinations) are an awareness of experiences from the past that come into the mind without complete loss of awareness of the present.

DISCUSSION

What, then, is the function of the interpretive cortex? This is a physiological question that follows the foregoing observations naturally.

An electrode, delivering, for example, 60 electrical pulses per second to the surface of the motor cortex, causes a man to make crude movements. When applied to the various sensory areas of the cortex, it causes him to have crude sensations of sight or sound or body feeling. This indicates only that these areas have something to do with the complicated mechanism of voluntary action or conscious sensation. It does not reveal what contribution the cortex may make, or in what way it may contribute to skill in making voluntary movement or qualify the incoming sensory streams.

In the case of the interpretive cortex, the observations are similar. We may say that the interpretive cortex has something to do with a mechanism that can reactivate the vivid record of the past. It has also something to do with a mechanism that can present to consciousness a reflex interpretation of the present. To conclude that here is the mechanism of memory would be an unjustified assumption. It would be too simple.

What a man remembers when he makes a voluntary effort is apt to be a generalization. If this were not so, he might be hopelessly lost in detail. On the other hand, the experiential responses described above are detailed reenactments of a single experience. Such experiences soon slip beyond the range of voluntary recall. A man may summon to mind a song at will. He hears it then in his mind, not all at once but advancing phrase by phrase. He may sing it or play it too, and one would call this memory.

But if a patient hears music in response to the electrode, he hears it in one particular strip of time. That time runs forward again at the original tempo, and he hears the orchestration, or he sees the player at a piano "over there." These are details he would have thought forgotten.

A vast amount of work remains to be done before the mechanism of memory, and how and where the recording takes place, are understood. This record is not laid down in the interpretive cortex, but it is kept in a part of the brain that is intimately connected with it.

Removal of large areas of interpretive cortex, even when carried out on both sides, may result in mild complaints of memory defect, but it does not abolish the capacity to remember recent events. On the other hand, surgical removals that result in bilateral interference with the underlying hippocampal zone do make the recording of recent events impossible, while distant memory is still preserved [12, 13].

The importance of the hippocampal area for memory was pointed out long ago in a forgotten publication by the Russian neurologist Bechterew [14]. The year before publication Bechterew had demonstrated the case before the St. Petersburg Clinic for Nervous and Mental Diseases. The man on whom Bechterew reported had "extraordinary weakness of memory, falsifications of memory and great apathy." These defects were shown at autopsy to be secondary to lesions of the mesial surface of the cortex of both temporal lobes. The English neurologists Glees and Griffith [15] reported similar defects, a half century later, in a patient who had symmetrical lesions of the hippocampus and of hippocampal and fusiform gyri on both sides.

The way in which the interpretive cortex seems to be used may be suggested by an example: After years of absence you meet, by chance, a man whose very existence you had forgotten. On seeing him, you may be struck by a sudden sense of familiarity, even before you have time to "think." A signal seems to flash up in consciousness to tell you that you've seen that man before. You watch him as he smiles and moves and speaks. The sense of familiarity grows stronger. Then you remember him. You may even recall that his name was Jones. The sight and the sound of the man has given you an instant access, through some reflex, to the records of the past in which this man has played some part. The opening of this forgotten file was subconscious. It was not a voluntary act. You would have known him even against your will. Although Jones was a forgotten man a moment before, now you can summon the record in such detail that you remark at once the slowness of his gait or a new line about the mouth.

If Jones had been a source of danger to you, you might have felt fear as well as familiarity before you had time to consider the man. Thus, the signal of fear as well as the signal of familiarity may come to one as the result of subconscious comparison of present with similar past experience.

One more example may be given from common experience. A sudden increase in the size of objects seen and in sounds heard may mean the rapid approach of something that calls for instant avoidance action. These are signals that, because of previous experience, we sometimes act upon with little consideration.

SUMMARY

The interpretive cortex has in it a mechanism for instant reactivation of the detailed record of the past. It has a mechanism also for the production of interpretive signals. Such signals could only be significant if past records are scanned and relevant experiences are selected for comparison with present experience. This is a subconscious process. But it may well be that this scanning of past experience and selection from it also renders the relevant past available for conscious consideration as well. Thus, the individual may refer to the record as he employs other circuits of the brain.

Access to the record of the past seems to be as readily available from the temporal cortex of one side as from that of the other. Auditory illusions (or interpretations of the distance, loudness, or tempo of sounds) have been produced by stimulation of the temporal cortex of either side. The same is true of illusional emotions, such as fear and disgust.

But, on the contrary, visual illusions (interpretations of the distance, dimension, erectness, and tempo of things seen) are only produced by stimulation of the temporal cortex on the nondominant (normally, right) side of the brain. Illusions of recognition, such as familiarity or strangeness, were also elicited only from the nondominant side, except in one case.

CONCLUSION

"Consciousness," to quote William James [16], "is never quite the same in successive moments of time. It is a stream forever flowing, forever changing." The stream of changing states of mind that James described so well does flow through each man's waking hours until the time when he falls asleep to wake no more. But the stream, unlike a river, leaves a record in the living brain.

Transient electrical potentials move with it through the circuits of the nervous system, leaving a path that can be followed again. The pattern of this pathway, from neuron to neuron along each nerve-cell body and fiber and junction, is the recorded pattern of each man's past. That complicated record is held there in temporal sequence through the principle of durable facilitation of conduction and connection.

A steady stream of electrical pulses applied through an electrode to some point in the interpretive cortex causes a stream of excitation to flow from the cortex to the place where past experience is recorded. This stream of excitation acts as a key to the past. It can enter the pathway of recorded consciousness at any random point, from childhood on through adult life. But having entered, the experience moves forward without interference from other experiences. And when the electrode is withdrawn there is a likelihood, which lasts for seconds or minutes, that the stream of excitation will enter the pathway again at the same moment of past time, even if the electrode is reapplied at neighboring points [17].

Finally, an electric current applied to the surface of what may be called the interpretive cortex of a conscious man (i) may cause the stream of former consciousness to flow again or (ii) may give him an interpretation of the present that is unexpected and involuntary. Therefore, it is concluded that, under normal circumstances, this area of cortex must make some functional contribution to reflex comparison of the present with related past experience. It contributes to reflex interpretation or perception of the present.

The combination and comparison of present experience with similar past experience must call for remarkable scanning of the past and classification of similarities. What contribution this area of the temporal cortex may make to the whole process is not clear. The term *interpretive cortex* will serve for identification until students of human physiology can shed more light on these fascinating findings.

REFERENCES AND NOTES

1. W. Penfield, *J. Mental Sci.* **101,** 451 (1955).
2. These patients, designated by the same initials, have been described in previous publications in much greater detail. An index of patients (designated by initials) may be found in any of my books.
3. This case is reported in detail in W. Penfield and H. Jasper, *Epilepsy and the Functional Anatomy of the Human Brain* (Little, Brown, Boston, 1954) [published in abridged form in Russian (translation by N. P. Graschenkov and G. Smirnov) by the Soviet Academy of Sciences, 1958].
4. The forebrain, or prosencephalon, properly includes the diencephalon and the telencephalon, or higher brain stem, and hemispheres. Flourens probably had cerebral hemispheres in mind as distinguished from cerebellum.
5. "Within the brain, a central transactional core has been identified between the strictly sensory or motor systems of classical neurology. This central reticular mechanism has been found capable of grading the activity of most other parts of the brain"— H. Magoun, *The Waking Brain* (Thomas, Springfield, Ill., (1958).
6. W. Penfield, *The Excitable Cortex in Conscious Man* (Thomas, Springfield, Ill., 1958).
7. It did more than this; it produced illusions or hallucinations that had never been experienced by the patient during a seizure.
8. J. Taylor, Ed., *Selected Writings of John Hughlings Jackson* (Hodder and Stoughton, London, 1931), vol. 1, *On Epilepsy and Epileptiform Convulsions.*
9. Twenty-one years later this young woman, who is the daughter of a physician, was present at a meeting of the National Academy of Sciences in New York while her case was discussed. She could still recall the operation and the nature of the "dreams" that had preceded her seizures [W. Penfield, *Proc. Natl. Acad. Sci. U.S.* **44,** 51 (1958)].
10. In a recent review of the series my associate, Dr. Phanor Perot, has found and summarized 35 out of 384 temporal lobe cases in which stimulation produced experiential responses. All such responses were elicited in the temporal cortex. In a study of 214 consecutive operations for temporal lobe epilepsy, my associate Sean Mullan found 70 cases in which interpretive illusion occurred in the minor seizures before operation, or in which an interpretive response was produced by stimulation during operation. In most cases it occurred both before and during operation.
11. S. Mullan and W. Penfield, *A.M.A. Arch. Neurol. Psychiat.* **81,** 269 (1959).
12. This area is marked "Hipp" and "Hipp. G" in Fig. 2 (bottom) and "g. Hippoc." and "amygdala" in Fig. 3.
13. W. Penfield and B. Milner, *A.M.A. Arch. Neurol. Psychiat.* **79,** 475 (1958).
14. W. V. Bechterew, "Demonstration eines Gehirns mit Zerstörung der vorderen und inneren Theile der Hirnrinde beider Schläfenlappen," *Neurol. Zentralbl. Leipzig* **19,** 990 (1900). My attention was called to this case recently by Dr. Peter Gloor of Montreal.
15. P. Glees and H. B. Griffith, *Monatsschr. Psychiat. Neurol.* **123,** 193 (1952).
16. W. James, *The Principles of Psychology* (Holt, New York, 1910).
17. Thus, it is apparent that the beam of excitation that emanates from the interpretive cortex and seems to scan the record of the past is subject to the principles of transient facilitation already demonstrated for the anthropoid

motor cortex [A. S. F. GRÜNBAUM and C. SHERRINGTON, *Proc. Roy. Soc. (London)* **72B,** 152 (1901); T. GRAHAM BROWN and C. S. SHERRINGTON, *ibid.* **85B,** 250 (1912)]. Similarly subject to the principles of facilitation are the motor and the sensory cortex of man [W. PENFIELD and K. WELCH, *J. Physiol. (London)* **109,** 358 (1949)]. The patient D. F. heard the same orchestra playing the same music in the operating room more than 20 times when the electrode was reapplied to the superior surface of the temporal lobe. Each time the music began in the verse of a popular song. It proceeded to the chorus, if the electrode was kept in place.

18. W. PENFIELD and L. ROBERTS, *Speech and Brain Mechanisms* (Princeton Univ. Press, Princeton, N.J., 1959).

19. G. JELGERSMA, *Atlas anatomicum cerebri humani* (Scheltema and Holkema, Amsterdam).

Unit Three | DISCUSSION QUESTIONS

8. *DNA's Code: Key to All Life*
What is meant by the term "the genetic code"?
Support the view that most behavioral characteristics are acquired.

9. *That Odd Chemical Complex, the Human Mind*
What does the author mean when he refers to "instant education"?
What is the effect of a hallucinogen on the human mind?

10. *How the Machine Called the Brain Feels and Thinks*
What is meant by "double-consciousness"?
What does "machine" mean in this sense?
How are experiments dealing with lower animals proving to be beneficial to man?

11. *The Interpretive Cortex*
Do we forget? Why are some people able to remember better than others?
What is the "déjà vu" phenomenon? Give examples.

Unit Four *Maturation and Learning*

Heredity is fixed at the moment of conception; maturation begins at the time of conception. Maturation is a physiological growth process that is closely related to age. Maturation is characterized by its orderly sequence of events. For example, the prenatal stage, identified by the *germinal, embryonic,* and *fetal* periods, is a time of rapid growth and development. During these periods, various structures of the organism take form; each is dependent upon the successful prior development of other structures. In order for the nervous system to reach functional maturity, it is necessary for the spinal cord to be developed. If one stage is slowed or delayed, for one reason or another, so are succeeding functions which are dependent on it. This is further illustrated during adolescence when sexual maturity is reached. The onset of sexual maturity, called *puberty,* sets the stage for other forms of maturity, such as physiological growth and emotional development. The sequences of development are generally the same for all; however, individuals may and often do differ in the rate of development. Recognition of the varying patterns of development offers invaluable knowledge for understanding the behavior of individuals.

Maturational readiness refers to periods of life in which it is easier for a person to learn particular tasks. For example, teaching a child to say *da-da* and *ma-ma* is appropriate during the baby's babbling stage because these words are much like the sounds he is making. Any attempt to teach other words, at this stage, generally ends with failure.

Varying skills that call for muscular coordination are most easily learned when muscular maturation is at its peak. It is apparent that learning and maturation are interwoven and related.

Since Pavlov's first experiments with dogs salivating to the sound of a bell, behavioral scientists have been working to create satisfactory *laws* of learning. Many *theories* have been created with varying degrees of interpretation; for example, one psychologist, Clark Hull, attempted to explain learning through the use of mathematically stated formulas. Whether man will be able to establish *laws* of learning remains to be answered; however, there is much we have already gained in the understanding of learning. In the first article, *What Do We Know About Learning?,* Goodwin Watson presents a brief and concise evaluation about some of the facts that scientists know about learning and behavior.

The second paper, *Formulas for Learning,* is concerned with the field of computer-assisted instruction (CAI) as it is applied in the classroom. The author discusses how conditioning theory is unlocking the mystery of the acquisition of new skills.

The remaining brief articles illustrate various stages of maturation throughout the life span and the problems that are encountered. N. J. Berrill's *Sex and the Nature of Things* is an interesting discussion of the physical differences of the sexes during conception. Elizabeth B. Hurlock in *The Sex Ratio* illustrates the impact sex differences have upon the survival rates of the different sexes. David Elkind, in *Middle-Class Delinquency,* introduces interesting environmental factors that contribute to delinquency among middle-class families. The number of individuals reaching later maturity is growing and the problems are likewise increasing. *Geriatrics,* the science of treating the old, is attempting to understand these problems and offer solutions for creating an enjoyable life for senior citizens. *Golden Years?* presents research carried out by certain behavioral scientists and the methods they have developed to cope with the economic and social difficulties of older people.

---

12 | What Do We Know About Learning?

Goodwin Watson

What do we really know today about learning? Although no scientific "truths" are established beyond the possibility of revision, knowledgeable psychologists generally agree on a number of propositions about learning which are important for education. The educator who bases his program on the propositions presented below is entitled, therefore, to feel that he is on solid psychological ground and not on shifting sands.

Behaviors which are rewarded (reinforced) are more likely to recur.

This most fundamental law of learning has been demonstrated in literally thousands of experiments. It seems to hold for every sort of animal from earthworms to highly intelligent adults. The behavior most likely to emerge in any situation is that which the subject found successful or satisfying previously in a similar situation. No other variable affects learning so powerfully. The best-planned learning provides for a steady, cumulative sequence of successful behaviors.

Reward (reinforcement), to be most effective in learning, must follow almost immediately after the desired behavior and be clearly connected with that behavior in the mind of the learner.

The simple word, "Right," coming directly after a given response, will have more influence on learning than any big reward which comes much later or which is dimly connected with many responses so that it can't really reinforce any of them. Much of the effectiveness of programed self-instruc-

---

From *National Education Association Journal,* March 1963. Reprinted by permission of the author and publisher.

tion lies in the fact that information about success is fed back immediately for each learner response. A total mark on a test the day after it is administered has little or no reinforcement value for the specific answers.

Sheer repetition without indications of improvement or any kind of reinforcement (reward) is a poor way to attempt to learn.

Practice is not enough. The learner cannot improve by repeated efforts unless he is informed whether or not each effort has been successful.

Threat and punishment have variable and uncertain effects upon learning: They may make the punished response more likely or less likely to recur; they may set up avoidance tendencies which prevent further learning.

Punishment is not, psychologically, the reverse of reward. It disturbs the relationship of the learner to the situation and the teacher. It does not assist the learner in finding and fixing the correct response.

Readiness for any new learning is a complex product of interaction among such factors as (a) sufficient physiological and psychological maturity, (b) sense of the importance of the new learning for the learner in his world, (c) mastery of prerequisites providing a fair chance of success, and (d) freedom from discouragement (expectation of failure) or threat (sense of danger).

Conversely, the learner will not be ready to try new responses which are beyond his powers or are seen as valueless or too dangerous.

Opportunity for fresh, novel, stimulating experience is a kind of reward which is quite effective in conditioning and learning.

Experiments indicate that lower animals (rats, dogs, monkeys) will learn as effectively when they receive rewards of new experience or satisfied curiosity as they will when the rewards gratify physical desires. Similarly, stimulating new insights have been found to be effective as rewards for the learning efforts of human beings.

The sense of satisfaction which results from achievement is the type of reward (reinforcement) which has the greatest transfer value to other life situations.

Any extrinsic reward—candy, or stars on a chart, or commendation—depends on its dispenser. There is no need to strive if the reward-giver is out of the picture. Also, cheating can sometimes win the extrinsic reward. The internal reward system is always present for the learner, and he sees little gain in fooling himself.

Learners progress in an area of learning only as far as they need to in order to achieve their purposes. Often they do only well enough to "get by"; with increased motivation, they improve.

Studies of reading speed show that practice alone will not bring improvement; a person may have read books for years at his customary rate, but with new demands and opportunities he may be able to double that rate.

The most effective effort is put forth by children when they attempt tasks which are not too easy and not too hard—where success seems quite possible but not certain. It is not reasonable to expect a teacher to set an appropriate level of challenge for each pupil in a class; pupils can, however, be helped to set their own goals to bring maximum satisfaction and learning.

Children are more likely to throw themselves wholeheartedly into any learning project if they themselves have participated in the selection and planning of the project.

Genuine participation (not pretended sharing) increases motivation, adaptability, and speed of learning.

Excessive direction by the teacher is likely to result in apathetic conformity, defiance, scapegoating, or escape from the whole affair.

Autocratic leadership has been found to increase dependence of members on the leader and to generate resentment (conscious or unconscious) which finds expression in attacks on weaker figures or even in sabotage of the work.

Overstrict discipline is associated with more conformity, anxiety, shyness, and acquiescence in children; greater permissiveness is associated with more initiative and creativity.

In comparisons of children whose parents were most permissive in home discipline with those whose parents were most strict (both groups of parents loving and concerned), the youngsters from permissive homes showed more enterprise, self-confidence, curiosity, and originality.

Many pupils experience so much criticism, failure, and discouragement in school that their self-confidence, level of aspiration, and sense of worth are damaged.

The pupil who sees himself at his worst in school is likely to place little value on study and to seek his role of importance outside the classroom. He may carry through life a sense of being not good for much. He is likely also to feel resentment at schools, teachers, and books.

When children or adults experience too much frustration, their behavior ceases to be integrated, purposeful, and rational. The threshold of what is "too much" varies; it is lowered by previous failures.

Pupils who have had little success and almost continuous failure at school tasks are in no condition to think, to learn, or even to pay attention. They may turn their anger outward against respectable society or inward against themselves.

Pupils think whenever they encounter an obstacle, difficulty, puzzle, or intellectual challenge which interests them. The process of thinking involves designing and testing plausible solutions for the problem as understood by the thinker.

It is useless to command people to think; they must feel concerned to get somewhere and eager to remove an obstruction on the way.

The best way to help pupils form a general concept is to present the concept in numerous and varied specific situations—contrasting experiences with and without the desired concept—and then to encourage precise formulations of the general idea and its application in situations different from those in which the concept was learned.

For example, the concept of democracy might be illustrated not only in national government but also in familiar situations of home, school, church, jobs, clubs, and local affairs. It is best understood when it is contrasted with other power structures such as autocracy, oligarchy, or *laissez faire.*

The experience of learning by sudden insight into a previously confused or puzzling situation arises when (a) there has been a sufficient background and preparation, (b) attention is given to the relationships operative in the whole situation, (c) the perceptual structure "frees" the key elements to be shifted into new patterns, (d) the task is meaningful and within the range of ability of the subject.

The term "cognitive reorganization" is sometimes applied to this experience. Suddenly the scene changes into one that seems familiar and can be coped with.

Learning from reading is facilitated more by time spent recalling what has been read than by re-reading.

In one experiment (typical of many), students who spent eighty percent of their learning periods trying to remember what they had read surpassed those who spent only sixty percent of the time on recollection. The students who spent all the time reading and re-reading the assignment made the poorest record.

Forgetting proceeds rapidly at first—then more and more slowly. Recall shortly after learning reduces the amount forgotten.

Within twenty-four hours after learning something, a large part is forgotten unless efforts are made to prevent forgetting. A thing can be relearned more quickly than it was learned originally, however, and if it is reviewed several times at gradually increasing intervals, it can be retained for some time.

People remember new information which confirms their previous attitudes better than they remember new information which runs counter to their previous attitudes.

Studies consistently show that individuals who feel strongly on a controversial issue, and who are asked to read presentations of both sides, remember the facts and arguments which support their feelings better than they recall those on the opposite side.

What is learned is most likely to be available for use if it is learned in a situation much like that in which it is to be used and immediately preceding the time when it is needed. Learning in childhood, then forgetting, and later relearning when need arises is not an efficient procedure.

The best time to learn is when the learning can be useful. Motivation is then strongest and forgetting less of a problem. Much that is now taught children might be more effective if taught to responsible adults.

If there is a discrepancy between the real objectives and the tests used to measure achievement, the latter become the main influence upon choice of subject matter and method. Curriculum and teaching geared to standardized tests and programed learning are likely to concentrate only on learnings which can be easily checked and scored.

The most rapid mental growth comes during infancy and early childhood; the average child achieves about half of his total mental growth by age five.

In the first two years a normal child transforms the "big, buzzing, blooming confusion" of his first conscious experience to organized perception of familiar faces, spoken words, surroundings, toys, bed, clothing, and foods. He differentiates himself from others, high from low, many from few, approval from disapproval. He lays a foundation for lifelong tendencies toward trust or mistrust, self-acceptance or shame, initiative or passivity; and these vitally condition further growth.

Not until adolescence do most children develop the sense of time which is required for historical perspective. The so-called facts of history—1492, 1776, and all that—can be learned by children but without any real grasp of what life was like in another period or in a different country. Most instruction in ancient, medieval, and even modern history is no more real to children than are fairy tales.

Ability to learn increases with age up to adult years. The apparent decline is largely the result of lack of motivation. We can coerce children into school activities; adult education is mostly voluntary. Men and women *can,* if they wish, master new languages, new ideas, and new ways of acting or problem-solving even at sixty and seventy years of age.

---

13 | Formulas for Learning

When Newton discovered gravity, he discovered something that could be quantified, tested, applied, reworked and reapplied by anyone who followed.

But scientists looking into human behavior have had no such certainty. They may reach great insights into human processes, but rarely can they be sure. Because the insight usually lacks the precision of physics, it can be neither measured nor tested for universality.

Such has generally been the fate of learning theory. Descriptions of intuitive and cognitive learning processes abound. They may be valid, but at their present stage of development, they are virtually useless, not only for such things as programming a computer to teach first grade arithmetic, but for establishing guidelines for teaching at all. And that is the problem.

A revolution in education called computer-assisted instruction is surely coming. Congressmen favor it, corporations are backing it and the U.S. Office of Education is spending several million dollars for its development.

From *Science News,* **91**, April 1967. Reprinted with permission of *Science News,* weekly summary of current science, © 1967 by Science Service, Inc.

But there is a gap between learning theories and their practical application. It must be narrowed if computers are to be a boon to education—the greatest thing since printed textbooks—and not just overpaid drill masters.

Despite the lack of a solid theoretical base, the field of computer-assisted instruction (CAI) appears to be moving rapidly, with some justification.

Though three-fourths of the programs so far developed in CAI are little more than computerized versions of present classroom practices, they do offer the student more individualized material than he now receives in most classrooms. They offer to relieve teachers of tedious drilling tasks, and they promise better education to slum children.

Perhaps even more important, the computers may themselves help fill the theory gap. In the long run, computers in the classroom should build an unprecedented research base for learning about learning, as the data from thousands of students pours in. It is from this expectation that much of the enthusiasm for CAI stems. As Dr. Louis Bright, director of research at the Office of Education, put it, "CAI is the most valuable instrument ever devised for the study and testing of learning theory."

But he says a learning theory is not essential now. Computerized teaching programs can be devised without it. Through a process of trial and error, they will eventually produce deeper understanding of the learning process, says Dr. Bright. And with the exception of one theoretically oriented project at Stanford, all the universities working with CAI—some seven or eight—are proceeding on that assumption.

Theory or no theory, computer-assisted education is in the throes of a classic struggle at the moment—how to get program development out of the hands of technicians and into the hands of educators.

Dr. Francis Keppel, onetime Commissioner of Education, solved the problem for his corporation earlier this year by firing 60 employes. In so doing, he rechanneled the energies of General Learning Corporation, a subsidiary of General Electric, from computer technology to education.

It is an aim shared by Congress. Last year, after several days of testimony on technology in education, the Joint Economic Committee noted that engineers, not educators, were writing most of the programs.

"It appears that the vital function of programming—preparation of the content of education—is falling too frequently to the 'hardware' manufacturers when it should be handled by educational experts." The report went on to note "insufficient coordination" between industrial manufacturers who are creating and selling the programs and the educators.

Much programming of teaching devices was described as poor, the Committee observed. One witness labeled the result "a shallow penetration by the technologists into education." On the other hand, educators themselves "show little extensive long-range planning," said the Committee.

The report also called for more research "not only in the application of technological devices, but on the learning process itself."

Such research is underway at Stanford University. There at the Institute for Mathematical Studies in the Social Sciences, Dr. Patrick Suppes and his colleagues are combining theory, intuition, computers and children in a $2 million project to break ground on a mathematical understanding of human learning.

It is a step by step process. The Stanford group has begun with a simple, conditioning theory—that humans learn basic concepts and facts in an all-or-none fashion. That is, the learner directly associates a right answer with a specific question. But before that association takes place, there is no evidence of learning whatsoever. Very simply, "either you've got it, or you don't," and if you don't, your odds of hitting the right answer are at chance level.

An alternative theory, which the Stanford group has considered, represents the exact opposite. Here learning supposedly increases in a smooth upward line, by increments. Each time a problem appears, the learner has a better chance of answering it correctly, even though he has not yet done so.

But both concepts, however, still suggest some kind of unexplained process—intuition for want of a better term. And intuition, in Dr. Suppes' opinion, is a suspicious word. "It should be a signal to the behavioral psychologist," he says, "that unexplained and ill-understood learning behavior is about to be mentioned, and unfortunately, often described as if it were understood."

In his experiments on the way students learn elementary concepts in mathematics or foreign languages, Dr. Suppes has, in fact, not found a smooth upward curve. But he has found all-or-none learning, in addition to a kind of half-breed—slight incremental increase and then a sudden learning leap.

Psychologists occupied with describing the total range of human intellect view the all-or-none theory with some disdain.

"It's a simplistic kind of notion," says Dr. Jerome Bruner, learning theorist at Harvard University. "I can't believe the nervous system has evolved through the ages to this."

Such criticism misses the point, answers Dr. Suppes. "I don't want to claim I have an overriding theory," he says. It is a "first approximation only," but one that can be used and hopefully shaped into more sophisticated levels of understanding.

Actually, whether or not all-or-none adequately describes complex learning processes is irrelevant to the Stanford work. The concept is a tool, a framework for organizing lessons in a computer and a means of computing the probabilities that a student has learned something. After that comes the arduous task of revising programs on the basis of returned data.

Dr. Suppes, who is both director of the Institute and chairman of the department of philosophy, has developed drill and practice programs in mathematics and foreign languages since he began working with Palo Alto children and computerized instruction four years ago.

The programs are not meant to teach, only to drill; consequently they require no particular theoretical basis.

Now, however, Dr. Suppes is working toward a more elegant program in mathematics. "If it works, it will be a very pretty thing indeed," he says. Rather than lumping problems into blocks of difficulty and then giving a student one or another block according to his ability—as CAI programs now do—the new computer program ranks each and every problem. A student would receive a sequence of problems unlike the sequence of any other student. As he gets better, the problems get harder, but since they do not follow an obvious pattern, the student cannot find tricky shortcuts to the answers.

Given, say, 2,000 problems and a hundred students, such a program represents highly complex computer strategy and a startling degree of adaptability to individual differences.

The total effect is to turn learning theory on its head and make computers learn about students, says Dr. Suppes.

In addition, he wants the machine to adapt to the speed of the response, as well as its correctness. There is evidence, he points out, that speed is a more sensitive index to learning than correctness—at least for the skill subjects.

While Dr. Suppes has concentrated on mathematics and logic, his colleague, Dr. Richard Atkinson, has attacked the problem of teaching children to read.

Still experimental, the project should give some basis for evaluating different reading theories, says Dr. Atkinson. But first, he must find ways of mathematically describing and spanning the diversity of concepts and skills that children bring to elementary reading.

Eventually, Dr. Atkinson hopes to reach a "rich and highly structured theory of learning."

That is, in fact, the promise computers hold out to psychology—that for the first time a workable, measurable principle of learning will be found—one as mathematically rigorous and elegant as the law of gravity.

---

14 | Sex and the Nature of Things

The Virgin Egg

N. J. Berrill

If nature as a whole can be said to have an obsession it lies in the need to produce fertilized eggs and to launch them upon their career. And it calls attention to the difference between the sex cells—why should they be so different? The perennial human question concerning the equality of the sexes goes far beyond sex as we know it and finds its roots in the sex cells as such. Why are eggs and sperm so unlike, and what are their respective contributions to the organisms-to-be?

Much of it is simply a division of labor. It is difficult to be a jack-of-all-trades and do any particular job well. And the cell that is to develop into a new plant or animal must unite with another cell, and between them they must possess enough material to make something much more complex than they are to begin with. So one kind stores the substance and the other does the traveling. In this way they get together and have enough to build with.

Even the smallest egg is large for a cell, many times larger than a white corpuscle in your blood, while the egg of an ostrich may well be the largest cell in the universe. We will never know. But storing up material makes eggs round and large, and this alone puts any movement on their part to meet a sperm completely out of the question. So it is all left for the sperm to do. All the responsibility for reaching an egg is theirs and theirs alone. They are simply cells with a delicate tail for swimming and everything else reduced to a minimum.

Numbers are important too. At the best the chances are slight that any particular sperm will ever make contact with an egg, and astronomical numbers are always necessary for successful fertilization. The largest possible number, and therefore the smallest possible size, is the rule. In the case of eggs the problem is different—in fact it is a dilemma. For the larger the individual egg becomes, the farther it can progress along its course before it has to be an organism fending for itself. Large eggs are better than small eggs. Yet every animal and plant works on a budget and can set aside just so much material for producing sex cells. Large eggs means fewer eggs and that is not so good. The greater the number of eggs produced the more likely some of them will survive to carry on the race. And so every race and species is torn between producing large eggs and enough eggs. It is a difficult choice and there is no single answer—it all depends on circumstances, one creature does this and another does that, and one thing leads to another.

Cell for cell the sexes are not equal—a sperm is minute compared with even the smallest egg. Yet a male may hope to console himself with the thought that matter is not everything. What else is there? As a rule an egg must be fertilized by a sperm in order to develop, but it is only as a rule and far from being always. Masculine self-esteem gets shakier the more you look into the question.

It all started more than half a century ago when biologists were looking closely for the first time into the nature of the fertilization of an egg and of the processes involved—sheer curiosity of the kind that killed the cat and led to the making of an atomic bomb. Only in this case it merely puts the male in his place.

The experiments made at that time have been repeated ever since. Every summer in marine laboratories on the coasts, students and others place ripe starfish eggs in sea water that has been tampered with, usually by the addition of a little organic acid, and they watch the eggs develop in consequence without the aid of spermatozoa at all. Apparently all the potentiality for development and the making of a new starfish is there in the egg by itself. All it needs is a little push to get it started.

Frog eggs are equally susceptible, although they need a somewhat different kind of push. It is a fascinating process and its practice is a common classroom exercise in most of the colleges throughout the land. It gives you an unwarranted god-like feeling. You need only some female frogs a month or two before the onset of their breeding season. If you inject one of them with extract of pituitary gland—that small but all-important gland that lies beneath the brain of every backboned animal from fish to man—the frog lays her eggs within twenty-four hours. It works almost every time and it is about the only way you can get fully ripened eggs entirely free from any sperm. For once they have been laid in a pond it is too late, and there would be spermatozoa around to confuse the issue.

The release of the eggs by pressing a physiological button is impressive enough, but making them develop by mechanical means is more than that. The jelly that surrounds each egg is carefully removed by rolling it gently on blotting paper, so that the naked egg is exposed. Then, with extreme care, you prick its surface with the point of a fine glass needle. It is a delicate operation and the steadiest hand is all too clumsy, but out of a hundred so treated a score or two will start to divide and develop into tadpoles. And all such tadpoles will be males.

Only the human male seems inclined to play tricks with eggs like this—women are either busier or have more important things to do. Female frogs are made to lay eggs before their time, the eggs are made to develop without benefit of spermatozoa, but only males result. There is a suggestion of irony somewhere.

Actually there is a clue here to sex as distinct from sex cells. The fully ripened egg of almost any kind of animal, if it will develop at all without being fertilized by a sperm, develops into a male. It takes a double dose of something to become a female. In the case of frogs and human beings there are two kinds of sperm, although they all look alike. One kind carries that extra component that added to an egg makes a female, the other kind does not. Since the two kinds are produced in approximately equal numbers, the chances are the same that one or the other kind will fertilize an egg. The result is that males and females are normally produced in equal numbers. Pricked frog eggs lack the spermatozoan contribution and are doomed to develop into males, if they develop at all.

Parthenogenesis—the long name for a short process, and meaning origin from a virgin—has been brought about by methods such as these in a number of different animals, particularly among the so-called lower forms. Simply raising the temperature will often do it in the case of frog eggs. It has been only natural to wonder if it can be accomplished in a mammal.

In spite of ancient notions concerning conception and the general belief that all conceptions in human beings were the result of a spirit of some kind entering the womb of the woman, there is no good evidence that in mammals, whether human or otherwise, eggs ever naturally develop without being fertilized by spermatozoa. Such an occurrence is not implausible for it does happen in bees and other creatures, but not in mammals. And I doubt whether it is ever a natural event in frogs or starfish.

Yet the thought lingers and sooner or later as you might expect, someone would attempt to make mammalian eggs develop without benefit of paternity. The victims have been rabbits. Ripe but unfertilized mammalian eggs, whether a rabbit's or some other's, are notoriously hard to obtain, and they are always few in number. Nearly thirty years ago in France the embryologist Champy discovered among a group of unfertilized rabbit eggs cultivated outside the body—although at the body temperature—that some eggs underwent divisions as though they had been fertilized. Gregory

Pincus, in America, followed this up and tried out all the tricks we know that have made the eggs of lower animals develop spontaneously. But only an occasional egg ever reached a recognizable stage in embryo formation. The possibility of parthenogenesis seemed to be present, yet something was wrong.

Apparently it is one thing to cause a mammalian egg to divide, it is another entirely to keep it going in a normal manner; which is not surprising when you consider that the mammalian egg is adjusted to develop in the tubes and womb of the mother. So Pincus treated the unfertilized eggs as before and then transplanted them into virgin rabbits. Out of a large number of trials, some of these virgins bore normal rabbits. In many others the embryos were well advanced but died prematurely. It is not very promising, though perhaps one day we may breed our cows without utilizing bulls. Perhaps it would be better if we cannot, for the human race so far shows no sign of knowing when or where to stop.

The immediate interest of these rabbit experiments, to me at least, is that all the born and unborn offspring that have come from these unfertilized eggs have been females.

The explanation goes back to the ripening of the egg. Starfish eggs, frog eggs, rabbit and human eggs all ripen normally in essentially the same way. When the fully grown egg leaves the ovary, whether to be shed into the sea if it is a starfish or to enter and lie in the oviduct if it is a mammal, it has to go through a process of division before it is ready to be fertilized. It divides not into two equal parts as a cell usually does, but into a minute polar cell and one so large it looks like the original egg. And the event is important out of all proportion to its magnitude.

This particular division of the egg cell is possibly the most important in all of nature and throughout earthly time. For it is during this division that the differences arise that make one egg different from the next, that supply the raw material for evolution and adaptation to a changing world. This is the general importance of it. The egg is different because of this division, and the polar cell is simply a by-product of the process. Yet sometimes the polar division is suppressed and the egg may still develop. This, according to another French investigator, is exactly what happens in those eggs that produce parthenogenetic female rabbits. The eggs retain a double quantity of the female component and develop into females. The rabbit eggs that do not retain the substance of the polar cell but ripen fully, do not develop at all unless they are fertilized by a sperm. I doubt if this indicates the final fate of the human male, but it does suggest that if we ever succeed in producing a race with eggs that develop spontaneously the result will be a purely female population capable of carrying on more or less indefinitely without the male—in fact no males could be expected, unless the system became elaborated.

15 | The Sex Ratio

Elizabeth B. Hurlock

SEX RATIO

According to the law of chance, there should be an approximately equal number of children of both sexes conceived. As a matter of fact, medical science reports that there are between 120 and 150 males conceived for every 100 females. The reason for this difference is unknown, although a number of suggestions have been advanced to explain it. Of these, the most credible though still unproven possibility is that since the spermatozoon bearing the Y sex chromosome (the one that produces the male offspring) is slightly lighter and hence swifter in movement than the spermatozoon bearing the X sex chromosome (the type that produces a female offspring), the Y-bearing type has a better chance of reaching the ovum sooner and fertilizing it.

Another reason that has been suggested for this difference in sex ratio is that a "canny Nature starts the sexes off with a surplus of males to partly provide for the greater drain upon their number later" [7]. It has been reported that during the prenatal period, 50 per cent more male fetuses die than female. By the time of birth, there are approximately 105 to 106 male babies, as compared with 100 female. This means that of the males conceived, between 15 and 45 die before birth, as compared with a relatively small number of females [4].

During the first four weeks of postnatal life, 40 per cent more male babies die than female, while among the prematurely born, 50 per cent more males than females die. In the first year of life, 33 per cent more male babies die than female; between five and nine years of age, 44 per cent more boys than girls; between ten and fourteen years, 70 per cent more boys than girls; and between fifteen and nineteen years, 145 per cent more boys than girls [8]. The result is that by the time a male child reaches adulthood, his sex is literally the "minority" sex.

In commenting on this, Montagu has said:

> Whatever the physical reasons may be which result in more eggs being fertilized by Y-bearing spermatozoa the evolutionary "reason" would appear to be that *since the male is the constitutionally weaker organism he must be conceived in greater numbers than the female if a relatively harmonious numerical balance is to be achieved between the sexes during the reproductive life of the female* [4].

From Elizabeth B. Hurlock, *Child Development,* 4th edition, McGraw-Hill Book Company, 1964. Reprinted by permission.

According to traditional belief, more boys are born in wartime than the normal 105 or 106 boys for every 100 girls. Data from the United States, Great Britain, Canada, Australia, and New Zealand, however, showed that the ratio did not change appreciably during the war years. Thus there is no evidence to support this belief [6]. Neither has the traditional belief that young fathers produce more male offspring than older fathers stood up under scientific study. Evidence seems to indicate that there is no relationship whatever between the sex of the offspring and the age of *either* the mother or the father [2].

Another tradition is that boys (or girls) "run in some families." As Spencer has pointed out, "Of course the sex distribution among the children of a given family will be subject to the usual chance fluctuations observed when small samples are used. Even in large families, a certain small proportion of these will be expected to be all of one sex purely by chance" [9]. Studies of sex distribution in families have shown that there is an excess of unisexual sibship in two-child and three-child families [1, 5].

In the upper socioeconomic groups, there is some evidence that there is a sex ratio of 120 to 125 males born for every 100 females, but the groups studied have, to date, been too small to warrant much confidence in the results. While reports have indicated that men in the "masculine" occupations have a higher percentage of male offspring than men in "feminine" occupations, there is no conclusive evidence that this is true.

REFERENCES

1. Bernstein, M. E., Studies in the Human Sex Ratio. II. The Proportion of Unisexual Siblings, *Human Biology,* **24,** 35–43, 1952.
2. Bernstein, M. E., Parental Age and Sex Ratio, *Science,* **118,** 448–449, 1953.
3. Bernstein, M. E., Studies on the Human Sex Ratio. Evidence of Genetic Variation of the Primary Sex Ratio in Man. *Journal of Heredity,* **44,** 59–64, 1954.
4. Montagu, A., *Human Heredity.* New York: Harcourt, Brace & World, 1959.
5. Myers, R. G., Same Sexed Families, *Journal of Heredity,* **40,** 260–270, 1949.
6. Myers, R. G., War and Post-War Experience in Regard to the Sex Ratios at Birth in Various Countries, *Human Biology,* **21,** 257–259, 1949.
7. Scheinfeld, A., *The Human Heredity Handbook.* Philadelphia: Lippincott, 1956.
8. Scheinfeld, A., The Mortality of Men and Women, *Scientific American,* **198,** 22–27, 1958.
9. Spencer, W. P., Heredity: Facts and Fallacies. In M. Fishbein and R. J. R. Kennedy (Eds.), *Modern Marriage and Family Living.* Fair Lawn, N.J.: Oxford University Press, 1957, pp. 341–356.

16 | Middle-Class Delinquency

David Elkind

The research literature on juvenile delinquency is already vast and continues to grow at an increasing pace [1]. By and large, however, this research tends to deal with lower-class children living in slum areas of large cities. Much less is known about the young people from suburban, middle-class homes who also get into trouble with the law.

Some writers [2, 3] have suggested that delinquent youngsters from "respectable homes" are acting out the parents' repressed antisocial impulses and are subtly encouraged by the parents in this regard. Although this explanation probably holds true in a certain number of cases, my own experience (as consulting psychologist to a suburban juvenile court) suggests that the vicarious satisfaction of needs is but one of many forms of parental exploitation that can lead to delinquent behavior on the part of children. In what follows I shall elaborate on some of the forms of parental exploitation and some of the possible adolescent reactions to such exploitation.

Before proceeding, however, it is necessary to distinguish among three quite distinct groups of middle-class delinquents. There are, first of all, those adolescents whose delinquency is a direct manifestation of a long-standing emotional disturbance and for whom the remedy is usually psychiatric rather than probationary. Secondly, there are those young people who come before the court almost by accident—quite often for pulling some prank that turned out to be more serious than they had anticipated—and who are seldom, if ever, adjudicated for a second time. By far the largest group, however, are those adolescents who get into trouble more or less regularly and who have a series of past charges filed against them. Although these young people do not appear to have serious internalized conflicts, they are usually in quite open conflict with their parents.

It is with the etiology of delinquent behavior in this third group of young people that the present paper is primarily concerned.

THE CONTRACT

The concept of parental exploitation makes sense only if there is an implicit contract between parents and their offspring. In middle-class families such a contract does exist. For their part, the parents agree to provide for the physical and emotional well-being of their children, who, in return, agree to abide by the norms of middle-class society. Although minor infractions

From *Mental Health,* January 1967, p. 80. Reprinted by permission of the author and Mental Health, Inc.

of this contract on the part of both parents and children are to be found in most middle-class families, they tend to be temporary. For the most part, the contract is honored on both sides.

This appears not to be true in the families of the delinquent children under discussion. If one inquires deeply enough into the family relationships of these children, one finds that the contract has been broken by one or both parents *over a prolonged period of time.* More particularly, that part of the contract is broken which ensures that the parent will take responsibility for the emotional well-being of his child. What one finds in these cases is that the parent not only puts his own needs before those of the child, but, more significantly, attempts to use the child as an instrument in the satisfaction of those needs. It is because the parent violates the contract with his child while demanding that the child hold to his end of the bargain that such violations are legitimately called "parental exploitation."

FORMS OF PARENTAL EXPLOITATION

Although particular instances of parental exploitation are almost infinite in their variety, they can nonetheless be grouped under a few reasonably comprehensive headings. We have already noted that the *vicarious satisfaction of parental needs* is one frequent form of exploitation.

This form of exploitation is illustrated by a case in which a sexually frustrated mother encouraged her daughter to act out sexually. When the daughter returned from a date, the mother would demand a kiss-by-kiss description of the affair and end by calling the girl a tramp. When I saw the girl, who was being adjudicated for sexual vagrancy, she told me, "I have the name so I might as well play the role." When she left my office, her mother, who had been waiting outside, teasingly asked her how far she had gotten with the "cute psychologist."

A somewhat different form of parental exploitation might be called *ego bolstering.* In this category fall those parents who demand academic or athletic achievement far beyond what the young person is able, or has the capacity, to produce. This form of exploitation has an element of vicarious satisfaction in it, but the dominant affect seems to be the need to bolster flagging parental self-esteem. Although it is normal to want to take pride in one's child's achievements, it becomes pathologic when the parents' own needs to bask in reflected glory take precedence over the emotional welfare of the child.

A somewhat different variety of this form of exploitation is illustrated by the father who encouraged his 17-year-old son to drink, frequent prostitutes, and generally "raise hell." This particular father was awakened late one night by the police who had caught his son in a raid on a so-called "massage" parlor. The father's reaction was, "Why aren't you guys out catching crooks?" This same father would boast to his co-workers that his son was "all boy" and a "chip off the old block."

Still another form of parental exploitation occurs when parents use their youngsters as *slave labor.* In one instance, a father who owned a motel demanded that his son do all the lawn work and help to clean up the rooms and make the beds. To top it off, he insisted that the boy take the lids off all the cans in the trash barrels and then flatten the cans so that the volume of trash, and hence the cost of disposal, would be lessened. The boy barely had time to do his homework, much less to visit with his friends. Mothers who get their teenage daughters to do more of the housework and the baby-sitting than is reasonable or equitable provide another example of slave labor exploitation.

A fourth form of parental exploitation is frequently encountered in broken homes in which the mother, who usually retains custody of the children, is relatively young and attractive. In one case a mother took a lover, much younger than herself, into her home over the protestations of her teenage daughter, who had to cope with the curiosity of friends and the indignation of neighbors. Another young divorcee had a baby out of wedlock whom she kept in the home without any explanation to her teenage children. Still another mother, who had lost her husband under tragic circumstances, took to drinking away her afternoons with a younger man, to whom she gave large sums of money. She could not understand why her teenage son ran off to Mexico.

In all such cases, the mothers demand not only that their children accept the situation, but that they condone it. By demanding that their children accept and condone their behavior, these mothers hope to use their children to *assuage their own consciences.*

One of the saddest forms of parental exploitation is engaged in by parents who are very much in the public eye, particularly school principals, clergymen (of whatever faith), and judges. If a parent in one of these professions sees his child's behavior primarily in terms of what it means to his career, he may demand a degree of conformity to middle-class mores that is quite unreasonable from the young person's point of view. When young people of this kind get into trouble, it is not because the parents are too strict, but rather because the parents are using their children to *proclaim their own moral rectitude.* As in all cases of parental exploitation, the dominant affect in such children is not so much the feeling of being restricted as it is the feeling of being *used.*

REACTIONS TO PARENTAL EXPLOITATION

When a worker is exploited he has at least four courses of action open to him. He can either quit, go out on strike, sabotage the plant, or passively submit to the exploitation.

Parallel types of reaction are found in middle-class delinquents. Some young people literally quit the scene. They may quit school and become truant, quit the home and become runaways, or quit the family psychologically and become incorrigible. Other adolescents go on strike. They continue to go to school, but refuse to perform; they stay in the home, but refuse to do their fair share of the chores; they stay out late, and they go with a group of whom the parents don't approve. In short, they defy parental authority generally. More serious reactions are observed in young people who wish to sabotage their parents. These kids get pregnant, steal cars, vandalize schools, get drunk, sniff glue, or take drugs. Such reactions cost the parents plenty in worry, time, money, and bad publicity. The saddest reaction of all is that of the youngsters who passively submit to parental exploitation in the hope of winning or regaining parental love.

Despite the variety of these reactions, they all have one feature in common: parental exploitation is essentially private and is seldom recognized by anyone outside the home. Whereas the worker often has a union to voice his grievances and to stand up for his rights, there are no unions for children. Consequently, the delinquent behavior of adolescents who are being exploited by their parents often serves as a kind of "cry for help." Put differently, delinquent behavior often has as one of its components the desire to make the exploitation public, to let the world know what is happening behind the drawn drapes and closed doors. The sad thing about such cries for help is that they are as injurious to the young person as they are to the parents.

TREATMENT

To say that middle-class delinquency is difficult to treat psychotherapeutically is a gross understatement. The major reason for this is the fact that, *although the pathology exists in the parents, the symptoms appear in the children.* Since it is the children who are in trouble, the parents find it hard, except on a superficial basis, to accept their responsibility in the matter. Blind to their own violation of the parent-child contract, they insist that the young person live up to his side of the bargain. For his part, the young person feels that he has been used and abused and generally will not take responsibility for his actions.

With both parents and children blaming each other for the difficulty, there is little motivation for change on either side. Usually, however, the children are more tractable than the parents on this score. In many cases all that one can do is either remove the young person from the home, or help him to understand and deal with the exploitation in a more effective and less self-injurious way.

SUMMARY AND IMPLICATIONS

In the foregoing discussion, I have argued that middle-class delinquency is essentially a reaction to parental exploitation and have tried to enumerate some of the forms of exploitation as well as some of the reactions to it. Such a position clearly places the burden of blame for middle-class delinquency upon the parents. To some extent, this is perhaps unjust, since children may encourage exploitation on their own behalf and may well exploit their parents in return. In many cases the exploitation is as likely to be circular as it is to be unidirectional. And yet, my impression is that in the majority of cases the parents are much more to blame than are their children.

It should be said, too, that I don't offer the notion of parental exploitation as a complete explanation of middle-class delinquency. It is probably true that many of these young people have ego and superego defects of long standing. It is also true that we don't know why one form of exploitation will lead to a particular kind of delinquency and not another. In some cases, the connections seem direct and clear-cut, whereas in others they remain obscure. Unknown, too, is how prolonged the exploitation must be and how much of it is needed to incite an adolescent to delinquent acting-out. Such threshold values are probably a joint function of the child's personality and the quality of parental exploitation.

In short, a detailed understanding of any particular case of middle-class delinquency will have to involve a psychodynamic evaluation of the personalities of both parent and child. On the other hand (or so it seems to me), a psychodynamic evaluation of the parent-child interaction, although providing an explanation in a particular case, may well miss the common theme that seems to run through all cases of middle-class delinquency, namely, parental exploitation. Taken together, however, the concept of parental exploitation and psychodynamic evaluations may well provide a general, as well as a specific, explanation for middle-class delinquency.

The value of such a general explanation of delinquency as parental exploitation is shown in the way it helps to make plausible why certain familial conditions are regularly associated with delinquent behavior. Broken homes, for example, have routinely contributed more than their fair share to the delinquent population [4–7]. It seems reasonable to assume that in broken homes one is more likely to find unmet parental needs than would be the case in intact families. Under these conditions, the temptation to put one's own needs ahead of those of the child and to use the child as an instrument in the satisfaction of those needs would probably be greatly enhanced. In short, the concept of parental exploitation might allow one to predict, or at least hypothesize, the kinds of family constellations that would be most likely to produce delinquent behavior.

Before closing, I want to take up one more point that has been raised by those who attribute middle-class delinquency to the antisocial impulses of parents that are vicariously satisfied through the child. It has already been noted that the vicarious satisfaction of parental needs is indeed one form of parental exploitation. Where I disagree with this position is in the implication that middle-class delinquency is antisocial, regardless of whether or not this is true of the parental need. If antisocial means the intent to harm or injure society in general, then I do not believe middle-class delinquency is antisocial. I do believe it is antifamilial. Looked at from the point of view of the adolescent, and not necessarily from the point of view of society, delinquent behavior may be the most psychologically adaptive action a young person can take in the face of parental exploitation. Delinquent behavior not only calls attention to his plight, but also may remove him from the home on temporary or permanent basis.

Although I have limited the application of the concept of exploitation to the question of middle-class delinquency, it is possible that all delinquency is, at least in part, a reaction to exploitation and that society, as well as parents, can be culpable in this regard.

REFERENCES

1. Quay, H. C. (ed.), *Juvenile Delinquency.* Princeton: Van Nostrand, 1965.
2. Giffin, M. E., Johnson, A. M., and Litin, E. M., *American Journal of Orthopsychiatry,* 24:668, 1954.

3. Johnson, A. M., and Burke, E. C., *Proceedings of the Staff Meetings of the Mayo Clinic,* ***30***:557, 1955.
4. Burt, C., *The Young Delinquent.* New York, Appleton, 1929.
5. Glueck, S., and Glueck, E. T., *Unraveling Juvenile Delinquency.* New York: Commonwealth Fund, 1950.
6. Monahan, T. P., *Social Forces,* **35**:250, 1957.
7. Nye, F. I., *Family Relationships and Delinquent Behavior.* New York: Wiley, 1958.

---

17 | Golden Years?

Ford Foundation

WORK AND RETIREMENT

Some older people are happy to sit in a rocking chair and rock. Some remain active in their jobs, others busy themselves in the affairs of the community. But for many people, old age means two things: too little money and too much time on their hands. They find it hard enough to slough off the work habits of a lifetime, and resent enforced idleness.

Here are some basic facts:

• Four out of every five workers, willingly or not, are out of the labor market by the age of sixty-five. Of the remainder, fewer than half have full-time, year-round jobs.

• Most retired workers find their incomes cut in half. They may save on food, transportation, occupational expenses, personal taxes, and life insurance. But medical bills and housing costs are sometimes significantly higher.

• Despite such continuing claims on the older person's budget, basic Social Security benefits reach a maximum of $190 a month for a married couple. Some 14 per cent of the aged receive additional Old Age Assistance payments, which vary from state to state. A few receive assistance from relatives. About one in four lives with children, but this is a declining trend.

"Many men over sixty-five would like to go on working," says Juanita M. Kreps, associate professor of economics at Duke University. "But the older worker is part of an enormously complex system. Little is known about the relationship of work and retirement, and the chances of successful adjustment to the latter. While a growing awareness has resulted in some

---

From *Golden Years,* November 1963. Reprinted by permission of Ford Foundation.

serious study of the problem, there is still a reliance on the Pollyanna approach in campaigns to hire the older worker. Such emotional appeals are no substitute for facts."

A number of efforts are under way to marshal the skills of economists, sociologists, and psychologists in building a base of knowledge from which industrial and governmental policy can proceed. Among these are studies at five universities—Brown, Cornell, Duke, Washington (St. Louis), and Wisconsin—assisted by the Foundation.*

At Duke University, a study of the probable state of the nation's economy in the next fifteen years is providing a backdrop against which to view the future of the older worker. Faculty members of the university's department of economics made forecasts of the demand for manpower in each of the sixty-two sectors of the economy—from metal mining and railroads to banking and printing—corresponding to the Department of Commerce National Income Division industrial classification.

They found that employment in the 1960s is expected to decline in many sectors of the economy, as more goods are produced by fewer workers; that employment in professional services and in government will double in the same period. Unemployment, currently 6 percent, could easily rise to 8 percent by 1970, the study reported.

Professor Kreps sees unmistakable implications for older people in these findings. "The possibility that a growing percentage of the labor force will be unemployed," she says, "suggests that the older person will be discouraged by both public policy and business practice from working in his later years. So far, no solution to this problem has been found. To reduce unemployment by such measures as extending the school age or cutting down the hours worked by the mass of the labor force would bring little advantage to the older worker in general. To stimulate the economy by an increased demand for manufactured goods would make for few extra jobs in an economy where goods are produced increasingly by mechanical means."

In this setting, Brown and Washington Universities are studying some specific problems of the older worker—his chances in the labor market, and the role of unions and employment agencies in the field.

The trade union is an important influence on the hiring and retention of older workers in industry. To discover to what extent unions protect the older worker, Prof. Philip Taft, Brown's veteran labor-relations expert, interviewed local, regional, and national officers of labor organizations in several states.

His conclusions so far indicate that union collective bargaining with employers is severely limited in value in solving the problems of the older

---

* Grants were as follows: $160,000 to Brown University for research on the employment problems of older workers; $190,000 to Cornell University for a survey of retirement policies and practices in industry and other organizations; $200,000 to Duke University for studies of the socio-economic problems and potentials of older people; $177,000 to Washington University for research on improving job-placement services for older workers; and $250,000 to the University of Wisconsin for a study of the economic impact of private pension plans on the older worker.

worker in general. "Unions have struggled mainly to achieve the rule of seniority—that employees with the longest tenure should have preference in maintaining their jobs," he explains. "However, workers with the longest tenure are not always the oldest. Also, the seniority system is limited in its protection; it can only protect against layoffs in a particular plant or, even more narrowly, in a seniority unit.

"Attempts to widen the application of seniority so as to protect older workers are likely to face opposition not only from employers, who feel that they are prevented from hiring the most efficient labor available, but also from union members who may not wish to share their tenure advantages with workers transferred from another plant of the same company. Finally, the seniority system may increase the obstacles facing older men trying to get back into the labor market. The union is geared mainly to protecting those already employed and can regard the problems of others as of secondary importance.

"Then, too, the resistance of younger workers to the introduction of exceptions that dilute their right to employment makes it extremely difficult for many unions and firms to insist upon liberal transfer rules for older and partially incapacitated workers."

What part, then, *do* older people play in the labor force? Brown University economists are analyzing a mass of data from the 1960 census, the Old Age and Survivors Insurance records, and the Internal Revenue Service, to find out.

Their studies are divided into three parts:

• First, in which industries does the older worker have the best chance of employment? For example, there are indications that the older worker may have difficulty in adapting to new machinery, and may lack the manual dexterity needed in such fields as electronics. However, he may have better opportunities in some types of service jobs where stability may count more than manual skill.

• Second, how many older workers migrate to other states? Moving costs for an older worker, who is more likely to have a settled home and family than a younger man, are usually greater. Also, he has fewer years ahead to reap the advantage of better income and conditions. To what extent do such factors control the older worker's decision to relocate?

• Third, what is the relation of technological change to choice of jobs? The vital question: Are declining occupational fields forcing more men out of work than can be absorbed by new industry?

While the Brown study is concerned with the over-all employment problem of the older worker, Washington University is studying the effectiveness of public and private job-placement programs already in operation. The research, coordinated by Professors Irvin Sobel of Washington University and Richard Wilcock of the University of Illinois, is being done by teams of labor-market economists in Arkansas, California, Illinois, Massachusetts, Missouri, and Pennsylvania. After evaluating employment practices in their areas, these teams will single out the most effective programs. From these, business and labor leaders, academic economists, and employment-service officials will attempt to develop recommendations to improve older-worker placement methods.

"We are fairly certain that several things are *not* the answer," Sobel says. "With a present unemployment rate of 6 percent, few changes that we can now anticipate in the pattern and structure of industry can produce other than marginal results. Again, if new industries are established in areas with a surplus of older workers, younger workers will move in. Public employment agencies, too, have found that too great an emphasis on special programs to place older workers may boomerang if employers come to see an employment service as a means of foisting off less capable workers on them."

Sobel points out that if an older employee returns to the labor market after a period of unemployment, he tends to do so at a lower level. Technological change and merger of industries have decreased the demand for unskilled labor. Administrators, once out of a job, have difficulty in selling their skills elsewhere, or obtaining jobs at comparable levels of authority. Many workers are squeezed out of the labor market before the age of sixty-five, and to all intents and purposes, join the ranks of the retired.

Retirement, then, is for most workers a fact of life. How satisfactory can it be, and what is being done to prepare a worker for it?

Studies at Duke University have pointed out that there is rarely a complete break between working life and retirement, as is often supposed. Friendships and interests formed during working life tend to remain the same. But people with certain characteristics find retirement unsatisfactory because they are not easily able to substitute new interests for time spent at work.

For purposes of studying adaptability to retirement, Duke sociologists categorize people according to whether they work primarily with ideas, people, or things. For those concerned with ideas—teachers and writers, for example—there are few problems. Such people usually know where to look for new sources of interest. For those working primarily with people, retirement seems to present difficulties. "The retired foreman who goes down to the plant every day is a good example," says Ida Simpson, assistant professor of sociology. "Such people could become the successful Scout leaders of the community. But too often they find no substitute interest for the camaraderie found in work."

In the final category also, Professor Simpson has found little evidence of new interests. Asked to describe a typical day in retirement, former manual workers show an inordinate emphasis on routine activities—getting up, having meals, and going to bed. "For many people, the problems of an unsatisfactory working life are merely continued into retirement," Professor Simpson says.

These conclusions agree with the findings of Karl U. Smith, professor of psychology at the University of Wisconsin, who has developed his own "behavorial feedback" theory—that things that people do habitually, they do well, and that physical fitness, learning ability, and satisfaction in old age depend on the type of work done in earlier years.

Education for aging, then, must become a new feature of our society. If habits learned in working life are continued into retirement, then preparation for retirement should begin in the fifth, if not the fourth, decade of people's lives.

E. B. Shultz, of the New York State School of Industrial and Labor Relations at Cornell University, stresses the need for anticipating retirement psychologically. "Employers seldom attempt to justify the practice of compulsory retirement at sixty-five on any other ground than ease of administration," he says. "But a retiree feels just as badly when told that he can no longer be employed because he is over sixty-five as when he is told that he is incapable of doing the job. A desire or even a genuine willingness to retire at sixty-five can be a positive step toward successful retirement adjustment.

"The task of our society, then, is to provide a new enthusiasm for successful retirement. This is a complicated process—and involves much more than informing the worker about his pension rights and warning him of some of the difficulties inherent in retirement."

The Cornell unit, with its grant from the Foundation, is making the first national survey of retirement policies and practices, based on analyses of questionnaires sent to industry and nonprofit organizations. It is also evaluating the effectiveness of various retirement-age policies on the basis of interviews with middle management and foremen, and on questionnaires sent to workers and retired workers.

In a parallel study, the Cornell unit is attempting to assess the use made of preretirement counseling in industry. A survey indicated that most firms rely on individual discussion between personnel representatives or supervisors and the worker about to retire. Some companies, however, had group discussions for prospective retirees on taxes, health and economic problems, and the best use of leisure.

"These programs are not in themselves a complete answer," Shultz stresses. "But they contribute to the understanding and enrichment of retirement, which is, after all, a relatively new characteristic stage of life in our industrial society."

A retirement study supported by the Foundation was also made by the California Institute of Technology.* The study, which had a wide circulation in industry, found broad acceptance of the idea that advance preparation was needed to help industrial workers adjust to retirement, but some disagreement about who was responsible for providing this assistance. Some managers thought that industry had the responsibility of helping their workers adjust to retirement, and that it was to their interest to do so; others thought that "this kind of social work," as one manager described it, was the responsibility of the church or the community at large.

Using ideas from the industries that answered its questionnaires, the research group outlined a model program that could be adapted by various

---

* Michael T. Wermel and Geraldine M. Beideman, *Retirement Preparation Programs: A Study of Company Responsibilities:* Pasadena, California Institute of Technology, 1961.

industries. The program begins with a letter mailed to each employee on his fiftieth birthday, in which the president of the company invites the employee to take part in the firm's retirement program. In the next eight years, literature on retirement planning is sent periodically to those in the program. They are invited to join a long-service club to which active and retired employees may belong. Employees are offered free physical examinations to encourage them to take a greater interest in their fitness and correct any disorders.

When an employee reaches fifty-eight, he is invited to weekly group discussions on such topics as planning and budgeting, housing, health, leisure-time activities, and community resources. At age sixty-four, he has an interview with his personnel officer to discuss retirement benefits. In some cases, employees are permitted to continue work until age sixty-eight (taking successively longer vacations each year) and train their replacements during this period.

The part played by pension plans to retirement is the focus of a series of studies now under way at the University of Wisconsin.

Private pension plans have grown phenomenally since World War II, with pension fund assets totaling about $40 billion and benefits being paid to one and a half million retired workers. While the effect of these funds on the economy in general has been the subject of several studies, the *adequacy* of pension plans from the viewpoint of the older worker had hardly been studied at all.

Wisconsin researchers have been concerned with such problems as safeguarding pension benefits for the older worker. For example, what is the cost, effect, and extent of "vesting"—enabling an employee who changes his job to retain his pension rights—in pension planning? The study assessed the cost effect on pension plans of providing vesting after differing periods of employee service, under various assumptions as to the rate of interest and the amount of employee turnover.

Studies indicated that workers in slow-growth industries were sometimes reluctant to sacrifice pension rights to move to more promising jobs. Research in this field also pointed up the need for retraining workers in slow-growth industries who became unemployed before they had earned adequate retirement benefits.

The Wisconsin group has also explored the problem of protecting a worker's pension rights when his firm goes out of business or is merged with a larger one. A study pinpointed the factors involved, so that better legal draftsmanship can make clearer in the original pension contract the order in which pension-plan participants should share in the assets of a firm that goes out of business.

As more people in the work force learn to plan for retirement, future generations of older people may adapt more easily to their leisure years.

At the moment, however, research in such fields as employment and retirement has uncovered more complexities than were suspected before the problems were first tackled.

Similarly, growing concern over the problems of the aging has disclosed their ample dimensions. Concern must be followed by action programs aimed at better methods to meet the housing, social, and health needs of older people. And research must underpin improved local, state, national, and individual and corporate policies on housing, retirement, and employment.

In this effort, the Ford Foundation program in problems of the aging has been only one chapter. The program sought to stimulate attention and action on strategic needs by means of research, training, and community experiments. It sought to draw to problems of the aging the talents of economists, sociologists, businessmen, labor leaders, and others, and the attention and resources of other groups and agencies.

During the seven years of the Foundation program, it became clear that the nation recognizes aging as a major, continuing social issue affecting all American families. A start has been made on action and research that may turn "the golden years" from a period of problems into a time of opportunity, in which the older person has greater measure of well-being and dignity.

Unit Four | DISCUSSION QUESTIONS

12. *What Do We Know About Learning?*
    What are the personality effects of overstrict discipline in young people?
    What are the advantages of "reward" in terms of a learning situation?
13. *Formulas for Learning*
    Discuss the "all-or-none" theory in computerized instruction.
    How are computers helping psychologists understand more about learning?
14. *Sex and the Nature of Things: The Virgin Egg*
    Discuss why the division of labor is so significant in the egg cell.
    What is "parthenogenesis"?
15. *The Sex Ratio*
    What are the reasons for the higher death rate in the male?
    Discuss your views on whether or not the male is the "constitutionally weaker" organism.
16. *Middle-Class Delinquency*
    Discuss what is meant by "parental exploitation." Does it exist?
    What does the author mean by the statement "middle-class delinquency is not anti-social, but anti-familial"?
17. *Golden Years?*
    Describe the "model retirement program" devised by one of the leading universities.
    What are the main problems facing old age?

Unit Five *Individual Differences*

When we observe friends, neighbors, or people from distant lands, speaking different languages, exhibiting different cultures, and representing varying ethnic backgrounds we are aware that individuals are more alike than they are different. Differences in individuals are differences in degree rather than in kind of traits or attributes. Differences are based on *units* rather than on *wholeness* of behavior. It is these units of behavior which affect the perception we have of one's total behavior. Differing capacities for hate, greed, love, friendliness, and coordination are examples of interpersonal, or social, variables. Such physical differences as skin, hair, eye color, height, and weight are determined by heredity. When these differences vary minutely, we are able to notice the human varieties. Variances prove to be helpful in selecting desirable traits. For example, different strains of plants yield healthier crops and are more resistant to disease. We select these traits to reproduce more plants of this kind. Likewise with human beings, society emphasizes the importance and need for certain qualities, and we attempt to cultivate these traits in ourselves and in our children. Traits which society considers detrimental are discouraged and an attempt is made to correct or alter such behavior.

Attributes of masculinity and femininity are differences which, for the most part, are learned cultural demands. In western cultures, masculinity is related to aggressiveness, competitiveness, and strength. Femininity, on the other hand, is often related to submissiveness, weakness, and dependence. As a result, females are often referred to as the "weaker sex." *How Different Are They?* is an exploration by Stanley F. Yolles into the relative differences of the sexes as related to the demands of our culture. Interestingly enough, the author illustrates that many of the so-called masculine tasks are accomplished readily and efficiently by females. The same is true for so-called feminine tasks when performed by males.

Wagner H. Bridger investigates *Individual Differences in Behavior and Autonomic Activity.* Bridger suggests that human infants are born with certain predetermined temperamental differences and he points out that while the origins and consequences of these differences are not known, significant implications for the future are possible.

Biological and Environmental Interchange in the Development of Children by John B. Reinhart and Elizabeth Elmer discusses the biological endowment with which we are born and its interaction with the environment. The authors detail the various facets of the mother-child unit as it relates to the development of children.

In 1936, Harold M. Skeels reported the impact of environment on intelligence. His report was based on a painstaking study of selected Iowa orphanage children. The final reading, *Environment Important* [in intelligence], is an interesting follow-up made on these same orphanage children.

---

18 | How Different Are They?

Stanley F. Yolles

Experts on behavior hesitate when Henry Higgins asks, "Why can't a woman be more like a man?" Parents who wonder why little girls don't act like boys are assured by one authority that the differences are of "no consequence." A Stanford University professor of psychology now documents what little boys and girls are made of. The details, distilled from some 900 studies, show that boys and girls are indeed quite different. This notion is hardly a news bulletin for parents, but science has documented the obvious generalizations with facts and has also uncovered some fresh answers to the eternal question of Henry Higgins. Here they are as outlined in the book, "The Development of Sex Differences," written in part with National Institute of Mental Health support and edited by Dr. Eleanor E. Maccoby:

Little boys start more fights, make more noise, take more risks, think more independently, are harder to educate and are the more fragile of the sexes. While many more males are conceived, more miscarried fetuses are male. More males than females die in the first year of life and in each decade after that. They are much more likely to stutter, to have reading problems and to suffer emotional quirks of every sort. They lag a year or more behind girls in physical development. By the time they start school, even their hand muscles are markedly less mature.

In contrast, little girls are more robust and mature, yet much more dependent, passive, submissive, conforming, unadventurous. They are more interested in people than in things, show more concern for others and are more sensitive to their reactions and are more likely, by far, to remember names and places.

Science has found no difference in I.Q. between boys and girls in childhood, yet their styles of thinking and learning are different. Girls excel in verbal abilities—even before they know they are girls. They talk first, and later on they spell better and write more. Boys outclass them in abstract thinking including math and science. Boys are also more likely to be creative.

How do we explain the basic and early differences? Some experts believe most of these differences are taught to the child. Other experts, such as

---

From *New York Times Magazine,* February 5, 1967.

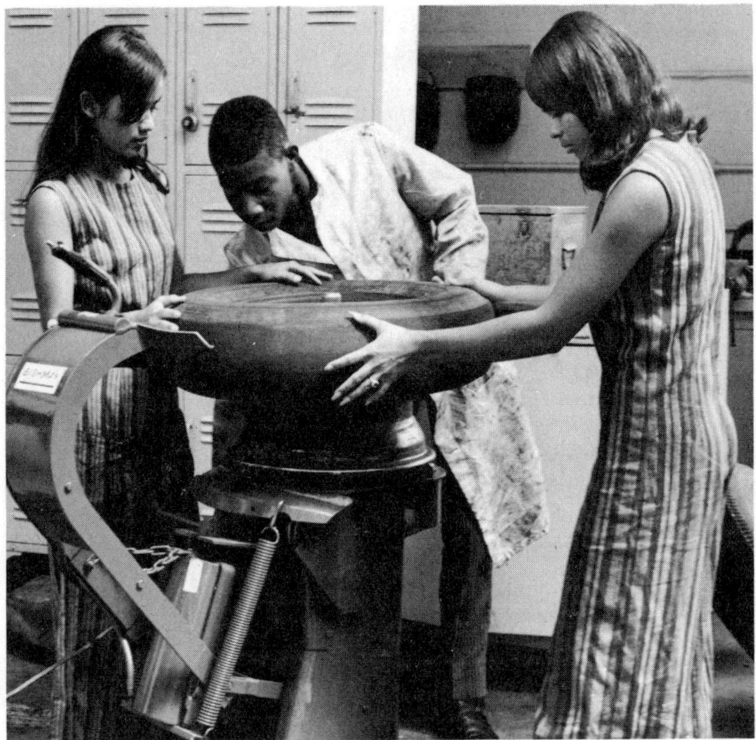

(*San Diego City Schools*)

"Science has found that the brightest girls are those whose interests extend into the masculine range." Above, girls repair tire in an auto mechanics class.

Dr. David Hamburg, chairman of the department of psychiatry at Stanford, think there may be hormonal and genetic causes. Dr. Hamburg writes that hormones may act on the brain even before birth or right after, to organize certain circuits into male or female patterns. The evidence for this comes from experiments with the hormonal systems of newborn rats. When male rats are castrated within the first 24 hours after birth, they retain a basic female-type system for regulating hormonal secretions later in life. If castration is delayed until the second 24 hours, only a few males retain the female patterns. By the third day, all male rats have developed a male-type pattern.

In addition, Dr. Hamburg points out that their genetic make-up is different. The female has a chromosomal composition that seems to lend her protection against disease and infection. It protects her against blood-clotting disorders, color-vision defects and one type of rickets.

Scientists at the National Institute of Mental Health who have observed infants right after birth and in the weeks that follow have seen sharp differences too early in life to have been caused by the environment. These differences have been uncovered through ingenious tests. Drs. George Weller and

Richard Q. Bell hooked up recording devices to 40 newborns by placing sensors on their skins. By this method they were able to detect the faint electrical activity of the skin called "conductance," a property which turned out to be greater in the female. Since this increases as the baby gets older, it is taken as a sign of maturity. The female infant, therefore, is more mature than the male of the same age. The females also show more sensitivity to contact and the temperature changes on the skin, more proof of their greater maturity in this very early period of life.

Dr. Howard Moss, an institute psychologist who has watched three-week-old and three-month-old infants for seven and eight hours at a time is impressed with the "striking differences" between boys and girls. Boys sleep less, cry more, demand more attention. "Much more is happening with the male infants," he reports. Some boys, he found, also seem to be much more "inconsolable" than the girls, a sign of lesser maturity.

When children go to school, their differences become magnified. From first grade until well into high school, the girls usually make better grades. One ingenious researcher found that as early as the second grade, little boys think of school as a female institution and, therefore, one which is hostile to them. Our psychologists at the N.I.M.H. asked teachers in Arlington County, Va., to write their impressions of 153 seventh-graders.

According to the teachers, girls are 20 per cent better than boys at sticking to a task. They are more conscientious, compliant, methodical. They are also friendlier to the teacher, and more attentive. And boys are 35 per cent more hostile, domineering, aggressive, also more irritable, boastful, argumentative, quarrelsome. Paradoxically, boys are more introverted—depressed, sad, withdrawn.

Several years ago, educators in Fairfax County, Va., near Washington, D.C., decided to experiment with separate elementary classes for boys and girls.

One teacher said: "I learned things about boys and girls that I had never understood before. I had spent years trying to keep boys from disturbing everyone. This was just wasted effort. I found that boys can still concentrate even when they are noisy. You can learn to work in a boiler factory, if you have to, and that is just what I have done."

Another said: "I always liked girls best until I got a whole classful of them. In the beginning of the experiment, it dawned on me that the girls were not doing their own thinking. Parrot-like, they repeated everything that the teacher had ever said. What are we doing to these girls, I began to wonder, to make them so conforming?"

The results of the experiment were impressive. Both sexes did significantly better in their studies. The boys became much more interested in school. The girls grew more independent and original in their thinking.

Since it is scarcely practical to separate the boys and girls in most of our school systems today, educators might consider what they can do to achieve some of the same results. Principals and teachers can keep the differences in school performance between boys and girls in mind when they deal with problems in the classroom—either of discipline or of underachievement.

Devices such as all-boy or all-girl contests, debates, or dramatic and musical clubs might give students the sense of confidence and enthusiasm found in the separate classes.

If schools can capitalize on the differences between boys and girls, parents can do so, too. Parents of a boy can now see that he may be at a disadvantage in early years at school, under the twin burden of the girls' better performances and the teachers' disapproval. If parents don't expect their sons' reading or handwriting to be of the best, it may take some unnecessary pressure off the boys.

The girl's problem is even more complex. Many families feel that education is not so important for a girl as a boy. Today, only one in 10 Ph.D.'s is a woman, a drop from the one in seven of the nineteen-thirties. Teen-age marriages are on the rise, with an accompanying rise in the divorce rate. The question is, are we properly fitting girls for a woman's life as it really is?

After raising a girl to conform and to be subordinate we expect her to face problems that require education, originality, dominance and drive. A new study of young married people points out that conformity and submissiveness often lead only to boredom in marriage.

Science has found that the brightest girls are those whose interests extend into the masculine range. They like math, motors and abstract problems. The brighter boys also show a sensitivity and responsiveness we call "feminine" although these children are by no means effeminate. The most creative boys, for example, are dominant and aggressive, yet show much more sensitivity to their surroundings than other boys.

In my experience, the most successful personalities are those who have the widest range of interests and abilities. I would like to see our boys and girls brought up with as broad and varied an experience as possible, with attention to the many facets of the human mind. This includes insight into the thinking of the opposite sex.

What can parents do to offer this kind of insight to the young child? One psychologist bought his 3-year-old girl a truck when she asked for it, to the consternation of her grandmother. Another brought home an abandoned engine his pretty 12-year-old daughter had longed to tinker with. One father makes a point of answering his girls' questions about science and about his business world, although he has to fight an ingrained tendency against it. He tries to pique them into forming interesting solutions to problems, and to build self-confidence in their mental abilities.

As for the boys, one mother encourages hers to experiment with cooking. She enjoys giving them the benefit of her feminine insight into human behavior and motivation. This insight into the female skills will stand them in good stead professionally as well as in their marriages. It augments rather than reduces their manliness, she argues.

It might be in order to revise our ideas about what the proper sex role is for our boys and girls, and how best to train them for it. Society needs men who are not limited to the so-called tougher masculine characteristics of aggressiveness and dominance. It needs men who are capable of showing the more "feminine" traits of warmth and sensitivity toward the feelings of others. And we need women who are less conforming, more original and daring, women who can think hard and straight.

Henry Higgins, who yearned for more "logic" in women, and Eliza Doolittle, for "a little kindness" in men, surely would agree.

---

19 | Individual Differences in Behavior and Autonomic Activity in Newborn Infants

Wagner H. Bridger, M.D.

Before the turn of the century, it was rather common practice to ascribe to temperament and biological predispositions the origin of both mental and medical illnesses. In the twentieth century the emphasis has turned from these intrinsic factors to a search for extrinsic or environmental factors. In the field of mental health and personality development, both Watsonian behaviorism and Freudian psychoanalysis have put prime responsibility upon the parents for the personality, health, or ill-health of their offspring.

In recent years there has been a trend away from this unilateral approach, since specific environmental variables that would be responsible for many psychiatric and medical syndromes have not been found. The possible role of biological predispositions in interacting with environmental factors has been gaining a theoretical acceptance. This new emphasis seems particularly applicable to the psychiatric syndromes of schizophrenic and manic-depressive psychoses and the psychosomatic syndromes of hypertension and peptic ulcer.

The return of the potential significance of intrinsic factors is also true in regard to personality development. Several investigators, Bayley, Escalona, Thomas, and Schaeffer, have emphasized the probable role of intrinsic factors in the individual personality differences they found in the children of their respective studies. In particular, at least one factor—the infant's activity level—is predictive of subsequent behavior in childhood. However, all studies were started after the children were a few months old, and thus there is no conclusive evidence that these individual differences were present at birth.

It is within this framework that our laboratory at Albert Einstein College of Medicine has been intensively studying the human neonate for the past five years. Specifically, we were interested in determining whether or not there are individual differences in behavioral and autonomic functions at birth, which may influence later personality development and which may represent predisposition to later psychosomatic illnesses.

From *American Journal of Public Health,* **55,** 12, December 1965, p. 1899. Reprinted by permission of the author and publisher.

TYPES OF EXPERIMENTS

The following types of experiments have been performed: Our basic technic is to take two-to-five-day-old infants, Apgar above 8, and, using a team of raters, make a series of repeated behavioral rating and heart rate measurements. When studying day-to-day constancy, we rotate observers to diminish halo bias. The ratings are on a 6-point scale, 1 = quiet, no movement to 6 = extreme agitation with severe crying. We rated the infants' responses to a loud sound, a soft sound, an air puff applied to the abdomen, a cold disc applied to the thigh, and a pacifier inserted into the baby's mouth. With this last procedure the vigor of the sucking was monitored on a polygraph.

Using correlational technics, we found that there are significant individual differences between these babies in behavioral response to these stimulations, and these differences are consistent during the first few days of life. The babies were ranked according to their median behavioral ratings to the stimuli, and the analysis revealed that a baby who gave intense responses to the soft sound also gave intense responses to the loud sound and cold disc and also sucked vigorously on the pacifier. The babies who gave gentle responses to the soft sound also gave gentle responses to the loud sound and cold disc and sucked weakly. Thus, most babies could be characterized as being either slightly, moderately, or intensely responsive to stimuli, regardless of the modality or nature of the stimulus. In addition, this characteristic behavior was present on successive days. The baby who responded vigorously on the second day of life also responded vigorously on the third, fourth, and fifth days.

In addition to these behavioral ratings, the heart rate of the babies was monitored on a polygraph. The experimental question being investigated was whether or not the neonates showed individual differences in autonomic lability, a possible predisposition to psychosomatic disorders. The infants' heart rates were compared at the same behavioral states. The babies were ranked according to their heart rates when they were asleep, active, and crying. The data revealed consistent individual differences between the babies in cardiovascular functioning. Infants who slept with relatively high heart rates (e.g., 140 beats per minute) had high heart rates when active and when crying (e.g., 220). Infants who had relatively low heart rates when asleep (e.g., 70 beats per minute) had low heart rates when active and when crying (e.g., 150). The autonomic and behavioral factors seemed to be independent in that the behavioral hyperreactor did not necessarily have a labile autonomic nervous system. The individual differences just described were in response to excitatory stimuli.

The next experiment investigated whether or not there were individual differences with respect to inhibitory stimuli. In other words, do infants differ from one another in their ability to be soothed when in a state of distress? In this study, the babies were brought to a high level of excitation by flicking the soles of their feet. Then, an inhibitory stimulus was applied for one minute each. Among these stimuli were continuous low-pitch sounds, rocking, warmth, and sucking on a pacifier. The results indicated that, in general, all these experimental manipulations were equally effective in soothing the infants as compared to a control period during which no stimulus was applied.

DATA EVALUATED

While the analysis of the data from this study is not complete, it appears that there are consistent individual differences in soothability. In addition, some babies have a predisposition to be more effectively soothed by one or another of the stimuli. For example, one baby was most effectively soothed by the loud sound, another by rocking, still another by sucking a pacifier. We are in the process of analyzing whether or not there is a relationship between individual differences in excitability and soothability. During these soothing studies, we also recorded the heart rate. Some babies demonstrated a labile cardiovascular reaction in that while showing behavioral inhibition, their heart rates reached the same level as when they were crying.

Summarizing the results of this research, it is evident that human infants show stable temperamental differences right after birth. These differences are present in respect to levels of behavioral activity, reactivity, soothability, and autonomic lability. The implications of these findings can only be tentative at this time, because we do not know their origin or the consequences of these differences. In view of these differences, however, it seems likely that similar maternal behavior will have a different affect upon different babies. In addition, the behavior of the neonate may determine in part the behavior of the mother. In any case, it seems obvious that advice in regard to child-rearing practice might best be adjusted in each instance to the specific qualities of the individual child.

In conclusion, it is suggested that the role of environmental variables in growth and development must be evaluated in the context of the biological endowment of the individual. There are significant implications for public health if we can find controllable pre- and perinatal factors, which may be important determinants of neonatal individual differences.

This paper was presented before a Joint Session of the American Orthopsychiatric Association and the Mental Health Section of the American Public Health Association at the Ninety-Second Annual Meeting in New York, N.Y., October 7, 1964.

---

20 | Biological and Environmental Interchange in the Development of Children

John B. Reinhart, M.D., and Elizabeth Elmer, M.S.S.

Historically, pediatrics and child psychiatry centered their interests on the child himself. For instance, in the period 1900–1920, major concerns were about the composition of the food that went into a baby and the composition of the bowel movements that came out. This attention was not unwarranted,

From *American Journal of Public Health,* **55,** 12, December 1965, p. 1902. Reprinted by permission of the author and publisher.

and investigations led to the evolution of infant feeding from an extremely complex and difficult task to its present-day simplicity. The discovery of vitamins and more recent investigation into enzyme activity have made diseases such as rickets and scurvy almost nonexistent in the United States, and will make possible the prevention and treatment of more complicated and bizarre disorders, such as PKU and histidinemia. Infectious and nutritional diseases are no longer the scourge they once were, and studies in child behavior, growth, and development are of current interest.

Just as pediatrics changed its focus from the individual child, child psychiatry became aware that the consideration of the child and his environment and the interaction of the two were absolutely necessary. This was common sense, of course, for even the understanding of the diphtheria bacillus and its mode of action depends on the understanding of the environment in which it lives.

Theresa Benedek [1], some years ago, used the term "mother-child unit" to point out that the child functioned as a part of the mother just as the mother functioned as a part of the child. The behavior and development of each depended upon the other, and observation of one without observation of the interaction with the other was not productive. That there are individual differences in infants seems to be a fact. The identification and measurement of these differences are the problems. Anna Freud, in a lecture to first-year medical students at Western Reserve in October, 1952, told the story of two young nurses in an institution for infants. As they were changing duty, one said to the other, "If Jimmy cries, you must go to him immediately. He gets very frightened just before falling asleep. You know many infants, just in the few moments before dropping off, get very frightened. You must comfort him and then everything will be all right and he will go to sleep. But if Johnny cries, don't go to him. He just whimpers for a little while before dropping off, and if you go in and try to comfort him, you will just wake him up." In Anna Freud's opinion, these nurses had had very good training if they were able to distinguish between those two crying infants. Studies today, such as being done by Chess and Birch [2, 3], Richmond and his group [4], Bridger [5], and others, will eventually identify and help us measure these individual differences.

Some years ago, fresh in pediatric practice, one of us (J.B.R.) had referred to him a forty-year-old mother who had just delivered twins. She had had one child twenty years previously who was then in college, and she had suggested to her obstetrician that she would need pediatric help since "things are different since I had my first baby." She used her pediatrician as a consultant in raising this little boy and girl, and taught him a good deal about child development. From the beginning, she saw the little boy as aggressive, active, flamboyant, and she encouraged him in the behavior with which he seemed to be born. However, she devoted as much attention to her daughter, but seemed to enjoy her in terms of her quiet, demure, and placid disposition, her prettiness, her softness, and her femininity. This mother delighted in her little boy's screaming at the doctor when he received his immunization and enjoyed his scolding of the physician. She also had a tear in her eye and was sympathetic when her little girl whimpered at receiving her shot. These two babies behaved quite differently even from their first day of life, but also were handled quite differently by their mother. The boy was seen as an active, aggressive, stubborn, intense, persistent individual with a low threshold for all stimuli. His sister was a more passive, quiet, adaptable, mild little girl who seemed to have a high threshold for stimuli and not easily upset. This mother, who had a professional life of her own, spent a good deal of time finding a woman who was motherly, adaptable, flexible, and interested in the care of tiny children so that she could pursue her own life and still be certain that her children received good care.

An old pediatrician for whom the same physician (J.B.R.) had a great deal of respect, once told him that on a few occasions he had seen mothers whom he felt "didn't have it in them to be good mothers," and for such families he strongly recommended and, indeed, on his own engaged women he considered to be "good mothers" to care for these infants. He said that he felt that he had saved many babies and their families from considerable distress, and as the years have gone by we suspect he may well have been right. We are not certain we agree with his method of treatment, but some babies from the day they are born are not "easy babies to take care of." Such babies need confident, adaptable, and flexible people to care for them. Other babies are easy to care for, and even the most frightened and insecure of parents can weather it through with them.

PATTERNS OF RESPONSE

A recent study on the patterns of response to physical contact in infants revealed that of a group of 37 babies, nine, consistently and without any modification, resisted being cuddled and held by their mothers [6]. Nineteen of the 37 babies actively and consistently sought contact with their mothers and enjoyed being held at all times. The other nine babies were in an intermediate group who enjoyed being held, if tired or at a certain age and for a certain amount of time. It was not just contact per se that these noncuddling babies avoided, but only the restriction of movement that is involved in certain contact situations.

Their mothers also were divided into two groups of "handlers" and "nonhandlers." The mothers who were handlers enjoyed physical contact in contrast to the nonhandling mothers who made contact with their babies in aural or visual terms or through the medium of toys. Those babies who were cuddlers seemed to be less active, less protesting and resistive, slept longer, and seemed less restless than those babies who were not cuddlers. There are many ways of making contact with babies, in rough play such as fathers are inclined to, by carrying or walking around, and interaction through toys which are alternate ways of relating to children. It is unlikely that in all human infants there is a need for a great deal of physical contact in order to develop properly. The noncuddling infant has difficulty only if his mother is rigid to the use of alternate ways of relating or where she interprets the infant's behavior as rejection of her.

Maternal attitudes about children and the child caretaking abilities of mothers vary and are dependent upon many factors. Some of this has to do with the mother's own past history of being cared for herself. It is dependent upon the support system which she has available to her at the time, the attitudes of her husband, her mother, her mother-in-law, and their availability to her in supportive fashion. Not the least of these is the attitude of the physicians who care for her, her obstetrician, her pediatrician, or her family doctor, as well as others in the health professions such as the visiting nurse.

CASE HISTORIES

In the past few years, we have been following a family which was brought to our attention when one of their children was admitted to our hospital because he was gaining weight very slowly. At the age of nine months, he weighed only seven and a half pounds. All examinations and studies of this child were within normal limits, other than for his obvious lack of development. We learned that his mother was 19 years old, had three children, the youngest of whom was our patient, David. She was pregnant again and married to a young man who was immature, worked infrequently, drank too much, ran around, and kept the family in a constant state of chaos. We were unable to involve the father of David in our discussions, but his mother did agree to a voluntary placement and he was entered into a foster home. There he spent about two months and did very well, gained weight, and learned to respond to other people. In view of his improvement, the agency talked the situation over with the court because they did not think the parents were able to care for this child. However, the court felt the parents must be given the chance to take care of the child before any radical step could be made, and the family agency followed this child until David was about two years old. It was their opinion that the family was not amenable to help, and that David's mother seemed willing to continue her life with her husband as he was.

A few months later, David was seen by a pediatrician because of a fractured forearm and at the time of x-rays, and on review of other x-rays, it was felt that this child might have multiple trauma. Arrangements were made to have all of the children seen. David was admitted to the hospital when we found that he had injuries to the long bones in his arm, minor damage to the bones of his legs, and a small rib injury. At the age of two, he would sit very quietly in his chair without reaching out for any kind of attention. He showed no sign of affection, played very little with his siblings, and on the whole was inactive and appeared remote. His mother was vehement in her denial of having beaten or having mistreated this boy, and could only account for his fractures in terms of the way in which she handled him by lifting him. Later, she informed us that David had fallen from the bed several times and, although told by the visiting nurse to get sides for the bed she had just never thought of this. She also regarded David as "different" in that he did not respond to her from the beginning as did the other children. He never seemed to ask for affection, was hard to understand, and because of his failure to demand attention he had been slighted and passed over in the family.

We learned that David's mother was the youngest of four, with a difference of nine years between herself and her next oldest sister. She had always been her father's favorite and he, like her husband, was a very heavy drinker. He was occasionally abusive, sometimes silly, and sometimes slept only when he had been drinking. When she was six, her parents were divorced; when she was ten, her father died. Her mother had had to go to work to support the family, and it was interesting that her mother had always liked her husband and seemed to excuse his poor behavior.

David's parents had to get married because of the mother's first pregnancy with her oldest child, now five. With each pregnancy, the father caused some disturbance. One time, he was arrested for drunken driving and in jail at the birth of the baby; another time, he was drunk and in an automobile accident; subsequently, he was involved with another woman. This behavior caused these parents to become estranged from both their families.

From our standpoint the situation seemed rather hopeless, for we felt the child's family situation was a poor one and we saw no way to help them change. Both the father and mother resisted the idea of having David placed in a foster home again, and the agency involved with the family found their trailer home to be neat and clean and were reluctant to proceed further. After several other tragedies, such as losing their home, having no furniture, and so forth, life continued on for this family. The pediatrician who had been caring for this family and the visiting nurse, however, continued to lend a great deal of support. The physician talked with the mother about birth control and even provided her with the means. The visiting nurse made frequent visits, and spent a great deal of time doing what many grandmothers do to help young women learn to be mothers.

A few months ago, in a follow-up visit, we examined David and found him to be in good health physically, but to be retarded in his mental development. The most amazing development, however, was that the father had now been employed at the same place of work continuously since our last contacts. The family seemed much better organized, more mature, and David's mother decided not to have children for a while. The visiting nurse, who had had contact with this family throughout their worst days, apparently had been an important factor in giving them continuous mature adult help during a very stressful period in their lives. This was a family that could not use "psychiatric treatment," but needed a great many people involved in a helpful, noncritical way to give them the attention and support they may not have received in their own childhood. They needed this in order to become parents to their own children. Today, this family seems to be on their feet and recovering; however, they bear the scars of the tragedies they have experienced, and David will require a great deal of help from both educators and his family, and even then may never become self-supporting.

Another patient was a boy born in a home for unwed mothers. The story of his mother's pregnancy was said to be uneventful. The mother's serological report was negative and his delivery was by low forceps with a "fairly difficult forceps pull," and forceps marks were noted on the sides of both ears. However, his condition at birth, after a labor of five hours, was described as good and his birth weight was 6 lb 4 oz. He cried spontaneously and there was no report of any neonatal difficulty. He ate well and, at the end of two weeks, weighed 6 lb 14 oz.

He was followed in the Well Baby Clinic and, at the age of six weeks, weighed 9 lb 12 oz, had a hemoglobin of 8.5 with a hematocrit of 28 per cent, and was described as "healthy." He gained weight well and, at 3½ months, weighed 15 lb and had a hemoglobin of 10 with hematocrit of 35 per cent. He received his immunizations to DPT and polio, and from the hospital chart there is no evidence of difficulty. The usual description of the child was "skin clean, fontanelle flat, ENT negative." He had some fussiness after his second DPT shot, but no fever and at the visit of 18 weeks it was remarked that "he hears and sees." At 5½ months, shortly before adoption, he was described as healthy and the only abnormal finding was a diaper rash with the description "uses plastic diapers all the time."

When he was 3½ years, his adoptive parents had him tested by a psychologist who diagnosed him as retarded. He attended a diagnostic nursery school in a speech clinic from 3¾ to 4¾ years, and then transferred to another speech program for a few months. At age five, he was referred to our hospital for diagnostic work-up because of psychotic symptomatology, as well as his retardation. Referring statements were: "Psychological evaluation was not possible with this boy because of an extremely short attention span. His language development was retarded, and it was noted that his voice inflection was inappropriate to communication. He echoed single words out of context in a high shrill tone. He was generally not interested in the activities of his peers, but engaged in solitary play that appeared to have no meaning beyond random movements. It was stated, "His interest may be described as focused on objects rather than people." He seemed to lack some physiologic reflective responses, such as failure to blink, even when hit in the head with a ball, and appeared to be the victim of unreasonable fears and response to internal stress."

Physically, he was a handsome young boy with large expressive eyes. His examination was completely within normal movements and the neurological findings were not remarkable, other than for his hyperactivity and short attention span. His weight was 45 lb which was in the 70th percentile, and his height was 42¼ inches, which was in the 20th percentile. It was felt that this boy was performing at a severely retarded level, and the question of autistic behavior was raised.

Psychiatric consultation was requested and a history was obtained from the parents. His mother told a very dramatic story of having picked the boy up at the foster home. It was her impression at the time that the boy had received minimal care, seemed wide-eyed and apprehensive. On coming through tunnels, the baby was described as "very frightened" and stiffened in the mother's arms and cried. In retrospect, in comparing him with a younger adopted sibling, they saw him as having been quite different. The mother had a great deal of difficulty in getting the baby to take the bottle well, until she speculated that perhaps he had not been well-cared for and that he had been given a bottle which was propped, so that he may well have been fed while lying down and that his milk may not have been warm. Accordingly, she tried him, in desperation, in a feeding situation in which he was lying flat on the kitchen table with a bottle of cold milk. He took this well, and over a period of some weeks she gradually tilted him more and more into a sitting or semi-reclining position and gradually heated the milk.

His physical development went on at a rapid rate from that point on, and by the time he was nine months old he had "trained himself" and he was walking alone before one year. At the age of 20 months, his parents adopted a little girl, three months old, and the mother noted a change in this boy in that he began to cling to her much more constantly. Both parents saw him as a sensitive child, that is, easily upset by discipline and hyperexcitable and hyperactive. They felt he had undergone "marked improvement" in the six months before he was seen at the age of five, since he had been involved in the group situation both in the nursery school and the program for delayed language.

It was the psychiatrist's impression that this child was an autistic child. The unanswered questions about him are many. We have good observations of his physical growth and he had good medical care in the sense that he was protected from infections, was given adequate nutrition, and his body grew properly.

We have less information about the development of his sensory awareness, his motor development, and his interaction with his environment. There is a single statement at age five months that he can "see and hear." This is the kind of child for whom we wish we had information of an observational nature, such as that in the studies of Chess and Birch [2, 3], and others.

We would also want to know about this child's environment and about the caretaking he received and his reaction to this caretaking. Were we dealing with a child whose primary reactions were those of withdrawal rather than of approach? Was he a child who tended to be nonadaptive rather than adaptive, a child with high threshold so that the lack of stimulation he received caused an atrophy of response? Were we dealing with a child whose attention span as a tiny infant was less than most of the other babies in the nursery in which he lived?

The adoptive mother's approach to this baby was of real interest in formulating his eating problem and in the way in which she tended to correct his disability. That he is no feeding problem today is obvious, both from his nutritional status and from the family story of his appetite and food habits. He presents no serious variation from the physical norm.

It is in terms of his mental ability, his relationship to other human beings, and his social behavior that this boy has his defects, and we are dealing with the problem of whether this boy was defective to begin with in this respect or whether he did not receive the right amount or the quality of stimulation in care that the ordinary child needs. Was this child prone to be injured by lack of stimulation or was the lack of stimulation so great that most children might suffer similarly?

SUMMARY

We can say that human behavior is a product of the biologic-neurologic system with which we are born and the interaction of this system with its environment. The mother-child unit, in order to be understood, will need critical evaluation of the behavioral abilities, physical and psychologic, of the child as well as study of the child's environment—the mothering.

Mothering is a product of the mother's own past history of being taken care of herself, the development of her motherliness, and the support—or lack of support—she receives from the environment in her caretaking role.

We need to identify as well as possible what kind of a child we have to deal with, as well as what kind of environment, what kind of mothering he will receive. When we know what is on both sides of the equation, we will then be able to get closer to the correct answer about what kind of behavior we may expect. Then we can be more rational in planning for interaction and support of the child and his family as they go through critical periods of development, so that optimum growth is possible.

REFERENCES

1. BENEDEK, T. The Psychosomatic Implications of the Primary Unit: Mother-Child. *Am. J. Orthopsychiat.* **19**:642–654, 1949.
2. THOMAS, A., *et al. Behavioral Individuality in Early Childhood.* New York: New York University Press, 1963.
3. CHESS, S., *et al.* Interaction of Temperament and Environment in the Production of Behavioral Disturbances in Childhood. *Am. J. Psychiat.* **120**:142–147 (Aug.), 1963.
4. RICHMOND, J. B., *et al.* Observations on Differences in Autonomic Nervous System Function Between and Within Individuals During Early Infancy. *J. Am. Acad. Child Psychiat.* **1**:83–91 (Jan.), 1962.
5. BRIDGER, W. H. Sensory Discrimination and Autonomic Function in the Newborn. *J. Am. Acad. Child Psychiat.* **1**:67–82 (Jan.), 1962
6. SCHAFFER, H. R., and EMERSON, P. E. Patterns of Response to Physical Contact in Early Human Development. *J. Child Psychol. and Psychiat.* **5**:1–13, 1964.

---

21 | Environment Important

Thirty years ago a psychologist made what was then a radical and rather daring change in the lives of 13 Iowa orphanage children. Within five years his study was completed, the results were obvious and the children disappeared into the mainstream of American life.

In 1965, Dr. Harold M. Skeels, now with the National Institute of Mental Health, began the onerous task of tracking down the orphans to discover what, if any, impact his controversial experiment had had in their adult lives.

The results of his follow-up testify to the strong relationship between intelligence and environment.

All 13 children were less than three years old and mentally retarded when Dr. Skeels began his experiment. Three of them were "imbeciles" with IQ ratings around 40.

At the time, normal orphanage procedure was simply to keep those unadoptable children whose development was delayed, and if they did not become normal, eventually transfer them to a nearby institution for the mentally retarded.

But by chance, two little girls, emaciated, undersized, colorless and obviously retarded, got transferred to the institution at very young ages. Within a year they were alert and mentally normal.

Viewing this inexplicable change, Dr. Skeels discovered a major distinction between the orphanage and the institution: the degree of tender loving care. Each girl had been "adopted" by an older institution inmate while others in the ward "served as adoring aunts." The children were pampered, played with and taken on excursions.

By contrast, the orphanage, though standard and designed for mentally normal children, was so overcrowded with youngsters that they had no chance to form intense relationships with an adult.

As Dr. Skeels described it: "Human interactions were limited to busy nurses who, with the speed born of practice and necessity, changed diapers or bedding, bathed and medicated the infants, and fed them efficiently with propped bottles." Few toys were available.

Dr. Skeels decided to try something new. Throughout the wards of the state institution he placed the 13 orphans, using a classification of "house guest" to avoid later stigmatization as "retarded."

As with the two little girls, 11 of the 13 children attained normal intelligence, including the three imbeciles, who more than doubled their IQ scores. Once normal, the 11 were put up for adoption.

Meanwhile, Dr. Skeels found a similar group in the orphanage to use for comparison. Though this group had originally been fairly well off intellectually (nine were of average intelligence), their IQs dropped as dramatically and as quickly as those of the first group rose.

In two years, the groups literally switched positions intellectually, the first gaining an average of 28 IQ points, the second losing 26. One 10-month-old boy in the orphanage, starting with good average intelligence (IQ 109), became an imbecile in five years. By the time he was 19 he had an IQ score of 19 and a speech defect so severe he could not make himself understood.

Dr. Skeels was successful in locating all the children in the original study, and reports that they have continued these same patterns into adulthood. All 13 "houseguests" are self-supporting. None is a ward of any institution, public or private. By contrast four of the orphanage group are in institutions or hospitals of some kind. In education and level of occupation the same difference exists. Those in the contrast group who do support themselves have only menial jobs, while the "houseguests" entered middle-class occupations.

"In no instance," Dr. Skeels said, "was there any indication of mental retardation" in the 28 children born to these "houseguests" who were themselves so markedly retarded as young children.

Lest the study should be misinterpreted, it should be noted that the orphanage was no snakepit, nor was the home for the mentally retarded a palace. Simply, the quality of orphanage life would be described today as "deprived."

It was a depersonalized, affectionless existence—by necessity, regimented. Like domitory living, the children were mass handled in groups of 30 or so, headed by one adult.

At the institution, each child became the recipient of much attention. The wards competed, said Dr. Skeels, to "see which one would have its 'baby' walking or talking first."

Although the study describes conditions of thirty years ago, it seems obvious, said Dr. Skeels, that "there are still countless infants born" with full normal capacity who will become retarded (and expensive) wards of society unless intervention occurs.

His findings have been published as a 65-page monograph by the Society for Research in Child Development.

Unit Five | DISCUSSION QUESTIONS

18. *How Different Are They?*
Discuss how a revision of our ideas concerning the proper sex role will improve our society.
What are some of the early differences between boys and girls in learning ability?

19. *Individual Differences in Behavior and Autonomic Activity in Newborn Infants*
What effects of the environment affect temperamental differences?
Give examples of maternal behavior that affects temperamental differences in young babies.

20. *Biological and Environmental Interchange in the Development of Children*
Explain how mothers' caring ability for babies depends much on the mothers' own past history.
How important is the "mother-child unit" in understanding human behavior?

21. *Environment Important*
What information gained from this study can contribute to work with "deprived children"?
What effect does "love" have upon "intelligence"?

Unit Six   Evaluating and Measuring Behavior

The fact that employers generally ask job applicants for references or past employment records is an indication that employers attempt to predict future performance on past behavioral patterns. Many colleges and universities require prospective students to present certain high school grade point averages and certain psychological test scores. This, too, is an indication that probable academic success is predictable on the basis of past performance. Even at race tracks people buy racing forms on the assumption that future expectations of horses and dogs can be determined by past experiences. Installment-buying customers are evaluated by their past payment records. All these examples are indications that prediction is an integral part of our way of life.

Approximately 200 years ago astronomers discovered that seemingly inaccurate recordings of astronomical events were in reality individual differences in reaction timing. Wundt's laboratory of the late 1800's concentrated on behavioral differences found in human beings. Ruby Yoshioka's *What Can We Predict?* is a knowledgeable discussion of the history of probability theory which was founded on a gambler's curiosity.

During the first decade of this century the French government solicited the services of two psychologists, Binet and Simon, to devise a method that would identify intellectual differences of Paris youngsters. The American revision of this test in 1916 ushered in an era that was destined to make the United States the leading proponent of psychological testing.

Evaluating and measuring human behavior are based on the assumption that heredity imposes certain limitations on one's intellectual abilities as well as his physical skills. That these limits are affected by environmental factors has led to many classical studies illustrating the effects of heredity and environment upon intelligence and other abilities. The Psychological Corporation's *Methods of Expressing Test Scores,* which presents the meaning of test scores in relation to sampling and norm models, stands as an outstanding reference in psychometry.

In recent years, a number of critics have voiced concern about the mass testing movement in this country. In 1964, the New York City Board of Education acted on a controversy which has long been brewing across the country. It decided to abolish IQ tests in New York public schools. This action was taken in response to charges that the tests were middle-class oriented and were therefore slanted against disadvantaged children. David Wechsler, who has given his name to several IQ tests, discusses the validity of the test in *The IQ Is an Intelligent Test.*

Banesh Hoffmann presents a penetrating criticism of the mass testing movement in *Psychometric Scientism.* This article is an abridgment of a paper delivered at an American Psychological Association symposium in 1966.

Since Hermann Rorschach, the Swiss psychiatrist, published a set of inkblots, personality testing has also become a popular aspect of psychological evaluation. Rorschach died in 1922 at the age of 37 and he had barely begun to extend the application of his tests from mental patients to normal subjects; however, since that time, individual and group personality testing has become widespread. An appendix to William Whyte's book, *The Organization Man,* is the subject of the final article in this unit. Whyte's *How to Cheat on Personality Tests* is reprinted to illustrate how some observers have viewed this aspect of psychological testing.

---

22 | What Can We Predict?

Ruby Yoshioka

A mathematical system which was born in order to predict the probable winnings of gamblers is now helping man predict the path of atomic particles, the color of a hybrid flower, the odds against quintuplets or whether an eel will swim to America or to Europe.

Aside from gambling, our daily lives are full of probabilities. Will it rain? Will I pass the science exam? Will a surgical operation be successful? At best what we decide will or will not happen is based on some previous experience or just a guess as to the outcome or a "feeling" of what probably will take place. This is the common conception of probability.

But for mathematicians and statisticians, probability is more than a guess or intuition. They have devised mathematical systems, some of which are very complex, whereby the chances of an event occurring can be predicted.

HOW THEORY AROSE

The theory of mathematical probability arose from the studies of games of chance, early in the 17th century. Blaise Pascal, a French mathematician, scientist, and philosopher, and creator of the famous Pascal triangle based on the binomial theorem, was asked by a gambler friend, who was interested in the "why" of gambling chances, to figure out why certain odds were more favorable to a gambling house than other odds. This Pascal undertook with the help of Pierre Fermat, another French mathematician, and developed probability theory.

From *Science News,* **85,** 139, 1964. Reprinted by permission of *Science News,* weekly summary of current science,

Since that time, probability theory has become increasingly important and many mathematicians have contributed to its advancement.

Probability theory today has applications in virtually every field from atomic physics and biology to social science.

Predictions of weather, population increase, the number of accidents that may occur during a holiday weekend and the probable outcome of elections are all examples of the application of mathematical probability, as are the estimation of insurance rates.

The classic example to explain probability theory is in tossing coins. If a coin is flipped, what is the chance that it will turn up heads? Since it must turn up either heads or tails, the probability is $\frac{1}{2}$; in 100 throws the probability is 50 heads and 50 tails in an ideal situation.

This does not mean that if heads shows in the first throw, tails will turn up in the next. Each throw is independent of the previous throw, since coins do not have a memory. However, in the long run, that is, after many tosses, say 100,000, the ratio of heads to tails tends to be 1 to 1.

Thus, if in 100 throws, there are 45 heads, heads could turn up about 450 times in 1,000 throws. It would be most unusual and highly improbable that in 1,000 throws the number of heads would be only 45. Actually tossing the coin and recording the result would show this to be true.

Taking another example, if a die is thrown, the chances of any one of the numbers, 1 through 6, appearing is $\frac{1}{6}$. This means that after many throws, or in the long run, any single number, say 3, will appear in $\frac{1}{6}$ of the throws.

If you throw two dice, one blue and one white, the chance of 3 appearing on a blue die is $\frac{1}{6} \times \frac{1}{6}$ or $\frac{1}{36}$, but a sum of 3 can be produced in two ways, with a 2 and 1, both equally likely. Thus its probability is $\frac{2}{36}$, or $\frac{1}{18}$, so a sum of 3 may be expected to occur once in every 18 throws.

As the number of throws increases, the chances of occurring at this ratio increase.

MORE COMPLEX PROBLEMS

These simple applications of probability theory as shown in the tossed coins and the throwing of dice have been applied to more complex problems of probability. James Bernoulli, later in the 17th century, clearly defined probability theory in relationship to large numbers of cases, applying the same mathematical equation.

As a result of Bernoulli's law and subsequent related laws, the central limit theorems were derived. These theorems state that as the number of trials increases, the predictions made by probability theory can be more and more closely satisfied.

For example, taking coins again, the ratio of heads to tails tends to come closer to 1 to 1 as the number of throws is increased. However, an interesting point is that the actual numerical difference between heads and tails tends to become greater with the greater number of trials. In 100 throws, if tails show 45 times and heads 55 times, the difference is 10. But, if 1,000 throws are made and the ratio is 450 to 550, the numerical difference is 100.

WHY GAMBLERS LOSE

Thus, the best lesson a gambler can learn from probability theory is that if he continues to play, he will always lose. Mathematicians have shown, since the time of Bernoulli, that the chances of loss become greater and greater as the gambler continues to play and the resources of the house increase compared to those of the gambler.

This is also true in a slot machine. The more quarters a player puts into the machine, the slimmer become his chances of becoming a winner.

A curve can be drawn from a table of the various ways in which an event may happen, such as the tossing of coins. The probability distribution curve is bell-shaped and is known as the normal distribution curve, or Gaussian curve after Karl Friedrich Gauss.

The normal curve is used extensively in many applications, for example, in showing the variations of I.Q. in a certain age group or the heights of different races. Where natural phenomena can be measured, such as the number of peas in a pod or the weight of children of a certain age, the normal probability distribution is closely followed.

In genetics, the Mendelian theory of the transmission of traits can be predicted by probability theory.

If a red flower is crossed with a white flower, the red gene will unite with the white gene to form a pink flower. If two pink flowers are then crossed, the next generation will produce one red, one white and two pinks, following the pattern of the probability distribution of heads and tails when two coins are tossed.

This ability to predict offspring of plants is most useful to agriculturists and botanists in hybridizing and improving plants and animals.

RANDOM SAMPLING

It is often desirable to know how a population will vote or how well a machine is turning out a product. A system of random sampling has been devised.

The straw vote taken before an election is an example of random sampling. From such a vote, the trend of the election can be predicted.

If the product of a new machine is to be tested, samples selected at random can give the manufacturer an indication of the quality of the whole.

Sampling is a convenient and oftentimes the only method by which a study of large groups can be made.

In physics the behavior of atoms and molecules and the paths of electrons and protons are determined probabilistically. Since it is impossible to determine the exact position or exact motion of an electron at a particular moment, its position or direction of movement must be based on probability and must be estimated.

Most physicists believe that probability behavior governing electrons must also apply to the universe, but the late Prof. Albert Einstein, among other scientists, believed there is an underlying order in the universe that does not involve probability.

Astronomers apply probability statistics when determining the position of stars and space scientists calculate travels in outer space on a probabilistic basis.

NEW METHOD OF CALCULATION

A new method of calculating probability that uses only existing factors rather than previous events has been recently devised by Prof. Marcel Neuts of Purdue University, Lafayette, Ind.

Prof. Neuts reported that his method can be applied to actual biological and physical phenomena as well as purely theoretical mathematical problems.

The concept of mathematical probability is far reaching and enters into virtually all phases of our lives, from birth rates to death rates, with all the probabilities and statistics that can happen in between.

Since this is so, an early introduction to the concept of probability and statistical methods would be extremely valuable to students in almost every field of study. To help make this important step in the introduction of probability theory to younger students, SCIENCE SERVICE has issued a THINGS of science kit on probability containing problems and explanations of elementary mathematical probability and the materials necessary to perform the experiments. The unit is available at 75¢ each from SCIENCE SERVICE, Washington, D.C. 20036.

---

23 | Methods of Expressing Test Scores

An individual's test score acquires meaning when it can be compared with the scores of well-identified groups of people. Manuals for tests provide tables of norms to make it easy to compare individuals and groups. Several systems for deriving more meaningful "standard scores" from raw scores have been widely adopted. All of them reveal the relative status of individuals within a group.

The fundamental equivalence of the most popular standard score systems is illustrated in the chart on the next page. We hope the chart and the accompanying description will be useful to counselors, personnel officers, clinical diagnosticians and others in helping them to show the uninitiated the essential simplicity of standard score systems, percentile equivalents, and their relation to the ideal normal distribution.

Sooner or later, every textbook discussion of test scores introduces the bell-shaped normal curve. The student of testing soon learns that many of the methods of deriving meaningful scores are anchored to the dimensions and characteristics of this curve. And he learns by observation of actual test

---

From *Test Service Bulletin,* **48,** January 1955. Reprinted courtesy of *Test Service Bulletin* of The Psychological Corporation.

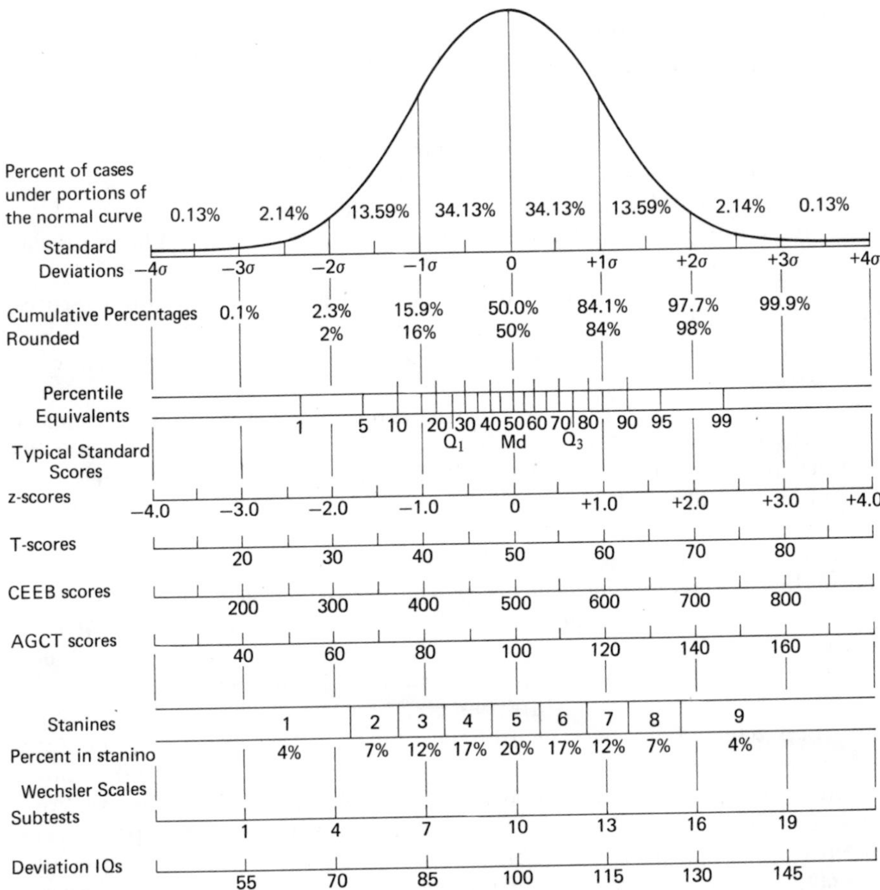

Note: This chart cannot be used to equate scores on one test to scores on another test. For example, both 600 on the CEEB and 120 on the AGCT are one standard deviation above their respective means, but they do not represent "equal" standings because the scores were obtained from different groups.

score distributions that the ideal mathematical curve is a reasonably good approximation of many practical cases. He learns to use the standardized properties of the ideal curve as a model.

Let us look first at the curve itself. Notice that there are no raw scores printed along the baseline. The graph is generalized; it describes an idealized distribution of scores of any group on any test. We are free to use any numerical scale we like. For any particular set of scores, we can be arbitrary and call the average score zero. In technical terms we "equate" the mean raw score to zero. Similarly we can choose any convenient number, say 1.00, to represent the scale distance of one standard deviation.* Thus, if a distribution of scores on a particular test has a mean of 36 and a standard devia-

* The mathematical symbol for the standard deviation is the lower-case Greek letter sigma or σ. These terms are used interchangeably in this article.

tion of 4, the zero point on the baseline of our curve would be equivalent to an original score of 36; one unit to the right, $+1\sigma$, would be equivalent to 40, $(36 + 4)$; and one unit to the left, -1σ, would be equivalent to 32, $(36 - 4)$.

The total area under the curve represents the total number of scores in the distribution. Vertical lines have been drawn through the score scale (the baseline) at zero and at 1, 2, 3, and 4 sigma units to the right and left. These lines mark off subareas of the total area under the curve. The numbers printed in these sub-areas are per cents—*percentages of the total number of people.* Thus, 34.13 per cent of all cases in a normal distribution have scores falling between 0 and -1σ. For practical purposes we rarely need to deal with standard deviation units below -3 or above $+3$; the percentage of cases with scores beyond $\pm 3\sigma$ is negligible.

The fact that 68.26 per cent fall between $\pm 1\sigma$ gives rise to the common statement that in a normal distribution roughly two-thirds of all cases lie between plus and minus one sigma. This is a rule of thumb every test user should keep in mind. It is very near to the theoretical value and is a useful approximation.

Below the row of deviations expressed in sigma units is a row of per cents; these show *cumulatively* the percentage of people which is included *to the left* of each of the sigma points. Thus, starting from the left, when we reach the line erected above -2σ, we have included the lowest 2.3 per cent of cases. These percentages have been rounded in the next row.

Note some other relationships: the area between the $\pm 1\sigma$ points includes the scores which lie above the 16th percentile (-1σ) and below the 84th percentile $(+1\sigma)$—two major reference points all test users should know. When we find that an individual has a score 1σ above the mean, we conclude that his score ranks at the 84th percentile in the group of persons on whom the test was normed. (This conclusion is good provided we also add this clause, at least subvocally: *if this particular group reasonably approximates the ideal normal model.*)

The simplest facts to memorize about the normal distribution and the relation of the *percentile* system to deviations from the average in sigma units are seen in the chart. They are

Deviation from the mean	-2σ	-1σ	0	$+1\sigma$	$+2\sigma$
Percentile equivalent	2	16	50	84	98

To avoid cluttering the graph reference lines have not been drawn, but we could mark off ten per cent sections of area under the normal curve by drawing lines vertically from the indicated decile points (10, 20, . . . 80, 90) up through the graph. The reader might do this lightly with a colored pencil.

We can readily see that ten per cent of the area (people) at the middle of the distribution embraces a smaller *distance* on the baseline of the curve than ten per cent of the area (people) at the ends of the range of scores, for the simple reason that the curve is much higher at the middle. A person who is at the 95th percentile is farther away from a person at the 85th percentile in units of *test score* than a person at the 55th percentile is from one at the 45th percentile.

The remainder of the chart, that is the several scoring scales drawn parallel to the baseline, illustrates variations of the *deviation score* principle. As a class these are called *standard scores.*

First, there are the *z-scores.* These are the same *numbers* as shown on the baseline of the graph; the only difference is that the expression, σ, has been omitted. These scores run, in practical terms, from -3.0 to $+3.0$. One can compute them to more decimal places if one wishes, although computing to a single decimal place is usually sufficient. One can compute *z*-scores by equating the mean to 0.00 and the standard deviation to 1.00 for a distribution of any shape, but the relationships shown in this figure between the *z*-score equivalents of raw scores and percentile equivalents of raw scores are correct only for normal distributions. The interpretation of standard score systems derives from the idea of using the normal curve as a model.

As can be seen, *T*-scores are directly related to *z*-scores. The mean of the raw scores is equated to 50, and the standard deviation of the raw scores is equated to 10. Thus a *z*-score of $+1.5$ means the same as a *T*-score of 65. *T*-scores are usually expressed in whole numbers from about 20 to 80. The *T*-score plan eliminates negative numbers and thus facilitates many computations.*

The College Entrance Examination Board uses a plan in which both decimals and negative numbers are avoided by setting the arbitrary mean at 500 points and the arbitrary sigma at another convenient unit, namely, 100 points. The experienced tester or counselor who hears of a College Board SAT-V score of 550 at once thinks, "Half a sigma (50 points) above average (500 points) on the CEEB basic norms." And when he hears of a score of 725 on SAT-M, he can interpret, "Plus $2\frac{1}{4}\sigma$. Therefore, better than the 98th percentile."

During World War II the Navy used the *T*-score plan of reporting test status. The Army used still another system with a mean of 100 and a standard deviation of 20 points.

Another derivative of the general standard score system is the *stanine* plan, developed by psychologists in the Air Force during the war. The plan divides the norm population into nine groups, hence, "standard nines." Except for stanine 9, the top, and stanine 1, the bottom, these groups are spaced in half-sigma units. Thus, stanine 5 is defined as including the people who are within $\pm 0.25\sigma$ of the mean. Stanine 6 is the group defined by the half-sigma distance on the baseline between $+0.25\sigma$ and $+0.75\sigma$. Stanines 1 and 9 include all persons who are below -1.75σ and above $+1.75\sigma$, respectively. The result is a distribution in which the mean is 5.0 and the standard deviation is 2.0.

Just below the line showing the demarcation of the nine groups in the stanine system there is a row of percentages which indicates the per cent of the total population in each of the stanines. Thus 7 per cent of the population will be in stanine 2, and 20 per cent in the middle group, stanine 5.

---

* T-scores and percentiles both have 50 as the main reference point, an occasional source of confusion to those who do not insist on careful labelling of data and of scores of individuals in their records.

Interpretation of the Wechsler scales (W-B I, W-B II, WISC, and WAIS) depends on a knowledge of standard scores. A subject's raw score *on each of the subtests* in these scales is converted, by appropriate norms tables, to a standard score, based on a mean of 10 and a standard deviation of 3. The sums of standard scores on the Verbal Scale, the Performance Scale, and the Full Scale are then converted into IQs. These IQs are based on a standard score mean of 100, the conventional number for representing the IQ of the average person in a given age group. The standard deviation of the IQs is set at 15 points. In practical terms, then, roughly two-thirds of the IQs are between 85 and 115, that is, $\pm 1\sigma$.* IQs of the type used in the Wechsler scales have come to be known as *deviation IQs,* as contrasted with the IQs developed from scales in which a derived mental age is divided by chronological age.

Users of the Wechsler scales should establish clearly in their minds the relationship of subtest scaled scores and the deviation IQs to the other standard score systems, to the ordinary percentile rank interpretation, and to the deviation units on the baseline of the normal curve. For example, every Wechsler examiner should recognize that an IQ of 130 is a score equivalent to a deviation of $+2\sigma$, and that this IQ score delimits approximately the upper two per cent of the population. If a clinician wants to evaluate a Wechsler IQ of 85 along with percentile ranks on several other tests given in school, he can mentally convert the IQ of 85 to a percentile rank of about 16, this being the percentile equal to a deviation from the mean of -1σ. Of course he should also consider the appropriateness and comparability of norms.

Efficiency in interpreting test scores in counseling, in clinical diagnosis, and in personnel selection depends, in part, on facility in thinking in terms of the major interrelated plans by which meaningful scores are derived from raw scores. It is hoped that this graphic presentation will be helpful to all who in their daily work must help others understand the information conveyed by numerical test scores.

---

* Every once in a while we receive a letter from someone who suggests that the Wechsler scales ought to generate a wider range of IQs. The reply is very simple. If we want a wider range of IQs all we have to do is to choose a *larger arbitrary* standard deviation, say, 20 or 25. Under the present system, $\pm 3\sigma$ gives IQs of 55 to 145, with a few rare cases below and a few rare cases above. If we used 20 as the standard deviation, we would *arbitrarily* increase the $\pm 3\sigma$ range of IQs from 55–145 to 40–160. This *is* a wider range of numbers! But, test users should never forget that adaptations of this kind do not change the responses of the people who took the test, do not change the order of the persons in relation to each other, and do not change the psychological meaning attached to an IQ.

24 | The I.Q. Is an Intelligent Test

David Wechsler

It is now two years since the New York City school system eliminated the I.Q. from pupils' records. Banned under the pressure of groups that claimed the I.Q. was unfair to the culturally deprived, it has been replaced by achievement tests. Meanwhile, a great deal of effort is being put into developing new, nonverbal scales to measure schoolchildren's abilities while eliminating the troublesome factor of language.

Neither of these substitutes is an adequate replacement for the I.Q. In my opinion, the ban was misdirected in the first place and we should restore the I.Q. to its former position as a diagnostic tool as soon as possible. The substitutes simply do not test enough of the abilities that go to make up individual intelligence.

To understand what I.Q. tests do, and why they are valuable, we must first be clear about what intelligence is. This is a surprisingly thorny issue. Too much depends upon how one defines intelligence. In this respect psychologists are in no better agreement than the lay public. Divergency of view stems largely from differences in emphasis on the particular abilities thought to be central to the definition one envisages. Thus, an educator may define intelligence primarily as the ability to learn, a biologist in terms of ability to adapt, a psychologist as the ability to reason abstractly and the practical layman as just common sense.

One difficulty is similar to what a physicist encounters when asked to state what he means by energy, or a biologist what he means by life. The fact is that energy and life are not tangible entities; you cannot touch them or see them under a microscope even though you are able to describe them. We know them by their effects or properties.

The same is true of general intelligence. For example, we must assume that there is something common to learning to count, avoiding danger and playing chess which makes it possible for us to say that they are evidence of intelligent behavior, as against learning to walk, being accident prone and playing bingo, which seemingly have little if anything to do with it.

Intelligence, operationally defined, is the aggregate capacity of the individual to act purposefully, to think rationally and to deal effectively with his environment. Although it is not a mere sum of intellectual abilities, the only way we can evaluate it quantitatively is by the measurement of various aspects of these abilities.

Any test is primarily a device for eliciting and evaluating a fragment of behavior. An intelligence test is one by which an examiner seeks to appraise this bit of behavior insofar as it may be called intelligent. Various abilities can be used for this purpose because manifestations of ability are the means by which a subject can communicate and demonstrate his competences. To this end it is not so much the particular ability that is tested which is important, as the degree to which it correlates with posited criteria. A test is considered a good measure of intelligence if it correlates, for example, with learning ability, ability to comprehend, evidence of capacity to adjust and so on. If it does so to a satisfactory degree it is said to be valid. But, even when a test has been established as valid, there still remains a question: For what class of subjects is it valid? The answer will depend in a large measure upon the population on which the test was standardized—for example, middle-class white children, Southern Negro children or recently arrived Puerto Ricans.

Thus I.Q. tests are attacked on the ground that they are overweighted with items depending on verbal ability and academic information. Individuals with limited educational backgrounds are obviously penalized, and non-English-speaking subjects are admittedly incapable of taking the tests at all. This is an important stricture and test makers, contrary to some opinion, are fully aware of it. One way of "solving" the problem would be to provide separate normal or average scores for different populations, but apart from the practical difficulty of obtaining such norms, there is always the stricture that they bypass rather than meet the central issue. A compromise approach is practiced in some school systems, where intelligence tests continue to be used—under the more acceptable name of "aptitude tests."

Almost from the start, psychologists have sought to cope with the problem of literacy and language disability by devising nonverbal tests of intelligence. Thus, soon after the Binet tests were introduced more than a half-century ago, two American psychologists, Pintner and Paterson, developed the Non-Language Individual Performance Scale for non-English-speaking subjects. Similarly, when the Army Alpha (the main verbal test of World War I) was devised for the military services, a companion nonverbal test (the Army Beta) was prepared along with it.

The Pintner-Paterson scale required the subject to give evidence of his capacities by filling in appropriate missing parts on familiar pictures, putting together form boards, learning to associate signs with symbols, etc. The Army Beta consisted of such tasks as following mazes, reproducing picture designs, counting cubes, etc.—with directions presented to the subject by gesture or mime.

Many similar tests—the so-called "culture-free" or "culture-fair" tests—have followed. The most recent one reported is the Johns Hopkins Perceptual Test devised by Dr. Leon Rosenberg and associates at the Johns Hopkins School of Medicine. This test was initially developed for children who did not speak or who were handicapped by certain functional or organic disorders; it has also been recommended as a more effective intelligence test for the very young and for culturally deprived children.

The Johns Hopkins Perceptual Test consists of a series of designs from which a child is asked to choose appropriate patterns to match others shown to him. Its primary merit is that it eliminates the factor of language. It is also claimed to be less dependent than verbal tests upon acquired skills, which, of course, depend to some extent upon a child's environmental experience. But this test, like other performance tests, does not measure a sufficient number of the abilities that go to make up the total picture of intelligent behavior.

Contrary to claims, the results of performance tests have been generally disappointing. The findings indicate that while they may be useful in certain situations, and for certain diagnostic groups, they prove quite unsatisfactory as alternates for verbal scales. They correlate poorly with verbal aptitudes and are poor prognosticators of over-all learning ability as well as school achievement. Above all, they have turned out to be neither culture-free nor culture-fair.

Culture-free tests fail to attain their end because, in the first place, the items usually employed are themselves subject to particular environmental experiences. A circle in one place may be associated with the sun, in another with a copper coin, in still another with a wheel. In some places a dog is a pet, in others a detested animal. Pictures, in the long run, are just symbols and these may be as difficult to understand and recognize as words; they have to be interpreted, as anyone who has attempted to learn sign language knows. Putting together blocks may be a challenge or a threat, working fast a sign of carelessness or an incentive to competition. Nonverbal, even more than verbal tests, need to be related to particular environments and, from a practical point of view, are both limited in range and difficult to contrive.

Finally, many performance items when increased in difficulty tend to become measures of special abilities rather than having any significant correlation with over-all measures of intelligence. Thus, while tests of visual motor coordination may be useful items on intelligence tests for young children they are no longer effective at later ages. Copying a diamond is a good test at the 7-year level, but whether a child of 12 can reproduce a complicated design has little to do with his general intelligence and represents at most a special ability.

The effect of culture on test performance is a subject that demands serious concern, but here one deals with the problem of what one understands by the word "culture." In the United States there is a strong trend among contemporary writers to identify the term with socio-economic levels. This is in contrast to the historic and broader meaning of the term, which covers all human as well as environmental influences that serve to characterize the intellectual and moral status of a civilization.

Not all the poor are culturally deprived. Although standards may differ widely, "culturally different" does not mean "culturally deprived." The Jews and Italians who lived on the Lower East Side had their culture, and so have the Negroes in the slums of Harlem. They differ widely in respect to almost any variable one might employ, and culture is no exception. What this implies is that "culture" no more than color of skin should be a basis for assessing individuals.

The comments relating to the question of cultural impact apply with equal force to the problem of racial and national differences. One may start with the hypothesis that such differences exist and not necessarily be overwhelmed by their importance. This, in the writer's opinion, is a reasonable position.

This opinion is based on studies done in the field and, in particular, on data from World War I and World War II United States Armed Forces testing programs. The data from World War I included not only tables for the overall draft population but for a great many subgroupings. Among these were separate test-score summaries according to national origin of the draftees, and a particularly detailed one comparing Negroes and whites. As might have been expected, differences between groups compared were found, and as might also have been expected invidious comparisons were immediately made and exploited. Particularly emphasized were the lower scores made by Negroes as compared with those made by white soldiers. Neglected, on the other hand, were the differences found between occupational levels and the more general ones between urban and rural populations.

It was not too difficult to correct the erroneous inferences made by the racists. But, in disposing of the racial claims, some authors went much beyond what the data warranted. Eventually, statements were made that other test findings revealed no significant differences between any national or racial groups—a fact which is equally questionable, and in any event still needs to be demonstrated. In the author's opinion, national and racial differences do exist—probably of both genetic and environmental origins, in varying degree. But the fact is that these differences are not large or relevant in the individual case.

We now come to the biggest bugaboo of intelligence testing—the I.Q. itself. The scientific literature on it is as large as its assailants are numerous. It has been attacked by educators, parents, writers of popular articles and politicians. During the Korean War it was investigated by Congress. Now that we are once more having trouble with draft quotas, the I.Q. will most likely be investigated again. It is doubtful whether the I.Q. can be brought into good grace at this time, but perhaps much of the fire sparked by the I.Q. can be quenched by an objective explanation of what it really is.

An I.Q. is just a measure of relative brightness. It merely asserts that, compared with persons of his own age group, an individual has attained a certain rank on a particular intelligence test. For example, a 10-year-old takes the Stanford-Binet test and attains a certain score, which happens to be that for the statistically average 8-year-old. We then divide the child's mental age (8) by his chronological age (10) and obtain a quotient, which we multiply by 100 simply to remove the inconvenience of decimal points. The result is called the Intelligence Quotient (or I.Q.)—in this case, 80. This particular figure tells us that, as compared with others in his age group, the child has performed below normal (which would be 100).

When this procedure of comparative grading is applied to a geography or bookkeeping test—when a teacher apportions class grades on a bell curve or a sliding scale—nobody gets excited. But when it is used with a mental test the reaction is quite different.

Opposition is generally focused not on the way that I.Q.'s are computed, but, more pointedly, on the way they are interpreted and utilized. One interpretation that has caused understandable concern is the notion that a person is "born with" an I.Q. which remains immutable. This is an allegation proclaimed by those who are opposed to the I.Q. rather than a view maintained by psychologists. What is asserted by psychologists, and supported by test-retest findings, is that I.Q.'s once accurately established are not likely to vary to any considerable degree. This does not mean that an I.Q. never changes, or that the conditions under which it was obtained may not have affected its validity.

The so-called constancy of the I.Q. is relative, but compared with other commonly used indexes, it is surprisingly stable. It is much more stable, for instance, than an individual's electrocardiogram or his basal metabolism level, which are accepted without question.

There are always exceptional cases which cannot be overlooked or bypassed. But one does not throw out the baby with the bath water. When for any reason a subject's I.Q. is suspect, the sensible thing to do is to have him retested. I.Q.'s, unlike the laws of the Medes and the Persians, are not irrevocable, but they should be respected.

While retest studies show that I.Q.'s are relatively stable, they also reveal that in individual cases large changes may occur—as much as 20 points or more. Thus, conceivably, an individual could move from the "dull normal" group to "average," or vice versa.

Much depends upon the age at which the original test was administered and the interval between testings. In general, I.Q.'s obtained before the age of 4 or 5 are more likely to show discrepancies between test and retest; those in the middle years least. Discrepancies are also likely to be larger as the intervals between retests increase. All this evidence points to reasons for not making a definitive intelligence classification on the basis of a single test, and more especially on one administered at an early age. This precaution is necessary not because the tests are unreliable but because rates of mental maturity are often factors that have to be taken into account. Such variations tend not only to penalize slow developers but also to overrate early bloomers.

Various skills are required for effective test performance at different age levels. The fact that they are not present at a particular age level does not indicate that a child who lacks them is necessarily stunted. It may only be that these skills have not as yet emerged. Early training has a bearing on test readiness, but it is not true that if a child has not had this training at one age, he will not develop the skills required at a later age. On the other hand, deliberately teaching a child skills in order to have him "pass" an intelligence test, as now seems to be the vogue, is not the answer to acquiring a high I.Q.

An important conclusion to be drawn from the above is that more, rather than less, testing is needed. Unfortunately, when this is suggested, one encounters the objection that extended testing programs in public schools would be too costly. The expensiveness of school testing has been greatly exaggerated, especially when considered in relation to the over-all cost of keeping a child in school (an average of $600 to $700 per child per year in most parts of the country).

Particularly neglected is the individual intelligence examination, which at present is administered in most public schools only to "problem cases."

In the author's opinion, an individual intelligence examination ought to be given to all children as they enter school. Most private schools require such an examination, and there is good reason why the public schools should also provide it.

Allowing $50 per examination administered once over a four-year period, the cost would be a minuscule addition to the school's budget. In return, a systematic individual examination could serve as a means of evaluating a child's assets and liabilities before he was subjected to the hazards of arbitrary placement. Finally, it must be borne in mind that intelligence tests are intended as a means not merely for detecting the intellectually retarded, but also for discovering the intellectually gifted.

In discussions of the merits and limitations of intelligence tests, one important aspect, frequently overlooked, is their basic aim. This objective is most effectively summed up in the late Prof. Irving Lorge's definition of what intelligence tests aim to measure—namely, "the ability to learn and to solve the tasks required by a particular environment."

This definition implies a multiple approach to the concept of intelligence and intelligence testing. In the latter process, one is of necessity engaged in evaluating an individual's particular abilities. Of course, in doing so, one obtains information regarding a subject's liabilities and handicaps. This information is both useful and important, but is really only an incidental aspect of what one wishes to discover from an intelligence test.

When it is asserted that intelligence tests are unfair to the disadvantaged and minorities, one must be mindful of the fact that they are simply recording the unfairness of life. They show also, for example, that our mental abilities, whoever we may be, decline with advancing age—as demonstrated in the chart below, based on the author's Adult Intelligence Scale. (Of course, this decline is in many cases counterbalanced by increased experience.)

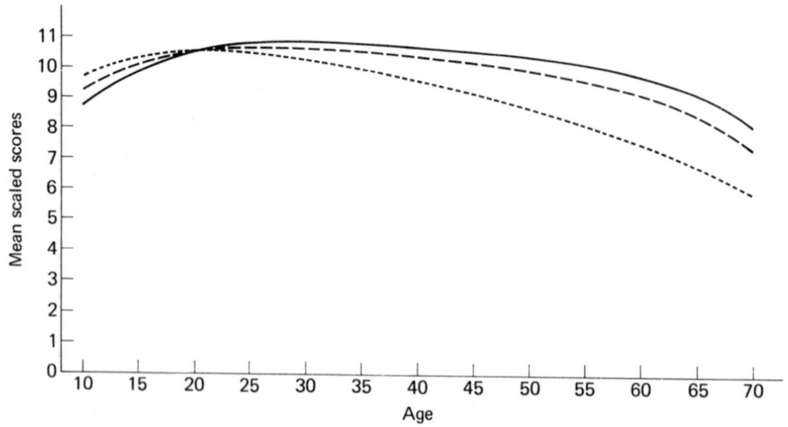

Decline. Scores, by age, as registered on the Wechsler Adult Intelligence Scale. Solid line represents results on information tests; dashed line, arithmetic; dotted line, block design.

Intelligence tests were not devised for the handicapped alone but for everybody. What then can be the reason for believing they may not be suitable for the major segments of our population—or for prohibiting their administration to the majority of children in a school system? The current New York City I.Q. ban is a case in point, and especially discouraging when one sees what is being used instead.

The tests that have been substituted are a series of achievement tests—in particular, reading tests. Of all the possible choices, one can hardly imagine a worse alternative. For of all areas in which the disadvantaged child is handicapped, reading heads the list. The main difference between an intelligence (or aptitude) test and an achievement test is that the former is less tied to curriculum content. If it is true that a low score on an intelligence test presents a misleading picture of a pupil's learning capacity, how much more unfair would be an even lower score on an achievement test. It is possible that the I.Q. was banned in New York because those who supported the ban wished primarily to combat what they believed to be a widespread view that the I.Q. is "somehow a fixed, static and genetic measure of learning ability." One may wonder, however, whether political pressures may not have played some role in the decision—and one may hope that the ban will soon be retracted.

The I.Q. has had a long life and will probably withstand the latest assaults on it. The most discouraging thing about them is not that they are without merit, but that they are directed against the wrong target. It is true that the results of intelligence tests, and of others, too, are unfair to the disadvantaged, deprived and various minority groups but it is not the I.Q. that has made them so. The culprits are poor housing, broken homes, a lack of basic opportunities, etc., etc. If the various pressure groups succeed in eliminating these problems, the I.Q.'s of the disadvantaged will take care of themselves.

RECOMMENDED READINGS

Getzels, J. W., and P. W. Jackson, *Creativity and Intelligence: Explorations with Gifted Students.* New York: Wiley, 1962.

Hunt, J. McV., *Intelligence and Experience.* New York: Ronald, 1961.

Jenkins, J. J., and D. G. Paterson, eds., *Studies in Individual Differences: The Search for Intelligence.* New York: Appleton-Century-Crofts, 1961.

Pinneau, S. R., *Changes in Intelligence Quotient: Infancy to Maturity.* Boston: Houghton Mifflin, 1961.

Taylor, C. W., and Frank Barron, eds., *Scientific Creativity: Its Recognition and Development.* New York: Wiley, 1963.

Terman, L. M. and Maud A. Merrill, *Stanford-Binet Intelligence Scale; Manual for the Third Revision, Form L-M.* Boston: Houghton Mifflin, 1960.

Wechsler, David, *The Measurement of Adult Intelligence,* 4th ed. Baltimore: Williams and Wilkins, 1958.

25 | Psychometric Scientism

Banesh Hoffmann

Last month bright juniors at nearly 18,000 high schools took the National Merit Scholarship Examinations. More than 2,000,000 college hopefuls will take the SAT this year. Since Vietnam, thousands of young college men have been screened for deferment by Selective Service tests. Next year 6,000,000 youngsters and adults may fill out some part of the national assessment scales produced by the four major U.S. testing services. All in all, testers hold almost godlike power over individual lives.

How good are even the best multiple-choice tests, and how scientific are their makers, not only in their statistical procedures but also in their response to sharply defined criticisms? In this article Mr. Hoffmann raises new doubts about what the test-makers are doing in the name of science.

Although this article is concerned primarily with academic testing, it has wider implications. First let us be clear on a crucial point: There is no generally satisfactory method of evaluating human abilities and capabilities. The detection and evaluation of other than superficial ability is inevitably an art demanding insight, taste, and knowledge. Current attempts to reduce it to a science and then mechanize it are not only dangerous but in a profound sense unscientific.

These are hard words, and it would be too much to expect psychometrists to find them pleasing. Yet the psychometrists' defensive reaction to past criticism has been unfortunate. By it the psychometrists have not only prevented a significant confrontation of issues; they have unwittingly advertised their own insecurity.

Most of the weaknesses of psychometrists' current methods have to do with the manner in which they use statistics. They seem unaware of the fallacies in their procedures. To illustrate some of these, consider the following skeleton of a multiple-choice question. One is required, essentially, to say which one of the words, if any, in the following sentence makes it defective and should thus be changed:

Among them Tom and Dick could not find enough money.

It does not take long to pick *among* on the ground that Tom and Dick are two persons and the preposition should therefore be *between*. On a pretest of this question the statistics would strongly support this as the key.

But if one pauses just a little to think—and has the ability to do so—one concludes that the question is ambiguous. For Tom and Dick might have been holding up a large group at gunpoint and "among *them*" could not find enough money.

Abridged from *Phi Delta Kappan,* April 1967, p. 381. Reprinted by permission of the author and publisher.

(San Diego City Schools)

The tyranny of multiple-choice tests. High School students take college qualifying tests in one of many centers across the nation.

Would this ambiguity show up in the statistics? Think before you answer. There is a trap in all of this. I have tried this question verbally on various groups. Some people, unaware that *among* and *between* mean different things, see nothing wrong with the sentence. The question discriminates excellently between these people (call them Group I—for ignorant) and those who say *among* should be *between* (call them Group K—for knowledgeable). Only a small percentage of the people seem to see the alternative meaning fairly quickly and to conclude therefore that the question is ambiguous (call them Group D—for deep). Since Group D is small, it has no great effect on the pretest statistics. These statistics, therefore, will not reveal to the test-maker that the question is defective. Since this is by no means an untypical situation, we have the following important theorem: *pretest statistics are significantly misleading.*

Test-makers sometimes argue that they do not rely solely on pretest statistics to eliminate defective items: that they also use their own judgment and that of their expert consultants in the subject of the test. But the fact that defective questions nevertheless appear on tests—and not rarely—shows that this judgment too is by no means to be relied on. Because space does not permit a full analysis of this point, I confine myself to two reasons.

One is that the testers and their expert consultants often know beforehand which is the wanted answer, and this destroys their objectivity. Another is that they have a psychological set as to the answer they think would be wanted even when they are not told which one it is. Since the testers may believe that they can make the necessary allowances for this and thus retain objectivity, I should like to demonstrate here that this is almost certainly not the case.

For the purposes of this demonstration let us return to the question about Tom and Dick and the word "among." We said that deep people quickly decide that the question is ambiguous. But in fact there is no ambiguity in it at all—except for doubts we may have as to what is in the tester's mind. Not only is there only one logically correct answer, but that answer is different from the keyed answer. Why? Because *the sentence is a good sentence as it stands.* It reads, "Among them Tom and Dick could not find enough money," and the word "among" shows that "them" does not refer to Tom and Dick but to a larger group. True, we also get a good sentence—though one with a different meaning—if we change "among" to "between," just as we would if we changed "Dick" to "Harry" or "money" to "food," but such possible changes are irrelevant. The sentence is good as it stands and therefore the only logically correct response—as distinguished from the officially wanted response—is to leave the sentence unchanged.

Only an extremely small percentage of people (call them Group P—for profound) realize this on their own. Why do so many people miss it? Why do most readers feel that the matter has been fully discussed at the Group D stage and thus believe the question ambiguous? Because of their psychological set. They sense what is in the tester's mind and they cannot easily rid their own minds of the bias this induces—despite my early mention of a trap.

So much for the demonstration. But there are further important conclusions to be drawn from the above. One is a deepening of the theorem that pretest statistics are significantly misleading, for those statistics would not reveal this new and crucial facet of the item. The other major point is that the item itself fails to discriminate between members of Group I (for ignorant) and of Group P (for profound) but gives them all the same score of zero.

Though the preceding considerations were illustrated in terms of a single item, they are of general validity. They demonstrate fundamental defects in current psychometric procedures and are part of the reason for the choice of the title of this article. They are not the most important defects, though, as we shall see.

Why do the pretest statistics perform so badly on this question, and thus on many others? There are two main reasons. First, in the usual statistical sample, the percentage of people in Group P, and even in Group D, is apt to be very small. These people thus have little effect on the statistics—a fact that is particularly unfortunate because we would do better to cherish such people for their depth than to dismiss them, as at present, as a negligible minority of statistical misfits.

The second reason is that the process of statistical pretesting suffers from the fundamental deficiency of the mechanized, multiple-choice tests themselves: It concentrates solely on the choices of answers and ignores the reasons for these choices. Even though the tests themselves ignore the reasons for choices, the sensible thing would surely be to pretest the items by asking not just for the choices but for the reasons. In this way many major defects visible to, say, one percent of the students, and thus undetected statistically, would become sharply evident to any sufficiently intelligent psychometrist who cared—or dared—to look at the reasons. Besides, this would open his eyes, if they were not already opened, to the extraordinary variety of reasons, both good and bad, for making particular choices. Indeed, psychometrists who have never looked seriously into students' reasons for their choices would find this a most salutary experience, because it would strikingly exhibit once again one of the fundamental fallacies we have discussed of the standard multiple-choice method of testing.

Only exceptional students are apt to see the deeper defects of test items. Since these important people form a small minority, both the pretest statistics and the validation statistics, as currently used, are insensitive to their presence; and since these exceptional students often pick better answers than the official so-called "best" answers that are supported by the mass statistics, these very statistics contain a built-in bias against the deep students. Clearly, if both the pretest statistics and the validation statistics contain this bias, so do the tests themselves.

The principal objection to mechanized testing as currently practiced, and indeed to the general procedures of the multiple-choice psychometrists, is the fallacy of the statistical criterion. This goes beyond the matters of misguidance and bias discussed above. It has to do with the limitations of statistics themselves. To bring in statistics, one must first quantify, however crudely. Until something has been somehow reduced to numbers it can not be handled statistically.

The multiple-choice psychometrist confines himself, in the name of Science, to those criteria that he can readily reduce to statistical form, and closes his eyes to criteria that require subtle evaluation, even though just those criteria are apt to be the important ones. By so doing, he introduces a further and graver bias in his statistical criteria, this one arising from the very fact that the criteria he uses are purely statistical.

That is the first part of the fallacy of the statistical criterion. But there is a second part that is far more important: Not only does the statistical criterion ignore crucial aspects of ability; it also ignores the side effects of the tests.

Gifted teachers well know, for example, that the prevalence of mechanized tests corrupts education. But the multiple-choice psychometrist brushes such things aside and evaluates tests by means of their reliability and validity correlation coefficients. In so doing he believes he is behaving scientifically. When pressed, he asks for statistical evidence of the side effects before he, as a Scientist, will believe they exist. Yet he can easily obtain evidence that undesirable side effects exist, if only he can gain the confidence of gifted teachers and gifted students so that they will talk to him freely. He might be surprised to learn, for example, that such teachers often feel it necessary to warn precisely their intellectually liveliest students not to think too precisely or deeply when taking mechanized tests. The causes of the corruption of education by mechanized tests are many. Among them are such things as the use of ambiguity as a substitute for worthwhile difficulty, the fostering of intellectual dishonesty, the ignoring of taste, style, and quality of reasoning, the rewarding of superficiality, the penalizing of depth, and so on. The list is a long one, and not the least items in it are the evaluation of educational experiments by means of such tests, and the sheer poor quality of actual test questions.

If multiple-choice tests corrupt education, their worth certainly can not be properly evaluated by statistical criteria that ignore this and other far from negligible side effects.

It is no defense to say, as has been said, that the only function of a test is to test, and that a test can indeed be properly evaluated solely by means of such statistical criteria as validity correlation coefficients. The fallacy of a pseudo-scientific argument of this sort is easily seen by applying it to a test for the presence of cancer. By the statistical criterion of validity the best method of testing would be to kill the patient and perform a post-mortem—indeed, there would be no statistical advantage at all in killing him painlessly.

Evaluating the merits of different types of tests is not as simple as multiple-choice psychometrists seem to imagine. To confine oneself to simple correlation coefficients, costs per pupil, and other narrow figures of merit, while ignoring not only the inherent biases in the statistics but also the crucial side effects of the tests, is hardly to be scientific. Far too many psychometrists and their supporters are unaware how treacherous are the grounds on which they conduct their activities and reach their conclusions.

I have already mentioned the poor quality of test items, and a few remarks on the subject of quality will not be irrelevant. After all, test items made by leading test-making organizations are a product of what is widely regarded as an objective, scientific procedure, and if the quality of items leaves something to be desired it is an indication if not of the quality of the procedure then at least of that of some of its leading practitioners and thus of the fallibility of the procedure itself.

Because of the almost complete refusal of leading test-making organizations to permit verbatim publication of actual test items, I have, in my various writings on the subject, had to confine myself almost entirely to their official sample questions. Several instances are given in my book [1].

In a more recent article [2] I exhibited and analyzed in detail four seriously defective questions taken from the most recent booklet then available [3] describing the College Entrance Examination Board's *Scholastic Aptitude Test.* Though the College Board had every opportunity, in its response to the article [4], to deny that the four questions were seriously defective, it did not do so. We may take it as a reasonable conclusion, therefore, that the questions were indeed seriously defective.

Since the booklet contained 127 sample questions, a psychometrist, in conversation, made the point that four out of 127 is only about three percent and thus of little consequence, a view that others may be inclined to share. Let me explain, therefore, why the four defective questions loom much larger than this simple statistic suggests.

Of the 127 sample questions, 76 pertained to verbal aptitude and the other 51 to mathematical aptitude. The four defective sample questions were chosen solely from the 76 verbal aptitude ones, and four out of 76 is approximately five percent.

But there were more than just four defective sample questions dealing with verbal aptitude. The 76 verbal aptitude questions were of only four different types. The four seriously defective sample questions that I analyzed were selected to fulfill three conditions simultaneously. First, there had to be one question of each type; second, each question had to illustrate a different sort of defect; and third, the defect had to be so sharply defined that my detailed critical analysis of it would be logically unassailable.

Is it likely that only four of the sample questions were defective, and that by the merest chance they happened to meet these three stringent criteria? Enough, then, of the argument, all too often put forward, that the number of defective questions in tests made by leading test-making organizations is negligible.

To make a strong case, I have, in my various writings, directed my main criticisms of sample questions, procedures, and the like against the College Board and Educational Testing Service because I regard them as among the very best major organizations in the field, and I say this in all sincerity. If their influential booklets contain defective sample questions, do not the booklets themselves set an example of intellectual quality that contributes in its own way to that corruption of education to which I have already referred?

Nothing I say here is to be construed as implying that ETS and the College Board are inferior to analogous organizations that I have not discussed. To be fair, let me mention briefly the Selective Service pamphlet describing the draft deferment test made by Science Research Associates, now a subsidiary of IBM. The problems of draft deferment are many and profound, and the officials whose unenviable task it is to struggle with them deserve our fullest support. My remarks here are concerned solely with the technical quality of the 30 sample questions in the pamphlet. I have specified elsewhere [5] three of these questions that were defective, each in a different way, and three is 10 percent of the supply. In a situation of such national importance, one would hope that special pains would have been taken to make the sample questions impeccable. That it should be possible to take significant exception to 10 percent of them is surely unfortunate enough. Yet the situation is actually markedly worse than this, since there are more like 20 percent of such questions among the samples. One wonders how the test itself, in its various forms, compares in quality with the samples, but, if my understanding of the situation is correct, the test itself will not be released even after its use is discontinued.

I come now to my penultimate point. It concerns the reactions of psychometrists to criticisms. For brevity I shall confine myself to two incidents connected with my experiences with Educational Testing Service.

Having noticed a tendency of some psychometrists to try to over-awe critics by citing statistics that were not always relevant, I devised a statistics-proof strategy to demonstrate that all was far from well in current testing. Exhibiting defective sample questions made by outstanding organizations, I challenged them to defend their own questions.

In Chapters 16 and 17 of my book, I tell in full detail how ETS reacted to the challenge in the case of two of their own sample questions in science taken from a College Board booklet.

In seeking to defend the first of these questions, ETS argued to the effect that the student who understood $E = mc^2$ ought to realize that he should ignore Einstein's formula in answering the question. Apparently ETS did not realize that, among other things, this was tantamount to an admission that the question penalized the superior student.

In seeking to defend the other question, ETS gave an invalid defense, made scientific errors, used an intendedly clinching argument that proved to be a boomerang; and, as if this were not enough, showed throughout its argument that it did not even understand what its own question was asking.

These are fully documented facts, and they have not been denied by ETS. Indeed, in a public debate an executive of ETS had the grace and the courage to admit their validity.

The point I wish to stress here is that ETS decided to attempt to defend the questions, and to do so in words suggesting that the questions were not in the least defective: instead of frankly conceding that the questions were defective, it sought to brazen the matter out.

I realize how natural it is to react defensively. Certainly, in this case the reaction was neither scientific nor objective. One of its results has been to increase the logical vulnerability of ETS, and thus, because of the deservedly high standing of ETS, of multiple-choice testers in general.

The second incident has to do with the penalizing of deep, subtle, creative students by multiple-choice and similar tests of convergent thinking. It is an old charge, but when I discussed it in detail with a group of ETS executives some 10 years ago they expressed doubt as to its validity, saying they would need to look into the matter experimentally.

Since then I have repeatedly explained, among other things, how multiple-choice tests penalize depth, subtlety, and the like; and to make a strong case I have mainly used sample questions prepared by ETS. If the charge were false, the obvious strategy for ETS would have been to make experiments and prove it false forthwith. Yet there are reasons to believe from an article in *Science* by Chauncey and Hilton [6], both of ETS, that as late as 1965 ETS had made no such experiments despite the seriousness of the charge.

I therefore pointed out in a letter to *Science* [7] that the charge that multiple-choice tests penalize depth, subtlety, and the like prevailed not only on its own merits but also by default.

If ETS had any evidence to offer against this charge of default, one would have expected it to have responded at once by presenting the evidence. But although the editor of *Science* specifically invited ETS to respond to my argument and to a criticism by another person, no official response from ETS was forthcoming. *Thus the original charge of default now itself prevails by default.*

Let me add a brief coda to this episode. An ETS study, only recently completed, of the validity of the Graduate-Record Examination Advanced Physics Test [8] showed that scores from about 625 to the top, while indicating superiority, gave so little discrimination among students with these scores that using the scores for discriminating among them might just as well be replaced by drawing lots.

My final point has to do with the behavior of ETS and the College Board in the matter of evaluating ability in English composition.

When, on the basis of experiment, ETS and the College Board gave up the use of essay examinations for evaluating ability in English composition, there was an outcry. To overawe the objectors, ETS and the College Board made an elaborate new experiment pitting an essay examination against both the SAT Verbal and their so-called "English Composition Test," which last involved no English composition. They found that the SAT Verbal had the highest statistical validity, the misbranded "English Composition Test" the next, and the essay test—called the General Composition Test—the lowest. They then used these validity statistics as an argument for giving up essay examinations in the evaluation of ability in English composition. And by this display of pseudo-science they overawed the objectors and gained their point.

Having overawed the objectors, ETS and the College Board, by their own actions, immediately repudiated their statistical argument. How? By retaining the misbranded "English Composition Test" that involved no English composition. Had they really believed in the statistical argument with which they had overawed the objectors, they would have had to give up not only the essay examination but also the misbranded "English Composition Test" and used the SAT Verbal instead—perhaps calling *it* the "English Composition Test." For had not the SAT Verbal come out best according to their statistical criterion?

I doubt that ETS and the College Board were aware of the illogic of their various actions in this matter. But the illogic does suggest that they were aware, at least subconsciously, of what I have been referring to as the fallacy of the statistical criterion.

Space does not permit a discussion of the gradual reintroduction of essays and the illogic that has attended it. Nor of the recent ETS experiments that now show—statistically, of course—that essays are after all of value.

Let me proceed at once to the recent experiments on the grading of essays by computer [9], these being sponsored by the College Board. The computer, of course, had no basis for judgment of its own. It had to have values fed into it by the programmer. How were these values arrived at? By scientism masquerading as objective science. From such things as the statistical analysis of samples of good prose, the experimenter obtained a plentiful yield of objective criteria: for example, the average length of sentence, the number of commas, the number of prepositions, the number of dashes, and other objective criteria too numerous to mention, each criterion having its established weighting factor.

Since a computer cannot understand, a student could bring in an essay on any subject, prepared so as to have just the right number and distribution of commas and the like. To prevent this, a list of relevant words was fed into the computer. Absence of such words would immediately reveal the deception, while the number of such words in the essay became a further criterion of merit, with its own statistical weighting.

When the computer produced ratings of essays that turned out to be *statistically* indistinguishable from those produced by experienced human graders, the experimenters were so delighted that they opened a bottle of champagne by way of celebration and rushed into print with arrogant pride.

That the essentials were missing was apparently of no concern. Since such crucial things as meaning, style, wit, whimsy, rhythm, emphasis, nuance, felicity of image, and the careful use of words could not be quantified, they could presumably be ignored as scientifically undefinable and thus of no interest to a true scientist.

According to the statistical criterion used by the experimenters, the computer itself could turn out gibberish that would rate higher than any man-made prose.

I have my own ideas as to the relative values of human and computer grading, and of their effects on the teaching of English composition, and on education in general. I find them far from comparable. My preference is, of course, a matter of taste, and yours may be diametrically opposite to mine. But we will surely agree that the two methods are widely dissimilar and that their effects on the identification and fostering of talent and on the whole of education would be widely different. *Yet the statistical criterion rates them as equal,* and it is in the basic fallacy of the statistical criterion that I see the major peril arising from the methodology of psychometry.

REFERENCES

1. BANESH HOFFMANN, *The Tyranny of Testing.* New York: Crowell-Collier, 1962; Collier Books, 1964.
2. BANESH HOFFMANN, The College Boards Fail the Test, *The New York Times Magazine,* October 24, 1965, p. 52. See also College Boards and Our Nation's Scholastic Profile, Extension of Remarks of Hon. Lee Metcalf, October 22, 1965, *The Congressional Record,* October 27, 1965.
3. *A Description of the College Board Scholastic Aptitude Test,* College Entrance Examination Board. Princeton, N.J., 1964.
4. RICHARD PEARSON (President, College Entrance Examination Board), *The New York Times Magazine,* November 7, 1965, p. 40.
5. BANESH HOFFMANN, *The New York Times Magazine,* May 8, 1966, p. 36.
6. HENRY CHAUNCEY and THOMAS H. HILTON, Are Aptitude Tests Valid for the Highly Able? *Science,* June 4, 1965, p. 1297.
7. BANESH HOFFMANN, *Science,* July 16, 1965, p. 245.
8. WALTER C. MICHELS, Graduate-Record Examination Advanced Physics Test as a Predictor of Performance, *American Journal of Physics,* September, 1966, p. 862.
9. ARTHUR DAIGAN, Computer Grading of English Composition. *English Journal,* January, 1966, p. 46; ELLIS B. PAGE, The Imminence of Grading Essays by Computer, *Phi Delta Kappan,* January, 1966, p. 238.

---

26 | How to Cheat on Personality Tests

William H. Whyte, Jr.

The important thing to recognize is that you don't win a good score: you avoid a bad one. What a bad score would be depends upon the particular profile the company in question intends to measure you against, and this varies according to companies and according to the type of work. Your

---

score is usually rendered in terms of your percentile rating—that is, how you answer questions in relation to how other people have answered them. Sometimes it is perfectly all right for you to score in the 80th or 90th percentile; if you are being tested, for example, to see if you would make a good chemist, a score indicating that you are likely to be more reflective than ninety out of a hundred adults might not harm you and might even do you some good.

By and large, however, your safety lies in getting a score somewhere between the 40th and 60th percentiles, which is to say, you should try to answer as if you were like everybody else is supposed to be. This is not always too easy to figure out, of course, and this is one of the reasons why I will go into some detail in the following paragraphs on the principal types of questions. When in doubt, however, there are two general rules you can follow: (1) When asked for word associations or comments about the world, give the most conventional, run-of-the-mill, pedestrian answer possible. (2) To settle on the most beneficial answer to any question, repeat to yourself:

a) *I loved my father and my mother, but my father a little bit more.*
b) *I like things pretty well the way they are.*
c) *I never worry much about anything.*
d) *I don't care for books or music much.*
e) *I love my wife and children.*
f) *I don't let them get in the way of company work.*

Now to specifics. The first five questions in the composite test (Table 1) are examples of the ordinary, garden variety of self-report questions.* Gen-

---

* Leading tests of this type include:

The Personality Inventory by Robert G. Bernreuter. Published by The Stanford University Press, Stanford, California. Copyright 1935 by The Board of Trustees of Leland Stanford Junior University. All rights reserved. *125 questions.* Measures several different things at once; scoring keys available for neurotic tendency; self-sufficiency; introversion-extroversion; dominance-submission; self-confidence; sociability.

Thurstone Temperament Schedule by L. L. Thurstone. Copyright 1949 by L. L. Thurstone. Published by Science Research Associates, Chicago, Ill. *140 questions.* Measures, at once, seven areas of temperament: to wit, degree to which one is active, vigorous, impulsive, dominant, stable, sociable, reflective. "The primary aim of the Thurstone Temperament Schedule . . . is to evaluate an individual in terms of his relatively permanent temperament traits. One of the values of the schedule is that it helps provide an objective pattern, or profile, of personal traits which you can use to predict probable success or failure in a particular situation."

Minnesota T-S-E Inventory by M. Catherine Evans and T. R. McConnell. Copyright 1942 by Science Research Associates, Chicago, Illinois. *150 questions.* Measures three types of introversion-extroversion—thinking, social and emotional.

The Personal Audit by Clifford R. Adams and William M. Lepley, Psycho-Educational Clinic, Pennsylvania State College. Published by Science Research Associates, Chicago, Ill. Copyright 1945 by Clifford R. Adams. All rights reserved. *450 questions.* Nine parts, of 50 questions each. Each part measures "a relatively independent component of personality." Extremes of each trait listed thus: seriousness-impulsiveness; firmness-indecision; tranquillity-irritability; frankness-evasion; stability-instability; tolerance-intolerance; steadiness-emotionality; persistence-fluctuation; contentment-worry.

erally speaking, they are designed to reveal your degree of introversion or extroversion, your stability, and such. While it is true that in these "inventory" types of tests there is not a right or wrong answer to any *one* question, cumulatively you can get yourself into a lot of trouble if you are not wary. "Have you enjoyed reading books as much as having company in?" "Do you sometimes feel self-conscious?"—You can easily see what is being asked for here.

Stay in character.

The trick is to mediate yourself a score as near the norm as possible without departing too far from your own true self. It won't necessarily hurt you, for example, to say that you have enjoyed reading books as much as having company in. It will hurt you, however, to answer every such question in that vein if you are, in fact, the kind that does enjoy books and a measure of solitude. Strive for the happy mean; on one hand, recognize that a display of too much introversion, a desire for reflection, or sensitivity is to be avoided. On the other hand, don't overcompensate. If you try too hard to deny these qualities in yourself, you'll end so far on the other end of the scale as to be rated excessively insensitive or extroverted. If you are somewhat introverted, then, don't strive to get yourself in the 70th or 80th percentile for extroversion, but merely try to get up into the 40th percentile.

Since you will probably be taking not one, but a battery of tests, you must be consistent. The tester will be comparing your extroversion score on one test with, say, your sociability score on another, and if these don't correlate the way the tables say they should, suspicion will be aroused. Even when you are taking only one test, consistency is important. Many contain built-in L ("lie") scores, and woe betide you if you answer some questions as if you were a life of the party type and others as if you were an excellent follower. Another pitfall to avoid is giving yourself the benefit of the doubt on all questions in which one answer is clearly preferable to another, viz.: "Do you frequently daydream?" In some tests ways have been worked out to penalize you for this. (By the same token, occasionally you are given credit for excessive frankness. But you'd better not count on it.)

Be emphatic to the values of the test maker.

Question five asks:

"Do you prefer serious motion pictures about famous historical personalities to musical comedies?" If you answer this question honestly you are quite likely to get a good score for the wrong reasons. If you vote for the musical comedies, you are given a credit for extroversion. It might be, of course, that you are a very thoughtful person who dislikes the kind of pretentious, self-consciously arty "prestige" pictures which Hollywood does badly, and rather enjoy the musical comedies which it does well. The point illustrated here is that, before answering such questions, you must ask yourself which of the alternatives the test maker, not yourself, would regard as the more artistic.

Choose your neurosis.

When you come across questions that are like the ones from 6 to 11—"I often get pink spots all over"—be very much on your guard. Such questions were originally a by-product of efforts to screen mentally disturbed people; they measure degrees of neurotic tendency and were meant mainly for use in mental institutions and psychiatric clinics.* The Organization has no business at all to throw these questions at you, but its curiosity is powerful and some companies have been adopting these tests as standard. Should you find yourself being asked about spiders, Oedipus complexes, and such, you must, even more than in the previous type of test, remain consistent and as much in character as possible—these tests almost always have lie scores built into them. A few mild neuroses conceded here and there won't give you too bad a score, and in conceding neuroses you should know that more often than not you have the best margin for error if you err on the side of being "hypermanic"—that is, too energetic and active.

Don't be too dominant.

Question 12, which asks you what you would do if somebody barged in ahead of you in a store, is fairly typical of the kind of questions designed to find out how passive or dominant you may be. As always, the middle course is best. Resist the temptation to show yourself as trying to control each situation. You might think companies would prefer that characteristic to passivity, but they often regard it as a sign that you wouldn't be a permissive kind of leader. To err slightly on the side of acquiescence will rarely give you a bad score.

Incline to conservatism.

Questions 13 through 17, which ask you to comment on a variety of propositions, yield a measure of how conservative or radical your views are.† To go to either extreme earns you a bad score, but in most situations you should resolve any doubts you have on a particular question by deciding in favor of the accepted.

Similarly with word associations. In questions 18 through 23, each word in capitals is followed by four words, ranging from the conventional to the somewhat unusual. The trouble here is that if you are not a totally conventional person you may be somewhat puzzled as to what the conventional response is. Here is one tip: before examining any one question closely and

---

* Outstanding example is the *Minnesota Multiphasic Personality Inventory,* Revised Edition, by Starke R. Hathaway and J. Charnley McKinley. Published by The Psychological Corporation, N.Y. *495 questions.* This yields scores on hypochondriasis, depression, hysteria, psychopathic deviation, masculinity and femininity, paranoia, psychoasthenia, schizophrenia, hypomania. It also yields a score on the subject's "test-taking attitude," with a score for his degree of "defensiveness-frankness." If the subject consistently gives himself the benefit of the doubt, or vice versa, the scoring reveals the fact. This is not a test for the amateur to trifle with.

† An example of this kind of testing is the *Conservatism-Radicalism Opinionaire* by Theodore F. Lentz and Colleagues of The Attitude Research Laboratory. Published by Character Research Association, Washington University, St. Louis, Mo., Dept. of Education. Copyright 1935. 60 statements are given; the subject indicates whether he tends to agree or disagree. His score is obtained by checking the number of times he sides with the conservative statement side vs. the radical one.

reading it from left to right, read vertically through the whole list of questions and you may well see a definite pattern. In making up tests, testers are thinking of ease in scoring, and on some test forms the most conventional responses will be found in one column, the next most conventional in the next, and so on. All you have to do then is go down the list and pick, alternately, the most conventional, and the second most conventional. Instead of a high score for emotionalism, which you might easily get were you to proceed on your own, you earn a stability score that will indicate "normal ways of thinking."

Don't split hairs.

When you come to hypothetical situations designed to test your judgment, you have come to the toughest of all questions.* In this kind there are correct answers, and the testers make no bones about it. Restricted as the choice is, however, determining which are the correct ones is extremely difficult, and the more intelligent you are the more difficult. One tester, indeed, states that the measurement of practical judgment is "unique and statistically independent of such factors as intelligence, and academic and social background." He has a point. Consider the question about the woman and the baby at the window of the burning house. It is impossible to decide which is the best course of action unless you know how big the fire is, whether she is on the first floor or the second, whether there is a ladder handy, how near by the fire department is, plus a number of other considerations.

On this type of question, let me confess that I can be of very little help to the reader. I have made a very thorough study of these tests, have administered them to many people of unquestioned judgment, and invariably the results have been baffling. But there does seem to be one moral: don't think too much. The searching mind is severely handicapped by such forced choices and may easily miss what is meant to be the obviously right answer. Suppress this quality in yourself by answering these questions as quickly as you possibly can, with practically no pause for reflection.

The judgment questions from 25 through 28 are much easier to answer.† The right answers here are, simply, those which represent sound personnel

---

* Two tests of this type are:

Test of Practical Judgment by Alfred J. Cardall, N.B.A., Ed.D. Published by Science Research Associates, Inc., Chicago, Ill. Copyright 1942, 1950 by Science Research Associates, Inc. All rights reserved. *48 Forced-choice questions* "designed to measure the element of practical judgment as it operates in everyday business and social situations." How were the "best" answers chosen? "Rigorous statistical analysis was supplemented by consensus of authority. . . ."

Practical Social Judgment by Thomas N. Jenkins, Ph.D. Copyright 1947. All rights reserved. Executive Analysis Corporation, N.Y. *52 questions* about hypothetical situations; subject must choose the "best" and the "poorest" of given answers.

† An example of this kind of test is *How Supervise?* by Quentin W. File, edited by H. H. Remmers. Published by The Psychological Corporation, N.Y. Copyright 1948, by Purdue Research Foundation, Lafayette, Indiana. 100 questions on management policy and attitudes.

policy, and this is not hard to figure out. Again, don't quibble. It is true enough that it is virtually impossible to tell the worker why he didn't get promoted unless you know whether he was a good worker, or a poor one, or whether Jones's uncle did in fact own the plant (in which case, candor could be eminently sensible). The mealy-mouthed answer d)—"Let's figure out how you can improve"—is the "right" answer. Similarly with questions about the worker's home life. It isn't the concern of the company, but it is modern personnel dogma that it should be, and therefore "agree" is the right answer. So with the question about whether good supervisors are born or made. To say that a good supervisor is born deprecates the whole apparatus of modern organization training, and that kind of attitude won't get you anywhere.

Know your company.

Questions 29 and 30 are characteristic of the kind of test that attempts to measure the relative emphasis you attach to certain values—such as aesthetic, economic, religious, social.* The profile of you it produces is matched against the profile that the company thinks is desirable. To be considered as a potential executive, you will probably do best when you emphasize economic motivation the most; aesthetic and religious, the least. In question 29, accordingly, you should say the skyscraper makes you think of industrial growth. Theoretical motivation is also a good thing; if you were trying out for the research department, for example, you might wish to say that you think Sir Isaac Newton helped mankind more than Shakespeare and thereby increase your rating for theoretical learning. Were you trying out for a public relations job, however, you might wish to vote for Shakespeare, for a somewhat higher aesthetic score would not be amiss in this case.

There are many more kinds of tests and there is no telling what surprises the testers will come up with in the future. But the principles will probably change little, and by obeying a few simple precepts and getting yourself in the right frame of mind, you have the wherewithal to adapt to any new testing situation. In all of us there is a streak of normalcy.

Table 1. Composite Personality Test

Self-Report Questions

1. Have you enjoyed reading books as much as having company in?
2. Are you sometimes afraid of failure?
3. Do you sometimes feel self-conscious?
4. Does it annoy you to be interrupted in the middle of your work?
5. Do you prefer serious motion pictures about famous historical personalities to musical comedies?

---

* *A Study of Values,* Revised Edition, by Gordon W. Allport, Philip E. Vernan, and Gardner Lindzey. Copyright 1951, by Gordon W. Allport, Philip E. Vernan, and Gardner Lindzey. Copyright 1931 by Gordon W. Allport and Philip E. Vernan. Published by Houghton Mifflin Co. *45 forced-choice questions.* Answers are scored to give a measure of the relative prominence of six motives in a person: theoretical, economic, aesthetic, social, political, and religious. A profile is charted to show how he varies from the norm on each of the six.

Indicate whether you agree, disagree, or are uncertain:

6. I am going to Hell.
7. I often get pink spots all over.
8. The sex act is repulsive.
9. I like strong-minded women.
10. Strange voices speak to me.
11. My father is a tyrant.

Hypothetical Question—Dominance Type

12. You have been waiting patiently for a salesperson to wait on you. Just when she's finished with another customer, a woman walks up abruptly and demands to be waited upon before you. What would you do?
    a. Do nothing
    b. Push the woman to one side
    c. Give her a piece of your mind
    d. Comment about her behavior to the salesperson

Opinion Questions: Degree of Conservatism

Indicate whether you agree or disagree with the following questions:

13. Prostitution should be state supervised.
14. Modern art should not be allowed in churches.
15. It is worse for a woman to have extramarital relations than for a man.
16. Foreigners are dirtier than Americans.
17. "The Star-Spangled Banner" is difficult to sing properly.

Word Association Questions

Underline the word you think goes best with the word in capitals:

18. UMBRELLA (rain, prepared, cumbersome, appeasement)
19. RED (hot, color, stain, blood)
20. GRASS (green, mow, lawn, court)
21. NIGHT (dark, sleep, moon, morbid)
22. NAKED (nude, body, art, evil)
23. AUTUMN (fall, leaves, season, sad)

Hypothetical Situations—Judgment Type

24. What would you do if you saw a woman holding a baby at the window of a burning house:
    a. Call the fire department
    b. Rush into the house
    c. Fetch a ladder
    d. Try and catch the baby
25. Which do you think is the best answer for the executive to make in the following situation:
    Worker: "Why did Jones get the promotion and I didn't?"
    Executive:
    a. "You deserved it but Jones has seniority."
    b. "You've got to work harder."
    c. "Jones's uncle owns the plant."
    d. "Let's figure out how you can improve."

Opinion Questions: Policy Type

26. A worker's home life is not the concern of the company.
    Agree............... Disagree...............

27. Good supervisors are born, not made.
Agree.............. Disagree..............

28. It should be company policy to encourage off-hours participation by employees in company-sponsored social gatherings, clubs, and teams.
Agree.............. Disagree..............

Opinion Questions: Value Type

29. When you look at a great skyscraper, do you think of:
a. our tremendous industrial growth
b. the simplicity and beauty of the structural design

30. Who helped mankind most?
a. Shakespeare
b. Sir Isaac Newton

Unit Six | DISCUSSION QUESTIONS

22. *What Can We Predict?*
Discuss how modern science has used "probability" theory.
If it is a fact that the gambler will eventually lose, why is the gambling profession so lucrative?

23. *Methods of Expressing Test Scores*
How can information gained from the "bell-shaped" curve be utilized in fields other than testing?
Discuss the meaning of "norms," "standardization," and "central tendency."

24. *The I. Q. Is an Intelligent Test*
Discuss the advantages and disadvantages the IQ test has over achievement tests.
Should Intelligence Tests be used in public and private schools?

25. *Psychometric Scientism*
On the basis of your own experiences, would you attack or defend the author's view of the mass testing movement? Discuss.
Distinguish between "convergent" and "divergent" thinking.

26. *How to Cheat on Personality Tests*
What do you think is the general public's opinion regarding personality tests?
Should personality tests be used in personnel hiring? Why?

Unit Seven *Extrasensory and Subliminal Perception, Dreams, and Hypnosis*

Responses do not occur without stimulation; sensation is the result of specific receptor activity. Sense modalities include: vision, hearing (audition), smell (olfaction), taste (gustation), pressure, temperature, pain, kinesthesia (stretching of muscles and joints), and equilibrium (balance). Parapsychology investigates the possibility that some individuals can be aware of events or capable of influencing physical objects without the use of known senses. Parapsychology studies these forms of perception known as "extrasensory perception (ESP)." Mental telepathy (communicating by thought transference), clairvoyance (perception without sensory knowledge), precognition (foretelling the future), and psychokinesis (influencing physical objects by mental powers) are forms of ESP.

Critical evaluations of collected data are being made and there is little doubt that some ESP is genuine. Nevertheless, many scientists refuse to accept the existence of ESP because it appears to be contrary to the basic laws of science. Yet, mounting evidence makes it increasingly difficult to ignore the validity of ESP. Ian Stevenson's evaluation of this exciting possibility is entitled *The Uncomfortable Facts About Extrasensory Perception.*

The phenomenon of "extra-ocular vision," the ability to detect color in the dark with the fingertips, was reported by Russian scientists in 1963. A Russian housewife had the ability to run her fingers over printed text and "read" a newspaper! In November, 1964 a housewife of Flint, Michigan, proved to Barnard College psychologists that she, too, had the same ability. Scientists in many countries are working to evaluate this strange and interesting ability. The second reading of this unit, *A Sixth Sense?,* is a Russian report that discusses the testing methods for measuring extra-ocular vision and offers possible explanations for this phenomenon.

Reports of sensory stimulation, involving the interpretation of fast exposures flashed on a theater screen, is the subject matter of Ann Anastasi's *Subliminal Perception.* Since 1957 many experiments evaluating subliminal perception have been conducted. This brief analysis is an accumulation of the reported results.

Since Sigmund Freud wrote his treatise on *Interpretation of Dreams* in 1900, scientists as well as laymen have been concerned with understanding the mystery of dreams. Dreaming is behavior, and there is little doubt that it can be motivated by unconscious material. One form of psychotherapy called "psychoanalysis" utilizes the technique of dream analysis. *The Reality of Dreams* by Edith Lederer reveals what research psychologists are discovering about dreams.

Although hypnosis has been known and practiced since ancient times, it still escapes exact definition; however, most scientists agree that it is an extreme state of suggestibility. Hypnosis is used in psychotherapy (hypnoanalysis), dentistry, surgery, and research. Many have the ability to hypnotize, but, like a potent drug, it should be used with caution by a qualified person. The final article, *Regarding Hypnosis,* is a statement by the American Psychiatric Association declaring its position on the subject of hypnosis.

---

27 | The Uncomfortable Facts About Extrasensory Perception

Ian Stevenson, M.D.

For centuries some persons have believed they could perceive or influence events at a distance without known physical means of communication or action.

Scientific investigation of such claims began about seventy-five years ago. The branch of science born then, known variously as psychical research and parapsychology, has slowly developed in method and productivity. Two veteran parapsychologists, Dr. J. B. Rhine and Dr. J. G. Pratt, recently published the first avowed textbook on the subject. The publication last year of this book and of another, *ESP and Personality Patterns,* by G. R. Schmeidler and R. A. McConnell, indicate the increasing maturity of the subject and also a shift in emphasis on the part of parapsychologists.

For both these books depart from tests and proofs of whether extrasensory perception occurs, and chiefly report studies of when and how it occurs. I do not mean that the mere occurrence of extrasensory perception has lost its novelty or its interest for parapsychologists. Striking demonstrations are still too rare to be taken for granted—indeed they may always be so. But parapsychologists believe the case for the occurrence of extrasensory perception is so solidly established that they see no reason to engage in further combat with die-hard skeptics who remain obdurate not—as the proponents see it—from lack of evidence, but rather from failure to examine or accept the evidence already abundantly available. Today parapsychologists insist that the fact of extrasensory perception is beyond debate, and they are therefore working more and more toward *understanding* extrasensory perception (and kindred phenomena) with regard to its processes and its relations to other parts of scientific knowledge. At this turning point, then, interested laymen may find useful a review of present knowledge of the subject.

This knowledge derives from a great many sources, but we can divide these conveniently into two large groups: (1) naturally occurring events and

---

(2) planned experimental observations. As in other branches of science, the experimental aspects developed as men tried to understand better their observations of spontaneous occurrences.

Unfortunately, most of the vast literature of the past about spontaneous occurrences of extrasensory perception has no value today, because the reporters did not adopt what we would now consider proper scientific precautions in recording their observations. Most witnesses of strange, ghostly events did not write down their accounts until considerably after the events. Many such events have had only one witness. Such conditions would permit both a free play to the imagination and also the kind of inaccurate recollection which frequently obscures even the records of ordinary happenings which originally occurred under controlled circumstances.

Many modern experiments, moreover, have shown that nearly everyone will hallucinate when his expectation of seeing something becomes sufficiently heightened. For example, one experimenter arranged for a group of persons to bring pressure on one of their number (left out of the conspiracy) to say that he had seen what they pretended to see. Almost invariably the victim yielded and denied his own senses.

This kind of influence can work both ways. We know, for example, that the Middle Ages venerated and encouraged visions. Subsequently, the churches—both Catholic and Protestant—turned against persons who claimed to have visions and accused them of witchcraft. Many burned to death in the fires of the Inquisition. A reaction to this cruelty set in, and also some enlightenment developed, so that from the eighteenth century to the present persons who have had visions have generally been thought not wicked but sick. This attitude has led to more humane treatment but not necessarily to greater understanding of their experiences. The power of such cultural influences—either to stimulate perceptions or to force their concealment—has made many students conclude that we should believe nothing of what has come down to us on this subject from its pre-scientific period.

THE BEGINNINGS OF SCIENTIFIC INQUIRY

Yet even before the modern period of scientific inquiry, some instances of extrasensory perception were witnessed and recorded by able observers. For example, we have a number of accounts attested to by reliable witnesses, of exhibitions of clairvoyant powers by the Swedish mystic and scientist, Emanuel Swedenborg. In 1759, for instance, he returned from a trip to England and dined with friends in Göteborg.

> About six o'clock, Swedenborg went out, and returned to the company quite pale and alarmed. He said that a dangerous fire had just broken out in Stockholm, on Sodermalm (where his house was), and that it was spreading very fast. He was restless and went out often. He said that the house of one of his friends, whom he named, was already in ashes, and that his own was in danger. At eight o'clock after he had been out again, he joyfully exclaimed, "Thank God! The fire is extinguished, the third door from my house." On Tuesday morning (three days later) the royal courier arrived at the Governor's with the melancholy intelligence of the fire, of the loss which it had occasioned, and

of the houses it had damaged and ruined, not in the least differing from that which Swedenborg had given at the very time when it happened, for the fire was extinguished at eight o'clock.

I have quoted the description of this incident by the philosopher Kant, who although not himself a witness, took great pains to inquire through an agent of those who had witnessed the episode.

Until the late nineteenth century, no one had ever studied in a systematic way the numerous incidents of apparitions and clairvoyant powers which seemed to call for scientific scrutiny. Then a group of men, mostly scholars of Cambridge University, organized the Society for Psychical Research in England. Its declared purpose, from which it has not since departed, was to study all such phenomena without officially formulating any opinion as to their nature. Individual members have naturally formed and independently published their own opinions—but the Society (and the similar American Society for Psychical Research) has remained a scientific agency and a forum for discussion and review; it does not promulgate a settled opinion on any issue which might come to its attention. This attitude has earned the Society the contempt of many who believe the evidence, for example, of human survival of physical death already beyond dispute. On the other hand, it has won the praise of those who believe that only the most rigorous scientific method will advance the subject. William James said of the Society for Psychical Research:

> According to the newspaper and drawing-room myth, soft-headedness and idiotic credulity are the bond of sympathy in this Society, and general wonder-sickness its dynamic principle. A glance at the membership fails, however, to corroborate this view. [James then lists some of the distinguished scientists and philosophers who were active in the early days of the Society.] . . . In fact, were I asked to point to a scientific journal where hardheadedness and never-sleeping suspicion of sources of error might be seen in their full bloom, I think I should have to fall back on the Proceedings of the Society for Psychical Research.

Shortly after the founding of the Society, the members undertook what was called a census of hallucinations. This began with the questioning of about 17,000 people regarding any quasi-sensory experiences (without any apparent physical cause) which they had while awake. About 10 per cent said that they had had some such experience. Similar questionnaires since then have produced approximately the same percentage of affirmative replies. For this reason and because the inquirers adopted certain precautions in sampling, the census of hallucinations probably studied an adequately representative group of people.

The investigators made further detailed inquiries concerning the experiences of those who had reported seeing apparitions or having other hallucinations. They rapidly eliminated a great many cases where the testimony might be fallacious. The inquirers believed that the remaining experiences could not reasonably be explained as having occurred through normal physical channels of communication. The societies in England and the United States have continued to study such cases.

TYPES OF APPARITIONS

Emotional crises seem to promote extrasensory communications. Many, although by no means all, instances of apparitions relate to persons who are dying or dead. In a large number of the cases collected by the Society for Psychical Research, a person is "seen" in an entirely different place, perhaps hundreds of miles away, just before or after his death. I have already mentioned that expectation can certainly promote hallucinations. But in the best cases, the person seeing the apparition has no knowledge whatever that the person seen is dying or even ill. Indeed, often the person of the apparition has not even been known to the percipient and is only subsequently recognized from details in a photograph or description.

Some of the most interesting cases collected by the Society describe experiences in which a person believes himself out of his physical body and able to look at it, as if from the point of view of another person. Some of these experiences we can attribute to a simple dream. In others, however, the person having the experience becomes aware of objects or events of which he could have had no normal knowledge and which could be later verified. These cases are by no means restricted to those collected by the Society for Psychical Research. Recently, for example, a clergyman who underwent an operation afterwards reported in detail what had happened while he was clearly anesthetized and ostensibly unconscious. He accurately described the surgeon's having left the operating room to get another instrument, and the details of the conversations of those in the operating-room.

Sometimes such "out-of-the-body" experiences, as they are called, occur when several persons simultaneously observe another person whose physical body is actually elsewhere. An example involving three persons occurred in the nineteenth century. A Mr. Wilmot was crossing the Atlantic from Britain to rejoin his wife in the United States. He shared a cabin with another man. The cabin had a sloping side so that the upper berth was set back from the lower one. One night during a storm, Mr. Wilmot thought he dreamed that his wife came to the cabin, hesitated at the entrance, then entered and kissed him. When he awoke, his cabin-mate reproached him for having a female visitor and then described the appearance of his wife exactly as Mr. Wilmot had seen her in his dream.

When Mr. Wilmot landed and met his wife, to continue the story in his own words, ". . . almost her first question when we were alone was, 'Did you receive a visit from me a week ago Tuesday?' 'A visit from you?' said I. 'We were more than a thousand miles at sea.' 'I know it,' she replied, 'but it seemed to me that I visited you.' 'It would be impossible,' said I. 'Tell me what makes you think so.' My wife then told me that on account of the severity of the weather and the reported loss of the 'Africa' . . . she had been extremely anxious about me. On the night . . . when the storm had just begun to abate, she had lain awake for a long time thinking of me, and about four o'clock in the morning it seemed to her that she went out to seek me. Crossing the wide and stormy sea, she came at length to a low, black steamship, whose side she went up, and then descending into the cabin, passed through it to the stern until she came to my stateroom. 'Tell me,' she said, 'do they ever have staterooms like the one I saw where the upper berth extends further back than the under one? A man was in the upper berth looking right at me, and for a moment I was afraid to go in, but soon I went up to the side of your berth, bent down and kissed you and embraced you and then went away.' "

It seems that the circumstances of dying not only favor the appearance of the dying person as an apparition, but also sometimes give the dying heightened powers of extrasensory perception. Usually, deathbed visions comprise only ramblings of delirium like Falstaff's "babbling of green fields." But occasionally they seem to include communications of a paranormal kind.

An elderly woman in this country became seriously ill. When the doctors said that she did not have long to live, the family gathered around her bed. Suddenly she seemed much more alert and the expression on her face changed to one of great pleasure and excitement. She raised herself slightly and said: "Oh, Will, are you there?"—and fell back dead.

Of the many members of the family who were present, no one was named Will. After her death, the family questioned who Will might be and found that the only Will in the family was a great-uncle who lived in England. Not long after the grandmother's death, word was received from England that her brother Will had died about two days before her death.

This little story strongly suggests the occurrence of extrasensory awareness in the dying woman of the recent death on the other side of the Atlantic of her brother. However, it also illustrates some of the difficulties in the investigation of spontaneous cases of extrasensory perception. Although more than one witness heard the dying woman, none of them made a written record of the event before word came from England of the brother's death. Thus the whole story might be explained as a retrospective falsification of memory.

Many instances of such retrospective distortion have occurred. I am not suggesting that this is always a satisfactory explanation. On the contrary, the evidence in many cases quite clearly supports their interpretation as instances of paranormal communication. Yet the difficulties of obtaining reliable testimony—and the small returns—have dissuaded many investigators from investing the extraordinary effort, time, and patience required to sift the evidence carefully.

ENTER DR. RHINE

This discouragement was itself helpful, however, in turning the investigators in another direction, that of experimental testing. Some of the early research workers of the nineteenth century studied extrasensory perception by quantitative methods, which included attempts at card-guessing. However, serious quantitative studies began with the work of Dr. J. B. Rhine in 1930 at Duke University. For almost thirty years now, Dr. Rhine and his colleagues have conducted an extensive series of experiments exploring many aspects of the subject. The scientific scope and discipline of these experiments have slowly won respect from many other scientists.

Dr. Rhine's experiments have mostly used the technique of having the percipient guess cards which an experimenter has shuffled into a random order. The percipient may call his guesses while someone else—an "agent"

—looks at the cards one after the other (telepathy); or he may guess the order without anyone else's looking at the cards while he does so (clairvoyance). In either case, the order of the cards and of the guesses are independently recorded before being compared. Some of Dr. Rhine's earlier experiments used procedures which critics objected could not absolutely exclude sensory cues, errors, or other factors which would permit attributing the positive results to normal perceptions.

By separating constructive criticism from mere invective, Dr. Rhine and others working in this research have slowly tightened the conditions of the experiments until they seem to have eliminated alternative explanations of the results. Some of the adopted precautions may seem unnecessary to those unfamiliar with the range of normal perceptions, the possibilities of self-deception, and the temptations for fraud to be found in this work. To give one example only, it might be thought sufficient—and was at first—to keep the cards to be guessed by the subject face down on a table even if their backs remained visible to him. But printing can emboss a pattern on cards which can show through, so that some persons have read cards through their backs. Now screens separate the subject and the cards if they are in the same room.

In addition, the experimenters have further excluded the possibility of sensory cues by conducting a number of successful experiments with percipient and agent separated by distances of from several hundred yards to several hundred miles. By using additional witnesses they have controlled errors in recording the guesses and comparing them to the "target" cards. They have also given much attention to the statistical problems involved in estimating the likelihood that a percipient might come up with seemingly high scores on the basis of chance alone. Some subjects show such slight capacities for extrasensory perception that it is hard to refute this possibility in their cases. However, certain unusual subjects have shown such extraordinary ability at card-guessing that the odds against their having done so without some extrasensory knowledge of the cards are astronomically high.

A number of able mathematicians beginning as far back as the 1930s have acknowledged publicly the soundness of the statistical procedures used in parapsychology. However, the interpretation of the results with regard to probability remains controversial for some scientists. Critics have sometimes alleged that parapsychologists say the results of the experiments they cite as evidence of extrasensory perception could not have occurred by chance. In fact they say no such thing, because one can never say *anything* could not have occurred by chance. Obviously a great many unusual events—such as drawing a hand of thirteen spades at bridge—do occur by chance. Accordingly, parapsychologists simply calculate the probability that the scores in their experiments would occur by chance alone. In experiment after experiment the probability has been exceedingly small.

Recently Mr. Spencer Brown in England has challenged the use of current concepts of chance and its statistical evaluation in parapsychology. In this he has received attention but little support from other scientists—not that a majority vote should decide such a matter. The reluctance of other scientists to discard the statistical methods used in parapsychology derives from the support which many other branches of science obtain from these methods. Only a Samson of theory could bring down the temple erected on this foundation.

Dr. Rhine's experiments, as I have mentioned, showed that extrasensory perception does not depend upon space. Those of Dr. S. G. Soal in London showed that it apparently does not depend on time. Dr. Soal is an experimenter of extraordinary tenacity who worked to duplicate Dr. Rhine's results for five years without success. He had almost abandoned the attempt when another investigator, Mr. Whately Carington, persuaded him reluctantly to review his data for the possibility that percipients might have guessed not the "target" card up for guessing at that moment, but one or several cards before or later. Carington had already found evidence of this effect in experiments of his own.

The task of rechecking Dr. Soal's data for this "displacement" effect proved a tedious chore, but resulted in the discovery of two remarkably gifted subjects. These showed unusually high scores in the guessing of the cards immediately ahead of the target cards.

Following this discovery, Dr. Soal recalled one of these subjects and in a further and most carefully controlled series of experiments repeated the observations of the displacement effect, thus demonstrating that it was not due to a *post hoc* interpretation of the data in the first series of experiments. These experiments of Dr. Soal provide an experimental confirmation of precognition, of which a number of spontaneous cases had already given some evidence. Since the work of Dr. Rhine and Dr. Soal, other independent investigators have provided further confirmation of the occurrence under controlled conditions of extrasensory perception.

INFLUENCING THE DICE

Dr. Rhine's group seems to have demonstrated also that some persons have a capacity to influence physical objects without physical means—a process called psychokinesis. The usual experiments call for attempts to influence the fall of dice in particular ways. These experiments have included the standard precautions against error and have also received confirmation from other investigators, notably Mrs. Laura Dale in New York City and Dr. R. A. McConnell of the University of Pittsburgh. However, the evidence for psychokinesis is generally considered less substantial than that for ESP.

Much of the recent work on extrasensory perception has studied not its occurrence as such, but its processes—what facilitates it and what inhibits it. The newness of this work forbids more than tentative conclusions. It appears that some ability in extrasensory perception is widespread and indeed all people may have it at some time or other in their lives. However, marked degrees of it occur only rarely. Also, the capacity fluctuates rather widely and may vanish altogether. The novelty of tests of extrasensory perception stimulates many beginning subjects to performances which are well above chance but which they do not sustain after the initial enthusiasm wears off.

Dr. Gertrude Schmeidler has just summarized, in the book mentioned earlier, an extensive series of experiments on the relationship between the capacity for extrasensory perception and certain features of personality, especially the attitude which the subject has toward extrasensory perception itself. In experiments conducted over more than ten years, she has found significant differences between those who accept the possibility of their having an ability to demonstrate extrasensory perception (sheep) and those who deny this possibility (goats). "Sheep" score on the average significantly above chance, "goats" below chance. The scoring below chance of many of the goats seems to indicate—paradoxically—that they use some extrasensory communication in order to do this. They must know what *not* to guess in order not to guess at a chance level.

The processes of extrasensory perception apparently are unconscious and can rarely be modified by conscious efforts or training. In altered states of consciousness—induced by barbiturates or by hypnosis—some subjects score better but the changes are rarely spectacular.

SENDERS AND RECEIVERS

Of special importance is the relationship between the percipient and the sender (or "agent"), and often also that between either of these and the experimenter. Investigators have known for many years that some subjects reached high scores with one sender but not with another. Recently, a Dutch investigator who is also an inspector of schools in Amsterdam, Mr. J. G. van Buschbach, made extensive studies of extrasensory perception in children of elementary and junior high schools when their teachers acted as agents. He found highly significant above-chance scores among the elementary school children—but not among the older children. These differences he attributed to the greater emotional closeness of the pupils and teachers in the younger group.

Two American experimenters, Miss Margaret Anderson and Miss Rhea White, have sharpened this a little by studying extrasensory capacity in relation to the expressed liking or disliking of the pupils and teachers for each other. They found that when pupils liked teachers the scores with the teachers as co-experimenters were higher than when the pupils disliked the teachers. Even better results occurred when the teachers also liked the pupils.

This kind of relationship psychiatrists have called rapport. They would like to know much more about it, because they believe that successful psychotherapy requires the attainment of rapport between the psychotherapist and his patient. But to name a relationship does not explain its processes. In studying relationships between persons who have a higher-than-average degree of communication by extrasensory perception, psychiatrists can perhaps help the parapsychologists as well as learn from them. A number of psychiatrists have reported instances of extrasensory perception in their patients under circumstances which permitted rather close study of the current personal relationships of the patient. These few studies have illustrated also the occurrence of transient extrasensory perceptions during periods of strong emotional involvement with another person, often the psychotherapist.

The foregoing absurdly condensed survey of parapsychology shows that its work is little more than started. But at least it seems to have arrived as a respectable branch of science. Professor Henry Sidgwick of Cambridge, one of the founders and the first president of the Society for Psychical Research, said at the time of its founding that he aimed at finding evidence about psychical matters of such strength that his critics would accuse him of fraud. This exalted, if perhaps masochistic, wish has often come true.

The most recent instance occurred in an article in the professional journal of American scientists, *Science,* in 1955. The author, Dr. G. R. Price, said that the apparent evidence for extrasensory perception, if accepted, will require a drastic revision of our current concepts of physics. He found this impossible to contemplate, and therefore proposed that the apparent evidence for extrasensory perception derived from the deliberate practice of fraud. He could not specify any particular fraud, but believed this the only sensible explanation. The wrath of parapsychologists found expression in subsequent correspondence about this article, but was not unmixed with some satisfaction that the matter had been put by Dr. Price with such clear alternatives.

For indeed, it seems that scientists must soon accept and incorporate in their concepts the data of parapsychology. Many continue intransigent but necessarily uncomfortable. Professor C. D. Broad, of Cambridge University —one of a handful of philosophers who have recognized the importance of these phenomena—has described their position as follows:

> It compels one either to ignore all the phenomena in question, or to be continually occupied in explaining them away. The former course is not scientifically respectable; for it is quite certain that many people quite as sensible as oneself and far more expert, have personally investigated these matters and have persuaded themselves of the genuineness of these phenomena and of the impossibility of explaining them completely by fraud or mistake. And the latter course may at any moment be barred by some fact which we simply cannot explain away.

I do not mean to suggest that the opposition to the data of parapsychology derives exclusively from the ignorance or prejudice of other scientists. I hope I have made sufficiently clear that the investigators of the last seventy-five years have only made a modest beginning. Data are still scant and so are successful repetitions of the same experiments. Critics often complain about the lack of repeatability of the parapsychological experiments. But as I have tried to make clear, many experiments have been repeated both by the same experimenter and by different experimenters. Yet it remains true that the capacity for extrasensory perception frequently fades even in high-scoring subjects and parapsychologists are far from being able to turn it on at will. We know much more about what interferes with the capacity than about what facilitates it.

And we know even less about the nature of the capacity for extrasensory perception. Some students of the subject have theorized that current human capacities for extrasensory perception are a faint residue of a once much stronger power which has gradually diminished with evolution—being displaced by the known sensory capacities which can locate the origin of stimuli and thus may serve man better in his adaptation to his current environment. But this is pure speculation. Parapsychologists have no really satisfactory theory of extrasensory perception to market even to available buyers.

ENEMY OF SCIENCE?

It is unfortunate for the progress of the subject that parapsychologists remain few in number and short of funds. We can still count on the fingers of one hand the number of laboratories engaged in parapsychology across the world. And even these sustain a precarious life through the generosity of a few ardent supporters. Fortunately, the subject has happened to interest a number of remarkable people whose energy has compensated partly for their lack of numbers and money. The work continues and slowly expands, in the discovery of fundamental data and in making ties with other branches of science for which it may become increasingly relevant.

Both enthusiasts and skeptics sometimes state that the acceptance of parapsychology implies an overthrow of the present scientific view of the universe. This opinion seems to have impelled Dr. Price to his accusations of fraud since for him the alternative seemed so improbable and appalling. Such delights or alarms may prove unjustified.

The facts of extrasensory perception and kindred phenomena may not alter greatly our view of the physical world. They will, I believe, revolutionize our view of man. It is perhaps not more surprising that a man should influence the fall of dice thrown by a machine than that he should activate his own hand to throw the dice. In either case, a man's mind acts on a physical object whether dice or his own hand. But we do not know how mind acts on matter—whether part of the same organism or outside it.

Many persons have thought that mind is merely a name for certain kinds of experiences; that minds have no real existence; and that mental activity cannot occur apart from the brain. A number of evidences interfere with the acceptance of this view. Parapsychological studies provide one group of such evidences. For they show that the mind can function without its physical senses. Thus they open—or re-open as religious believers would say—the possibility that the mind can also function without the brain or body to which those senses are attached.

---

28 | A Sixth Sense?

Rosa Kuleshova was blindfolded. She ran the fingers of her right hand over the printed text and "read" the newspaper. Again blindfolded, she "looked" at a photograph with her fingers and accurately described the posture and appearance of the figure in the picture. Pieces of colored paper were placed in an opaque paper envelope. She touched each piece and called its color directly.

Reprinted by permission from *Soviet Life,* February 1964.

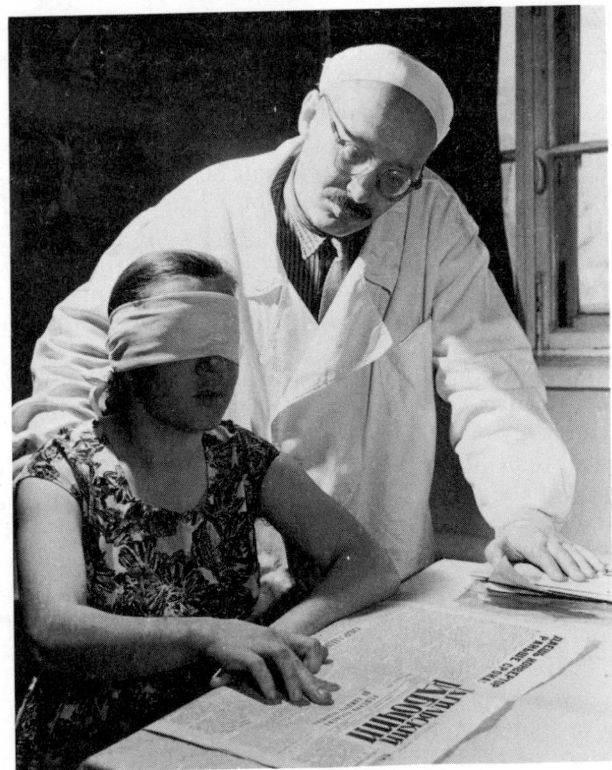

(*Novosti Photo Service, Moscow*)

Reading with fingertips. A neuropathologist observes Rosa Kuleshova reading newspaper with the help of her fingers.

In a demonstration at a meeting of the Ural Branch of the USSR Psychological Society, Rosa dug into a closed bag and without a single error pulled out the colored spools of thread and playing cards she was asked for. She described what was pictured on a postage stamp merely by feeling it.

This is how Rosa herself explains her remarkable gift. When she touches a colored surface, she perceives one color as a wavy line, another as points, the third as crosses. Simultaneously a visual concept of the color comes to her mind.

Rosa developed an unusual tactile sense by persistent training when she worked at a school for the blind in the city of Nizhni Tagil. After an attack of rheumatic encephalitis, her sense of touch became more acute, to the point where she could "see" color with her fingers.

VISION IN THE FINGERTIPS (AS REPORTED IN THE NEWSPAPER *IZVESTIA*)

Early in December Rosa Kuleshova came to Moscow at the invitation of the Information Transmission Problems Institute of the USSR Academy of Sciences. The light-sensitivity hypothesis was checked by the Biophysics

Institute. This incredible fact emerged after a whole series of tests—Rosa had real light receptors, organs of vision, in the skin of her fingers.

Hard to believe? Here are the experiments.

The first was to determine whether Rosa distinguished dark spots from light spots by the relative roughness of the surface. When the picture was projected on frosted glass, it was apparent that the gradations of roughness of the polished surface had no relation whatsoever to its illumination. Rosa differentiated the dark and light spots on the glass screen with her fingers. Only one conclusion could be drawn: The tips of Rosa's fingers, like our eyes, react to ordinary light; to put it more plainly, they *see*. It was all so extraordinary that even the experimenters for the first few minutes did not believe their test results.

But, it occurred to them, Rosa's fingers may not be reacting to light, but to temperature changes. The light sections of the screen are warmer than the dark, even if only by a hundredth of a degree.

Two special light filters settled that hypothesis. First one of them was placed in front of the objective to block the infrared (heat) rays. Rosa accurately differentiated the dark and the light sections as she had before. Then a filter was placed so that it stopped the light but let the infrared rays through almost without interference. Although a sort of heat image showed up on the screen, Rosa could not detect it. Thus the experimenters had to reject the supersensitive heat sense as well as the supersensitive tactile sense hypotheses. There remained only vision—vision in the fingertips!

When the young physicists working on problems of vision finally accepted the idea that Rosa's fingers constituted an organ of sight, they decided to measure its possibilities objectively. For the purpose they carried through a series of tests of the kind usually given in eye examinations.

Back away slowly from an open newspaper. The outlines of the letters will blur first, and then the lines too will merge into one gray spot. When do the eyes distinguish two closely placed points, and when are the points merged? The image of the points, much reduced in size, of course, is focused on the retina—the light-sensitive cone layer at the back of the eye—by the crystalline lens. If the points strike different cones, they will each be distinguishable; if they strike the same point, they will not. What follows is this simple conclusion: The higher the density of the light sensory elements in the retina, the sharper the vision.

How does that apply in Rosa's case? Are her fingers sharp-sighted or does each finger have only one light receptor? With special drawings—lines consisting of points located at different distances—it was established that Rosa had about 10 light sensory elements in each square millimeter of her fingertips!

The next question was one of the most difficult: How does Rosa differentiate color? We know that man's color vision is three-dimensional. Each cone has three light receptors—one reacts better to blue, the second to red and the third to green. Each of these receptors also "senses" the other colors, but the reaction to them is noticeably weaker. Therefore a spectral characteristic can be formed for each receptor that will show how much it is excited by one or another color.

Any light falling on the cone acts on its receptors, and, as a result, two or even three different signals appear. The intricate computer of the brain differentiates colors by the manner in which the strength of these signals correlate.

The conclusion for Kuleshova is that her fingers have three types of light receptors—for red, blue and green—whose graph of spectral sensitivity corresponds exactly to the cones of the human eye. With every experiment the similarity between the sensitivity to light of Rosa's fingers and our organs of sight became more evident.

If we shift rapidly from red to gray, we see blue. Rosa perceives the same color changes with her fingers.

One other observation was made—that her fingers operate within the same limits as our eyes do with regard to light inertia, a phenomenon we are familiar with in ordinary vision. Light inertia explains why we do not notice fluctuations on the movie or TV screen. The eye, though we are not aware of it, is in constant motion—if the motion stops, we also stop seeing. For the same reason Kuleshova must keep her fingers moving for them to "see."

Rosa's authentically established second vision has bearing on the work of scientists in many fields, particularly those who are studying the evolution of the living organism. It can help them to understand how the systems for perceiving light and color developed, what form they had initially, and how the specialized organ of sight, the eye, evolved. Histologists will undoubtedly try to find out where the light-sensitive elements are located and how they are formed. Cybernetics specialists have a whole series of new riddles—how the color signal is transmitted from the eye to the brain, how it is coded and decoded, how it interacts with other signals, and how the process of recognizing images takes place.

Among the large number of problems the Tagil phenomenon raises is this one, perhaps the most important: Are other people's fingers also sensitive to light or is this a gift only Rosa Kuleshova has?

Shortly afterward that question was answered by another group of tests. Here is what the popular Soviet magazine *Science and Life* wrote about it:

DISTINGUISHING COLORS WITH THE FINGERS

Docent Abram Novomeisky, head of the psychology laboratory of the Nizhni Tagil Teachers Training School, visited our editorial offices to tell us about the conclusions reached by the Ural scientists who studied "the Tagil phenomenon."

When he concluded his story, he suggested to those assembled that they try to see whether they too could learn to differentiate color with their fingers. Boris Malyshev, an artist, volunteered for the test. Docent Novomeisky blindfolded him with a dark cloth which let no light through. "I do this not so much to prevent you from taking a peek," the scientist explained, "as to switch off your instrument of sight and force you to concentrate on tactile sensations."

A carefully wiped glass was placed on the desk, and on it two sheets of colored paper: yellow and red. "At first the colors have to be pure, not mixed, and the surface of the paper must be uniform," Novomeisky explained. "It is important that the fingers of the subject be dry."

Novomeisky first tried to get his subject to relate the tactile sensation to the color. He put Malyshev's hand on the yellow sheet and told him to rub the surface lightly with three fingers—the index, third and fourth—while Novomeisky said several times in succession, "This is yellow." The procedure was repeated with the second color.

Then Novomeisky fixed in the subject's mind the difference in the sensations that the yellow and red colors gave him. He suggested that Boris touch the sheets alternately and try to determine the difference in his perceptions. While Malyshev did this, Novomeisky told him the color of the sheet he was touching.

In about five minutes Malyshev had begun to feel something of the difference between the colors. He said: "The yellow paper seems to be more porous and smooth, and the red sticky."

"All right," Novomeisky said. "What we have done is establish a reflex action in a rough way. Now let us get on to the tests." He changed the places of the two sheets on the glass and asked the artist to say which color was which. In a matter of seconds Malyshev accurately called the colors.

Then the scientist made the test more difficult. He slipped a third sheet on the glass, mixed them all up and asked Boris what the colors were. Malyshev rubbed the sheets alternately and then said: "This one is yellow, this one is red, and this is also red." All correct.

"Now try to determine the color of the paper without the help of comparisons," the docent suggested.

He placed a single sheet on the glass. Boris rubbed it, thought for a second, rubbed it again and called the right color.

"Very good," the scientist said, obviously pleased. "Your passing this test means that you are beginning to fix the colors in your mind not by the difference in sensations but by associating a definite sensation with a definite color. Now I'll give you a more complicated task."

He covered the colored sheets lying on the glass with transparent tracing paper, rough side up. "The tracing paper will make it a bit more difficult to perceive the colors," he explained, "but we want to make the test more rigorous by excluding any influence the structure of the colored surfaces themselves might have on your perception."

And this time Malyshev did have to take a much longer time figuring out the difference in his sensations before he called, correctly again, the colors of the sheets under the tracing paper.

Then another artist sat down to do the tests. He passed all of them and did better than his predecessor by this additional test.

"If we place two sheets of colored paper on top of each other," the docent told his audience, "for some strange reason the dominant sensation will be produced by the color of the bottom sheet."

He placed two sheets, yellow and red, in front of the subject and asked him to identify the colors. The answers were correct. Then Novomeisky mixed the sheets, slipped a red sheet under the yellow, and under the red another yellow sheet. The subject felt the top sheets and without hesitation named the colors of the two lower sheets.

"So you see," Novomeisky summed up, "the fingers of your artists are not at all inferior to Kuleshova's."

"Can Rosa distinguish the form of the image in addition to the colors?" someone asked him.

"That can be learned too," the docent replied. "I did some experimenting with my students. After some training they were able to determine the limits of two colors and then the shape of the image.

"Here is how it was done. We placed sheets of black and white paper on a glass. The subject tested learned how to differentiate one color from another. After he had mastered that, he was asked to determine the limits of the image of a simple black figure (but one he did not know) on a white background. After repeating experiments with various simple figures, we went on to large black letters on a white background."

Ural scientists believe that all this points to a tactile-optical sense that we did not know man possessed. And Rosa Kuleshova is not the only possessor of this sense; many people have it. The tactile-optical sense is very similar to vision, for it is connected with the visual centers of the brain. It differs, however, in that it is more tactile than visual. Eye vision embraces the whole object at once, but the fingers unfold the image, just as in a TV kinescope. The new discovery is being studied. It is too early yet to make any predictions about the secrets it will yield, but it is certain to enrich optics, the physiology of the sense organs, psychology, pedagogy and the theory of cognition.

---

29 | Subliminal Perception

Ann Anastasi

In the fall of 1957 widespread public alarm was aroused by the announcement of an "experiment" conducted by a commercial firm in a New Jersey motion-picture theater. During the showing of the regular film, the words "Eat Popcorn" and "Drink Coca-Cola" were flashed alternately on the screen every 5 seconds for 1/3,000th of a second. Because of the ex-

---

tremely brief exposure, these stimuli were described as "subliminal," that is, below the limen, or threshold, of perception. Nevertheless, the firm claimed that over the six weeks when this procedure was followed the sale of popcorn from the lobby refreshment stand rose 57.5 per cent and that of Coca-Cola rose 18.1 per cent. The report of these results aroused widespread comment in the popular press. This type of advertising was variously described as "the super-soft sell," "the invisible sell," and "the little ad that wasn't there." Dismal pictures were painted of a nation of robots whose behavior could be controlled by suggestions of which they were not even aware. The protests and charges soon reached such proportions as to come before the United States Congress and the Federal Communication Commission.

The specific claims made regarding the New Jersey motion-picture demonstration could not be evaluated because of the refusal of the commercial organization to reveal the necessary details of procedure and results. Without such knowledge it is impossible to determine whether the reported increase in sales resulted from the subliminal advertising or from other uncontrolled factors. We would need to know, for instance, whether the size and nature of the audience were in any way unusual during the experimental period. Because of weather conditions, time of year, or the particular films shown, the audience might be larger than usual or might include a larger proportion of teen-agers, who are more likely to buy popcorn and Coca-Cola. Similarly, any changes made in the display of merchandise or in the operation of the sales booth itself would need to be investigated. It would also help to have more direct information on the buying behavior of the audience. Was there an increase in purchases made on the way in, before exposure to the subliminal advertising? How many customers made their purchases during the film showing and how many on the way out?

In the absence of adequate information on the above demonstration, we may turn to some recent well-controlled investigations. Designed to test specific claims about the subliminal control of behavior, these experiments have yielded largely negative results. In one study, two groups of students watched the same 30-minute instructional film. During the showing of this film, a slide was projected on the screen for .01 second at 10-second intervals. The slide used in the experimental group showed a spoon of rice with the words "Wonder Rice" printed below it; the slide used in the control group contained only four lines arranged in a meaningless way.

At the conclusion of the film, all subjects were shown a picture of the spoon of rice without the name and were asked whether they had ever seen it in a rice advertisement. A few individuals in both groups said they had seen it, but the proportion did not differ significantly in the two groups—in fact, it was slightly *higher* in the control group. Regardless of their answer to the first question, all subjects were asked which of two brands (Monarch or Wonder) they believed was more likely to be associated with the picture. Both groups chose Monarch much oftener than Wonder, but the difference between the groups was insignificant. Thus the experimental subjects' subliminal exposure to the words "Wonder Rice" failed to increase the probability of their associating this brand name with the picture.

In another experiment, the word "beef" was superimposed on a classroom film in flashes of 1/200th of a second every 7 seconds. The control group was shown only the film, with no additional stimuli. After viewing the film, the experimental and control groups showed no significant differences in their references to beef in sentence completion and word-association tests. Nor was there a significant difference in reported preferences for roast beef sandwiches, out of a given list of five common types of sandwiches. The experimental subjects, however, rated themselves as significantly more hungry than did the control group, even when time of day and interval since last meal were equated. Three of the original 108 subjects were eliminated from the analysis of results because when questioned they said they had seen a word on the screen. But it is interesting to note that only one saw "beef"; the other two perceived the word as "beer."

In still another experiment, subliminal perception was found to have no significant effect upon the subject's choice of "right" or "left" circles when required to guess which was correct in each trial. Unknown to the subjects, the words "Choose right" and "Choose left" were exposed tachistoscopically for durations of .01, .02, and .03 seconds in different parts of the experiment. The only subjects whose individual performance was better than chance later reported that they had seen the words and had followed the suggestion deliberately. In a learning experiment, performance in two different learning tasks was not significantly affected by the subliminal exposure of either correct or incorrect suggestions. In this experiment, the duration of subliminal exposure was based on an individually determined threshold for each subject.

Quite apart from its use in advertising and its potential dangers as a devious means of "behavior control," subliminal perception has been extensively studied in the psychological laboratory. Research on subliminal perception dates back fully 100 years. Many experiments have demonstrated that subjects do respond in various ways to stimuli of which they report no awareness. Stimuli may fall below the "awareness" threshold because of low intensity, brief duration, or other characteristics. To understand the subject's reaction to such stimuli, it is essential to consider the nature of a sensory threshold. There is no single intensity such that stimuli above it are always perceptible and those below it always imperceptible. Sensitivity varies along a continuum; the transition from perceptible to imperceptible is gradual.

The specific threshold established for a given subject depends in part upon the *standard of accuracy*. If the subject must give a correct response 75 per cent of the time, he needs a more intense stimulus than he would need to give 50 per cent correct responses. The threshold also depends upon the nature of the *response indicator*. For instance, a stimulus may be too weak for the subject to report awareness of it. Nevertheless, if he is told to guess its location, he may be right significantly more often than by chance. Even weaker stimuli may lead to autonomic responses, such as a galvanic skin reaction to a word previously conditioned to an electric shock. Flashing such a word on a screen may evoke the conditioned galvanic response even when the word is too faint to be perceived in terms of other response indicators.

The problem of so-called subliminal perception thus reduces to that of threshold differences found with different response indicators. Reported awareness is a relatively crude and unreliable indicator. Such an awareness threshold will vary with the kind of directions given to subjects, the number and nature of available response categories, the serial position of stimuli, and other extraneous factors. This irrelevant variance tends to raise the threshold. An analogy may help to clarify the relationship among thresholds. Suppose you weigh yourself on an ordinary scale and find your weight to be 118 pounds. If you weigh yourself ten times during the day on such a scale, your weight will probably remain at 118 pounds. But repeated weighings on a highly sensitive laboratory scale will reveal systematic weight changes in the course of a 12-hour period. The latter could be described as "subliminal weight changes," which can be detected only with a delicate indicator.

By modifying the relative sensitivity of the two response indicators employed in a perception experiment, an investigator may artificially vary the extent of "subliminal perception" he finds from zero to any desired amount. It can thus be seen that subliminal perception is not a special phenomenon but a methodological artifact. It is not a mysterious technique for "beaming ideas directly into the mind" while bypassing the individual's conscious defenses. Research on so-called subliminal perception can be more accurately described as the study of diverse responses to *weak stimuli.* So far there is no evidence to suggest that weak stimuli exert more influence on behavior than do strong stimuli. In fact, the reverse is generally found to be true.

With regard to the use of subliminal stimulation in advertising, it should also be noted that individuals vary in their sensory thresholds. Hence a word flashed on a motion-picture screen may fall well above the awareness threshold of some persons and may be clearly read by them; for others, it may be totally imperceptible in terms of all response indicators; and for still others it may fall in the desired intermediate, or subliminal, zone. These thresholds also vary within the same person from time to time. When weak stimuli are employed, moreover, the probability of *misperception* increases. Remember the students who saw "beer" instead of "beef." The advertiser who hopefully flashes the words "Buy Tasty Tea" on a motion-picture screen may find that many subjects actually perceive "Burn Trashy Ties"—a suggestion they may feel strongly tempted to accept when opening Christmas packages.

If at some future time it should be adequately demonstrated that subliminal stimulation can seriously influence a person's actions, then psychologists should look to their code of professional ethics to make sure that they will use these techniques for the benefit of the individual and not for ulterior gains. Under such circumstances, too, legal controls should be instituted against misuse of the techniques by unscrupulous persons. But, in our present state of knowledge, subliminal perception does not constitute a social threat.

30 | The Reality of Dreams

Edith Lederer

Could it be that dreams do not depend on sleep at all?

Perhaps dreaming occurs when the body is not aroused by outside influences from the environment—regardless of the time of day.

If this is true, daydreaming might be more than just a figure of speech.

Since the Viennese father of psychoanalysis, Dr. Sigmund Freud, probed the world of dreams 65 years ago, scientific dream theory has come to replace the speculations of the poet and sage.

Freud believed that dreams were "wish fulfillments" that took place to safeguard sleep. Dream life, to him, was similar to many types of mental illness.

By encouraging a patient to recollect one of his trips into dreamland and, without reflection, report all his reactions to the physician, Freud thought he could reach the regions of the unconscious responsible for the mental ailments that plague modern man.

Recently, however, dream researchers have shifted their focus from the mind and its psychology, stressed by Freud, to the brain and its physiology.

TELLTALE EYE MOVEMENTS

In their University of Chicago "sleep laboratory," in 1953 Dr. Nathaniel Kleitman and Dr. Eugene Aserinsky ushered in the period of scientific dream measurement when they discovered that sudden bursts of rapid jerky eye movements in sleeping subjects were a clue to dreaming.

Their original method—still the basis of most dream research—utilized a sleeping subject who had tiny electrodes attached from his temples to an electroencephalograph (EEG) machine.

While he slept, instruments recorded his brain wave activity, heart and respiratory rates. What became evident almost immediately was that distinct breathing, heartbeat, rapid eye movement and brain wave patterns showed up at the same time during sleep.

The scientists decided to wake their sleeping subjects during the rapid eye movement periods to see if they were dreaming. Out of 191 arousals, 152 dreams were reported—a batting average of 80%.

Later, Dr. Kleitman and Dr. William Dement, now at Stanford University, Stanford, Calif., discovered that the subject's dream recall was almost 100% when he was awakened after a distinct brain wave pattern appeared on the EEG.

From *Science News Letter,* **87,** 282, May 1965. Reprinted by permission of *Science News,* weekly summary of current science,

Since the specific brain wave pattern seemed to be a better indicator of dreaming, Dr. Dement and his colleagues set out to find out what rapid eye movements actually did represent.

Rapid eye movements, they found, are indicators of visual events being experienced by the dreamer. The eyes of the man who is watching a tennis match in his dream will be moving back and forth across the court as the play progresses—stopping on one side when the ball bounces off the court.

"It appears that the dreamer is almost totally immersed in his dreaming consciousness. But he participated in the dream with both emotional and physiological responses as if it were a waking experience," these dream researchers point out.

As he does during waking hours, the dreamer watches or participates in a continuing, ongoing experience. However, sometimes he will shorten or leave out one part of the sequence. The girl who is getting dressed for a big dance in her dream may arrive at the ball without ever getting out of the car.

In dreams, everything does not happen in a flash, either. It takes as long to get dressed or undressed in a dream as it would in real life.

In calm dreams, the dreamer's pulse and breathing are fairly regular and he lies motionless. However, when he is physically active or under emotional stress in his dream, his breathing becomes irregular. The muscles he uses in the dream show weak movement, and his eyes gaze at the dreamed visual picture that he clearly "sees."

When Drs. Kleitman and Dement were recording the dreamer's activities on the EEG during sleep, they found that a repeated pattern of hills and valleys, varying in depth, regulated sleep and dreams.

They distinguished separate sleep stages, but found that only in one did dreaming take place. In this one, the lightest stage, everyone dreams. The flow of the sleep-dream cycle takes a person from the brink of sleep to deep slumber. From this depth he makes a rising approach to light, dreaming sleep.

This first dream is short, about nine minutes. When it ends, he falls into a deeper sleep, and returns to dream again about 90 minutes later, this time for about 19 minutes.

FOUR A NIGHT IS AVERAGE

The average adult will have four dreams every night, each one generally longer than the last. The third dream averages 24 minutes, and the fourth, 28 minutes—but dreams may last as long as an hour.

It seems, therefore, that the state of dreaming has its own unique set of physiological characteristics, which differ significantly from those of sleeping and waking.

This distinct "third state" associated with dreaming has led Dr. Frederick Snyder of the National Institute of Mental Health, Bethesda, Md., to theorize that an underlying physiological—rather than psychological—mechanism centered in the nerve fibers can explain the regular occurrence of dreaming.

Whatever this mechanism may be, Dr. Dement has found that it is essential. When he reversed the technique for recalling dreams developed by Drs. Kleitman and Aserinsky, the subjects were awakened at the beginning of an EEG dream-pattern period instead of at the end.

Although they got as much sleep as a control group that slept normally, the non-dreamers became irritable and upset during waking hours.

This reaction was similar to that of disc jockey Peter Tripp, who carried on a 200-hour sleep deprivation marathon in 1959. At the beginning of his no-sleep stint, he was easily upset, and by the fourth sleepless day he began to have hallucinations.

When Dr. Dement and Dr. Charles Fisher, Mt. Sinai Hospital, New York, allowed their dream-deprived subjects to sleep undisturbed, they noted an increase in their total dream time. Similar results were found after prolonged sleep loss.

The results of these dream deprivation experiments indicated to Dr. Snyder that something had interfered with the basic dream mechanism he had theorized.

Perhaps, he speculated, the conditions which produce mental illness—whatever they may be—could sufficiently interfere with the function of this mechanism to bring about dreaming when the patient was awake.

If this were true, the old Freudian belief that psychosis is a "waking dream" would gain new plausibility.

Since Freud, psychoanalysis has been used as a therapeutic tool to reach the unconscious mind of the psychologically disturbed person.

However, Drs. Roy M. Whitman and Milton Kramer with Bill Baldridge at the University of Cincinnati, who studied "which dreams are told and which are not in a psychotherapeutic session," throw out a word of caution to the therapist.

By recording a subject's dreams as they occurred during normal sleep, and discussing them during a later psychiatric session, the researchers found that portions of dreams, and whole dreams were omitted.

Dreams containing attitudes and experiences that the subject felt would bring a negative response from the psychiatrist were omitted. For one male subject these were strong homosexual feelings, and for a female subject they were initially guilt feelings about sex.

These scientists believe that there may be an automatic selection process determining which dreams are presented by the patient to the therapist. It could be the untold dream that contains the major interpersonal conflicts.

FREUD MAY HAVE BEEN RIGHT

Freud may have been right when he said "it is not only quite possible, but highly probable, that the dreamer really does know the meaning of his dream; only he does not know that he knows, and he thinks that he does not."

The question of dreaming has also been studied in newborns and animals. Many mammals such as monkeys, cats, dogs, goats, sheep and even the opossum show similar EEG brain-wave patterns to those of dreaming adults.

Dr. Howard Roffwarg of Columbia University, New York, has recently found that a low-voltage, fast-wave EEG pattern also exists in newborn infants. Their dream-sleep cycle is almost the exact picture of the dreaming sleep pattern in adults.

Although the infants show rapid eye movements, it is doubtful that they are experiencing visual dreaming. However, it would seem that the physiological mechanism is inborn.

Where does all this leave the dreamer and the dreaming mechanism that seems to be evident in many forms of life? Is the dreaming pattern in animals related to that of humans? If it is, how has it evolved, and what function does it play in animals and humans?

---

31 | Regarding Hypnosis

A Statement of Position by the American Psychiatric Association

February 15, 1961

Many inquiries requesting an official opinion of the American Psychiatric Association on hypnotic therapy have been received from local psychiatric and other medical societies and from individual members of the Association and others. These inquiries, in general, ask the following questions: Is hypnosis an acceptable psychiatric procedure? If so, who should teach it? To whom should it be taught? What should be the depth and extent of such teaching? When can adequate training be secured?

The following statement of position regarding these matters has been prepared by the Committee on Therapy of the American Psychiatric Association and is published with the approval of the Council of the Association for the information and guidance of all concerned.

STATEMENT

Hypnosis is a specialized psychiatric procedure and as such is an aspect of doctor-patient relationship. Hypnosis provides an adjunct to research, to diagnosis and to treatment in psychiatric practice. It is also of some value in other areas of medical practice and research.

Unfortunately, so little is known of the nature of the hypnotic state that definitions usually reduce themselves to mere descriptions of the various manifested phenomena. Few reports of controlled experiments into the nature of hypnosis have been published.

Hypnosis is appropriately and properly used in the course of therapy only when its employment serves therapeutic goals without posing undue risks to the patient. With selected patients, it can be used for sedative, anal-

---

Reprinted by permission of the American Psychiatric Association.

gesic and anesthetic purposes; for the relief of apprehension and anxiety; and for symptom suppression. It can also be used, but on a still more highly selective basis, as an adjunct in the treatment of patients with neurotic or psychotic illness.

Hypnosis or hypnotic treatment, as in any other psychiatric procedure, calls for all examinations necessary to a proper diagnosis and to the formulation of the immediate therapeutic needs of the patient. The technique of induction of the trance state is by far the least important of the many facets of the hypnotic procedure and under no circumstance should it be taught independently.

Whoever makes use of hypnotic techniques, therefore, should have sufficient knowledge of psychiatry, and particularly psychodynamics, to avoid its use in clinical situations where it is contraindicated or even dangerous. Although similar dangers attend the improper or inept use of all other aspects of the doctor-patient relationship, the nature of hypnosis renders its inappropriate use particularly hazardous. For hypnosis to be used safely, even for the relief of pain or for sedation, more than a superficial knowledge of the dynamics of human motivation is essential.

Since hypnosis has definite application in the various fields of medicine, physicians have recently shown increasing interest in hypnosis and have turned to psychiatrists for training in hypnosis.

To be adequate for medical purposes, all courses in hypnosis should be given in conjunction with recognized medical teaching institutions or teaching hospitals, under the auspices of the department of psychiatry and in collaboration with those other departments which are similarly interested. Although lectures, demonstrations, seminars, conferences and discussions are helpful, the basic learning experience must derive from closely supervised clinical contact with patients. Since such psychiatrically-centered courses are virtually non-existent, many physicians have enrolled in the inadequate brief courses available, which are taught often by individuals without medical or psychiatric training. These courses have concentrated on hypnotic-trance techniques and have neglected or covered psychodynamics and psychopathology in a superficial or stereotyped fashion.

Proper safeguards for the use of hypnosis are vitally important to the patient, to all physicians, and to psychiatry as a specialty. In the interest of encouraging the safe use of hypnosis, the following recommendations are approved.

RECOMMENDATIONS

1. Isolated courses limited to the teaching of trance induction techniques are strongly disapproved.

2. The teaching of hypnosis should take place in medical schools and other psychiatric training centers that have an interest in the teaching of hypnosis. When taught in such a climate, where students can acquire adequate knowledge of psychiatric principles, hypnosis may become a useful adjunct to therapy.

3. The teaching of hypnosis should be of sufficient duration and depth for students to acquire adequate understanding of its appropriate place in relation to other psychiatric treatment modalities; of its indications and contraindications; of

its values and its dangers. Decisions regarding the depth and extent of the teaching of hypnosis should remain flexible, and should be made by the psychiatric departments teaching such courses.

4. Training in all aspects of hypnosis should be made available to physicians and dentists requesting it.

5. An expansion of facilities for the teaching of hypnosis is needed particularly at the postgraduate level. The establishment of postgraduate courses in medical schools and other teaching centers under the direction of the department of psychiatry is recommended.

6. Physicians practicing hypnosis should do so only in their particular field of medical competence.

7. The need for continued study of hypnosis and for adequate research is emphasized, with particular reference to delineating its place in the total treatment program.

Unit Seven | DISCUSSION QUESTIONS

27. *The Uncomfortable Facts About ESP*

How do you explain the reasons why many psychologists refuse to accept the existence of ESP?

Do you believe that some individuals possess extrasensory abilities unexplainable by science? Support your answer.

28. *A Sixth Sense?*

Some blind people have been reported to possess the uncanny ability to distinguish colors by feeling. Would you explain this as a form of "extra-ocular vision"? Explain.

How do you account for the reported cases of "extra-ocular vision" in sighted people? Explain.

29. *Subliminal Perception*

Define "subliminal." Does this term refer only to vision?

What is the main difficulty in subliminal advertisement as a bona-fide technique of advertisement and communication?

30. *The Reality of Dreams*

What is the major difference between present-day dream researchers and Sigmund Freud in explaining the reasons for dreams?

Discuss the different stages of sleep and the physiological responses found in each.

31. *Regarding Hypnosis*

Should hypnosis be a form of nightclub entertainment? What are the advantages or disadvantages?

How do you explain why hypnosis is not used more by scientists in the treatment of human problems.

Unit Eight *Evaluating Abnormal Behavior*

As our society becomes increasingly complex and demanding, the problems of group living likewise increase. Strikingly different, strange, and unorthodox methods of coping with the environment are likely to be considered as abnormal behavior. When an individual's methods of adjustment are inefficient, he may have what is called a neurosis. A *neurosis* is a condition in which one does not require hospitalization; nevertheless, he fails to operate at full efficiency. One psychologist likens this condition to a poorly adjusted carburetor in an automobile. The engine is operative, but it fails to operate at full efficiency. If not attended to, the complete engine suffers and the problem is magnified. So, too, the neurotic fails to operate at maximum efficiency and his interaction with others is affected. (The terms *psychoneurosis* and *neurosis* are used interchangeably by many psychologists.) *Anxiety reaction* (extreme uneasiness in situations that are not dangerous), *phobia* (irrational fear), *amnesia* (loss of identity), *obsessions* and *compulsions* (recurrent irresistible ideas and acts) are the frequently encountered examples of neurosis.

On the other hand, a *psychosis* is a condition in which the maladjustment is so severe that hospitalization is often necessary. The distinction between neurosis and psychosis is easier to make in theory than it is in practice because many of the symptoms and conditions are not clear-cut and are borderline. A humorous distinction made between the psychotic and the neurotic is that "to the psychotic 2 and 2 make 5; to the neurotic 2 and 2 make 4, but he's unhappy about it!"

Schizophrenia (various reactions characterized by fundamental disturbances in reality relationships), *manic-depressive* (marked emotional oscillation), and *paranoia* (delusions) are frequently encountered examples of psychosis. Of all the psychotic disorders, schizophrenia makes up the largest group. The National Institute of Mental Health reports that 73% of all psychotics admitted to U.S. public mental hospitals were classified as schizophrenic.

In the first article, *One of the Great Mystery Stories of Medicine,* Lawrence Galton presents two theories concerning schizophrenia: (1) schizophrenia does not have an organic base and is considered functional, and (2) schizophrenia is an organic-based disorder and is considered organic. Recent experiments and therapeutic measures are also discussed.

Thomas S. Szasz' *Mental Illness Is a Myth* presents a case that mental disorder should not be classified as an "illness," but rather it should be categorized as "personal conduct." His viewpoint has been the center of current controversy among many behavioral scientists.

In the third article by Karl Menninger, *Psychiatrists Use Dangerous Words,* the author discusses some of the concepts and terms used in describing abnormal mental conditions, e.g., manic-depressive, schizophrenic, and psychotic. Menninger suggests healthier, and more useful, ways of viewing and discussing what he calls "human problems."

The involvement of behavioral scientists as "expert witnesses" has become a vital part of America's judicial procedures and the question of legal insanity is one of considerable debate in the courtroom as well as in the classroom. *Defense of Insanity: A Survey of Legal and Psychiatric Opinion,* the final article in this unit, is a presentation by Rita James Simon and Wendell Shackelford discussing opinions of psychiatrists and lawyers relating to the plea of insanity.

---

32 | One of the Great Mystery Stories of Medicine

Lawrence Galton

"Surely no other term in medicine rivals schizophrenia in the amount of confusion and despair it provokes. One of the great mystery stories of modern medicine, it is full of clues, rich in suspects, littered with victims, and with as yet no solution. The police as usual are busy but not impressive. . . ."

So, not long ago in the Journal of the American Medical Association, wrote Dr. Leston L. Havens of the Department of Psychiatry of Harvard Medical School.

And as if to exemplify the confusion and frustration involved in the policework—in the research into schizophrenia—almost simultaneously with the publication of Dr. Havens's observation a Canadian researcher at a New York scientific meeting was reporting, hopefully, the finding of a chemical, called NAD, which seemed able to erase the symptoms of the disease. But, a few months later, when a group of U.S. investigators tried NAD they got no results.

There have been two theories about schizophrenia. One—the still-prevailing—is that it is primarily psychological in nature, a matter of inadequate personality finally succumbing to some environmental stress.*

The other is that schizophrenia is physical—basically, a disorder of body chemistry. As proponents of this theory—the schizochemists, they are sometimes called—explain: "Before anyone can get schizophrenia, his body 'factory' must be different from that of a normal person; it must have the capacity to go out of order and set biochemical changes in motion. It may be triggered into going out of order by environmental stresses—but the physiological weakness must be there first."

From *The New York Times Magazine,* November 6, 1966.

* See cover illustration showing paintings produced by one patient at successive stages of schizophrenic disintegration.

The ranks of the schizochemists are growing. They include distinguished biologists, geneticists and psychiatrists. Recently, many joined to establish the American Schizophrenia Foundation, aimed at intensification of biochemical research. They see the psychological approach as sterile. They believe that, although there is as yet no definitive proof of a biochemical factor, there is growing evidence in favor, and that, despite difficulties and setbacks, it is in the biochemical search that the hope lies, perhaps not too remotely, for making understandable and manageable—as much so as diabetes, for example—one of the most widespread and devastating of illnesses.

Schizophrenia accounts for more than half of the mentally ill patients who fill more than half the hospital beds in this country. According to some estimates, it affects two million people in this country and Canada—and one of every 100 persons in the world today has, has had, or will have the disease. The 1 per cent incidence seems to prevail in all societies, cultures, racial and ethnic types and social classes.

Though it can develop at any time—even early in childhood—typically it overtakes people in the 16 to 30 age group.

Often it maims them for life. Although tranquilizing drugs have helped in many ways, they do not appear to have greatly changed the over-all recovery rate. According to Dr. Don D. Jackson of the Stanford University School of Medicine, a schizophrenic entering a state hospital has little better than an even chance of ever returning to society as a functioning member.

With or without treatment, according to the American Schizophrenia Foundation, about one-third of patients recover, a third remain totally disabled, and another third are discharged into the outside world "not sick enough to be institutionalized, not well enough to live healthy, happy lives."

Many of the last group, the foundation reports, will take their own lives to escape their pain and suffering. Schizophrenia is one of the reasons that suicide has become a major problem in the United States.

The symptoms of the disease are diverse. To the schizophrenic, the world may appear as though he were viewing it through a distorted looking glass; colors may assume unnatural brilliance or lose their brilliance; three-dimensional objects may look flat. Often the schizophrenic has illusions: A coat hanging in a closet may become a bear; a child may see a playmate turn temporarily into a lion. Frequently, there are auditory hallucinations: voices in the head—singing, or accusing or commanding. There may be changes in other senses—smell, taste, touch. Schizophrenics sometimes appear insensitive to pain yet may complain of bizarre sensations such as worms crawling under their skins.

There are disturbances in thought and thought content. Some victims experience a slow-down in the thinking process so that logical thinking becomes difficult or impossible. Others complain their minds are racing away from them. Some develop delusions of being persecuted; others, of being in positions of high authority. Sudden fear—nameless and overwhelming—is common; so, too, is deep depression.

In the 19th century, Emil Kraepelin, a European psychiatrist, distinguished four major subclasses of schizophrenia. His classification system is still in use:

In what Kraepelin called "hebephrenic" schizophrenia, silliness, abnormal pleasure in pranks and gaudy adornment, and hypochondria are among predominating symptoms.

The "catatonic" schizophrenic is mute, stuporous, withdrawn; and often assumes strange, uncomfortable positions he may maintain for long periods.

In "paranoid" schizophrenia, there are embittered, suspicious attitudes and feelings of persecution.

The "simple" type of schizophrenic reaction, gradual in onset, is marked by apathy and indifference, withdrawal, confusion and secret grandiosity.

One investigator, Dr. Robert S. de Ropp, has graphically described extreme cases of schizophrenia. A 28-year-old catatonic woman had been in a disturbed ward for eight years. "We find her huddled in a corner of a wooden bench, completely motionless, her knees drawn up under her chin and her thin arms clasped about her legs . . . her body so thin bones are visible through the flesh. . . . Most of the time she remains motionless, not moving even to satisfy calls of nature or take food. If you move her arm, it remains in any position in which you happen to place it. . . . The attendants have come to regard her as virtually an inanimate object, like a piece of furniture. Her husband has [divorced her] and married again. Her children do not remember her. Her illness began when she was 20. She may live on into her 60's. For all those 40 years she must be cared for—a living corpse, denied even the privilege of burial."

A second patient, a paranoid, is a man of 28, "very active but his activity has no connection with the realities of the world. . . . Everything he sees, hears, touches, even the food he eats, becomes endowed . . . with sinister, malignant significance. . . . The glance of an attendant, even a casual gesture by one of his fellow inmates, is interpreted as a threat. . . . He pushes food away . . . when they try to feed him by force he fights and screams and struggles. . . . He [too] may live for another 40 years, alone as only the mad can be alone, a curse to himself, a burden to those who care for him."

But if the disease can be totally disabling, it can also be mild and fleeting. Abraham Lincoln is believed to have experienced a schizophrenic breakdown as a young man. Kierkegaard, August Comte, Rousseau—many noted artists, writers, philosophers and scientists—suffered from time to time with schizophrenia.

A long-prevalent theory, as already noted, has been that it is an environmental-personality disorder—and that the stage may be set for it by a defective mother-child relationship. The child fails to develop normally. At some point, as the result of personality deficiency, he may become schizophrenic when life introduces a critical situation.

Recently, studies of sensory deprivation have led some investigators to postulate a mechanism through which schizophrenic symptoms may be brought on. The human organism appears to need a certain rate of sensory input. When the input is lowered—as in sleep, for example—dreams occur, and dreaming appears to be essential to physical well-being. In experiments, volunteers subjected to sensory deprivation—by being confined separately in rooms with hands isolated in special cuffs, eyes masked, sounds barred—have, in most cases, experienced hallucinations and psychosislike reactions after short periods. It has been suggested that schizophrenia may be triggered when the victim, experiencing severe anxiety, manages to reject the input of sensory experience from the environment that has provoked his anxiety—and then suffers hallucinations and the build-up of a delusional system.

Lately, going beyond mother-child interaction as the root cause of schizophrenia, some investigators have become convinced that an understanding of the disorder must be based on knowledge of total family interactions and behavior. They believe, for example, that the father's role is as important as the mother's in child development. One bit of evidence: research indicating that the highest probability of recovery in schizophrenics comes from homes in which the father had the dominant role.

There have been studies, too, indicating that, in some cases, the family system operates only at the expense of the schizophrenic's ill health. "Ulcers, heart attacks, gall-bladder disfunction and other disorders," observes Dr. Jackson of Stanford, "appear to afflict other members of the family with suspicious frequency just at that time in conjoint family therapy when the patient makes a significant change for the better."

But there is impressive evidence that heredity operates in schizophrenia —and a heredity factor suggests physical disorder. The classic study was done 20 years ago with identical twins by Dr. Franz J. Kallmann of the Columbia University College of Physicians and Surgeons. Dr. Kallmann was able to demonstrate that if one identical twin is in a state hospital suffering from schizophrenia, there is an 85 per cent likelihood that the other twin will be found to have the disorder.

In 1964, Dr. David Rosenthal of the National Institute of Mental Health was able to report on four young women, identical quadruplets now in their 20's, who constitute the first recorded case of quadruple schizophrenia. For three years, a team of 60 physicians and other specialists studied the girls, their upbringing and their genetic make-up, seeking an answer to the question of whether heredity or environment causes mental illness.

They found evidence of a single gene that might have been initially responsible. They found an abnormal brain-wave pattern shared in common by the quads—and by their father. And they found a mental-illness pattern in the father's family.

They also found abnormal environmental influences. The quads' parents were suspicious and would not allow them to have friends. The father drank heavily, and abused and frightened them.

Major conclusion of the study: schizophrenia results from an interplay of hereditary and environmental factors. Dr. Rosenthal reported: "In most cases, an inherited factor needs to be present for schizophrenia to develop. However, without severe environmental stresses the illness may not appear in those who have a predisposition to it."

If there is an inherited, or genetic, factor, it could very well manifest itself in a biochemical aberration. Sigmund Freud himself had mentioned the possibility of a biochemical answer to mental illness.

The ability of genetic errors to produce mental disease through physical mechanisms has become very clear in recent years. Phenylketonuria, or PKU, is one example. The child with PKU, once doomed to mental retardation, has lacking in the genetic blueprints in his cells the instructions to synthesize a specific chemical, a digestive enzyme—phenylalanine hydroxylase. Without the enzyme, his body is unable to metabolize phenylalanine, a constituent of many foods. The material builds up to abnormal levels in body and brain. Today, a widely used chemical test can spot the disorder in infants and, by special diet, retardation can be avoided.

Attempts to discover some biochemical defects in schizophrenics date back more than half a century. At one point, investigators observed that administration of thyroid-gland extract seemed to benefit some schizophrenics, and there was a feeling that thyroid derangement might be the key to the problem. It was not. Other investigations got nowhere.

Then, in 1943, the "chemistry of madness" search received a shot in the arm. Dr. Albert Hofmann, a scientist with the Swiss-based pharmaceutical firm, Sandoz, accidentally discovered that LSD—a chemical derivative of ergot, a fungus that grows on wheat—produced hallucinations resembling those experienced in schizophrenia. Ever since, entirely apart from the sociological implications of LSD, a growing corps of investigators has become increasingly sanguine about the biochemical hypothesis.

One startling fact about LSD was the tiny amount—less than one-70-millionth of a man's body weight—needed to distort ordinary perceptions. That made it seem not unreasonable to assume that naturally occurring materials, in extremely minute quantities, might also produce disturbances, and that chemical and other tests available in the past for detecting such materials had not been nearly fine enough.

LSD led Dr. D. W. Woolley of Rockefeller University to formulate what is known as the serotonin hypothesis. Serotonin is a chemical originally discovered in the lining of the intestine, and found to influence functioning of intestinal and other smooth muscle—the type not under voluntary control. Later, serotonin also was found in the nervous system and brain where, some investigators believe, it may act as an important hormone, or chemical messenger.

When, in a laboratory experiment, Dr. Woolley took a strip of smooth muscle and treated it with LSD, it went into contraction. But when serotonin had been applied to the muscle first, the muscle did not contract. Possibly then, LSD produced its bizarre behavioral effects because it antagonized or competed with serotonin in the nervous system. If this were so, schizophrenia might be caused by some disturbance in body chemistry which upset serotonin action.

Favoring the concept was research indicating that some tranquilizing agents and stimulating drugs, when they produced changes in behavior, also produced changes in the levels of serotonin. The serotonin hypothesis is being actively explored today.

Generally, in searching for biochemical clues, investigators have tried to find something unusual in the blood, urine or spinal fluid of schizophrenics—abnormal quantities of some natural substances, or something not present at all in normal people. They have tried to identify it, see if it causes temporary schizophrenic symptoms when given to normal volunteers, figure out why it is formed, where in the body chemical system something may have gone wrong, what might be done to correct the fault.

In the past 20 years, there have been many false leads. Often investigators at some one institution have turned up what seemed to be an abnormality in their patients but investigators at other institutions have not been able to find it in theirs. In some instances, abnormal urine or other findings have been traced to the poor diets of schizophrenics.

But out of such research have come a number of promising leads. About 10 years ago, Dr. Robert Heath and associates at Tulane University found evidence of a distinctive abnormality in one portion of schizophrenic blood. More than half of blood is plasma, a fluid that carries the red and white blood cells. Plasma also contains globulins, complex chemicals which serve such functions as controlling blood clotting and combating disease organisms. Something was wrong in one of the globulins in schizophrenics. When that globulin, taken from their blood, was injected into normal volunteers, it produced transient psychotic episodes. To the abnormal material in the globulin—still not clearly identified—the Tulane workers gave the name of taraxein.

The finding was greeted skeptically as one more false lead. When, at a national meeting of psychiatrists, Dr. Heath showed movies of the disorienting effects of taraxein on prisoner volunteers, one comment in the audience was: "The volunteers must have been crazy to begin with."

But by 1962, Drs. Jacques Gottlieb and Charles Frohman of the Lafayette Clinic in Detroit were reporting independent work with a factor in schizophrenic globulin, possibly the same factor as Heath's. The Detroit research indicated that the factor could modify the chemical reactions by which simple sugars are made to produce energy. If such a disturbance in energy production took place in the cells of the nervous system, message transmission might be altered. The altered transmission might account for the strange sights and sounds in schizophrenia. Conceivably, as a result of altered transmission, the messages received in the brain of a catatonic might not be stimulating or seem important, leaving the victim stuporous, almost inanimate.

Meanwhile, Dr. Hudson Hoagland and associates at the Worcester Foundation for Experimental Biology also were studying a suspect globulin factor. They trained rats to climb a rope for a food reward. When they injected them with globulin samples from either hospitalized schizophrenic patients or nonpsychotic control donors, the rats became confused and took longer to climb the rope. But the injections from the schizophrenic patients produced twice the climbing time delay.

Through a series of complex tests, the Worcester workers were able to establish some evidence that the factor may be an amine—one of a group of highly potent body chemicals. Amines, which are known to occur in brain areas concerned with mood and emotion, include among their number the hormone adrenalin, which is involved in the body's response to stress.

Almost at the same time, researchers elsewhere turned up an abnormal amine substance in the urine of schizophrenic patients but not in that of normal persons, and found that it was derived from the same material used in forming adrenalin. Worcester workers have reported that preliminary tests in their laboratories showed that the abnormal amine disturbs trained rat performance in much the same way as the factor from the blood of schizophrenics, and investigations are continuing.

Meanwhile, since 1952, the possibility that an adrenalin disturbance might have something to do with causing schizophrenia has been under study in Saskatchewan, Canada, by Drs. Abram Hoffer and Humphrey Osmond.

It was the late Aldous Huxley who, after taking mescaline, a prime hallucinatory drug derived from a Mexican cactus plant, commented that the "schizophrenic is like a man permanently under the influence of mescaline."

Before going to Saskatchewan in 1951, Dr. Osmond had experimented in London with mescaline, which has a chemical structure similar to adrenalin's. One day, while Osmond was playing back a recording of effects produced by mescaline in a volunteer during an experiment, it was overheard by a colleague, a severe asthmatic, who remarked that sometimes when he took very large doses of adrenalin for his asthma he experienced similar effects—feelings of unreality and colored visions.

Osmond and Hoffer had picked up the clue—especially after learning from a Canadian physician that during the war, for lack of adequate supplies of normal adrenalin, a pinkish kind sometimes had to be used during anesthesia and then when patients recovered they had hallucinations and other disturbances.

Adrenochrome is a chemical derived from adrenalin. When adrenalin decomposes, it may form adrenochrome. Perhaps adrenochrome was the hallucinogen in pink adrenalin. If so, it might be that under normal circumstances in the body adrenalin decomposition goes through an adrenochrome stage of very brief duration, but that in schizophrenics the stage might be prolonged because of a metabolic defect. That is, the schizophrenic may not have the proper body chemicals to dispose of the poison rapidly enough to prevent intoxication and bizarre symptoms.

Osmond became a guinea pig. Ten minutes after taking an injection of adrenochrome, he noticed the ceiling in the laboratory changing color. Outside, he found the corridors "sinister and unfriendly," and was unable to relate distance and time. After a second injection, he reported: "I felt indifferent toward humans and had to curb myself from making unpleasant remarks." In subsequent experiments with volunteers, Hoffer and Osmond found several becoming temporarily psychotic after receiving adrenochrome.

Assuming that adrenochrome might be the culprit in schizophrenia, the two investigators began to look for some method of treatment. Reasoning that something capable of slowing down formation of adrenalin might help, they thought of nicotinic acid, also known as Vitamin B3, which in large amounts might latch onto some chemical constituents needed to build adrenalin.

Results have been gratifying, according to reports published by Dr. Hoffer, who is director of psychiatric research for the Saskatchewan Department of Public Health, and Dr. Osmond, now director of the Bureau of Research in Neurology and Psychiatry at the New Jersey Neuro-Psychiatric

Institute in Princeton. In comparison studies covering hundreds of patients, 30 per cent of those who did not receive the vitamin eventually recovered; of those treated with nicotinic acid, 75 per cent recovered. When the vitamin was used within a year after onset of schizophrenia, symptoms often disappeared after a few months of treatment. For long-term schizophrenia several years of treatment were needed.

Some researchers in the field believe that use of the vitamin is worth further investigation, but that the studies done so far cannot be considered conclusive. For example, some patients who benefited after the vitamin therapy had also received other treatment—such as electro-shock, sedation or psychotherapy. Skeptics see a need for studies in which the vitamin would be used in large groups as sole treatment, to establish its effect clearly.

While this debate has been building up, Dr. Hoffer, at that aforementioned symposium in New York, reported early results of another new treatment. Late in December, 1965, NAD, a compound related to nicotinic acid, had become available. When he tried it with 17 patients, it appeared to melt away the disease in 13.

One patient had been hospitalized for almost 30 years, and had shown only minor response to tranquilizer treatment. Eventually, the tranquilizer had to be discontinued because it had begun to produce ill effects. At that point, treatment with nicotinic acid was started. After a year, there had been some improvement. After two weeks of NAD, the patient could contact relatives and leave the hospital. Another patient had been hospitalized 8 years and had not responded to tranquilizers, shock treatment and psychotherapy. Three days after NAD treatment was begun, she had almost completely recovered.

He was, Dr. Hoffer emphasized, making only a very preliminary report about NAD. The number of patients treated was small, the time short, but the results seemed impressive enough for a report so other investigators could try the chemical and study its possibilities.

How might NAD work? "NAD is the active form of nicotinic acid," Dr. Hoffer explained to this writer. He had an idea that schizophrenia might result from a defect in production of NAD, which the body normally makes from nicotinic acid, the vitamin coming in from food. With NAD lacking, too much adrenalin might be changed to adrenochrome. "As a result, electric transmission across the synapses [the points of connection between cells in the nervous system] is partially blocked and parts of the brain thrown out of phase. Perception becomes distorted; the subject believes he still perceives normally and, responding normally to abnormal perception, is judged abnormal."

But almost immediately after Hoffer's report, a group of workers in the United States set out to try NAD and found themselves unable to duplicate his results. At Rockland State Hospital, Orangeburg, N.Y., Dr. Nathan S. Kline and a team of investigators divided 20 male chronic schizophrenics into 10 matched pairs. They gave one patient of each pair NAD; the other, sugar pills prepared to resemble the drug. All were carefully evaluated before—and again after 15 days of treatment—through interviews, sound films of their behavior and psychiatric rating scales. No significant difference could be found between those receiving NAD and those getting the sugar pills.

As yet, there is no clear explanation of the striking results in Canada and the failure in New York. Although NAD apparently was not responsible for the improvement in Dr. Hoffer's patients, Dr. Kline has suggested, something else the Canadian psychiatrist may have done in the course of treatment—without realizing its importance—could have helped.

Dr. Kline, president-elect of the American College of Neuropsychopharmacology, remains, he has said, "as convinced as ever that a metabolic disorder is involved" in schizophrenia, and that drug treatment "is a major part of the answer," even though NAD apparently is not the right drug.

Meanwhile, another avenue is being explored. It, too, relates to mescaline and adrenalin. Two years ago, Dr. Arnold Friedhoff of New York University discovered a chemical, DMPE, in the urine of 15 out of 19 schizophrenics but not in 14 other subjects. It shows up as a pink spot when urine is put through a special analytical test. Its chemical structure is similar to that of mescaline, which is also similar to that of adrenalin. In animals, DMPE proved to have potent mind-altering properties.

At first, there was some tendency to regard it as another possible red herring. But late in 1965, Dr. Cyril A. Clarke and associates at the University of Liverpool reported hunting for pink spots in the urine of more than 800 individuals—schizophrenic, otherwise mentally ill and normal. They found a "clear-cut association" of pink spots with schizophrenia.

This past spring, Dr. John R. Smythies of the Edinburgh University Department of Psychiatry made another report to the annual conference of the National Association for Mental Health in London. Not only are DMPE and mescaline much alike chemically and closely related to adrenalin; the difference between the first two and adrenalin lies largely in certain added-on groups of atoms—methyl groups. Adrenalin does not have them; the other two do. Thus, a single faulty step in body chemistry—in the handling of methyl groups—might be enough to turn adrenalin into an agent, such as DMPE, that might be responsible for schizophrenia. It was time, Smythies declared, to look for possible new therapeutic agents that could correct the methyl-handling error, and perhaps overcome schizophrenia.

If, as of now, the biochemistry of schizophrenia still seems murky, it is hardly surprising. In few areas of scientific investigation are there so many difficulties. Much of the research has had to be carried out with patients long institutionalized, often under conditions of overcrowding which may allow chronic infections, especially of the digestive tract, to produce or spread metabolic changes that could be mistakenly attributed to the mental disease.

Many schizophrenics, too, have been exposed to multitudinous drugs and other treatments which may produce metabolic changes that could be attributed to the disease. Also, disturbances in behavior and activity in schizophrenia could possibly cause deviations from normal in many biochemical and metabolic measures.

Far from being discouraged, investigators are optimistic. They note that it took 25 years from the suspicion that the key to diabetes might lie in the pancreas to actual isolation of the key—insulin.

They believe that many of the findings of recent years in schizophrenia research point in the right direction. They see some likelihood that, with further studies, many of the seemingly unconnected findings—taraxein, adrenochrome, DMPE and others—may yet be fitted together to form a comprehensible pattern. Conceivably, for example, taraxein could act to sensitize the nervous system to such substances as adrenochrome.

Some of the more sanguine believe that, with intensified research, a clear biochemical understanding of schizophrenia could emerge within a decade, and that with it could come the means for making the disease not only a quickly remediable but also, quite likely, a preventable one.

---

33 | Mental Illness Is a Myth

Thomas S. Szasz

On Feb. 28, 1966, the United States Court of Appeals for the Second Circuit handed down a decision which displaced the time-honored M'Naghten Rule as a test of criminal insanity, and substituted for it a new rule recommended by the American Law Institute.

The M'Naghten Rule dates from 1843, when one Daniel M'Naghten shot and killed a man named Drummond, the private secretary of Sir Robert Peel, whom M'Naghten had intended to kill. At M'Naghten's trial, evidence was introduced showing that he "was laboring under an insane delusion" of being hounded by enemies, among them Peel. The jury found him "not guilty, on the ground of insanity."

De jure, M'Naghten was acquitted; *de facto,* he was sentenced to life imprisonment in an insane asylum. He died in 1865, having been incarcerated for the last 22 years of his life.

The new ruling (binding on Federal courts in New York, Connecticut and Vermont) provides that: "A person is not responsible for criminal conduct if at the time of such conduct as a result of mental disease or defect he lacks substantial capacity either to appreciate the wrongfulness of his conduct or to conform his conduct to the requirements of law."

Both of these tests—and others, whatever their semantic differences—rest on the premise that the human mind may become "diseased," and that a person who has a "diseased mind" may, because of it, commit criminal acts unintentionally, not know the difference between right and wrong, or be unable to restrain himself from engaging in conduct prohibited by law. The value of all psychiatric tests of criminal responsibility thus hinges on the soundness of this underlying concept of "mental disease."

But what exactly is mental disease? If it is an illness, what kind is it? And if it is not an illness, what is it and why is it called an illness? Because of the frequency with which issues of mental health and illness arise not only in criminal cases but in matters of everyday life, it is important that we ask these questions and intelligently debate various possible answers to them.

I submit that mental illness is a myth. Bodies are physical objects; minds, whatever they may be, are not physical objects. Accordingly, mental diseases (such as depression or schizophrenia) cannot exist in the sense in which bodily diseases (such as broken bones or ulcerated skins) exist.

My disbelief in mental illness does not mean that I reject any facts of human behavior. "A myth," says the British philosopher Gilbert Ryle, "is not a fairy story. It is the presentation of facts belonging in one category in the idiom belonging to another. To explode a myth is accordingly not to deny facts, but to reallocate them." To say that mental illness is a myth is therefore not to *deny* facts (such as sadness or fear) but to *reallocate* them (from the category of mental illness to the category of personal conduct). Insofar as men are human beings, not machines, they always have some choice in how they act—hence, they are always responsible for their conduct. There is method in madness, no less than in sanity.

As long ago as the early nineteen-twenties, George H. Mead formulated the thesis that social situations—and human behavior in them—are analogous to games which must be played by certain "rules." In life, the games are infinite. As social conditions undergo rapid change, old games are constantly scrapped and new ones started. But most people are totally unprepared to shift from one type of game playing to another. They have early in life learned one set of rules—or, at most, a few—and find themselves forced to play new games by the old rules. This fundamental conflict leads to various problems in living—some severe enough to be commonly diagnosed as "mental illness" or "disease." It is these problems in living that the psychiatrist is usually called on to treat.

"But surely," someone might say, "a dope fiend, a rapist, or a Lee Harvey Oswald is not a *normal* person. What difference does it make whether we call him sick or something else?"

It makes, of course, all the difference in the world, for what we call things, and especially people, will shape our attitudes and justify our actions toward them. For example, when socially threatening behavior is called "witchcraft," it is handled by means of theological sanctions; when it is called "crime," it is handled by means of judicial sanctions, and when it is called "mental illness," it is handled by means of psychiatric sanctions.

The practices of modern American psychiatrists originate from two principal sources: hospital psychiatry and psychoanalysis.

Institutions for the care of the insane have existed since antiquity. However, the systematic confinement of madmen in buildings labeled "hospitals" did not begin until the middle of the 17th century. For about 250 years, from 1650 to 1900, the psychiatrist worked almost exclusively in the mental hospital. The alienist, as he was then called, was employed by an institution—a private or, more often, a public insane asylum.

The historical model and social prototype of the modern mental hospital is the French Hôpital Général. According to the distinguished medical historian George Rosen, the purposes of this institutional system were threefold: "In part they were economic: to increase [the] manufacture [of goods], provide productive work for the able-bodied, and to end unemployment; in part social: to punish willful idleness, restore public order, and rid Paris of beggars; and in part, religious and moral: to relieve the needy, the ill and suffering, to deal with immorality and antisocial behavior, and to provide Christian instruction."

A few years after its foundation, the Hôpital Général of Paris alone contained 6,000 persons, or about 1 per cent of the population. Who were these "mentally ill" people? According to regulations issued in 1680, "children of artisans and other poor inhabitants of Paris up to the age of 25 . . . girls who were debauched or in evident danger of being debauched . . . [and] wayward children . . ." were among those listed as proper subjects for confinement. In addition, old people, persons with venereal diseases, epileptics, vagrants, prostitutes—in brief, all of society's *"misérables"*—were incarcerated in the Hôpital Général. Michel Foucault, a French student of psychiatric history, thus concludes: "The Hôpital Général is not a medical establishment. It is rather a sort of semijudicial structure, an administrative entity which, along with already constituted powers, and outside the courts, decides, judges and executes."

The facts I have cited are important in showing us one of the roles of the psychiatrist—indeed, his traditional role: He is a physician working in a mental hospital, employed, as a rule, by the state, and charged with the task of confining and "treating" people who are considered "insane." Although some of his methods have changed, the social role of the institutional psychiatrist has remained what it has always been.

Nor is its importance diminished. At the present time in the United States, approximately 750,000 persons are incarcerated in mental hospitals —90 per cent of them against their will. This is about three times the number of persons imprisoned in jails.

The mental hospital is also important for the psychiatrist: Of 15,200 practicing psychiatrists in the United States, approximately 50 per cent are in institutional practice, most of them in mental hospitals, or in related administrative positions.

I do not imply that the hospital psychiatrist does not try to help his patient, but rather that his interpretation of "helping" is different from the patient's. If one person has the power to confine another, and uses it, it seems inevitable that the confined person will consider the other his jailer. This point of view, often held by mental patients, was expressed by Valentine Alamazov, the protagonist of Valeriy Tarsis's autobiographical novel, "Ward 7." Finding himself incarcerated in a mental hospital, Alamazov had this to say to his psychiatrist:

"I don't regard you as a doctor. You call this a hospital, I call it a prison. . . . So, now, let's get everything straight. I am your prisoner, you are my jailer, and there isn't going to be any nonsense about my health . . . or about examination and treatment."

It was Sigmund Freud who created the second major form of contemporary American psychiatric practice—psychoanalysis.

In the eighteen-eighties, when Freud was a young physician, to be a psychiatrist was to be an alienist or hospital psychiatrist. Traditionally, the psychiatrist was called in by a "mentally healthy" member of the family to treat one of its "mentally sick" members; often this meant removing the sick member from the family and putting him in a mental hospital as a "patient."

Freud departed from this traditional approach. Instead of acting as the agent of the family—ostensibly caring for the patient, but actually protecting the family from him—Freud created a new professional role—the agent of the patient.

He did not accept the situation as it was presented to him, usually by the patient's family. Instead, he listened at length to the patient to ascertain how he perceived his problem; and he tried to help him realize his own aspirations and goals, even if these brought the patient, or Freud himself, into even greater conflict with the family or with society.

Thus, ethically, Freud acted like other physicians, but unlike other psychiatrists: He tried to help his patient, not someone else. By systematically refusing to "treat" patients who did not want to be treated by him, Freud departed from the accepted psychiatric methods of his day. Many psychoanalysts still adhere to this principle in treating patients. Most hospital psychiatrists do not.

It is important to note also that Freud characterized psychoanalytic treatment in humanistic and pedagogic terms and did not regard his work as medical. Psychoanalysis was never intended to make "sick" people "well" again. The analyst's task, in Freud's words, was "to serve the patient . . . as a teacher and educator."

Freud was emphatic that the analyst—and hence also the psychotherapist who only listens and talks and uses no "medical" methods—does not cure disease. Indeed, although the three great pioneers of psychoanalysis—Freud, Adler and Jung—had little good to say about one another's doctrines and methods in later years, they all agreed on one thing: that psychological methods of therapy are *not* medical procedures.

We are now ready to reconsider the question: What is mental illness? In order to do this, it is necessary to understand the principal uses of the concept of mental illness and their social consequences.

First, the term "mental illness" is used to refer to certain types of bodily diseases—that is, to diseases of the brain whose predominant symptoms are abnormalities of behavior (for example, neurosyphilis). According to one school of psychiatric thought, all mental diseases are of this type. Those who hold this view assume that some metabolic, genetic or neurological defect—perhaps a very subtle one—will ultimately be found to explain all disorders of thinking and behavior now called "mental illness."

No one would deny that, like any other part of the body, the brain may be injured or become diseased. Nor are there, to my knowledge, any psychiatrists who would deny that some of the people nowadays diagnosed as mentally ill (and free of demonstrable organic disease) might actually be suffering from the effects of as yet undiscovered neurologic or metabolic disease processes. But for those who regard mental illness as a type of brain disease, the concept of mental illness is unnecessary and misleading. If they mean that people labeled mentally ill suffer from diseases of the brain, it would seem better for the sake of clarity to say that and not something else.

The second major use of the term "mental illness" is to denote a "functional" or "psychological" disorder. Proponents of this view admit that patients called "mentally ill" do not suffer from bodily diseases, but they maintain that such individuals exhibit defects or deformations of their personalities so severe as to justify calling them "ill."

When physicians (or others) label people as "sick" merely because their actions differ from those of their fellows, they speak metaphorically—as poets, not scientists. To be sure, this kind of metaphoric use of the term "sick" is not limited to psychiatry: People also say that our economy is "sick," that a joke is "sick" or that someone they dislike makes them "sick." Yet only in connection with mental illness do we systematically act as if figure of speech were fact. No one believes that "sick economies" require medical help, but nearly everyone believes that "sick minds" do.

The power to name, or to classify, is the basis for the third use of the term "mental illness"—that is, to denote a deviant social role. For our purposes it is necessary only to distinguish between two types of social roles: those that are assumed voluntarily, such as husband or graduate student, and those that are ascribed to a person against his will, such as draftee or convicted criminal.

Roles are social artifacts. Role deviance, therefore, has meaning only in the context of specific social customs and laws. The criminal is deviant because he breaks the law; the homosexual because most people are heterosexuals; the atheist because most people believe—or say they believe—in God. In the same way, the so-called "potential killer" (who, however, has not yet killed anyone) is considered deviant because he appears to be more dangerous than most people; and so is the chronically withdrawn mental-hospital patient, because most people are—and are expected to be—socially more responsive. (I shall say more about the problems that such persons pose for those about them, and for society in general, later on.)

But which kinds of social deviance constitute "mental illness"? The answer is: that conduct which deviates from psychiatrically defined rules of mental health.

However obvious this may be, its implications for our understanding of mental illness seem to be vastly unappreciated. The fact is that every time psychiatrists formulate a new rule of mental health they create a new class of mentally sick individuals. For example, the proposition that prejudice against Jews or Negroes is a manifestation of psycho-pathology—one of many instances in the contemporary inflation of the concept of mental illness—is nothing but an attempt to expand the category of people who can be legitimately classified as psychologically sick.

Since the consequences of being labeled mentally ill include such penalties as personal degradation, loss of employment, loss of the right to drive a car, to vote, to make valid contracts or to stand trial—and, last but not least, incarceration in a mental hospital, possibly for life—the expansion of the category of people who can be so designated is useful for the increased employment of psychiatric methods of social control.

Labeling someone mentally ill is a special kind of name-calling. In other fields name-calling may constitute libel, but calling someone "mentally sick" does not. The main reason for this is that the psychiatrist who makes a diagnosis of mental illness (especially on an involuntary patient) has more social power than the person he diagnoses.

The role of power in the psychiatric diagnostic process becomes obvious only when the potential patient is a Very Important Person. When someone like Secretary of Defense Forrestal disturbs people by his ideas and actions, it is difficult to get a psychiatrist to label him mentally ill. The reason for this is that by casting the individual in a socially deviant role the psychiatric diagnostician imparts a negative, debased identity to that person. This he cannot do if his intended "patient" is socially more powerful than he is. When a mental-hospital superintendent in Louisiana tried to incarcerate and "treat" Gov. Earl Long, the Governor fired the doctor—and walked out of the hospital.

One of the traditional problems of legal psychiatry, as we saw at the outset, is the determination of criminal insanity. Lawyers and psychiatrists persist in trying to distinguish between "sane" and "insane" criminals, and in finding a "scientific" basis for determining which offenders ought to be "punished" with imprisonment and which "treated" with involuntary mental hospitalization.

I submit that criminal insanity is a metaphorical and strategic concept just as civil insanity is. The effort to distinguish, by psychiatric methods, among different classes of criminals is really an exercise in second-order classification: Having labeled some persons as "criminals," we have the option of labeling them also as "mentally healthy," and dealing with them by means of penal sanctions, or as "mentally ill" (that is, as "criminally insane"), and dealing with them by means of psychiatric sanctions.

I do not believe that insanity should be an "excusing condition" for crime. Lawbreakers, irrespective of their "mental health," ought to be treated as offenders.

Another classic dilemma of psychiatry is the problem of what society should do with its "insane" citizens who, while having committed no crime, lack "insight" into their "illness" and hence do not seek "treatment." Here we should distinguish between two fundamentally different types of psychiatric practice. The person who decides to consult a psychiatrist and pays him for his services is like a graduate student pursuing a course of study: he assumes the role of mental patient (if we wish so to label his role) *voluntarily* and is free to cast it off. By contrast, the person who is coerced into psychiatric treatment by his relatives or by the law, and who does not pay the psychiatrist for his services, is like a prisoner sentenced to a term of servitude; he is placed in the role of mental patient *against his will* and is not free to cast it off.

The psychiatrist thus has a choice between doing something *to* his patient and doing something *for* him. One of the things the psychiatrist can do to his patient is to prescribe certain life games, with the expectation that these will pacify the patient's family and social environment—and perhaps also "help" the patient. Since this kind of treatment is carried out against the wishes of the patient, it requires coercion.

One of the things the psychiatrist can do for his patient is to analyze his life games, with the expectation that this understanding will help the client to lead a life more free and responsible. To do this, however, requires a voluntary, cooperating client. Coercion has no place whatever in this type of psychiatric work. Such a psychiatrist aspires to be on tap, not on top.

The reader who finds this thesis persuasive might wonder about its practical application. If we look upon mental illness as a metaphor and a social role, rather than as a disease, how will this affect what we *do?*

For work with voluntary clients the consequences would be mainly professional and economic: The humanistic view of mental illness would open opportunities for training nonmedical persons (psychologists, social workers and others) in psychotherapy and psychoanalysis, and would eliminate the rationale for preventing such persons from engaging in the independent practice of these skills.

For work with involuntary clients the consequences would be mainly legal and social: The humanistic view of mental illness would remove the justification for involuntary mental hospitalization and treatment; accordingly, it would require the mobilization of fresh personal efforts and social resources to cope with problems now dealt with by means of traditional psychiatric methods.

It would be impossible suddenly to empty out our mental hospitals and to stop all commitments—though, to be sure, I consider these desirable goals. To attain them, however, we must provide suitable alternatives to the present social functions of involuntary mental hospitalization. I must limit myself here to mentioning only a few such alternatives, each directed toward ameliorating a specific type of human problem.

The usual justification for commitment is that the person whose confinement is sought is "dangerous to himself or others." My position is based on a principle enunciated more than 100 years ago by John Stuart Mill: "The only purpose for which power can be rightfully exercised over any member of a civilized community, against his will, is to prevent harm to others. His own good, either physical or moral, is not sufficient warranty."

Suicide, for example, should be recognized as a basic human right. The threat of suicide, or an attempt at suicide, should not be ground for involuntary mental hospitalization. (This does not mean that a physician should not treat a person who, say, is unconscious as a result of an overdose of barbiturates. It does mean that, after the patient has regained consciousness, he should not be confined in a hospital against his will.)

While being "dangerous to oneself" should never be considered a legitimate reason for depriving a person of his liberty, being "dangerous to others" —if it involves breaking the law—is the best reason for doing so. One of the main functions of society is to prevent violence among its members. Thus, if individuals commit violence, or threaten to do so, they should be treated for what they are—law-breakers.

Judicial sentencing of lawbreakers does not deprive us of the opportunity of also trying to help them. If we truly believe that some lawbreakers are "mentally ill," we could offer them psychiatric help in prison. As always, the clients ought to be free to accept or reject such help.

The social control, by means of psychiatric sanctions, of dangerous behavior is complicated by the fact that people often disagree on what constitutes "dangerousness," and, even if they agree on it, on how such "dangerousness" is to be established. Thus, one group of persons now often committed is composed of individuals who manage their lives more or less adequately, but who break certain laws or social customs, and are therefore considered "dangerous" and treated as involuntary patients.

If we wish to avoid using coercive psychiatric measures against persons of this type, we have two basic options. Instead of constantly proliferating legislation prohibiting various kinds of personal conduct not directly injurious to others (as we now do), we might consider repealing and eschewing such legislation. We would thereby eliminate many types of "crime," and hence the need to define such criminals (as "dope addicts," "homosexuals" and so forth) as mentally sick. Or, if we wish to persist in our efforts to control private behavior by means of criminal sanctions, we might decide that it is more humane to punish persons who transgress these prohibitions by means of penal rather than psychiatric sanctions; the result would be the jailing of many individuals now committed to mental hospitals. (The desirability of confining lawbreakers in mental hospitals rather than in prisons is sometimes advocated on the allegedly humanitarian ground that conditions in mental hospitals are better than in jails. Even if this were true—and as a rule it is not—it would not justify redefining lawbreakers as patients. The proper remedy for inadequate prisons is prison reform.)

In addition to persons whose dangerousness is actual, established by what they have done, there are those whose dangerousness is potential, who are feared for what they might do. We often hear of "potential troublemakers" who, however, have broken no laws, and hence could not be convicted of crime, but whom many would like to "diagnose" as "deranged" and restrain in mental hospitals.

We cannot eat our cake and have it, too: we cannot have a free society and imprison—in jails or mental hospitals—people who have broken no law. This does not mean that some people might not be "potentially" dangerous to others (indeed, many, like drunken drivers, are very dangerous); it means only that we cannot restrain such people through our mental-hygiene laws without gravely injuring the entire fabric of our society.

Another large group of persons confined involuntarily in mental hospitals is the aged; in some public mental hospitals as many as one-third of the inmates fall into this group. Yet, even hospital psychiatrists admit that many of these patients do not need mental-hospital care. "Only 50 per cent of the [elderly] patients . . . hospitalized required hospitalization in a mental institution," testified Dr. Dale C. Cameron, superintendent of St. Elizabeth's Hospital in Washington, before a House committee. "For many older patients," he added, "the primary need was found to be for physical rather than psychiatric care."

The fact that public mental hospitals accept geriatric patients—whose "mental illness" is so clearly a strategic concept designed to justify their forcible removal to places of custody—diminishes the pressure on society to provide suitable accommodations for them.

Still another group of involuntarily hospitalized patients is composed of individuals who present so-called psychiatric emergencies. Examples are the young man who becomes uncommunicative, does not leave his room, refuses to eat, perhaps even soils himself; or the young woman who faints and thereafter remains unresponsive and acts as if she were unconscious.

Patients of this type do not object to being hospitalized or to receiving medical care. Moreover, some of them suffer from bodily illness—brain tumor, head injury, uncontrolled diabetes. Others develop medical problems as a result of their behavior—severe dehydration because of failure to eat and drink, for example. Such patients should therefore be hospitalized in medical, not mental, hospitals, and should be treated as medical emergencies. Consent for hospitalization and treatment should be given by relatives, and confinement should last only until the patient has regained his powers.

The application of these principles to the care of chronic mental patients would help us to avoid coercion in their care as well. Regardless of the cause—subtle malfunctions of the brain, the effect of prolonged institutionalization or flight from communal existence into a world of private dreams—people who are almost completely unable to cope with their problems of living will no doubt always be with us. Such "nondangerous" but gravely disabled individuals could be dealt with by offering them care—good and attractive enough so that they would willingly accept it—while leaving them free to make other choices.

In short, the abolition of involuntary mental hospitalization and treatment would mean that psychiatric help, like medical, would (on the whole) have to be restricted to voluntary clients. Furthermore, some persons who are now cast in the role of involuntary mental patients would, if they broke laws, have to be dealt with as offenders, not as patients.

The nominal aim of psychiatry is the study and treatment of mental disorders. The consequences of subscribing to this apparently harmless, conventional definition of "mental health" work are, in our present age, momentous. Accepting the existence of a class of phenomena called "mental diseases," rather than inquiring into the conditions under which some persons may designate others as "mentally ill," has been the decisive step in embracing what I call the mental-health ethic. In so doing, the study of a large part of human behavior is subtly transferred from ethics to psychiatry, from the free marketplace of ideas to the closed wards of the mental hospital.

The psychiatrist deals with moral and social problems, not with medical diseases. Hence he cannot help being embroiled in the moral conflicts of his patient and of his society. The psychiatrist's role as moral legislator and social engineer is obscured, however, by the rhetoric of mental health and illness which makes his work appear as a species of medical therapy. This evasion of ethical judgments and choices may be reassuring to the laity and comforting to the profession. But can we, as individuals, afford it?

The individual can never escape the moral burden of his existence. He must choose between obedience to authority and responsibility to himself. Moral decisions are often hard and painful to make. The temptation to delegate this burden to others is therefore ever-present. Yet, as all history teaches us, those who would take from man his moral burdens—be they priests or warlords, politicians or psychiatrists—must also take from him his liberty and hence his very humanity.

A humanistic psychiatry must, therefore, repudiate its seemingly therapeutic mandate, the pursuit of which often results, intentionally or unwittingly, in moral tranquility gained at the expense of freedom and responsibility. Instead of trying to diminish man's moral burdens, such a psychiatry must aim at increasing his powers and so making him equal to his task.

And what is this task? No one has stated it better than Albert Camus when he wrote: "The aim of life can only be to increase the sum of freedom and responsibility to be found in every man and in the world. It cannot, under any circumstances, be to reduce or suppress that freedom, even temporarily."

---

34 | Psychiatrists Use Dangerous Words

Karl Menninger, M.D.

Every profession has its own jargon, and we psychiatrists have ours. But while the strange terms a lawyer or an archaeologist uses are harmless enough—the worst they do is mystify outsiders—the terms psychiatrists use can hurt people and sometimes do. Instead of helping to comfort and counsel and heal people—which is the goal of psychiatry—the terms often cause despair.

Words like "schizophrenia" and "manic-depressive" and "psychotic," for example, frighten patients and worry their anxious relatives and friends. The use of these alarming terms also affects us psychiatrists. They lead us back into the pessimism and helplessness of the days when mental illness was thought to be made up of many specific "diseases," and when each "disease" bore a formidable label and a gloomy prognosis.

Mental illness is not simple, but neither is it esoteric, weird and unhuman. We all know what it is from our own experience. We've all "had it"; we've all suffered from spells of mental illness of varying intensity and duration.

Occasionally they strike hard or last long. They may impel us to make serious mistakes and even do dreadful things. More often they only confuse or paralyze or frighten us; we become a bit demoralized. We fight against it and do the best we can. What we need from the outside world during our struggle is help. Not a "label" but *help*.

Psychiatrists are sometimes called "talking doctors," as opposed to "pill-prescribing doctors" and "baby-delivering doctors." In treating a patient we rely heavily upon his reactions to what we *say* to him. There is more to psychiatric treatment than talking, of course, but talking is a considerable part of it, and the psychiatrist's language must be carefully chosen. Nuances and implications that would be of no consequence in a discussion of surgical

---

From *Saturday Evening Post,* April 25, 1964. Reprinted by permission of the author.

procedures may be of critical importance in dealing with a case of mental illness. A single wrong word might ruin a recovery.

Every psychiatrist has had patients come to him with stories something like this: "I got upset and went to see a psychiatrist. He talked with me a couple of times and I felt better. But he told my parents that I had schizophrenia. And after that they seemed to think there was no use trying. I was in the hospital for a while, and now again I'm worried and depressed. Is this what you call 'schizophrenia'? Do I have it? Am I hopeless? Isn't suicide my only way out?"

In such a case—and there are many of them—the label applied to the illness becomes almost as damaging as the illness itself. The patient learns that he has "schizophrenic tendencies" (or "incipient schizophrenia," or some such malady) and assumes, with everyone else, that he has an incurable mental disease, one that will probably grow continually worse.

A label can blight the life of a person even after his recovery from mental illness. A young doctor I knew suffered for a time from some anxiety and indecision. He consulted a psychiatrist and soon recovered. Unfortunately, a "tentative" diagnosis of schizophrenia got abroad—I don't know how—and the young doctor's professional career was seriously impaired. He was injured, not by mental illness but by a word.

Certainly there are behavior patterns which can be described as schizophrenic, provided one defines the adjective. But schizophrenia is no more a clear-cut disease than "the falling sickness" or "biliousness" or "chronic endogenous indurative myelomalacia." I don't know what these names mean, but I don't know what schizophrenia really means either, because it means widely different things to different people and in different countries. The same can be said of terms like "neurotic," "extroversion," "catalepsy," "psychopathic" and many others.

Science in general and psychiatry in particular have come a long way since these words were coined. They no longer mean what they once did. "Dementia" and "demented," for example, used to mean literally the loss of one's mind, and "dementia praecox" was a supposed disease in which this "loss of mind" occurred precociously—that is, in young people, as compared with "dementia senilis," which occurred in old people. But gradually we came to realize that people didn't "lose" their minds, and that this was a misleading figure of speech. So another figure of speech was coined: splitting of the mind. And dementia praecox began to be called schizophrenia. It developed the same bad reputation, however, and the barest hint that someone was afflicted with this dreadful condition was enough to throw his loved ones into frantic despair, even though, as we now know, the collective symptoms called schizophrenia usually disappear.

I avoid using words like schizophrenia just as I avoid using words like "wop" and "nigger." I know what people mean by these names, but I dispute their specificity; they chiefly denote an attitude of the speaker toward skin color or foreign birth, and their use can do great harm.

I must frankly admit that many of my colleagues disagree with me. The American Psychiatric Association, in its official classification, lists only "schizophrenic reactions," but while some of us understand this to refer to one familiar pattern of behavior shown by an individual over a period of time, many others consider this a specific, well-defined *disease,* not a reaction or a pattern.

Those of us who use the outmoded terminology do so partly out of habit; it's easy to lapse into the established jargon. But it really comes down to one's attitude, or rather his conception of the nature of mental illness. I do not agree with certain writers that there is no mental illness. I would say rather that there is a great deal of mental illness. I agree with the American Medical Association and with the Joint Commission on Mental Illness and Health that mental illness is our No. 1 health problem. I do not think we help that problem by calling it a myth. But neither do I think we help it by persisting in obsolete terminology. Not only do these terms panic the patient but they discourage the doctor and permit him to justify a program of indifference and neglect.

In *The Vital Balance,* a book I wrote in collaboration with Drs. Martin Mayman and Paul Pruyser, we suggest that mental illness is not a "thing"—like a specimen in a museum—for which a label must be found. It is rather a state of functioning, a way of behaving. An individual having unusual difficulties in coping with his environment struggles and kicks up the dust, as it were. I once used the figure of a fish caught on a hook; his gyrations must look peculiar to other fishes that don't understand the circumstances. His splashings are not a *disease;* they are not the affliction. They are his efforts to get rid of the affliction. And as every fisherman knows, these efforts may succeed. To concentrate on patterns of splashing is an old-fashioned emphasis in psychiatry that is rapidly passing, although some still hold to it.

"What would you substitute?" I am sometimes asked. "What do you want to call these people—or these conditions?" Such questioners obviously have not caught my point. I wouldn't call them anything. I want us to emerge from the name-calling stage. Psychiatry should repudiate it. Some angry people don't call their opponents liars or skunks any more; they call them psychiatric names like "psychotics" or "psychopaths." Why? Because these technical words have become pejorative. They no longer mean merely psychiatric illness; they mean something despised.

These damning words were a great handicap to my brother William in World War II when, as assistant to the surgeon-general of the Army, he undertook to reduce the enormous manpower losses from mental illness. He found that many good soldiers were discharged after being labeled with old-fashioned designations implying incurable mental illness and personality disorder. With the aid of many colleagues over the country, Doctor Will radically revised and improved the Army classification of mental illness. (His revision was later adopted, in essence, by the U.S. Navy, the Veterans Administration and the American Psychiatric Association.)

"But," my questioner may continue, "if you are not going to call these conditions anything, how are you going to refer to them?" I think the answer is quite simple: How does the patient himself refer to his problem? "Oh, he says he is upset, he says he is nervous, and feels as if he were going to pieces. But these are lay terms; they are not scientific."

True, these are subjective expressions. They seem to be figures of speech. However, many psychiatric terms are figures of speech. Can a mind be split like a log of wood as the term schizophrenia implies? Actually the expressions coming from everyday life are often more accurate than the technical words and don't have the same dreadful or false implications. Some of them, like "going to pieces," imply those essential qualities of integration and steadiness which are the basis of our concept of the "vital balance." Things may happen today that so increase my tension that I feel as though I might explode. This tension is released in various ways—a game of cards, a concert or just a good night's rest. If these outlets don't restore the vital balance—if I can't listen to music, if I can't sleep—the threat of disintegration may increase, and I will feel worse and try harder to recover my equilibrium. I may even ask for help.

Any particular instance of such imminent "going to pieces" can be described scientifically—quantitatively and then qualitatively. We can say that a certain patient who has asked to be examined is indeed partially disorganized. This disorganization can be identified by anyone who has had experience in such things as being of severe degree, or moderately severe, or only slight.

But the most important thing the psychiatrist will try to do is to identify the factors in the environment and in the patient which combine to produce this picture of disturbance and distress. Where is the fishhook? Where does the shoe pinch? Where are the weak spots? And what are the forces bearing so heavily upon this individual as to get him out of line? This is psychiatric diagnosis in a new key—it includes prescriptions for treatment and it expects recovery. It may sound deceptively simple, but I prefer it to labels and concepts which sound deceptively complex.

To illustrate, let me cite the case of Helen D., the daughter of superior and ambitious parents. Even after careful study I do not know of anything they "did wrong." They were, like most parents, merely earnest, often puzzled, not perfect but trying hard. And Helen did well during her growing years. She was pretty and popular, studious and athletic. All was very promising, with a few minor, very human exceptions, until her senior year at college. Her letters home began to be irregular and infrequent. On the telephone she sounded preoccupied. She wrote her older brother that neither he nor their parents were aware of "the danger we are all in." She asked him why he did not love his country enough to join the John Birch Society or the Peace Corps. She missed classes; her grades declined. Her counselor referred her to the college psychiatrist who . . .

I stop in the middle of a sentence purposely. What do you want to read? What do you hope he did? Of course he recognized that she was confused and frightened and depressed and "morbidly preoccupied." Of course he prescribed temporary interruption of her schooling and intensive treatment.

But what did he tell her parents was "the matter" with her? Did he say she was afflicted with a "psychosis"? Did he call her affliction malignant and probably progressive? Did he diagnose it "manic-depressive" or "borderline"? Or did he describe it as a moderately severe personality disorganization related to certain excessive stresses, with such-and-such features amenable to treatment?

Fortunately he did the latter. Treatment was promptly instituted and she reentered college the following fall to graduate with honors a year later.

BRANDED AS INSANE

But suppose she had been officially labeled. Would her treatment have been so vigorously and expectantly pushed? More likely the parents and the college authorities would have reconciled themselves to the probability that this girl would never return to college. And even if she had been able to return, the college would probably have been reluctant to readmit her. And if she had been readmitted, it would have taken extraordinary courage for her to face her comrades as a "schizophrenic."

Contrast this with those who were not labeled and who this very minute can bravely say to their friends, "I had a severe spell of illness; I was quite depressed, but I got it straightened out. I'm fine now, and I think I learned a great deal from the whole experience."

To sum up, I think many words psychiatrists use are dangerous. They misrepresent mental illness and permit the public and even psychiatrists to entertain a pessimistic view of mental illness.

The widespread pessimism about mental illness may explain why so little is done about it. How shocking it is that for all the emphasis given the subject—by the late President Kennedy, for example, and by the A.M.A.—only about one fifth of the state hospitals for the mentally ill give patients any treatment.

In the past 10 years my brother, Doctor Will, has spoken earnestly to the legislatures of many states. What has he told them? Simply that mental illness is our No. 1 health problem; that the mentally ill can be helped and most of them cured; that it is more humane and less expensive to treat them scientifically than to confine them despairingly.

Why is this so hard for the public to believe? Why is the public so willing to retain its pessimism and cling to the ancient superstition that mental illness is incurable? For the mentally ill *can* be saved, most of them. They can be cured, but they need help. Their symptoms are a cry for help. We cannot plead ignorance to excuse our neglect, for we know what to do. It is not our helplessness that has deterred us so long but our hopelessness—and perhaps, in part, our dreadful vocabulary.

---

35 | The Defense of Insanity: A Survey of Legal and Psychiatric Opinion

Rita James Simon and Wendell Shackelford

This comparative and systematic survey of the opinions of lawyers and psychiatrists on thirteen searching questions relating to criminal cases involving the defense of insanity was started a few days after the Jack Ruby trial following President Kennedy's assassination. What qualifications should psychiatrists have to serve as ex-

From *The Public Opinion Quarterly*, **29**, 3, 411–424, 1965. Reprinted by permission.

pert witnesses? What effect does their testimony have on juries? Who should render the final verdict in an insanity trial? Was the decision that Ruby was sane a sound one? The answers to these and other questions are in many cases surprising.

Rita James Simon is associated with the Institute of Communications Research and the Sociology Department of the University of Illinois, and Wendell Shackelford is with the Annenberg School of Communications at the University of Pennsylvania.

The assassination of John F. Kennedy touched off a series of political and social consequences, one of which bears direct relationship to this paper. Jack Ruby, having committed murder before millions of television witnesses as he shot Lee Oswald, entered a plea of not guilty by reason of insanity. This act served as a dramatic reminder not only to the legal profession but also to the general public of one of the most disputed issues in legal history—the question of legal *responsibility* for a crime.

Our legal system traditionally has admitted the possibility of various defenses against punishment for committing a crime. One relatively uncontroversial example is the plea of self-defense. Just as we have generally accepted the idea that a person who has killed in order not to be killed should not be held responsible, we also have held that a person who is mentally ill or mentally defective is not punishable. One of the elements which must be proved in order to establish criminal guilt is *mens rea,* the willful *intention* to commit the crime, the active choice, and the "guilty mind" where the crime is concerned. It is *mens rea* which is challenged by the defense of insanity.

The decision as to the defendant's responsibility or lack of it rests with a jury. If the jury believes the defendant was responsible for his behavior at the time he committed the acts, it will find him guilty. If it believes he was not, it will acquit him on grounds of insanity.

Many people, among them judges, lawyers, psychiatrists, question the jury's ability to solve so complex and technical a problem as the determination of a defendant's mental state at the time he commits an unlawful act. Critics of the jury system argue that such decisions can be more intelligently made by a body of legal or medical experts or both.

Closely related to the issue of "who decides" is the problem of what should be done with a defendant if he is found not guilty by reason of insanity. Some jurisdictions have an automatic commitment procedure; others require a separate hearing before a judge, or a jury, or a group of medical experts. As a result of the hearing the defendant can be released or placed on "psychiatric probation," among other alternatives.

If the defendant is committed to a mental hospital, the problem does not end there. The length of the defendant's stay in the institution and the criteria for determining his release are frequently areas of controversy. In some states, the decision rests completely in the hands of the staff physicians. In other states, responsibility is shared between medical experts and the court. In still other states, a formal hearing is conducted and the decision is made by the judge.

What standards should govern the defendant's release? Some argue that the defendant should remain institutionalized until he is cured. Others believe this standard is too rigorous and urge that the criterion be whether the defendant is no longer dangerous to himself and to others.

Each of these problems—the appropriate criteria for criminal responsibility, commitment, and release, and who should determine responsibility, commitment, and release—are important practical issues about which most trial lawyers and psychiatrists are expected to have opinions.

PURPOSE OF STUDY

This study was designed to poll the opinions of lawyers and psychiatrists on topics about which they are believed to disagree, but where they must interact either as a team or as members of opposing teams. Specifically, it measures the amount of agreement and disagreement between the two professions on the following topics: the role of the psychiatrist as an expert witness in criminal cases involving a defense of insanity; the relationship between mental illness and criminality, with special emphasis on the defense of insanity; the Ruby trial.

We say that lawyers and psychiatrists are *believed* to disagree on these matters. But we know relatively little about the extent of the disagreement, the specific topics on which disagreement is sharpest, or the topics on which opinions may converge. We recommend that the psychiatrists' and lawyers' responses to this study serve as indicators of their desire for changes in public policy and courtroom procedure, or as indicators of their support for existing procedure.

SOURCES OF DATA

Respondents were obtained from two sources: psychiatrists from the *Biographical Directory of the American Psychiatric Association,* and lawyers from the Martindale and Hubbel directory of lawyers. The psychiatrists were selected by choosing every fourth listing in the American Psychiatric Association Directory in seven cities across the country: Baltimore, Chicago, Cleveland, Dallas, Denver, Fort Worth, and San Francisco. For each city, the number of lawyers was made to equal the number of psychiatrists by selecting every "n^{th}" name from Martindale and Hubbel. The sample consisted of 251 psychiatrists and 251 lawyers.

Each respondent was sent a twenty-item multiple-choice questionnaire with a letter explaining the purpose of the study and requesting cooperation. A stamped, self-addressed return envelope was provided. The rate of return was better among psychiatrists than it was among lawyers. One hundred thirty-nine (55 percent) of the psychiatrists returned their questionnaires, compared with 79 (31 percent) of the lawyers. Considering that no follow-ups were made, the rate of return was good for a mail survey.

PROFILE OF THE RESPONDENTS

Forty-six percent of the lawyers were partners in firms that range from two to more than fifteen people; 34 percent were in small firms that had between two and five people. Thirty-two percent were solo practitioners, and the remaining 22 percent worked for local, state, or Federal agencies. The lawyers were distributed almost evenly across four age categories, ranging from twenty-five years to over fifty-five. Only 35 percent had any experience with criminal cases involving a defense of insanity (almost all as defense attorneys) and 49 percent with civil cases involving an insanity issue.

Half the psychiatrists were in private practice exclusively, 30 percent combined teaching and private practice, and the remaining 20 percent were attached to private, veteran, or state hospitals. Fifty-two percent were between thirty-five and forty-five years old, 22 percent were between forty-five and fifty-five, and the rest were divided evenly between the youngest (twenty-five to thirty-five) and the oldest (over fifty-five) categories. Fifty percent had more than fifteen years of experience; 49 percent had appeared as witnesses in criminal trials involving a plea of insanity (mostly for the defense); and 43 percent had appeared in civil actions.

THE FINDINGS

The Psychiatrist as an Expert Witness

The procedure commonly used today in criminal cases involving the defense of insanity is for the defense to call one or more experts to testify as to the mental state of the defendant at the time of the crime. The state may or may not summon experts of its own. The practice of the courts has been to permit almost any person holding a medical degree to testify on any specialty, psychiatric or otherwise, in the field of medicine. When we asked lawyers and psychiatrists for their opinions concerning the qualifications of an expert psychiatric witness, we found that the majority opinion in both groups opposed the existing practice (question 1).

	Percent of	
	Psychiatrists	Lawyers
1. A psychiatric expert witness should be at least:		
a. A Ph.D. holder in clinical psychology	4.3	20.3
b. A medical doctor		13.9
c. A psychiatrist	77.0	44.5
d. A psychiatrist specializing in legal problems	18.0	17.7
e. No answer	.7	3.6

Ninety-five percent of the psychiatrists believe that only psychiatrists should qualify as expert witnesses, and 18 percent would restrict the qualifications to psychiatrists who specialize in legal problems. The 62 percent of lawyers who believe that only psychiatrists should qualify is considerably less than the 95 percent reported for psychiatrists,* but the significant finding is that 62 percent oppose and only 34 percent favor the prevailing practice of the courts. Thus most lawyers and psychiatrists recommend the adoption of more stringent qualifications than those presently applied.

* Lawyers v. psychiatrists favor psychiatrists: χ^2_{ldf} (.95) $= 3.8$; $\chi^2 = 36.2$ $p < .001$.

Another assumed point of disagreement centers around the adversary system now in use in our courts. Most psychiatrists are believed to be strongly opposed to it, claiming that it produces such tension between their usual role expectations and those expected of them in court that they seek to avoid all courtroom appearances. Most lawyers are believed to be strongly in favor of the adversary system, profoundly distrusting anything that cannot be exposed to adverse scrutiny. The lawyer is fearful that the psychiatrist's orientation, his view of human nature, and his beliefs concerning the origins of conforming behavior in contrast to deviant or criminal behavior will be so far removed from the legal orientation that his opinion would have no relevance for the trial. Lawyers also fear that, unless the function of the expert is carefully delineated, the combined effects of the latter's general prestige and his detailed technical knowledge can virtually dictate to the jury the outcome of the case. They want to have the expert available, but as a witness whose credibility is subjected to the usual scrutiny of the jury. Our findings confirm this difference of opinion and show that it is a powerful one (see question 2.)

	Percent of	
	Psychiatrists	Lawyers
2. *I prefer the following system of calling experts:*		
a. Only the defense should be allowed to call them		5.0
b. Both defense and prosecution should be allowed to call them	30.9	72.2
c. Both attorneys should agree on which experts are called	10.8	7.6
d. Only the court should be allowed to call experts	56.8	12.6
e. No answer	1.5	2.6

Two-thirds of the psychiatrists favor doing away with the adversary system and replacing it with a system where the court appoints the experts or the two attorneys agree on which experts will testify, presumably as impartial investigators.* Over three-quarters of the lawyers support their great invention, the adversary system.† When lawyers' and psychiatrists' responses were divided on the basis of prior experience with criminal cases involving the defense of insanity, lawyers with experience were more likely to endorse the adversary system than lawyers with no experience (85 to 73 percent), and psychiatrists with experience were more likely to endorse the court-appointed system than psychiatrists with no experience (63 to 54 percent). We see that on this matter the impressionistic accounts reflect accurately a true cleavage

* Lawyers v. psychiatrists favor nonpartisan experts: χ^2_{1df} $(.95) = 3.8$; $\chi^2 = 48.92$ $p < .001$.

† Baltimore is the only city in our study in which the adversary system has been replaced by court-appointed experts. We examined the responses of lawyers and psychiatrists from that city separately and found that the distribution was roughly the same as for the entire sample.

of opinion between the two professions. The lawyers favor the existing procedure; the psychiatrists recommend change.

Certain members of both professions have deplored the quality of psychiatric testimony that is obtained under the adversary system. Both Dr. Guttmacher and Judge Niles believed that the present system attracts the least able members of the profession and alienates psychiatrists who enjoy the highest prestige among their colleagues.* The responses to question 3 show that only a minority of the lawyers and psychiatrists in this study share Judge Niles's and Dr. Guttmacher's views.

	Percent of	
	Psychiatrists	Lawyers
3. Psychiatrists who most often act as expert witness generally have the following status within their profession:		
a. They tend to be held in low esteem	20.9	15.2
b. They are in neither the lowest nor the highest status group	26.6	32.9
c. They tend to be the most esteemed	2.9	1.2
d. Participation in court cases and professional status are unrelated	48.2	39.2
e. No answer	1.4	11.5

Over 70 percent of both lawyers and psychiatrists believe that professional status and courtroom activity are unrelated, or that persons who perform as expert witnesses are found in neither the highest nor the lowest statuses. We note, however, that 21 percent of the psychiatrists and 15 percent of the lawyers believe that psychiatrists who tend to make a career of appearing as expert witnesses are held in low esteem. By contrast, only 3 percent of the psychiatrists and 1 percent of the lawyers believe these experts enjoy the highest prestige.

A crucial issue in the defense of insanity trial is how the jury reacts to the expert's testimony. Do the jurors understand the testimony? Are they persuaded by it? Or do they ignore and reject it? The popular impression is that lawyers are fearful, on the one hand, that the jury will be overwhelmed by the expert's knowledge and prestige and will follow him blindly, and, on the other, that the jury will be so confused by the expert's erudition that it will ignore his testimony completely.

The typical procedure in trials involving expert testimony, psychiatric or otherwise, is for the judge to instruct the jury along these lines:

> You are not bound as jurors to accept the testimony of expert witnesses. You should certainly consider carefully the qualifications of the witnesses, their experiences. . . . You are to give to their testimony as experts such weight as in your judgment it is fairly entitled to receive. . . .

---

* Manfred Guttmacher, *The Mind of the Murderer,* New York, Farrar, Strauss, and Cudahy, 1959, p. 119; Emory H. Niles, "Impartial Medical Testimony," address before Section of Judicial Administration, American Bar Association, 1956, published in *Illinois Bar Journal,* Vol. 45, 1957, p. 282.

We asked the lawyers and psychiatrists the following question:

	Percent of Psychiatrists	Percent of Lawyers
4. *Which best describes the usual effect of psychiatric testimony on a jury?*		
a. Jurors are so impressed that they conform their verdicts to the expert's opinion	4.3	3.7
b. Jurors listen carefully to the expert but base their verdicts on all factors in the case	37.7	54.6
c. Jurors ignore expert testimony because they don't understand it	17.2	13.9
d. Jurors treat psychiatric testimony like any other testimony	30.0	21.5
e. No answer	10.8	6.3

Most lawyers and psychiatrists believe the jury follows the court's instructions. Fewer than 5 percent in each group believe that the jury becomes a rubber stamp to the expert and less than 20 percent believe that the jury ignores expert testimony. The great majority believe that the jury listens carefully to the expert and gives as much weight to his testimony as it believes it deserves.

The Defense of Insanity

We stated earlier that the lawyer is anxious to expose the psychiatrist's testimony to the adversary system because he is fearful that the psychiatrist's orientation, his view of human nature, and his beliefs about the origins of criminal behavior will differ radically from the legal orientation. The popular impression is that psychiatrists believe that all or most criminals are emotionally disturbed. But the responses to question 5 demonstrate that psychiatrists' opinions are far from unanimous on this matter.

	Percent of Psychiatrists	Percent of Lawyers
5. *Which best states the relationship between serious criminal activity and mental illness?*		
a. Anyone who commits a serious crime is mentally ill	8.0	3.7
b. Most people who commit serious crimes are mentally ill	41.8	29.2
c. Most people who commit serious crimes are *not* mentally ill	25.1	20.3
d. There is no relationship between mental illness and serious crime	15.1	34.2
e. No answer	10.0	12.6

Half the psychiatrists and a third of the lawyers believe that most or all people who commit serious crimes are mentally ill. These figures are surprising on two counts: the 50 percent figure for psychiatrists is lower and the 33 percent figure for lawyers is higher than expected. Lawyers and psychiatrists do not differ on this matter nearly so much as writers have warned.

Two other comparisons are worth making. A greater percentage of lawyers than psychiatrists believe there is no relationship between mental illness and serious crime; and respondents in both groups are unhappy with the choice of alternatives that the question provided. This is shown by the high proportion of "no answers" among both lawyers and psychiatrists.

In recent years the system of trial by jury has been the subject of considerable controversy and criticism. In the last three decades, the jury has been used less and less frequently. In England, jury trials have been virtually abandoned for civil actions and are used primarily in major criminal cases.

At the core of the criticism is the belief that the jury does not determine its verdict on the basis of the evidence and that the members of the jury do not have the special skills and training needed to make a rational decision about the kinds of disputes with which they are confronted. Many critics of the jury urge its replacement by a body of men selected on the basis of their expert knowledge of the particular issues raised by a given case, or by a bench trial in which the judge would be free to seek the advice and guidance of experts.

The substitute for trial by jury most frequently offered in trials that involve a defense of insanity is decision by a body of experts—medical, legal, or both. When the lawyers and psychiatrists were asked in question 6 who should make the final decision, the jury failed to receive majority support from either group, although they fared somewhat better among the lawyers.* Prior experience had no effect on preferences among either lawyers or psychiatrists. Both groups, the psychiatrists more strongly than the lawyers, favored decision by medical and legal experts over decision by the jury.

	Percent of Psychiatrists	Percent of Lawyers
6. The final verdict in a plea of insanity trial should rest with:		
a. A jury of laymen	27.3	39.2
b. A group of medical experts	12.2	11.3
c. A judge	5.0	7.6
d. A combined group of medical and legal experts	53.2	38.0
e. No answer	2.3	3.9

When we compared the responses of lawyers and psychiatrists to questions 4 (effect of psychiatric testimony on the jury) and 6 (decision as to final verdict), we found that respondents in both groups who believe that jurors listen carefully to the expert's testimony are much more likely to favor decision by a jury than are respondents who select other alternatives to

* Lawyers v. psychiatrists favor trial by jury: χ^2_{ldf} (.95) = 3.8; $\chi^2 = 2.8$ $p < .10$.

question 4 (58 compared with 29 percent among psychiatrists and 65 compared with 49 percent among lawyers).

Psychiatrists who believe that there is a relationship between mental illness and criminal behavior are less likely to favor decision by jury than are psychiatrists who see no relationship or who believe that most persons who commit serious crimes are not mentally ill (22 percent compared with 36 percent). Among the lawyers, there is no relation between responses on the two items.

In almost all jurisdictions, if a defendant is found not guilty by reason of insanity, he is committed to a mental institution. The commitment procedure, however, is not uniform. In some states it is automatic; in others, a separate hearing is held in front of a judge, a jury, or a group of medical experts.

In the figures in response to question 7 we note that there is relatively little disagreement between lawyers and psychiatrists as to which is the best system. Fifty-five percent of the psychiatrists in contrast to 42 percent of the lawyers believe that the decision concerning commitment should be made by medical experts.* Most of the lawyers favor automatic commitment or leaving the decision in the hands of a lay body.†

	Percent of Psychiatrists	Percent of Lawyers
7. *I think the following is the most sensible system regarding institutional commitment when the defendant is acquitted on grounds of insanity:*		
a. Commitment should be automatic in every case	23.7	29.1
b. Commitment should be at the discretion of the person or groups rendering the verdict	10.8	7.6
c. A separate hearing before a jury should be held to determine the question of commitment	6.5	17.6
d. Medical experts should determine	55.4	41.8
e. No answer	3.5	3.9

We found that both lawyers and psychiatrists who wish to see the jury retain power of decision in the original trial (question 6) are more likely to favor automatic commitment or a hearing before a jury than they are decision by medical experts—among psychiatrists, 63 compared with 41 percent, and among lawyers, 71 compared with 40 percent.

Two related problems that are frequently raised in connection with commitment procedures are (1) the criteria that should govern the defendant's commitment and (2) the length of his commitment. We dealt with the first problem in question 8. Half of the lawyers and 62 percent of the psychiatrists believe that the current mental state of the defendant should be

*Lawyers v. psychiatrists favor decision by medical experts: χ^2_{1df} $(.95) = 3.8$; $\chi^2 = 3.2$ $p < .10$.

† In almost all instances, alternatives a, b, and c would involve decision by a jury.

the most important criterion in determining his commitment. Respondents in both groups offer little support to the "dangerous in the past" criterion or to the "punishment for the sake of justice" standard.

	Percent of Psychiatrists	Percent of Lawyers
8. *The following is the* most important *criterion to be considered in deciding whether the defendant is to be committed:*		
a. He needs restraint because he is now dangerous to himself and others	26.6	27.8
b. He has been dangerous and needs to be deterred from becoming so again	9.3	16.4
c. Justice requires some form of penalty		2.5
d. He is mentally ill and in need of treatment	62.0	50.7
e. No answer	2.1	2.5

Question 9 compares the lawyers' and psychiatrists' reactions to the problem of release. Over three-quarters of the respondents in both groups agree that medical men rather than the court should make the decision about the defendant's release from a mental hospital. But lawyers and psychiatrists disagree about the standard that should be employed. Psychiatrists are more likely to favor the more realistic criterion of "no longer dangerous," while lawyers are more likely to recommend the more rigorous standard of "cure."* We are surprised that as many as 21 percent of the psychiatrists selected that alternative, because psychiatrists traditionally are extremely reluctant to describe a patient as cured.

	Percent of Psychiatrists	Percent of Lawyers
9. *A defendant who has been committed should be released from the hospital when:*		
a. He has stayed for a predetermined period of time		1.3
b. In the judgment of the *court,* he is no longer dangerous	15.8	20.3
c. In the judgment of *doctors* at the hospital, he is no longer dangerous	61.1	40.5
d. In the judgment of doctors, he is cured	20.9	35.4
e. No answer	2.2	2.5

In the responses to each of the items in this section, the lawyers were more willing to delegate responsibility and power of decision to medical experts than our review of the literature would have led us to expect. On specific issues the lawyers seem to have more faith in the psychiatrists' expertise than either the psychiatrists or the lawyers who write on these problems believe.

---

* Lawyers v. psychiatrists favor "cured" standard: χ^2_{1df} $(.95) = 3.8$; $\chi^2 = 4.8$ $p < .05$.

The Ruby Trial

The trial of Jack Ruby was the most dramatic courtroom event of the last thirty years. We started our research only a couple of days after the verdict in the Ruby trial was announced. The fact that the defendant entered a defense of insanity made it particularly convenient and pertinent for us to include items about the trial in our questionnaire. The responses to question 10 show that the decision in the Ruby case that he was legally sane was a popular one. Among lawyers and psychiatrists who had an opinion, the ratio was almost 2 to 1 in favor of the jury's decision. A quarter of the psychiatrists and a third of the lawyers claimed they had no opinion, and many of them wrote in that they felt they "could not have an opinion" without examining the record.

	Percent of Psychiatrists	Percent of Lawyers
10. *In Dallas, Jack Ruby was found legally sane and responsible. How do you feel about the decision?*		
a. I agree with the verdict	41.0	41.7
b. I disagree with the verdict	27.3	17.6
c. I have no opinion about the verdict	25.1	34.2
d. No answer	6.5	6.3

We compared the lawyers' and psychiatrists' opinions on the Ruby verdict with their beliefs about the relation between mental illness and criminal behavior in general (question 5). Respondents in both groups who believe that all or most persons who have committed serious crimes are mentally ill are more likely to disagree with the verdict in the Ruby case than are respondents who see no relationship between crime and mental illness or who believe most criminals are not mentally ill—among the psychiatrists, 35 compared with 16 percent, and among the lawyers, 39 compared with 9 percent.

We asked three additional items about the Ruby trial, questions 11, 12, and 13. About 15 percent of the respondents refused to answer (most of them on grounds that they had insufficient information about the trial). Among those who did respond, the modal category for both groups is that the defense's case on the whole was less impressive. We were surprised to find that the psychiatrists gave more weight than the lawyers to the impression the defense attorney made on the jury.* Only a small proportion of respondents in both groups feel that the jury acted out of anger and a desire to retaliate against Ruby for bringing additional bad publicity to their community.

	Percent of Psychiatrists	Percent of Lawyers
11. *Which was probably the most important factor in determining that verdict?*		
a. The defense's case as a whole was less impressive to an impartial jury	37.4	43.3

* Lawyers v. psychiatrists believe the tactics of the defense attorney alienated the jury: $\chi^2_{1df}\ (.95) = 3.8$; $\chi^2 = 5.1\ p < .05$.

b. Regardless of other factors, jurors were angry at Ruby for bringing bad publicity to Dallas	10.8	8.9
c. The tactics of defense attorney Melvin Belli alienated the jury	26.6	12.6
d. The battle of psychiatrists under the M'Naghten test confused the jury about the meaning of insanity	11.5	17.6
e. No answer	13.7	17.6

The remaining two items pertained to the expert testimony. Half the psychiatrists are divided almost equally in their evaluation of the effectiveness of the defense's expert testimony. Lawyers are less critical of the experts. Half of them believe that the defense's expert testimony affected the defendant's case, and by a ratio of almost 4 to 1 they believe that the influence was in the direction of increased effectiveness. The remaining half in both groups said that it was not an important factor, or refused to answer.

	Percent of	
	Psychiatrists	Lawyers
12. *The effect of the psychiatric testimony brought by the* defense *was:*		
a. To reduce the effectiveness of the defense's case	25.2	11.3
b. To increase the effectiveness of the defense's case	27.3	40.6
c. Not an important factor in the defense's case	31.0	25.4
d. No answer	16.5	22.7

A similar question was asked about the government's expert witnesses. Hardly anyone feels that the expert testimony detracted from the government's case, and about half the respondents believe that it increased the government's case. This is hardly surprising, since the jury brought in a verdict of guilty. About the same proportion as in the previous item felt that the expert testimony was not an important factor, or refused to answer.

	Percent of	
	Psychiatrists	Lawyers
13. *The effect of the psychiatrists' testimony brought by the prosecution was:*		
a. To reduce the effectiveness of the prosecution's case	3.7	6.3
b. To increase the effectiveness of the prosecution's case	49.6	48.1
c. Not an important factor in the prosecution's case	29.5	24.0
d. No answer	17.2	21.5

SUMMARY AND CONCLUDING REMARKS

This study surveyed the opinions of lawyers and psychiatrists on three issues: (1) the role of the psychiatrist as an expert witness in defense of insanity trials; (2) the relationship between mental illness and criminality, with special emphasis on the defense of insanity; and (3) the Ruby trial.

The topic on which disagreement was greatest pertained to the system of calling expert witnesses. Two-thirds of the psychiatrists advocated doing away with the adversary system in favor of a system of court-appointed or impartial experts. Over 75 percent of the lawyers supported the adversary system. Lawyers and psychiatrists with experience in defense of insanity trials disagreed even more sharply than respondents in each group who lacked experience.

This difference of opinion is more than a disagreement about procedure. It reflects the lawyer's doubts and fears about the quality of the expert opinion and of the psychiatrists' potential influence on the jury. On the part of the psychiatrist, it reflects his dislike for the role which he is forced to play in the proceedings and for the limitations which he believes are placed on the information that he can give to the court.

But on two related topics we found more agreement between lawyers and psychiatrists than we would have expected: (1) Most of the lawyers and almost all the psychiatrists advocated the adoption of more stringent qualifications by the court for the accreditation of psychiatric experts than exists presently. (2) Neither the lawyers nor the psychiatrists were as critical of the psychiatrists who testify under the present system as a review of the literature had led us to believe.

In general, the lawyers were somewhat more favorably disposed toward retaining the jury in defense of insanity trials than were the psychiatrists. To a slight extent, the lawyers were also more likely to believe that the jury listens carefully to the expert's testimony. They were also more willing to allow a jury of laymen to decide not only the responsibility question but the commitment issue as well. But the differences between lawyers and psychiatrists on these issues were not as great as we had expected. They did not, for example, attain statistical significance.

This study represents a relatively unusual attempt at collecting systematically the opinions of lawyers and psychiatrists on practical, professional issues that influence the day-to-day operations of the courts and the administration of justice. Our most important finding is that lawyers and psychiatrists agree much more on specific substantive issues pertaining to criminal responsibility, commitment, and release than the impressionistic literature would lead one to believe.

So much has been made of the differences in points of view that exist between the two professions that it is important to publicize the areas on which there is relative agreement. The points of agreement should serve as a stimulus for lawyers and psychiatrists to work together in bringing about those changes in courtroom procedure and atmosphere which would permit the fullest exploitation of psychiatric knowledge about mental illness and deviant behavior.

Unit Eight | DISCUSSION QUESTIONS

32. *One of the Great Mystery Stories of Medicine*
Discuss whether schizophrenia is an organic or environmental caused disorder. List and define three types of schizophrenia.

33. *Mental Illness Is a Myth*
The author feels that restraining individuals in mental hospitals is a risk to our society. Why?
Define and discuss the term "mental illness."

34. *Psychiatrists Use Dangerous Words*
What is the difficulty in using descriptive terms to define mental disturbances? Compare Menninger's view of mental illness with Szasz's views in the preceding article.

35. *The Defense of Insanity: A survey of Legal and Psychiatric Opinion*
Define "insanity." Do you think "insanity" is a valid plea in criminal cases?
Is a Ph.D. holder in clinical psychology qualified as an expert in the determinants of "insanity"?

Unit Nine *LSD, Alcohol, and Narcotic Addiction*

Man has used various drugs and alcohol for many years. As far back as we have a record of his fears and fancies, we know that he has always believed in secret potions and magic charms to ward off evil spirits and cure him of unwelcomed illness. It was later believed that only criminals, degenerates, and other undesirables were addicts. Today, we recognize that drug addiction and alcoholism know no class boundaries and are psychological as well as physiological and social problems.

Recently much discussion has been centered around LSD and drug usage. Newspapers, magazines, TV exposes, lectures, and classroom discussions have contributed to the impression that the problem is rampant among America's youth. A recent report of the San Mateo County (Calif.) Juvenile Justice Commission reported that one out of every seven high school students in that county had admitted using LSD or marijuana. A closer view of the commission's statistics reveals the ratio was one out of every five boys and one out of every ten girls. The report said, "Contrary to popular belief, these youngsters do not fit the stereotype . . . They not only range from welfare to upper class backgrounds, but their families range from severely troubled and broken to very stable and well-integrated." They also ranged from "dropouts to National Merit scholarship finalists." Although this sampling is not a valid assessment of the total population, it illustrates the magnitude of this growing problem.

Alcoholism has for some time been recognized as one of America's leading health problems. It, too, continues to spiral upward. The U.S. Department of Health, Education, and Welfare (HEW) reports not all alcoholics are addicted to alcohol, but over long periods of time, and with varying consequences are unable to stop whenever they want. HEW reports that approximately 5,000,000 Americans may be classified as alcoholics.

Addiction is one of this country's major medical, social, and economic problems. It affects males as well as females, in urban as well as rural communities, without regard for educational, religious, cultural, or financial status. The first reading, *Ours Is the Addicted Society,* by Leslie H. Farber, presents a timely discussion of drug and alcohol use in this country. Causes and effects of various kinds of addiction are presented along with some of the special problems that are created. Howard S. Becker's *Deviance and Deviates* investigates the wide variety of culturally and socially unacceptable behavioral patterns; special emphasis is on illegal drug usage. Becker offers an interesting analysis of "morality" when viewed by the general public.

Marijuana: Millions of Turned-on Users discusses methods, reasons and effects of marijuana. This article by Albert Rosenfeld discloses, via a question and answer section, that marijuana is becoming the "greatest mass flouting of the law since Prohibition."

Recent attention focused on hallucinogens such as Lysergic Acid Diethylamide (LSD) has created curiosity as well as concern in most Americans. *LSD: A Remarkable Mind Drug Suddenly Spells Danger* is an excellent discussion by the Staff of Life Magazine, into the known risks and benefits of the chemical.

Finally, Gerard Littman argues for a fresh view of the heavy drinker in *Bright Light on the Alcoholic.* The author discusses social and psychological problems as well as interesting therapeutic approaches to alcoholism.

A flower child.

36 | Ours Is the Addicted Society

Leslie H. Farber

This has been called the "Age of Anxiety." Considering the attention given the subject by psychology, theology, literature, and the pharmaceutical industry, not to mention the testimony from our own lives, we could fairly well conclude that there is more anxiety today, and, moreover, that there is definitely more anxiety about anxiety now than there has been in previous epochs of history. Nevertheless, I would hesitate to characterize this as an "Age of Anxiety," just as I would be loath to call this an "Age of Affluence," "Coronary Disease," "Mental Health," "Dieting," "Conformity," or "Sexual Freedom," my reason being that none of these labels, whatever fact or truth they may involve, goes to the heart of the matter.

Much as I dislike this game of labels, my preference would be to call this the "Age of the Disordered Will." It takes only a glance to see a few of the myriad varieties of willing what cannot be willed that enslave us: We will to sleep, will to read fast, will to have simultaneous orgasm, will to be creative and spontaneous, will to enjoy our old age, and, most urgently, will to will.

If anxiety is more prominent in our time, such anxiety is the product of our particular modern disability of will. To this disability, rather than to anxiety, I would attribute the ever-increasing dependence on drugs affecting all levels of our society. While drugs do offer relief from anxiety, their more important task is to offer the illusion of healing the split between the will and its refractory object. The resulting feeling of wholeness may not be a responsible one, but at least within that wholeness—no matter how perverse the drugged state may appear to an outsider—there seems to be, briefly and subjectively, a responsible and vigorous will. This is the reason, I believe, that the addictive possibilities of our age are so enormous.

Let me be more specific about the addictive consequence of this disability of will which, in varying degree, affects us all. Increasingly, I believe we are addicted to addiction. This is to say that, with few exceptions, we subscribe to the premise—whether implicit or explicit—that this life cannot be lived without drugs. And those who would repudiate this unpleasant premise by living without drugs are still more or less captive to it, in that so much of their consciousness must be given over to withstanding the chemical temptations that beset them. Withstanding is a lesser evil than yielding, but it is no escape from the issue of addiction, so that I would have to characterize the predicament as one of being addicted to not being addicted. I do not mean to suggest that we choose one course or the other, but rather that both the premise and its negative variation exist in all of us. Even the most debilitated heroin addict retains his pride in the few items to which he has not become addicted.

Not many years ago, we had best remind ourselves, the problem of addiction seemed confined to a few chemicals—narcotics, alcohol and, perhaps,

---

barbiturates—and it was then possible to make fairly clear distinctions between addiction and habituation, based mainly on the presence or absence of physiological withdrawal symptoms. However, today, even the well-publicized and allegedly extreme agonies of heroin withdrawal have been disputed by the Lazaruses who came back. Recently, a member of Synanon expressed to a reporter his disagreement with the fictional clichés which have acquired the status of scientific fact, remarking: "Kicking the habit is easy. It's not like that Frank Sinatra movie, crawling all over the walls. Sure, it's tough for a couple of days, but it's more like getting over a bad cold."

Fearing this view might be as extravagant in one direction as Nelson Algren's violent imaginings were in another, I checked with a friend who had been a staff member at Lexington. He thought the "bad-cold" analogy an accurate one, and added: "We had far more trouble with withdrawal symptoms in barbiturate users."

Our appropriation of the drug-user's vocabulary for our own purposes shows the extent to which the problem of addiction has invaded our daily existence. When our absorption with not only a chemical but a person, an activity, a distraction, an ideology seems to have more weight than is warranted, we say we are "hooked," meaning either that we wish we could be cured of our vice or else that we value the passion contained in our infatuation.

If someone or something excites us pleasurably, we say he or it "turns us on," but if our response is indifference or boredom, we are "turned off." Our extension of these terms for our own purposes is, to some degree, a fashionable reaction to the notoriety drugs have earned in the mass media. However, my own belief is that we resort to the junkie vocabulary because it expresses a metaphysical or addictive shift in our existence that the older vocabulary did not quite account for—at least in ordinary usage.

Even if we try to restrict ourselves to drug-taking, statistics about the extent and degree of addiction are hard to come by. Certainly we are no longer surprised to learn of the growing proportion of college students who resort to such drugs as marijuana, amphetamines, barbiturates, LSD, tranquilizers. One expert is quoted in The New York Times to the effect that about 40 per cent of the students at the University of California use drugs from time to time. This figure falls somewhat short of Timothy Leary's immoderate proclamation: "Today, in the molecular age, the issue is not what books you read or which symbols you use, but which chemicals are part of your life and your growth."

Numerical estimates notwithstanding, on the theory that convicts tend to riot for those privileges society deems essential, such as humane treatment, recreation, adequate food, civil rights, I am more persuaded by this news release:

> "WALPOLE, Mass., Aug. 13 (AP)—Inmates rioted outside a medication dispensary at the Massachusetts State Prison in an attempt to steal drugs late last night, injuring nine guards. . . Two guards were stabbed and five others beaten as the inmates pushed their way into the 'pill' room, yelling, thrashing and literally gobbling down as many pills as they could at one time . . . State Police Cpl. James Dunne, who led the squad equipped with 12-gauge shotguns, gas masks and crash helmets, said about 18 of the inmates were reeling 'on Cloud Nine' when he arrived . . ."

And from industry, where access to drugs is sufficiently relaxed not to require riots, I offer this item:

> "Los Angeles, Oct. 9 (Los Angeles Times)—Use of illegal drugs in industry, especially among production-line workers, is so common that to arrest everybody who sold or used them would mean some plants would have to hire whole new shifts of employes, according to a police narcotics specialist. The drugs most commonly used are amphetamine sulfate compounds and barbiturate derivatives, which keep workers awake, or put them to sleep. . ."

Since it is forbidden to peddle or "push" most drugs, including whisky, on television, Madison Avenue has responded to the double dilemma of addiction by advertising aspirin as though it were *the* drug for every tribulation we must undergo. On television we are shown scenes in which mothers snap at their children, employers lose their tempers with employes. With only an awkward swipe at the questionable ethics of permitting this poor old headache remedy to carry such a heavy burden, advertisers show these embattled and suffering creatures putting one hand to their heads while a kindly neighbor advises them that this new aspirin combination is the perfect cure for "tension." The happy scenes following their use of the drug are deliberate efforts to imitate the style in which the pharmaceutical companies persuade physicians of the virtues of their products.

Most touching are aspirin commercials in which an aging movie star, long past his prime and no longer regularly employed, sits thoughtfully in his well-appointed study, telling the television audience that movie-making is a hectic and demanding affair. To avoid tension and headache, intrinsic to such activity, he has always resorted to this particular remedy.

Although probably unintentional, such a commercial goes to the heart of addiction, for we must contemplate the pathos of this formerly glamorous creature whose powers have so dwindled that he is reduced to doing headache commercials in which, fooling no one, he pretends nothing has changed. As he holds his bottle of pills to the audience, he seems to say life is really impossible without these pills. But we know, and he knows, that aspirin is not enough; for the vast restitution he demands of life, more powerful drugs are needed.

Should he seek them, he will not have to resort to any illicit drug traffic. He will have no trouble finding a physician who will prescribe amphetamines or psychic energizers to brighten his mood as he waits for calls from his agent. And if the phone refuses to ring, one or several of the many tranquilizers can be prescribed so that he can endure the waiting. Whatever insomnia may have originally been his lot will now be painfully exacerbated by his drug-taking so that other sedatives, fortified often by alcohol, will insure his sleeping. As he moves from one drug to another, mixing and testing the chemicals he believes his state requires and countering their disagreeable effects with still other chemicals, from time to time the sheer immodest scope of his undertaking will strike him; he has become a deranged chemist, his only laboratory his own poor body.

No matter how haggard that body becomes, he must unfortunately depend on it for fresh chemical inspiration. And, if everything else fails, there is LSD for instant revelation, if not wisdom, about the pretentious games that have brought him to this impasse, allowing him the death and rebirth that are now accepted pieties of the LSD mystique.

While it is true that the medical profession and the pharmaceutical industry together are the largest and most powerful group of pushers for the new drugs, I see no conspiracy on their part to make addicts of us all. It has long been common knowledge that physicians are the most devoted users of the drugs they prescribe, unlike the more disreputable pushers whose livelihood depends on abstaining from the drugs they peddle. The men who devise and merchandise these pills and the physicians who dispense them are, by and large, decent human beings who share the same disability of will that afflicts everyone.

Believing, as we do, that we should be able to will ourselves to be calm, cheerful, thin, industrious, creative—and, moreover, to have a good night's sleep—they simply provide the products to collaborate in such willing. If the satisfactions turn out to be short-lived and spurious and if their cost in terms of emotion, intellect and physical health is disagreeable, these scientists are ready to concoct new drugs to counter this discomfort. In other words, they offer us always new chances—virtually to the point of extinction—to will away the unhappiness that comes from willing ourselves to be happy.

Recently, Dr. Carroll L. Witten, president-elect of the American Academy of General Practice, was quoted in the press as being in agreement with a report issued this year by the United Nations Commission on Narcotics which expressed concern over "the alarming rise in the sale of barbiturates, tranquilizers and amphetamines."

The report suggested further that the "explosive expansion of the use of drugs . . . was most likely a result of their being used less as medication than as agents for producing sleep, a sense of happiness and relaxation." Dr. Witten declared:

> "I believe these drugs are not only used wrongly, to excess and without adequate indication, but that in many cases their indiscriminate use has led to dependency, habituation and addiction, with all of the consequent results thereof."

Dr. Witten said he was referring specifically to the non-narcotic drugs used as "psychic energizers, stimulators, activators, deactivators, depressants, alleviators, levelers, elevators or in whatever imaginative category one might place them. One must note with a great deal of alarm," he declared, "that the vast majority of cases first obtained their drugs through the prescription of a physician."

If willing what cannot be willed has led us to being addicted to addiction, it would seem that our addictive appetite will always be more than a match for the ever-mounting number of chemicals that are fashioned to gratify that appetite. And even if we eliminate actual drugs from our consideration, the addictive possibilities are endless: cigarettes, chocolate, detective and spy stories, football on television, psychoanalysis—to mention only a few of my own excesses, which I would unhesitatingly characterize as addictive. Everyone, I am convinced, has his own list, as well as another more prideful list of those objects and activities whose addictive claims he has successfully withstood.

If the term is not to be altogether meaningless, some distinction must now be made between one addiction and another. Concretely, when it comes to putting myself to sleep, how shall I distinguish between detective stories and sleeping pills? Or between watching football on TV and enduring my Sunday with tranquilizers? Or completing a tedious chore on amphetamines and procrastinating as usual?

The first generalization I would make about these sets of alternatives is that in an immediate sense drugs are clearly more effective. Detective stories, for me at least, are not entirely reliable as sedatives. If the story is so poor as to outrage or challenge my diminished sensibilities, I am in trouble, whereas I can always take another sleeping pill.

Watching even an exciting, well-played football game on TV, I cannot entirely obliterate from my awareness the perception that there are other ways in which I could more profitably spend my time. And if the game is inept and boring and still I do not turn the set off, my view of my condition is grim indeed. On the other hand, with tranquilizers, I could achieve a state of not unpleasant relaxation, unruffled by the sort of nagging self-concern which interrupts my absorption with even a good football game.

It is the last set of alternatives that will prove the most troublesome. If I have a group of evaluations of psychoanalytic candidates to write, I am inclined to put it off. The reasons and/or rationalizations for my procrastination will be various: I don't feel well; such reports are too tedious to be endured; I resent the bureaucratic rule requiring these reports; I am reluctant to set myself up as a judge of the performance of these young men; I am convinced I am not equal to the imaginative discriminations that would do these human beings justice.

With a dose of amphetamine, however, my self-concern, with its associated fatigue and hesitations and doubts, will vanish, so that in a single-minded way I shall vigorously engage my task. Within a few hours all the evaluations will be completed. Like a schoolboy who has at the last minute finished his term paper, I shall feel relieved and virtuous to have at long last done what my organization demands of me.

Reading over my reports after I have recovered from the drug, I may be chagrined to note a breathless, assertive and yet self-indulgent quality to my writing that did not trouble me at the time. But I can counter my dissatisfaction by assuring myself these deficiencies matter very little, since I have done all that was asked of me. It was my own sin of pride that initially led me to regard my task as such an intricate and demanding responsibility. Besides, I will tell myself, wasn't it a choice between doing nothing and doing something, however imperfectly?

Thus will my mood of accomplishment prevail, helping me to disown my self-criticism and perhaps persuading me, since I won't have to read these reports again, that I had indeed been discriminating in preparing them. And my earlier doubts as to whether these evaluations should have been written at all can be postponed for another time.

The sensation of being a going, if unquestioning, member of society should not be slighted, because it is hard to come by these days. Nevertheless, we must concede that while the drugs in these sets of alternatives may be more effective, their effectiveness is largely dependent on the chemical deadening of important imaginative and critical capacities, whose privileges are admittedly problematic. Practically every drug invented, from opium to LSD, has had its champions in both science and the arts who insisted that their particular brew was not only not reductive but was actually heightening of human potentiality.

The objective evidence for their claims, however, has always been depressing, and of the same order as my own reports, whether it be the music played under marijuana or heroin, the pictures painted and the poetry composed under LSD, the deadlines met by means of amphetamines, or even—perhaps especially—the perceptions and insights granted by drugs.

At this point, the question must be raised: aren't other addictions—nondrug addictions—also reductive? The answer has to be a qualified affirmative. The friend watching me glued for hours to the television set, isolated from all intelligible life, impervious to the claims of my children who have waited all week to have a few moments with me, has to find my human condition bizarre, to say the least.

Far more seriously incapacitating, of course, are those nondrug addictions that involve ideas and habits of thought. Those who over the years develop an addiction to shopworn ideologies—religious, scientific, political, esthetic, psychological—in a sense forfeit, in willful dedication, the very capacities of spirit and intellect that might set them free.

Nevertheless, there is a difference between drugs and no drugs. While disdain and denial of these capacities will cause them to shrivel and grow ever more paralyzed as years go by, there remains the possibility of a response, however minimal at first, to some human claim. Chemical deadening, on the other hand, if pursued, will, by its very nature, render such capacities eventually heedless to any call.

But to return to my evaluations of those psychoanalytic candidates—my will, with the help of amphetamine, has had its undiscriminating way in my reports, without the reflective give-and-take between me and my writing that could be called dialogic, causing this enterprise to resemble other headstrong monologic sprees in which the speaker is deaf and blind to those about him at the same time that he is convinced of a singular openness and freedom and mutuality to the exchange.

The nonuser has a dispiriting effect on groups enthusiastically consolidated by such convictions, so that they would prefer him to find his own sober companions. And his response to them will be marked by his discouraged observation that, despite the cries of mutual congratulation, all he can hear are colliding monologues, breathlessly composed so that each participant gives in to his own worst headstrong and literal-minded inclinations.

The person who ordinarily must guard against his habit of vast abstraction now becomes even more abstract in his theoretical pronouncements. The person top-heavy with esthetic sensibility becomes even more indulgent to that side of himself, abdicating his ability to temper such estheticism with moral and psychological discriminations.

The most blatant examples of the literal-minded aspect of the drugged state come from the public writings on LSD, but it is by no means restricted to this particular drug. Under LSD, it would seem one is at the mercy of any fancy that strikes him, much like the hypnotic subject responding to the commands of the hypnotist. Should he note that his hand is ugly, that hand becomes literally swollen and grotesque. Should the thought strike him that he is alone in the world, he will quickly and literally find himself as one small mortal in the midst of an endless desolate landscape. In each instance, what properly should be no more than a beginning metaphor has been exalted, at the behest of the will, into physical reality. Similarly, the death undergone with LSD can be regarded as more deathly than death itself. In a section, jarringly titled "Running Smack Into Your Essence," of "LSD: The Acid Test," published in *Ramparts,* one evangelist, Donavan Bess, wrote:

> "The psychedelic death is especially lonely—lonelier, perhaps, than for the soldier who physically dies in a Vietnamese field hospital. He at least has the comfort of cuddling up in the image of his mother. Under LSD you have no such bourgeois comfort; you have no familial figure at all. You die grown up. If you can hang onto that, afterward, you can offer society some adult values. You came to this point in a rite of passage as explicit, as terrible and as meaningful as those rites used in aboriginal Australia."

In considering the addictive state which may result from drugs, narcotic and non-narcotic, I must of course neglect the specific effects each drug has or purports to have on the central nervous system. An unfortunate consequence of such neglect will be to give the false impression that my own addiction to nonaddiction has led me to advocate an impossibly ascetic life, requiring abstention from all chemical assistance, come what may. Let me quickly insist that all the drugs I have mentioned may be taken in nonaddictive ways for reasons that are appropriate to the effects of the particular drug. This is to say, there are times when prolonged sleeplessness can and should be interrupted by sedatives, just as there are painful occasions when morphine is the only answer. Even amphetamines may allow the completion of a low-level chore.

The difficulty, however, here, as indicated earlier, is that the mood of accomplishment may persuade us to disregard the quality, or lack of quality, of our performance, not to mention the disagreeable drug side-effects, so that we turn to the drug in situations that require more of our wits and equanimity than amphetamines will allow. Perhaps a greater danger, as the use of amphetamines becomes more widespread, is that the deadlines asked of us are increasingly determined by the amphetamine intoxications of those who ask. (Another illustration of the manner in which the drugged state influences social values is suggested by the aspirin commercials referred to in this article. The writers of these advertisements seem to be selling not only aspirin but also their conviction—possibly arrived at through their own experience with tranquilizers—that our ordinary difficulties, since they are only subjective and therefore not worth contending with, are best erased with drugs. Thus, an advertisement for meprobamate, addressed to physicians, shows a picture of an overwrought mother with a child, the caption reading: "Her kind of pressures last all day . . . shouldn't her tranquilizer?")

For the sake of completeness, alcohol and marijuana are two drugs whose object is explicitly pleasure, and which may be used nonaddictively. However, too much has been made recently by the younger generation of the nonaddictive properties of marijuana simply because its physical effects are less dramatic than those of alcohol and other drugs. More dramatic is its effect upon relation: the pleasures of monologue experienced as dialogue under the drug, persist as a habit of tolerance for such illusion—which in a sense is the very issue of addiction.

Let us consider briefly the addictive course—from initial pleasure to ultimate disaster—that will result from prolonged and excessive use of any of the drugs I have mentioned, singly or in combination.

The first subjective experience of wholeness and the pleasure accompanying it will acquire its intensity partly through contrast with the discomfort which preceded the use of the drug and partly through the manner a particular drug answers a particular person's need at a particular time. Thus, users are labeled according to their preferences as "Up-Heads" or "Speed-Heads," "Down-Heads," "Acid-Heads," "Pot-Heads," "Lushes," "Junkies."

With further sophistication and availability, and the cooperation of the medical profession, drug-users already are specializing less and availing themselves more of other products and mixtures of products. But the initial feeling of well-being is difficult to duplicate precisely, regardless of the ingenuity of the user. As the drug and the state associated with it begin to wear off, the user returns to a world which has lost none of its oppressiveness and with which, in the midst of the drug hangover, he feels less able to cope.

The distance between himself and the wholeness he sought has grown somewhat, so that he is now vulnerable to the beginning belief that the relief the drug afforded is an extraordinary sort of transcendence which his usual life with others cannot provide, except in the occasional unpredictable and surprising manner in which such moments arise. In other words, he has been burned by the demonic and addictive notion that he need not wait on life for the transcendence he seeks, that he may invoke it whenever he so decrees or wills by returning to the drug or drugs which first allowed him this remarkable feeling.

With this seeming triumph of his will, he will be more impatient of the often frustrating give-and-take of life without drugs, willfully demanding his well-being of those about him and thereby suffering even more the penalties of such willing. In a sense he insists futilely that life now be his drug.

Needless to say, his mounting impatience will be inimical to the exercise or development of such qualities as imagination, judgment, humor, tact. And should he glimpse, however dimly, his impoverishment, he may wish to believe these qualities at least can return with drugs, disowning the evidence accumulating to the contrary. However, without these qualities he is more and more confined to the exigencies of the moment, for he can no longer really remember his drug experience in the past nor can he imagine what may follow. As his intolerance for life without drugs increases, his competence for such life diminishes, so that with every return to the drug he is, in the spirit of Heraclitus, a different and lesser person who attempts to cross the same stream twice.

What seemed the feeling of transcendence at the beginning has long since been abandoned as his drug goal in favor merely of getting from one moment to the next, in favor of mindlessly and minimally staying alive. What began with his will to decree well-being for himself without having to wait on life now culminates in almost a paralysis of will for every trivial action, even getting dressed or feeding himself. It is as though all the taken-for-granted stream of activity had disintegrated into a swarm of tiny yet insurmountable enterprises for his will, every one seeming to require further drugs for its accomplishment.

As a result of the bombardment of his body by such large dosages of drugs, his physical debilitation grows extreme. Yet even this bodily exhaustion and derangement offers a last resort to the will which is now unequal to practically every small movement in his world. Unlike other depleting illnesses that mysteriously overtake us, this one has been induced by himself and seems to be within his control. That is, he may try to assuage his agonies with more chemicals or he can withdraw the noxious agent so that his body can slowly recover its strength.

All other dramas in which his will has been involved have given way now to the one small immediate drama of whether he shall live or die to this world. It is a far cry from the transcendence he sought originally, but every addict knows the drama of his failing body is the last plot his will must confront. Unlike the proponents of LSD, he is beyond metaphysical conceits about the meaning of dying to this world, nor will he glamorize recovery, to whatever degree it may occur, as spiritual rebirth.

Nietzsche, I believe, was not as interested in theological argument about the disappearance of the divine will in our lives as he was in the consequences of its disappearance. Today, the evidence is in. Out of disbelief we have impudently assumed that all of life is now subject to our own will. And the disasters that have come from willing what cannot be willed have not at all brought us to some modesty about our presumptions. Instead, we have turned to chemicals, which seem to enhance our willful strivings. It was only a question of time before man, in his desperation, would locate divinity in drugs and on that artificial rock build his church.

---

37 | Deviance and Deviates

Howard S. Becker

What is interesting about deviance is not what it is, but what people think it is. To be sure, there are such things as drug addiction and homosexuality, and they pose interesting problems for the physiologist, the bio-

Reprinted by permission of *The Nation,* **201,** 8 (Sept. 20, 1965), p. 115.

chemist and the psychologist. But interesting scientific problems do not create public concern. The still unexplained physiological mechanisms that produce heroin addiction do not generate newspaper headlines. What arouses the government, the press and the public is the crime attributed to addicts, the fear of attack by a drug-crazed kid on a lonely street, even though addicts engage mainly in shoplifting and other kinds of petty theft; the stories of high school students using marijuana, though there is no evidence that marijuana will harm them as much as the alcohol their parents allow them to drink; the fear even, for some, that the Chinese Communists are using narcotics to weaken the will of the American people.

Deviance, in general, as opposed to concrete forms of behavior like drug use or homosexuality, is a creation of the public imagination. The act of injecting heroin into a vein is not inherently deviant. If a nurse gives a patient drugs under a doctor's orders, it is perfectly proper. It is when it is done in a way that is not publicly defined as proper that it becomes deviant. The act's deviant character lies in the way it is defined in the public mind.

The public definition of an act as deviant has, of course, drastic consequences for the person who commits it. Under one definition, he may continue to live as an ordinary citizen. Under another definition, he may become a hounded criminal. A consideration of deviance in America over the last one hundred years must inevitably focus on what people have thought of deviance and how public thinking about it has changed, and must interpret what deviants do as a reaction to the way society reacts to them.

We have had drug addicts for a long time. Before the turn of the century, as a number of early studies show, many older people were addicted to patent medicines that were liberally laced with opium. Women helped themselves through menopause with the aid of opiates, and men and women alike alleviated their minor ills with such remedies. They came to depend on their "medicine" and were addicts without knowing it. We also had more self-conscious addicts: jockeys, gamblers, pimps, whores and others in the "sporting life," who smoked opium and became addicted.

Prostitution is, of course, the oldest profession. But prostitutes in earlier times were fallen women, fenced off (in red-light districts) from more respectable people.

Homosexuality is one of the oldest vices. Homosexual literature delights in naming the famous homosexuals of early times, from Nero to the present. But it seems likely that homosexual activity in an earlier day was usually practiced as a secret vice by those who lived in the conventional world.

The examples indicate the range of possibilities, in an earlier period, in the relations between respectable people and those they considered deviant. People who engaged in practices thought to be morally repellent either did not know that they were "doing wrong," like the patent medicine addicts; knew what they were doing, but did it secretly and despised themselves for it, as they would have been despised by others if their sin were known; or lived in a separate part of society, like the sporting world, segregated and isolated from the conventional society.

Have things changed? Yes and no. The same relationships can be observed today between some kinds of deviants and the rest of society. Large numbers of people are addicted to sleeping pills and tranquilizers; since the public has not yet been persuaded that these are dangerous drugs, they do not think of themselves, and are not thought of, as deviant. Yet the observation I heard attributed to a Kansas City tavern owner—"Everybody who doesn't drink takes pills"—becomes more true every day.

The practitioners of secret vices are still around, though the catalogue of vices involved has been enlarged. There are still secret addicts and "closet queens" who hide their homosexuality. There are, in addition, secret transvestites, secret devotees of sado-masochistic thrills, secret fetishists, and others whose kicks are mailed to them in plain brown envelopes with no return address.

But the analogue of the old red-light district, in which the deviant lived walled off from a society that might otherwise be contaminated by contact with him, is harder to find. Prostitutes inhabit most of the public places people go to for entertainment—bars, night clubs and hotels—at every level of society. Their way of life is not so different from that of other people as to mark them off as a special breed. It is difficult to think of any class of deviants so segregated and marked today.

Though some of the relations between deviants and respectable society characteristic of an earlier era can still be found, much has changed. Not only are deviants less segregated, but they have come, in increasing measure, to take a different view of themselves and of how they ought to be treated by others.

One component of the change is an increasing tolerance of deviance by respectable society. The deviant is no longer branded as a sinner whose consignment to hell is a foregone conclusion. Instead, ordinary people are willing to see extenuating circumstances that might account for the deviance, are willing to believe that deviants can be reformed, and are increasingly unwilling to take harsh punitive action toward deviants. Public beliefs have changed in this way, in part, because high court decisions have made it more difficult for the police to "roust" deviants in what used to be their customary fashion. Police habitually control deviance not by actually convicting people of crimes on the basis of evidence, but rather by harassing them with illegal and quasi-legal arrests that deviants are not disposed to fight because they cannot come into court with clean hands. But increasingly strict judicial interpretations of the search and seizure rule, and other decisions affecting civil rights in the area of vice and obscenity, have handcuffed the police so that these means are less available to them. (They have not, of course, given up completely; the nationwide harassment of Lenny Bruce, in clear contravention of Supreme Court decisions on obscenity, is a case in point.)

With the gradual lessening of police harassment, other influences have been at work. The rise of dimestore psychoanalysis—the easy explanation of deviant or odd behavior as the product of childhood traumas that might have happened to anyone—has helped the public to absolve deviants of responsibility for what they do. And, perhaps more important, it has helped deviants themselves to decide that what they do, right or wrong, is not their fault and, indeed, that it might not even be wrong. It is unlikely that any deviant believes this so completely that he never has a qualm about his deviant acts, but it provides the moral basis on which he can demand to be let alone.

Finally, various kinds of popular philosophical positions—the Eastern philosophies, psychological doctrines of self-development, and so on—have brought some people to see the means of salvation in what were formerly thought to be deviant practices. In particular, the use of drugs—both old-fashioned marijuana and heroin and such newer discoveries as peyote and LSD—has been seen as a way of expanding the consciousness and achieving higher levels of human experience. From this point of view, what ordinary people think deviant is not deviant at all; it is all a mistake and they need to be enlightened if they are capable of it and fought against if they attempt to interfere with one's own enlightenment.

In any case, for any or all of these reasons, deviants have become more self-conscious, more organized, more willing to fight with conventional society than ever before. They are more open in their deviance, prouder of what they are and less willing to be treated as others want to treat them without having some voice in the matter.

Homosexuals have organized what can be called "defense groups," very much on the model of such ethnic defense organizations as the Anti-Defamation League or the NAACP. The Mattachine Society (for male homosexuals) and the Daughters of Bilitis (for Lesbians) have branches in several large cities and publish magazines (*The Mattachine Review* and *The Ladder*); they hold annual conventions at which panels of experts and members discuss the biological, psychological, sociological and legal problems of homosexuality. Their magazines are filled with discussions of famous homosexuals in history, of civil rights cases and decisions involving them or applicable to their problem, and other matters justifying their right to be homosexual.

When I addressed a Lesbian group not long ago, I was surprised (a sign of how much I accepted conventional stereotypes) at how much the group looked like a middle-class women's club having a meeting to decide how to run the next charity bazaar. Since they were conventionally dressed, not in the least "butchy," I found myself amused by the disparity between my conception of them and the reality. But I stopped smiling when I realized the aggressiveness and courage it took to identify oneself publicly as the officer of a Lesbian organization and the risk these women were taking in doing so.

Homosexual organizations have won support from "straight" scientists, psychologists, lawyers and, most recently, the clergy. A group of San Francisco clergymen sponsored a homosexual New Year's Eve dance, a gesture deliberately designed to make the affair publicly respectable. Though the police had not bothered a Halloween dance at the Hilton (to which the guests came "in drag," to the great delight of news photographers), they saw a threat in this legitimately sponsored affair and moved in, taking pictures of everyone there. Lawyers, on hand to protest such maneuvers, were the only ones arrested. But the police, undoubtedly motivated by a wish to "keep them in their place," will not prevent homosexual defense groups from winning further allies in the respectable world and pressing their fight for equal rights. The militancy of the homosexual organizations has provoked a frightened warning from a committee of the New York Academy of Medicine.

Another version of the new self-conscious deviant organization is found in Synanon, a self-help organization of heroin addicts now more or less permanently settled in several places around the country, from Santa Monica and Marin County in the West to Westport in the East. The characteristic feature of Synanon is not that it thinks addicts ought to be allowed to take drugs in peace, even though many experts feel this is the most efficient and humane solution to the drug problem, but that it thinks addicts ought to break the habit with the help of ex-addicts rather than being cured forcibly by police or psychiatrists. With merciless discipline, Synanon forces the addicts who join to toe the line or get out. Since no professional group has very much success curing addicts, Synanon (whose successes are not yet reliably measured, if indeed there is any reliable measure) stands on solid ground when it demands that its members be given the right to help themselves. It has, of course, provoked strong reactions from many professionals in the drug-cure field, who cannot believe that any good can come of ex-addicts associating with one another. On the other hand, it has won strong support from many legislators and a few of the professionals who have had an opportunity to inspect its establishments.

Synanon is a grim operation. Not so the short-lived International Foundation for Internal Freedom (IFIF), headed by Timothy Leary and Richard Alpert, the psychologists who left Harvard after an extended battle over whether their experimental use of LSD and other psychedelic (mind-expanding) drugs with students was a proper professional activity. IFIF, in contrast to Synanon and the homosexual groups, is a frankly utopian organization. It looks forward to a radically changed society, in which people will see through the games of life they now play in deadly earnest—the family game, the work game, etc.—and, freed by the use of LSD, live in happier forms of human association, realizing at last the as yet untapped resources of the human mind and spirit.

Leary and Alpert attempted to found a colony embodying these ideas in Zihuatanejo, but the Mexican government drove them out. They are now giving seminars and lectures designed to let others in on the good news, and Leary has just published a book, based on the *Tibetan Book of the Dead,* of ritual and instruction to be used to enhance the LSD experience. They have had a fair amount of success, most of it with well-educated people, including many engineers and "hard" scientists, who seem especially drawn by the appeal of new kinds of mystical experience. Their success has been clouded, however, by the hostility with which officialdom greets them everywhere from Massachusetts to Mexico.

The LSD movement (if it is really big enough to merit being called a movement) differs from the organizations of drug addicts and homosexuals in being composed of people who were not, prior to their involvement with LSD, deviant in any sense. But all three groups exemplify the increasing militancy, organization and self-consciousness of deviant worlds and their growing unwillingness to let respectable society have its own way with them unchallenged.

A sense of what this might lead to (if every group engaged in deviant practices became self-consciously aggressive) comes from the recent light-hearted attempt in San Francisco to have marijuana legalized. One man staged a "puff-in" at the Hall of Justice, lighting up a marijuana cigarette in front of police officers so that he could become a test case. A local attorney has become interested in testing the legality of the law. A group of forty or fifty paraded around Union Square every Sunday for a month (some of the paraders were mothers pushing baby carriages) carrying signs advocating legalization. And when President Johnson spoke, during the campaign, in front of St. Peter and Paul's Church in North Beach, scattered among the "LBJ All the Way" signs that greeted him were a few that said, "Make Marijuana Legal."

Perhaps more interesting than the organization of deviant groups, though much harder to document, is the possibility that practices and beliefs formerly labeled deviant have spread to broad segments of the "normal" population. This possibility first became known to the public, I think, with the publication of the Kinsey Report, which reported surprisingly high percentages of men who had engaged in various abnormal forms of sex behavior. Although substantial questions have been raised about Kinsey's sampling and techniques, the figures were so much higher than anyone had suspected that it is a worthwhile hypothesis that there is a lot more deviance around than meets the eye and that Americans, while not advertising the fact, are by no means as straitlaced as we had thought.

With the Kinsey findings to point the way, a good deal more evidence, most of it quite impressionistic, can be cited in favor of such conclusions. As a simple example, note the mammoth sales of works like *Candy, Fanny Hill* and the *Tropics,* which had been smuggled in from France as pornography only a few years ago. Once the legal restraints were removed, there turned out to be a good many pornography fans around.

Other evidence is not hard to come by. Not long ago, police discovered that some sixty high school students in Woodside, an affluent suburb of San Francisco, were smoking marijuana supplied by a recent graduate. Similar stories could no doubt be told about hundreds of other communities. Marijuana use is not confined to Negroes, Puerto Ricans, musicians and show people. I know of no profession which does not have at least a few members who are at least occasional marijuana users. As an example, far out enough to make the point, one user I know was first offered marijuana by a clergyman, who himself saw nothing wrong with it, though he made sure that his congregation did not find out his views. (Perhaps because I have studied marijuana use and published on the subject, similar cases are constantly brought to my attention.)

Somewhat less direct evidence comes from a survey recently conducted by Paul Verden and Harold Hodges in Santa Clara County. They asked people a number of questions designed to measure "cultural orthodoxy," the tendency to be conservative in areas ranging from political and economic attitudes to attitudes toward sex. The results are somewhat surprising. There are a great many more people who are culturally unorthodox than one might have expected. In addition, the unorthodox are scattered uniformly through all the social classes of the community. In other words, this kind of deviance—and let us grant that asking people whether or not they agree with a number of unorthodox statements is at best a weak measure of actual deviant practice—is not the monopoly of any group in the community. People of all kinds, rich and poor, feel restive under the constraints of our Victorian public morality.

Given the growing underground of practicing deviants and adherents to the culturally unorthodox, what can we make of our official morality? Why does it receive overwhelming public support, even though many, probably a growing number, no longer believe in it or allow it to restrain their activity? The most likely answer is, of course, that official morality—preached by leading public figures, embodied in laws and enforced sporadically by police—is a political product. Politicians make laws embodying its precepts, or refuse to repeal laws which embody them, because organized pressure groups make that a wise course. Those in favor of a more relaxed official morality seldom organize in a way that makes them politically effective, although ministers, physicians or lawyers may occasionally act on their behalf, as when a New York county medical society issued a report advocating less punitive narcotics laws.

Public morality must, of course, keep itself in some sort of relation to "the times," to the slow drift of opinion and practice in the country. If it gets too far out of step, it creates the kind of situation we had during Prohibition; and public leaders do not care for the widespread disrespect for law such a situation engenders and soon put an end to it. But as long as some sizable and politically influential group demands a particular official morality, state legislatures and others are likely to bow to the demand, even if the consequence is simply a public affirmation of a way of life many no longer follow. If the laws embodying the morality are not enforced too strictly and if deviants do not mind being somewhat secretive in their activities, an accommodation can be worked out more or less to everyone's satisfaction.

But our public morality may have gotten too far out of step. Recent reports on college students indicate that a vast number of college girls, whatever their private beliefs and whatever their practice, simply no longer believe in chastity, virginity and the sexual double standard that once was the American way. Whether they "do" or "don't" they do not feel that they can successfully argue—either with the boys who pursue them or with other girls—that premarital intercourse is wrong in and of itself. In the same way, it seems likely that the general public is now prepared to accept revisions of our extremely punitive laws on homosexuality and addiction.

It is hard to say what things will be like if the trend toward relaxation of older standards of morality continues. We can get a clue, perhaps, from a look at the "swingers" of Los Angeles. Los Angeles is probably the most unorganized city in the country. It has a vast number of new migrants every year, no well-organized elites to absorb and tame the newcomers (as does the San Francisco Bay Area, which also has a large in-migration), and nearly perpetual summer. With none of the constraints that might be imposed by tightly organized neighborhoods, the presence of extended families close by, or even by a seasonal change that would get people off the beach, new kinds of manners and morals seem to have grown up.

A long-time resident of the Los Angeles beach communities told me the following tale. When he moved into a house already inhabited by three other bachelors, one of them handed him a pack of calling cards that had just a phone number, the number of the house phone, printed on them. He was told to hand the cards out to likely girls wherever he met them—on the beach, in bars, in department stores, wherever—and wait for the response. And, just as he had been told, within a week the phone started ringing and never stopped. Girls who couldn't even remember who had given them the card, girls he had thought attractive but unlikely to be intrigued, old ones, young ones—they all called and they all wanted to go to bed. Neither he nor his housemates have ever wanted for companionship.

While few Angelenos are so enterprising as to have cards printed up, and while such a story is a slim basis for generalization, a community where such a gimmick will work must surely be something new in American life. Though no one has really done a thorough investigation of the matter, the casualness about sex indicated by the story is said to permeate large segments of Los Angeles society. (This in a town whose police harass Lenny Bruce as efficiently and conscientiously as those of more puritanical eastern cities!)

David Boroff has suggested that sex is the politics of the sixties, and I think he is right, though perhaps not in the sense he meant. Sex of the Los Angeles variety, drugs (both the hipster's marijuana and the more intellectual drugs like LSD), and other varieties of exotic behavior may well come to be thought of as inalienable rights, not to be interfered with by either the police or self-appointed censors of family, neighborhood or community. Whether proponents take the low road of quiet evasion of existing moralities (like the quiet coteries of marijuana users found everywhere) or the high road of principled defiance (best exemplified by Leary and Alpert's open conflict with their Harvard colleagues), they will contribute to a growing tension between themselves and those who are not ready to countenance the new ways.

The newly organized deviant groups are making use of the potential for revolutionary change contained in our cultural emphasis on egalitarianism and our legal emphasis on due process. Our institutions can, when they are spurred into action by determined men, protect minorities of whatever kind from the restraints of cultural tradition and local prejudice. The civil rights movement has shown that. The techniques, legal and extra-legal, used by opponents of racial segregation, will probably be used more and more frequently by deviant groups in the years ahead. Recent events in Berkeley have shown that political freedoms and less conventional freedoms go hand in hand; the same powers use the same means to stifle both. As the indivisible nature of freedom becomes clear, even those who do not engage in forbidden activities will be drawn into the battle, just as physicians, lawyers and ministers have already been drawn into the fight for more humane and rational treatment of addicts and homosexuals. The seeds of independence planted in 1776 will yet bear some strange fruit.

38 | Marijuana: Millions of Turned-on Users

Albert Rosenfeld

A group of youngsters—the oldest was 14—formed a circle and solemnly inhaled on a Turkish water pipe until their eyes were glazed and distant. All of them were deep-tanned, sun-bleached, sports-playing, California-affluent junior-high-schoolers, good students and normal children whose parents thought they were off on a picnic. Instead they were stoned—laughing, excited, talking eagerly. Their talk turned to a zealous defense of pot, coupled with a scorn for the other world they see around them. "Just because 95% of the junkies who take heroin have smoked marijuana, everybody gets up in arms. . . . It's just not logical. It's not true. We're smarter than that," one boasted. "Kids are a lot more intelligent today," another claimed. "Smoking marijuana makes things look like they really are, and when you can see things clearly you can talk about them and learn."

This is childish bravado, heightened by the marijuana itself. The kids who are so sure they can handle it do not understand the nature of what they are dealing with, nor its effect on their attitudes and outlook. Carelessly tolerant grownups do not help either—nor do the older brothers who slip the kids marijuana. In California—and the problem is by no means limited to that state—marijuana arrests of juveniles last year were up 140%, and a state narcotics official predicts some 20,000 arrests by 1971. "It's going to take the combined effort of the whole society to cure this thing," says a Los Angeles police officer. But few people, even those now beginning to be deeply concerned, seem to know where to begin.

Almost overnight the U.S. was embarked on the greatest mass flouting of the law since Prohibition. Marijuana, a mild euphoric drug known and used throughout much of the world for centuries and long a part of the bohemian scene in the U.S., suddenly has become commonplace on college campuses, among intellectuals and suburbanites, and—most worrisome of all—even among subteen-agers. Some authorities estimate as many as 10 million Americans have tried marijuana at least once, and the number of users is increasing rapidly. Just how fast can be gauged from the fact that New York police last year seized 1,690 pounds of "pot"—17 times as much as in 1960—and concede this is only a fraction of the total coming into the city. Even more significant are the new openness with which the drug is used and the missionary fervor with which marijuana and its more powerful cousin LSD are extolled by an ever-widening circle of believers in mind-expanding drugs, which has now spread far beyond its base in the hippie ghettos. The use of marijuana is encouraged by rock 'n' roll groups, by the editorializing of underground newspapers and by "psychedelic shops."

One reason for the explosion is that old fears concerning marijuana have proved to be exaggerated. Pot is not physically addicting, nor need it lead to crime, immorality or stronger drugs. Other dangers, of course, remain: a driver who is high on pot is as lethal as a drunk, and the laws governing anyone caught possessing or peddling marijuana are extremely severe, often

---

with mandatory jail sentences. Despite the stringent laws, Federal Food and Drug Administration Director James Goddard admits that narcotics agents are unable to control the situation, and even so dedicated a drug foe as former Federal Narcotics Commissioner Harry Anslinger concedes that present penalties are unrealistically severe for youthful offenders. In fact, the very illegality of marijuana is part of its appeal for many young people. Seeing themselves in rebellion against the empty, materialistic striving of their parents, they turn the whole pot scene into a protest tool which they use to mock a middle-class culture they disdain. Used in this way, marijuana often leads them into a drug-culture shadow world and on to a psychological dependence whose implications for users—and for society—are disturbing indeed.

The marijuana underground used to be a brotherhood of nervous, secretive people. Even the buying of cigaret papers was feared as a dangerous giveaway. Now every city worthy of the name has at least one psychedelic store that sells everything a "head" could want, short of the grass itself. The soft sweet smell of marijuana hangs in the streets of San Francisco, New York, Atlanta, Detroit, Seattle. People pass on the sidewalk looking stoned, wearing buttons saying "Turned On" or "Let's Get Naked and Smoke." All this amazes the older heads; it seems too groovy to be true.

LSD is the force behind this surfacing, but marijuana is the day-to-day stuff of the psychedelic drug movement. Despite the boom, despite thrashing but futile police efforts to crack down, there is more around than ever and the price is going down. The best—from Morocco, Mexico, Panama, Colombia and half a dozen other places—never costs more than $25 an ounce, and on the West Coast the milder domestic grass can be had for as little as $7.50. An ounce lasts a devoted smoker a month or so, producing 80 to 100 cigarets. Making the connection, culling out the seeds and sticks, rolling the "joints," stoking and passing the pipe among friends—all this is part of the magic.

The effect of the drug varies with the smoker and his mood. In a circle of smokers there can be hilarity, a rush of talk or a solemn, ritualistic silence; almost never is there violence or trouble. Most smokers think of marijuana as a kind of lens through which they see more clearly, more beautifully. But this feeling of a heightened awareness is something that heads find hard to share with anyone but other heads, and from this comes their reverence for each other, their ironic detachment from the "straight" world, their zeal to turn everyone on.

To the police the heads are a dismaying, and often disarming, new criminal class. The crime rate in hippie communities is astonishingly low—apart from their massive violation of the drug laws—and their manner, when arrested, is often embarrassingly full of "love." Still, they are participants in what amounts to an insurrection, and it remains to be seen how socially damaged they will become by living in such outright violation of both law and cultural taboo. Those who pursue getting high to the point of "dropping out" find that an elaborate subculture has been constructed for them to drop into. Once inside it, they invariably adopt the apocalyptic vision of the underground, which preaches death to "repression" and doom for the American culture as it stands. Thus the allure of marijuana goes far beyond the subtle effects of a smoke. There is great exhilaration in joining a band of missionary-outlaws who are convinced that their psychic revolution will bring about the betterment of man. The underground has developed a powerful undertow, and a whole chorus of cult-heroes is helping to increase the pull. The Beatles, Donovan, Bob Dylan, the Jefferson Airplane, Allen Ginsberg, the booming underground press—their message is all the same: now is the time to turn on.

In the realm of marijuana, it is not easy to separate fact from myth. Still, facts do exist to dispel a great deal of the confusion about marijuana.

What, exactly, is marijuana?

It is one of the most ancient of the "psychochemicals"—the drugs that affect the mind. It is neither an opiate (such as heroin), nor an amphetamine (pep pill), nor a barbiturate (sleeping potion). It is rather one of the hallucinogens, or psychedelics, which include mescaline, psilocybin and LSD. (Life, March 25, 1966). LSD is the most potent and hazardous of these, marijuana the mildest and least harmful. It belongs to the family of intoxicating substances that go under the generic name of cannabis, because they all derive from the Indian hemp plant, *Cannabis sativa,* which is easy to grow in almost all tropical and temperate countries. From the flowering tops and leaves of the female plant oozes a pungent resin. It is this resin that contains the active intoxicant. When extracted from the plant and concentrated, the resin becomes the most potent of the cannabis drugs: hashish. Marijuana—known as *kif* in Morocco, *bhang* in India, and *dagga* in South Africa, among a whole lexicon of other names—is a smoking mixture made up of dried and crumpled parts of the hemp plant.

How potent is marijuana?

Since the resin content is low, it is perhaps one fifth as strong as hashish. But its strength varies considerably. If the mixture consists mainly of the cut tops of the plants, it will be richer in resins and therefore more powerful than if it is mixed with stems and seed pods. The potency varies, too, with conditions of cultivation, methods of preparation and the user's individual smoking style. The same dose affects different people differently, and can even give the same person different kinds of "highs," depending upon his mood, physical condition and surrounding circumstances. This is what leads a scientist like Dr. Edward Bloomquist of the University of Southern California to call marijuana "an unpredictable drug used by unpredictable people with unpredictable consequences."

Is it habit-forming?

No—not in the sense that heroin, morphine or the other "hard" narcotics are. The body develops no tolerance to marijuana—that is, the user does not have to keep increasing the dose to achieve the desired effect. When he quits, there are no withdrawal symptoms. But a man who likes it well enough to continue using it can be said to have formed the habit. "There is a moth and flame relationship between marijuana and unstable temperaments," says Dr. Henry Brill of New York's Pilgrim State Hospital, "and there are more of those than you might imagine. Pot-smoking will do nothing for instabilities but aggravate them." The user who develops a strong psychological dependence upon the drug may become a "pothead" who, rather than face his problem, prefers to escape regularly into a turned-on state.

Does it lead to narcotics addiction?

There is no biological effect that primes the marijuana user for the hard narcotics, and most marijuana smokers do not go on to become junkies. Nevertheless, a potential junkie is likely to get there faster if he starts on marijuana; and most junkies do in fact start that way. Moreover, the use of marijuana often leads to experimentation with other drugs, especially other psychedelics, and especially LSD.

Its physiological effects

Marijuana raises blood pressure and lowers body temperature somewhat, raises the pulse rate and slows breathing. It dehydrates the body and increases the need to urinate. It lowers blood-sugar levels and stimulates the appetite. It renders the hand less steady. All these effects are slight and transitory, lasting only a few hours. Continuous use, however, can irritate the eyes and lungs, thus possibly incurring some risk for anyone with eye trouble or pulmonary conditions—e.g., asthma or chronic bronchitis. No one has yet demonstrated any long-lasting deleterious effects on the body—though neither has anyone done enough research to provide assurance to the contrary.

Its effects on the mind and behavior

It acts on the nervous system as part relaxant, part stimulant, and the psychic effects may vary from sleepy contentment to wide-awake euphoria. It distorts perceptions and the sense of time and space, though not to the extreme degree LSD does. In unstable individuals marijuana has on rare occasions been known to cause anxiety and panic, and even to precipitate psychotic incidents. Repeated studies have failed to turn up any direct correlation between marijuana use and major crimes. As for sexual desire, or the energy to pursue it, marijuana is just as likely to diminish as to enhance it. A man high on marijuana is not the best judge of his own condition. He may feel sharper than normal though his perceptions are distorted, his judgment of distance faulty and his visual focus abnormal—and thus be a menace when driving an auto.

What happens to potheads?

In their own view, they may feel they are "getting out of the rat race" and closer to reality. "They believe," says Dr. Dana Farnsworth of Harvard, "that they belong to a superior order of human beings." But judged by any conventional standards they tend to be irresponsible, and uninterested in things like pursuing studies, keeping a job or supporting a family. Dr. Bloomquist says, "Kids who get high repeatedly don't want to come down. They don't want to do anything else. They find a world where they seemingly have no problems, and they become social bums."

Its legal status

The first federal legislation on marijuana was passed in 1937—after a wave of publicity about the "marijuana menace," which characterized the drug as driving its users to violent crimes, sex orgies and even outright insanity. In 1956 mandatory prison sentences were established: two to 10 years for the use or possession of even a tiny quantity of the drug; five to 20 years for its sale. Penalties go up after the first offense. Many state laws follow the federal but vary considerably in the severity of their penalties—some provide death for selling marijuana to minors.

Are current penalties too severe?

Yes. A young man may decide to try marijuana once, just to see what it is like. If he is caught, the experiment may cost him a long prison sentence in the company of hardened criminals and true addicts. Dr. James Goddard, head of the Food and Drug Administration, is one of many who advocate reduced penalties for the use or possession of marijuana—though not necessarily for its sale. A few authorities, such as Harry Anslinger, former chief of the Federal Bureau of Narcotics, and Dr. Robert Baird, director of the Haven Clinic in New York City, consider marijuana an unmitigated evil and are unalterably opposed to any relaxation of the laws. But Anslinger does worry about harsh sentences for youngsters who try marijuana innocently. "When it is a simple case of a kid using the stuff," suggests Anslinger, "instead of prosecuting, the case should be turned over to health and school authorities." Some feel that the very severity of the laws incites youngsters to try marijuana as a means of protest.

Arguments for legalization

Many creative people argue that marijuana expands their consciousness and appreciation of the world around them, including other human beings. Since it is not demonstrably harmful when used sensibly by normal people, they believe it should be freely available, with whatever restrictions are necessary to protect the young. A Boston attorney named Joseph Oteri will be challenging the constitutionality of the marijuana laws in both state and federal courts within the next few months. A standard argument for legalizing marijuana is: We accept potentially harmful commodities like tobacco and alcohol. We make them legal, warn people of the consequences, and hold them responsible. Why not take the same attitude toward marijuana? The whole argument was further complicated last May when, with little publicity, the U.S. ratified an international agreement on marijuana control accepted by 58 other countries. This would make it extremely difficult for the U.S. to legalize the use of marijuana.

Arguments against legalization

Nearly all authorities agree that the ready availability of marijuana would be certain to spread its use among all segments of the population, especially if it became an established and flourishing industry, advertising its product. Psychologically and socially, it is not a harmless drug. Many authorities are convinced that even more high school and college students would be driving around in a turned-on condition, even more people would be dropping out of schools and colleges and jobs and family responsibilities, if marijuana were legally sanctioned.

There are too many gaps in our knowledge about marijuana—some of which may now be closed, thanks to a new lab breakthrough. Substances called tetrahydrocannabinols, the active ingredients of marijuana, have now been synthesized, making it possible for the first time to measure accurately their effects on people. Meanwhile, until more is known, and until what is known can be effectively communicated to the public, most authorities opt for keeping marijuana laws. The consensus favors reducing punishments to realistically fit the nature of the offense.

"This does not mean we condone marijuana use," says Dr. Donald B. Louria of Cornell University Medical College. "It would be foolish at this point to knowingly add yet another intoxicant to a society already overburdened with them."

---

39 | LSD: A Remarkable Mind Drug Suddenly Spells Danger

The colorless, odorless, tasteless substance called LSD can be made in any college chemistry lab. A black-market dose costs only $3 to $5. But that is enough to send a person on a 10-hour "trip"—sometimes into a world of beatific serenity and shimmering insight, sometimes to frenzy and terror. In either case the person who has taken this remarkable drug never sees life quite the same way again.

Within the last three years the use of psychedelic (consciousness-expanding) drugs has exploded. No longer just a promising psychological research tool, LSD has been taken up by a large underground cult. Starting in artistic, bohemian and intellectual circles, the cult has now become a dangerous fad on the college campus. At least one million doses of LSD (which stands for lysergic acid diethylamide) will be taken in the U.S. this year. Hospitals and doctors are suddenly treating scores of panic-stricken young patients who have "taken a trip" on LSD with disastrous psychological effects. Some have been hospitalized for weeks. Now the federal Food and Drug Administration is moving in with new laws which will outlaw LSD's illegal manufacture, sale or transportation. Many states already make mere possession of the drug a crime. Only last week, former Harvard Psychologist Timothy Leary, a long-time user of and proselytizer for LSD, was sentenced to a 30-year prison term for smuggling marijuana and was pointedly held for psychiatric tests. The government crack-down has already cut heavily into legitimate research on LSD, but declaring it illegal may only make it more tempting to thrill-seekers who take it for kicks. At any rate, the genie of LSD, with all its tantalizing possibilities for good and evil, is out in the open.

THE VITAL FACTS ABOUT THE DRUG AND ITS EFFECTS

Ignorance about LSD is almost universal. Here is a medical report on the risks and benefits insofar as they are known.

What is LSD?

It is a relatively simple chemical compound, lysergic acid diethylamide. It is easily synthesized from lysergic acid, which comes from a parasitic fungus that grows on rye heads. It is called a hallucinogen and is similar in its effects to marijuana, peyote and certain "magic" mushrooms.

How potent is it?

A single ounce of it would provide an average dose for some 300,000 people. A few pounds of it dumped into the water supply of a major city would be enough to disorient millions.

How does it work?

This is only partially understood. It seems to affect those parts of the brain (the forebrain, midbrain, hypothalamus and hippocampus) where the input of information from the senses is decoded and processed. A substance that plays an important role in organizing and channeling this sensory information is serotonin. LSD is known to inhibit serotonin activity. But other substances inhibit serotonin function without producing the effects of LSD, so this cannot be the whole story.

What is the state of LSD research?

It is still primitive. Although the drug has been known for 28 years, it has attracted really intensive research interest only during the past few years. Medical science is still trying to determine just what it does to different people under different circumstances.

What are the physiological effects of LSD?

These are surprisingly mild, considering the monumentally disruptive nature of the psychic effects. There is an increase in blood pressure and heart rate, but not enough to be alarming. The blood sugar also goes up slightly. There may be other sporadic symptoms: nausea, chills, flushes, irregular breathing, sweating of palms, trembling of extremities. These manifestations are all transitory. Appetite is affected, but mainly because the subject is too enthralled by his own sensations to be interested in food; later he is ravenously hungry. Sleep is virtually impossible until at least eight or 10 hours after the whole LSD episode is over. The pupils of the eyes are widely dilated so that dark glasses are often worn even at night for protection against the light. With an average dose, .0001 of a gram, the effects begin within an hour and last for eight to 10 hours. A bigger dose speeds up and intensifies the experience, increasing the possibility of panic.

Does LSD cause hallucinations?

No. A true hallucination has no existence except in the imagination, yet the person experiencing it believes implicitly in its reality. The visions conjured up under LSD are usually based on something real. A stick may become a writhing snake, for example, and though the person may be frightened by the snake, he realizes that it is not a real snake but an illusory one.

Might there be long-range adverse effects on the brain?

Yes. In a small number of cases people under LSD, even people with no prior history or suspicion of epilepsy, have been seized with violent epileptic convulsions. A young bull elephant in an Oklahoma zoo was shaken with gigantic fits and died an hour and 40 minutes after the administration of what was mistakenly considered to be a moderate dose of LSD. Cats on high dosages of LSD for a three-week period underwent significant changes in their brainwave patterns, changes that persevered for six weeks after LSD was discontinued. No one knows what long-term changes would occur in the human brain as a result of sustained dosage, and no responsible scientist would dare carry out the experiments necessary to find out.

Is LSD habit-forming?

No. At least, it is not an addictive narcotic in the sense that heroin and morphine are. But the body builds up tolerances to it. Taken on successive days, larger and larger doses have less and less effect. Conversely, someone who has once been on LSD may, in the company of someone else who is on a "trip," undergo the experience on a very small dose—or even on none at all. Moreover, the psyche can build up a subtle dependence upon it.

Are there bona fide medical uses and benefits?

Yes, though these remain to be proven by further research. LSD may be extremely useful in psychotherapy. Some psychiatrists, using LSD in conjunction with hypnosis and standard psychiatric techniques, believe it has helped give their patients astonishing insights into themselves, thereby accelerating their recovery. LSD has been helpful in the treatment of alcoholism. It has also been used as "death therapy," to help dying people face the end more serenely and with less pain. Aldous Huxley, a dedicated advocate of such drugs, is reported to have taken LSD in his last days.

Are there really major risks?

Yes. They stem mainly from the bizarre psychic effects. A person whose sanity may be more precarious than he realizes can become permanently deranged through a single terrifying LSD experience. Hospitals report case after case where people arrive in a state of mental disorganization, unable sometimes to distinguish their bodies from their surroundings. To calm such patients, large doses of tranquilizers and barbiturates are usually given. There have been instances where LSD symptoms have recurred weeks after taking it, leading the victims to believe they were losing their sanity. A policeman took home some confiscated sugar cubes he did not realize were saturated with LSD. His 10-year-old son ate a sugar cube by accident, and it took weeks of treatment before he recovered his mental balance. People on LSD sometimes believe they have the power to fly, or to walk on water. One young Californian walked in front of a speeding car, convinced it could not harm him—and was killed. A woman in Europe, into whose drink a prankster dropped some LSD, thought she was going crazy and committed suicide. For these people and others like them, LSD was not merely dangerous—it was lethal. Anyone who drops LSD into someone's drink and thinks it is fun should not be surprised if the jury thinks it is murder.

Who should never take LSD?

People with any kind of heart trouble or liver malfunction, as well as epileptics or suspected epileptics, are routinely screened out of serious LSD experiments. LSD is especially risky for anyone with an unstable personality, and certainly for anyone who, knowingly or unknowingly, might harbor preschizoid tendencies. LSD can encourage weak and irresponsible people to even further irresponsibilities, and it can convince those with criminal propensities that they are above the law.

How important are setting and circumstances?

"Their importance," says Dr. Joel Elkes of Johns Hopkins University, "can hardly be overemphasized." Even when conditions are carefully controlled, mishaps occur. All the risks are intensified whenever LSD is used by an amateur. The appalling fact is that for every legitimate LSD experiment, a thousand or more probably are carried out by people experimenting on themselves, either alone (the most perilous circumstance) or in groups.

When will LSD be legally and generally available?

Perhaps never. LSD is considered so dangerous that its sole legitimate manufacturer, Sandoz Inc., has commendably limited its distribution even beyond government requirements. Even with a prescription it is not legally available over the drugstore counter. Whether it should ever be so available is considered questionable by Dr. Jonathan O. Cole of the National Institute of Mental Health. Anyone who has a strong desire to try the LSD experience is urged to seek professional assistance from a qualified scientist. Taking LSD, Dr. Elkes warns, "is not minor surgery."

Should everybody have the right to try LSD?

Emphatically not. Those who are vociferously pushing this point of view think of themselves as courageous, pioneering individuals. But an LSD trip is not always a round trip. What the LSD user may be buying is a one-way ticket to an asylum, a prison or a grave.

SCIENTISTS, THEOLOGIANS, MYSTICS SWEPT UP IN A PSYCHIC REVOLUTION

A Hard-headed Businessman's Vivid Memory

"I'm a hard-headed, conservative, Midwestern, Republican businessman. Under no circumstances would I consider myself a person who goes around taking strange drugs.

"But my wife took LSD at a friend's house, and in order to get her to agree to come home, I took the stuff myself.

"We got in the car, and I had only driven about three blocks, when suddenly the pavement in front of me opened up. It was as though the pavement was flowing over Niagara Falls. The street lights expanded into fantastic globes of light that filled my entire vision. I didn't dare stop.

"It was a nightmare. I came to traffic lights, but I couldn't tell what color they were. There were all sorts of colors around me anyway. I could detect other cars around me, so I stopped when they stopped, and went when they went.

"At home I flopped in a chair. I wasn't afraid. My conscious mind was sort of sitting on my shoulder—watching everything I was doing. I found I could make the room expand—oh, maybe a thousand miles—or I could make it contract right in front of me. All over the ceiling there were geometric patterns of light. To say they were beautiful is too shallow a word.

"My wife put on a violin concerto. I could make the music come out of the speaker like taffy, or a tube of toothpaste, surrounded by dancing lights of colors beyond description.

"A friend showed up. He was talking to me, and I was answering, all in a perfectly normal way. Then, I saw his face change. He became an Arab, a Chinese, a Negro. I found I could take my finger and wipe away his face and then paint it back again.

"I made a chocolate sundae and gave it to him for a head. A great truth appeared to me. The reason he had all those faces was this: he was a reflection of all mankind. So was I.

"I asked myself, 'What is God?' Then I knew that I was God. That really sounds ridiculous as I say it. But I knew that all life is one, and since God is Life, and I am Life, we are the same being.

"Then I decided to examine my own fears, because I wasn't really afraid of anything. I went down into my stomach and it was like Dante's inferno—all steaming and bubbling and ghastly. I saw some hideous shapes in the distance. My mind floated to each one, and they were horrible, hideous.

"They all got together in a mob and started to come up after me—a flood of bogeymen. But I knew I was stronger than all of them, and I took my hand and wiped them out.

"Now, I think there lies the real danger with LSD. Anyone who motioned with his hand and couldn't wipe out those creatures. He has to stay down there with them, forever."

"The game is about to be changed, ladies and gentlemen. Man is about to make use of that fabulous electrical network he carries around in his skull. Present social establishments had better be prepared for the change. Our favorite concepts are standing in the way of a flood-tide, two billion years building up. The verbal dam is collapsing. Head for the hills, or prepare your intellectual craft to flow with the current. . . ."

So ran the manifesto with which Drs. Timothy Leary and Richard Alpert embarked three years ago on what both continue to believe is the psychic revolution of man. Waves of odium have since washed over both of them, and Leary is now headed for jail with a sentence that suggests the government considers him a very dangerous man. But the revolution, if that is what it is, has long since slipped out of Leary's or anyone else's control. People are taking LSD for as many reasons as there are minds to imagine what lies in the universe behind the surface of the eye.

Leary and Alpert consider LSD "a sacred biochemical" that clears the path to mystic understanding. Normal consciousness, they say, is a dim and stunted thing, and LSD and the half-dozen other psychedelic drugs are the magic means of piercing through centuries of cultural conditioning to free, full psychic life. An all-fronts movement has sprung up around this view on big city campuses and in young intellectual circles all over the Western world, and it comes complete with quarterlies, lecture courses, a barrage of guide books to the cosmos and even two or three psychedelic churches.

There are many others whose interest in the drug has nothing to do with psychic revolution. Mathematicians have used it as a lens through which they sometimes glimpse the physical reality of concepts that the mind can only imagine—advanced number theory, for example. Theologians and divinity students have taken it as a Host, and most experience what they take to be direct evidence of their faith. There are psychedelic corporation presidents, military officers, doctors, teachers—each with a reason to risk a voyage on the unpredictable terrain of the deep brain dreamscape. And there are those, of course, who are taking LSD merely because it is the latest excitement around.

Official supplies of LSD are limited in the U.S. to 72 tightly controlled research projects. Anyone who sets out to experiment privately may do so with ease, however, by dealing in a vast and growing black market. As contraband, LSD cannot be improved upon: it is odorless, colorless and tasteless, and there are 300,000 doses in an ounce. Starting with ingredients freely available to anyone who knows where to shop—there are sources in Mexico, Canada and Czechoslovakia—a chemist can cook up pure LSD using nothing more complex than a vacuum pump. Single doses are absorbed and preserved almost indefinitely in a sugar cube or a sheet of blotting paper, and without leaving the slightest visible trace. One dealer had a six-gram bottle break inside his suitcase just after clearing customs with it, and for months thereafter he and his friends launched themselves into inner space simply by sucking on his suits.

LSD salesmen often have the air of men engaged in holy work, and they operate with a messianic conviction that is completely unknown in the rest of the drug world. Most LSD is sold or given away among friends, and it usually comes with a cautionary lecture—"Now you be cool with this." In New York, San Francisco or Los Angeles, though, a girl just off the bus from Boise can find it quicker than the YWCA merely by asking around for "a trip." There is nothing furtive about the "acid scene," as it is called, and in some places the cognoscenti even wear lapel buttons: LSD—SUPPORT YOUR LOCAL TRAVEL AGENT. A trip, which sells for 35¢ wholesale, brings $3 to $5 in major cities, and in other places as much as $10. The biggest black market dealer in the country sells a steady 50,000 doses a month, perhaps half the total market—for the moment.

Not many people take more than three or four trips a year. Some fast a little beforehand, or read Huxley or dwell on Zen *koan* to limber up the brain; others say they concentrate mainly on their own psychological "hang-ups." All but the real psychic desperados who try to stay high most of the time are careful to find someone they can trust to stay with them for the 10 or so hours of the trip—a "groundman" to keep trouble and distraction at bay. They wait for a long weekend, find a congenial spot, and . . . pull anchor.

A good experience is bizarre, extreme, profound. Thirty minutes after the exploding ticket is swallowed, life is dramatically changed. Objects are luminescent, vibrating, "more real." Colors shift and split into the spectrum of charged, electric color and light. Perceptions come as killing insights—true! true! who couldn't have seen it before! There is an oceanic sense of involvement in the mortal drama in a deeply emotional new way. Colors are heard as notes of music, ideas have substance and fire. A crystal vision comes: how full is the cosmos, how sweet the flowers!

The illusions beckoned to the surface by the drug are greatly influenced by expectation, atmosphere and the traveler's mental balance. Knots in the nervous system project out upon the universe, and a wife's face can be a blood tulip, a Greek coin, a glob of lazy ill-humor—all depending on how one feels about her. Forgotten secrets are found still glowing with pain behind the dissolved rock of Ego, and the discovery can be too much to bear. The voyager must be strong enough to drift through all manner of terrifying moments like a curtain blowing in the wind, and not everyone can manage it. There can be screaming and tears, trembling—misery throughout.

No matter how thrilling and illuminating a trip may be, only a good mind can return from it without some serious re-entry problems. Many perceive their past life as the pathetic, surrendering performance of an absurd cosmic clown, and they change it accordingly: get divorced, quit work, read aloud from *The Book of the Dead.* They discover that life is only a game, then begin playing it with less and less skill. Their vision becomes a beguiling scrim drawn over a life of deepening failure.

Others break bad habits or learn German in a week—really accomplish something of value in their lives. Yet nearly everyone who has taken LSD to whatever effect is left with a sense of mystic free-masonry about it. "Have you taken a trip?" is a question asked with unnerving frequency these days, and usually it suggests that if you haven't the conversation is about to end. LSD has become the cornerstone of a great many lives already, even among people who use it infrequently and with care. It can change their attitudes toward everything, transforming them into mumblers about Reality, sometimes with the merest terrestrial hook. "You may be making Buddhas out of everyone," Leary and Alpert were told when they were fired from Harvard, "but that's not what *we're* trying to do."

The highly circumspect research now being done on LSD touches very few of the questions raised by the arrival of the drug in the streets. There have been no studies on the effect of long-term use, and nothing at all is known of the subtle personality changes that are being witnessed inside the LSD culture. Does seeing with the Third Eye alter one's vision with two? Do easy, frequent visits with Reality genuinely heighten awareness or do they put odd new kinks in it? And what about the children? What becomes of visionary kids?

With so much LSD around, it becomes urgently important to learn how to aim it toward doing some good. There is no reason to suppose that doctors are the only men serious enough to approach the drug with official encouragement. Yet present restrictions have shut off a critical amount of study from everyone else—behavioral scientists, for example. Already it is evident that clinical research alone is insufficient, partly because it is so seldom concerned with social questions, partly because it is inimical to the psychedelic state of mind: a white-coated researcher seems the prince of fools to someone living inside a sugar cube.

The government has now arrived at the stage of declaring LSD "a problem worse than the narcotics evil," and there is reason to fear that it may soon become just that. After all, what are the police going to do? Odorless, colorless, tasteless, every scrap of paper suspect—what *are* the police going to do? Even the most active enforcement of the law as it stands may well have the effect of worsening the problem by driving away people with prudence and intelligence while scarcely inconveniencing the really reckless, dangerous ones.

It is frightening to think what will happen if this awesome drug becomes available only to those willing to risk jail for it. For it brings out the very worst in some people. LSD is being dropped in girls' drinks. Terrifying parties are being given with a surprise in the punch. The Humane Society is picking up disoriented dogs. People are even having "beautiful experiences" with their baffled children. "When my husband and I want to take a trip together," says the psychedelic mother of four, "I just put a little acid in the kids' orange juice in the morning and let them spend the day freaking out in the woods."

---

40 | Bright Light on the Alcoholic

Gerard Littman

In the United States today there are five million alcoholics, and their drinking directly affects the lives of another 15 million to 20 million people. Because the statistics are startling, there has been an outcry for quick and easy solutions to the problem of "alcoholism." But no easy answer is in sight.

To begin with, there is disagreement about just what alcoholism is. Excessive drinking in one cultural environment may be nothing more than

---

convivial imbibing in another, for drinking customs and the acceptance of intoxication vary widely from group to group. Even the World Health Organization used broad strokes in its definition. Alcoholism, it says, is "a chronic illness that manifests itself as a disorder of behavior. It is characterized by the repeated usage of alcoholic beverages to an extent that exceeds dietary use or compliance with social customs of the community and that interferes with the drinker's health or his economic or social functioning."

According to the United States Department of Health, Education and Welfare, "not all alcoholics are addicted to alcohol. Some people drink excessively over long periods of time and with serious consequences but are still able to stop whenever they wish. Others lose control over their drinking almost as soon as they start."

Any study of alcoholism quickly reveals that the reasons for drinking are many and diverse so that no one can point to a man and predict with certainty that he is a potential alcoholic. There are, however, some characteristics that many alcoholics have in common (many people who are not alcoholics also share these traits, so no hard and fast rules can be drawn from them). They suffer from much anxiety and often have deep feelings of inferiority and insecurity. Their tolerance of frustration is low; they are impulsive, fear rejection, feel lonely, isolated and dependent. They have unreal expectations of themselves and they are frequently beset with hostility, guilt and depression.

Many alcoholics had too much responsibility thrown on them early in life and never had a carefree childhood. All this makes it difficult in later life to behave appropriately and handle problems maturely. Often the patient's father was overly aggressive and stifled the development and growth of the child who, as an adult, resorts to drinking as a way of protesting his own independence and manliness. Because of his need to appear strong and because our culture emphasizes independence and self-reliance, the alcoholic finds it extremely difficult to admit that he requires help.

By drinking, the alcoholic attempts to cope with his fears and to face life's painful and stressful situations with less discomfort. Tensions are reduced and unacceptable impulses become acceptable. Although alcohol is really a depressant drug (an anesthetic) it is commonly and mistakenly thought of as a stimulant. Because of its effect on the central nervous system, inhibitions are released and repressed emotions can be more easily expressed. If the released impulses are too unacceptable to the person he will, after sobering up, forget much of what happened while drinking.

A woman who "blacked out" in this way told me how she had to have her telephone number changed every time she got off a binge because of the calls she received from men whom she did not remember having met. The entire episode had to be repressed because her conscience would not tolerate the anxiety, guilt and loss of self-respect that she would have suffered in recalling all the sordid details.

Some people drink because of their inability to assert themselves. A 35-year-old fireman would go to any length to avoid an argument, even with his wife, for fear that he would not be able to control his anger and that he might strike out physically. At times he became so shy and withdrew so completely that he was afraid to ask people for directions on the street or even tell a bus driver where he wanted to get off. But he had two outlets for his anger and hostility. He had his job—he gleefully related how much he enjoyed breaking windows with his ax, "the sort of thing you like to do as a kid." And he had drink; in the bottle he could find release.

While some people drink to be able to express aggressive or hostile feelings, others drink to drown their anger. I have seen people who drink because they are bored and still others because they are anxious. Some drink because they feel completely alone. They are unable to make friends and are so afraid of being rejected if they try that they cling desperately to the bottle rather than risk rejection by the world when cold sober and without alcoholic illusions.

Often the alcoholic is so guilt-ridden that he attempts to punish himself while he is drinking. One patient would pick fights with stronger and bigger men whenever he was on a binge; he regularly ended up severely battered. Another patient, with a similar personality, fell asleep with a lighted cigarette in his hand while drunk. He set his bed on fire and suffered severe burns. Still another had a serious automobile accident when he drove while drunk.

Paradoxically, excessive drinking is not necessarily the alcoholic's main problem. Recently, I received a call from the wife of a man who had been sober for four years. Though he appeared to be doing well, he had actually acquired a new symptom to replace the abandoned one. His wife had discovered that he had gambled away the family savings of $7,000. She wished, she said, that he were drinking instead "as he used to."

What happens, of course, is that unless the underlying causes of alcoholism are resolved, sobriety will often bring about only a change in symptoms, and the change is not always for the better. I have even seen cases where as long as the patient was drinking he could function at a certain minimal level; once he became sober, he turned openly psychotic. Dr. Carl Bowman of the University of California says: "You should be aware of the fact that you may bring harm to an alcoholic if you stop his drinking. You should remember that if you remove his drinking he may not be able to put together a life pattern nearly as satisfactory as the one he has."

It is too often assumed that the spouse is the innocent victim of the alcoholic's neglectful and irresponsible behavior. But, after all, the nonalcoholic spouse entered into and remains in the marriage, possibly for pathological reasons of his or her own, and unless treated the marriage will often break up at the very point where the alcoholic improves.

I have observed several wives who became more disturbed as their husbands improved. One wife complained that her husband wasn't the same any longer, and she even tried to get him to drink again by mixing two highballs and putting both glasses on the night table next to their bed. Gradually, she got used to a nondrinking husband and began meeting her unresolved needs by turning to their cat. The cat went on frequent nocturnal escapades, as the husband once had, and she would now wait up for him. When the cat came home at 3 A.M., she rewarded him with a can of tuna fish.

A woman alcoholic complained to me that, as she improved, her nonalcoholic husband did not want her to have any life outside. He wanted her to remain, as before, completely dependent on him. He told her he would rather have her drunk than sober. The 60-year-old wife of another alcoholic took up a life-saving course when her husband went on the wagon so that she would still have people to rescue.

In the face of such fundamental variations among drinkers and their families, it is obvious that, contrary to popular misconception, there is no one "best" way of treating alcoholism. Different alcoholics respond in different ways to different methods.

The most widespread approach to alcoholism in this country today is Alcoholics Anonymous. When an alcoholic seeks this kind of treatment, he must admit that he is powerless over alcohol and he must work toward a goal of complete sobriety. Once in A.A., he finds an equality of status among all members so that he can recapture his lost sense of identity and of belonging.

I remember a man who was desperately seeking help. He had wasted many weeks at unsuccessful psychotherapy until he admitted that he could never really feel accepted, could never really trust anyone, including his therapist, because he was afraid of being looked down on as a result of his "weakness." But once he joined A.A., he almost immediately identified with the group; he felt, he said, "like an outcast" who had gained acceptance in a group of outcasts.

This is not an unusual experience. Many alcoholics join A.A. because its members are ready and able to help each other in time of crisis and they will make emergency visits to the home and completely take over. A great many alcoholics continue to function adequately with the help of A.A. They meet their responsibilities without resorting to liquor. (Spouses can often benefit by attending meetings of Al-Anon, an organization similar to A.A. and designed especially for wives and husbands of alcoholics.)

But many alcoholics resent the religious overtones of the A.A. program. Others find it difficult to reveal their problems to a group of strangers, no matter how sympathetic the group may be.

For these, psychotherapy might prove a better way out of their alcoholism. It is the predominant treatment method at many alcoholism clinics, either as individual therapy or as group therapy. What psychotherapy can give some alcoholics is the opportunity to get at the root of their emotional problems and thereby remove the need to drink. The alcoholic can learn to accept life and gain confidence in his ability to handle difficulties.

As to how this works, let's take a particular case. At our clinic we saw a 40-year-old talented and imaginative commercial artist, who had once had great ambition to become a painter and despised himself for wasting his talents in an advertising agency. On his way home from work every evening, he would stop at a cocktail lounge; the intervals between the office and the home grew longer and longer as he began to drink more and more. At last, realizing that he felt frustrated in his job and bored at home, he came to the clinic.

For two years, he was counseled weekly, and during the sessions he revealed that he was from an upper-middle-class background and that he had always compared himself unfavorably with his father, a socially prominent judge, and depreciated his own achievements. As a result, he set unrealistically high goals for his children, demanding that they accomplish what he felt he had not. During his time in psychotherapeutic treatment at the clinic, he learned to respect himself and no longer to expect adult behavior from his preadolescent son and daughter. With the change in his behavior as a parent, the behavior of his children also improved.

While some alcoholism clinics emphasize psychotherapy, others use essentially a medical approach. The doctors may prescribe tranquilizers, vitamin B, or Antabuse, a drug designed to prevent an alcoholic from drinking. Some clinics combine the psychotherapeutic and medical approaches.

In an acute condition, the alcoholic often requires hospitalization. It takes only five to 14 days to "dry out," a process consisting mainly of rest, injections of vitamin B-complex and sedation, all to restore essential foods to the body and re-establish its physiological balance. But at times, when the patient is severely distressed, a longer period of hospitalization may be necessary, from several weeks to several months; the stay provides some relief and it allows the alcoholic to find himself by removing him from the stresses of everyday life. If the hospital stay is not followed up with consistent after-care, however, the effects are not likely to last.

We might draw upon the system followed by some mental hospitals in Britain. They have programs where patients can go to work in nearby towns and return to the hospital at night. Many people need this security and panic when confronted with the possibility of discharge. They simply cannot manage on their own.

In this country, we have been too unwilling to accept this unpleasant reality and we act surprised when an alcoholic goes on a binge within hours after his discharge from a hospital. The anxiety about an uncertain future is more than he can tolerate, particularly if his family is not emotionally prepared for his return. Illinois has developed a remarkable community placement program for former state hospital patients who wish to go into a nursing home or boarding home or to move in with a foster family at state expense instead of living alone or returning to their families.

Similar programs are needed throughout the country. And, as a practical matter, we have to create entirely new kinds of facilities and more imaginative approaches to suit those alcoholics who cannot be rehabilitated by current methods. We need day-care centers in addition to clinics and hospitals. We need half-way houses, where the single alcoholic can live after hospitalization. There he can get through the transition to a new job in a community more easily, for he will not have to face long nights and weekends alone. We also need more flexible insurance policies to enable patients to enter general hospitals.

Of considerable help would be more enlightened and flexible public assistance programs, particularly with regard to the nonresidents in a community. We must protect the many indigents, including alcoholics, from hunger and disease. The frustrations experienced by many people in making a necessary adjustment to a new and often alien and hostile environment frequently erupt into alcoholism. There is, further, little reason why the existing mental health clinics cannot offer more individual and group therapy to alcoholics.

Some of the things we are discovering in the study of alcoholism have far-reaching application to other emotional illnesses, just as what is learned in seemingly unrelated areas of human behavior has valuable meaning for those who work with alcoholics. Today, we may not have answers to all the questions about alcoholism, but at least we have enough knowledge to begin to throw away some of the myths.

Unit Nine | DISCUSSION QUESTIONS

36. *Ours Is the Addicted Society*
What does the author mean by "those who are addicted by not being addicted?"
Discuss the dangers in experimenting with drugs to satisfy curiosity.

37. *Deviance and Deviates*
Define and give two examples of "the self-conscious deviate."
How do the recently organized deviant groups affect public opinion?

38. *Marijuana: Millions of Turned-on Users*
What are the primary dangers of marijuana? Should marijuana be legalized?
How do you explain the upsurge in the use of marijuana among young people?

39. *LSD: A Remarkable Mind Drug Suddenly Spells Danger*
What are the major risks in using LSD?
Can LSD be used for beneficial purposes? Discuss.

40. *Bright Light on the Alcoholic*
Discuss the causes of alcoholism.
Can alcoholism be considered a mental illness? Discuss.

Unit Ten Preventive Measures and Psychotherapy

Prevention of mental illness is the cornerstone of mental hygiene. Historically, it was believed that demons and evil spirits were responsible for all mental illnesses. As a result, certain individuals believed to be endowed with mystical powers offered incantations and special potions to cure the mentally ill. Many years were devoted to ferreting out witches and evil spirits thought to exist in the mentally ill. As late as the 19th century, mental patients, thought to be voluntarily acting abnormal, were subjected to harassment and physical punishment designed to show them the error of their ways.

Dissenters such as the Dutch physician Johann Weyer (1515–1588), often referred to as the father of psychiatry, the French physician Philippe Pinel (1745–1826), the English physician William Cullen (1712–1790), and the American schoolteacher Dorothea Dix (1802–1887) called for humane treatment methods for the mentally ill. Yale graduate Clifford Beers is credited with initiating America's mental health movement in 1908 when he published his autobiography, *A Mind That Found Itself*. He wrote of the inhumane treatment he and other inmates had encountered in America's asylums. As a result, many committees were inaugurated for the promotion of mental hygiene. The Connecticut Society for Mental Hygiene (1908) and the National Committee for Mental Hygiene (1909) were forerunners for many current organizations that promote preventive measures in mental hygiene.

Today, behavioral scientists are not only involved in the search for environmental and organic causes of mental illness but in the application of treatment procedures. *Psychotherapy,* often referred to as "talk therapy," is concerned with psychological treatments used to help mentally distressed patients. Among the chief approaches are: psychoanalytic therapy, behavior therapy, family therapy, hypnotherapy, ego therapy, and client-centered therapy. Among the techniques used by behavioral scientists in psychotherapy are: group therapy, play therapy, psychodrama, and hypnosis.

Physical forms of therapy, distinguished from psychotherapy, involve: chemotherapy (medicines, e.g., tranquilizers and energizers), shock treatments (electroconvulsive and insulin), and the rarely used psychosurgery (lobotomies).

The first reading, *Prevention in Psychiatry* by Paul V. Lemkau, describes a broad overview of preventive psychiatry. The author centers his discussion on social deprivation, emotional conflict, and environmental stress as leading causes of pathological behavior.

Chandler Brossard's *Revolutionary Treatment of the Mentally Ill* is a discussion of how one scientist utilizes a special form of psychotherapy in dealing with psychosis. Brossard describes psychiatric care for the mentally ill at Delaware Valley Mental Health Foundation in Pennsylvania.

Transactional Analysis is the focal point of the third reading by Jack Langguth. *Dr. Berne Plays the Celebrity Game* presents Berne's threefold concept of the individual: the adult, the parent, and the child. The author illustrates how group therapy and the analysis of role-playing are utilized by Eric Berne.

Tracking Down the Causes of Birth Defects by Richard L. Masland is presented in this unit to illustrate how medical research programs are utilized to discover causes of mental, neurological, and sensory disorders in the newly born.

In the last article, *Children in Conflict,* Barbara Culliton describes the early identification and treatment of emotional disturbances of children. The author discusses how serious psychological problems encountered in adulthood may be prevented.

---

41 | Prevention in Psychiatry

Paul V. Lemkau, M.D., F.A.P.H.A.

It appears to be the fate of psychiatrists that each time an illness once freely admitted as belonging in their bailiwick yields up the secrets of its etiology, or even becomes subject to arrest by specific treatment, that disease is no longer considered psychiatric. At the moment, we are seeing the whole field of mental retardation being taken out of the psychiatric specialty which has struggled with it for a long time, and considered for transfer, in part to pediatrics and in part to education. The motivation for the shift appears to arise from two scientific advances, which, although they enlighten only an infinitesimal proportion of the whole scope of the problem, have given rise to the notion that enough is known to justify an approach more specific than is considered likely to be used by psychiatrists. Phenylketonuria and a few similar disorders are now reasonably well understood and are reasonably preventable; mongolism, which is not at all understood and quite unpreventable, is at least identifiable as a genetic error. On the basis of these scientific advances, the whole field of retardation has achieved a hopeful glow and it is proposed that it be transferred to another specialty.

A decade or so ago, the same thing happened in epilepsy. When treatment advances made hospitalization, or to be more accurate, institutionaliza-

---

From *American Journal of Public Health,* 55, 4, 1965. Reprinted by permission of the author and publisher. This paper was presented before the American College of Preventive Medicine at the Ninety-First Annual Meeting of the American Public Health Association in Kansas City, Mo., November 14, 1963.

tion, unnecessary for many cases, the illness drifted from the psychiatric specialist to the neurologist and pediatrician. A decade before that happened, general paralysis of the insane, central nervous system syphilis, a disease once considered the paradigm of psychiatric disorders, almost completed its transfer from the psychiatrist to the venereologist, a process which began when the Wassermann reaction in the spinal fluid was discovered, was furthered when Wagner-Jauregg discovered hyperthermia as a treatment, and completed its transfer when penicillin was discovered, which required no hospitalization at all unless there was marked behavior disorder. Delirium, which once presented such very severe psychiatric management problems in young pneumonia and typhoid patients, is rarely seen now because of improved treatment measures for infectious diseases. When it is seen, it occurs in disorders of which anoxia of the brain is a symptom, and these occur mainly in older people in whom the disorder is easier to manage.

Offhand, one could easily come to the conclusion that psychiatry will eventually be left with only diseases of which behavior disorders are outstanding symptoms and for which medical science has no explanation or effective treatment. There are enough of these to keep the specialty busy for a long time, but we in the field get a little discouraged when every medical advance shuts us away from a segment of the cases that could furnish us a glow of success.

While this process of cutting out groups of cases from the psychiatric specialty has been going on, psychiatry has been extending its responsibility in other directions which have had the effect of enlarging the total field of medical concern. The first step in this was the inclusion of the neurotic and psychosomatic syndromes in medicine. While ancient medicine considered such cases, it was only when Charcot, and later and more effectively Freud, studied these groups that they entered the range of medical responsibility. It was but another step, albeit a rather long one, when juvenile delinquency came to be looked upon as within the health field, to some extent, largely through the child guidance movement begun by William Healy. Douglas Thom and others brought childhood habit and behavior disorders under the medical umbrella. This trend is now so strong that the type of extension appears as a health goal; the World Health Organization speaks of health as social as well as physical and mental well-being.

Psychiatry seems to show a tendency to reach out for complex, intricate pathological problems and not to show much regret when illnesses for which it was once responsible are taken over by another specialty. This movement, however, brings to attention the likelihood that behavior disorders and psychiatric diseases are symptomatic, that all have a pathological base and that the triumphs of prevention (of psychiatric disorder) in syphilis, delirium, and phenylketonuric oligophrenia may be duplicated in senility, schizophrenia, depressive illnesses, and, perhaps, even the neuroses.

There is no type of pathological process that I have been able to discover which does not produce behavior disorders and psychiatric symptomatology. The model of competing biological systems exemplified in delirium has already been mentioned. So far as is known, delirium results in infectious diseases because some toxin alters brain function, probably in some way which interferes with cell metabolism. Such interference may be acute or chronic; some infectious diseases are followed by rather persistent depressions and slow recovery, as for example, in Icelandic disease epidemics. The process is probably not very different from the slow recovery that takes place in posterior column cells in poliomyelitis.

The model of genetically induced disease has also already been mentioned in connection with phenylketonuria. This model has certainly been considered applicable in psychiatry more often than the situation justifies. It appears traditional throughout all medicine to ascribe to heredity what cannot be explained at a particular stage of scientific development by other pathological models. In any case, there are many psychiatric illnesses in which genetics plays a part in the origination of pathological processes. Often this model is directly linked with peculiarities of enzyme action or with as yet less clearly understood metabolic dysfunctions as in the lipodystrophies. Along with these gross genetic disorders, there is the vexing and still completely unsolved problem of the inheritance of personality types which are more vulnerable than others to stress.

Trauma addles the brain and gives rise to behavior disorder which, if the destruction is severe, may be permanent or correctible only through long re-educating procedures.

Hormonal disorders result in behavior disorders in some instances, though frequently the disorder of behavior is secondary rather than primary. In diabetes, for example, the behavior disorder is likely to be more related to the acceleration of arteriosclerosis than directly to the hormonal disorder. Treatment-induced psychiatric illness when ACTH is used is well known, however, as are the psychiatric symptoms of hypo- and hyperthyroidism.

The nutritional model of pathological process also involves mental illness, witness the classical case of pellagra. Unfortunately, judgments as to the severity of nutritional disturbances are almost as difficult to make as are judgments on the severity of behavior disorders and this has retarded the identification of many specific relationships between nutrition and behavior. Some, however, are very clear as, for example, the association between psychosis and pernicious anemia.

Another model of pathological process which has had much publicity recently is the damage of the fetus by disease or disorder in the pregnant woman. The thalidomide incident reinforced what had been learned through experience with rubella and had been clarified by a great deal of animal experimental work.

The purpose of listing and illustrating these models of pathological process has been to demonstrate that the subject of this paper, preventive psychiatry, is not unitary. The concept implies that the prevention or arrest of any pathologic process whatever has a preventive effect in relation to psychiatric disorder. In some instances, the effect is direct, in some, indirect. The prevention of any disease is the prevention of psychiatric disorders. Any one who teaches preventive medicine teaches preventive psychiatry; he can do no other. Those of us most interested in the psychiatric symptomatology sometimes wish that our colleagues with other symptomatological interests would keep their preventive function for psychiatric disorders a little more in the forefront of their teaching than they do, but we appreciate the preventive job they are doing for psychiatry.

It is the model of psychological or environmental effect as a source of pathological process, however, which is usually thought of in connection with preventive psychiatry. Pathological processes of the sorts already alluded to rarely appear in solitary form; one or more processes frequently march along together in the production of disease states. Perhaps the most pervasive of all is this model of emotional conflict, environmental stress, and various kinds of psychological deprivation. It is the very pervasiveness that makes the field hard to keep in clear focus as an issue in disease prevention; what is everywhere is very hard to notice every time it appears. It is too easy to take for granted what must be looked at in every case. Like routine laboratory reports, it is very easy to paste the slip in the record without its being looked at very carefully. Furthermore, it seems so frequently that when the factors of emotional conflict, environmental stress, and deprivation are teased out for a case there is little to be done about it except feel frustrated. There is also the fact that these factors are cloudy and almost unquantifiable. It is often clear that something is going on that is important to some undetermined extent, but exactly what it is and how much effect it is having is indeed a frustrating problem to solve.

This problem, too, is not unique to psychiatry. It is present in most pathological conditions, such as arteriosclerosis, which have long periods of development before they make themselves apparent through symptoms. Presumably the etiological factors, whatever they may be, must act over a long period of time to produce symptomatic disease. And the factors are often not too specifically related to the particular form the disease takes. It is more common to hear the statement "we don't know what causes schizophrenia" than that "we don't know what causes arteriosclerosis," but the difference in frequency of the statements does not occur because more is known about one than the other. Furthermore, the fact that the cause or causes of schizophrenia are unknown is often, and very falsely, generalized to state "we don't know what causes mental disease." Such sloppy overgeneralization is rarely indulged in by saying that we know nothing about whole groups of illnesses of other types.

The model of disease production through psychological causes has been considerably refined and made more specific in the last few decades. Some of the vectors of this greater specificity have been suggested in the division of this general area used above—emotional conflict, environmental stress, and pathological deprivation. The latter has furnished very practical ways for preventive psychiatry to act, ways in which the output of personality function as behavior disorder is directly related to input factors, even though clarity is still clouded by the lengths of time over which the causes produce their results.

Psychological deprivation as a cause of illness seems to derive from the period in which Itard became interested in mental retardation in the 19th century. At that time a presumably feral child was found, "the boy of Aveyron," who could not speak, among other deficiencies. A little progress was made toward the use of language with elaborate training but the success was limited; it now appears that the training came too late. Later Chapin discovered that babies hospitalized for acute illness in the pediatric wards of that day would, if they remained in the hospital too long, develop marasmus.

This syndrome of low hemoglobin, diarrhea, emotional underactivity, and eventual severe weight loss and death could be prevented by early discharge from the hospital to home. It was this finding that led eventually to the colorful and active pediatric wards that are found in most hospitals today. Long before there was any research data to support his stand, in 1890, Homer Folks saw that children raised in institutions did not do well. He invented foster home care to prevent the underdevelopment he observed. His observations were later made again and subjected to investigation by Bender, Spitz, Goldfarb, Bowlby, and others. They have led to the massive reforms of children's institutions and to a great decrease in the number of such institutions.

The finding that relative social isolation inhibits mental and emotional growth has been confirmed in animal experimentation leading to refining notions of critical periods of development. The concept is that a capacity for development may be lost unless it has the opportunity to become active during a particular developmental period. When the lack of stimulation is severe enough, not only mental but physical growth is interfered with. Less severe deprivation leads, apparently, to inability to experience certain sentiments common to most people with the result that the deprived person cannot fit smoothly into his culture's pattern of living.

The "Guide to Control Methods for the Mental Disorders," recently published by the APHA, treats this sort of reaction in adults and for the first time gives it a name—the Social Breakdown Syndrome. School systems which, as is the case in many large cities, have been engulfed by populations in which the parents live by very low intellectual standards and have no habits of reading to pass on to their children are finding that the children are almost uneducable. They are turning to preschool education so that they may expose the child to some stimulation before the capacity to accept it is lost and it becomes impossible to learn what schools teach.

Those who have observed the sort of personalities developed in children who are socially isolated because of severe rheumatic heart disease will recall that they are usually quite restricted. Modern treatment of such cases includes much wider social and intellectual and emotional stimulation than previously; the preservation of breadth of personality is considered in treatment, along with the protection of the cardiovascular system. The same type of change has radically altered the treatment of all sorts of handicapped children in the last few decades.

The deprivation of mental stimulation is, then, a psychological factor in producing disease which has a great deal more specificity now than was the case earlier in the history of preventive psychiatry. To be sure, most of the research findings deal with extreme cases and the conclusion that milder deprivation leads to less severe underdevelopment requires some extrapolation from the data. Taking it all in all, however, this material offers a rather firm foundation for preventive psychiatry. The President's Panel on Retardation ascribes a considerable amount of the milder grades of mental retardation to this type of cause.

The types of programs necessary to prevent the Social Breakdown Syndrome vary, of course, depending upon when the opportunity is encountered. Because the parents are not easily available to work with, school systems have started to take children earlier, as already indicated. Children's institutions have broadened their programs, getting children out into the community more, and furnishing more continuous contact with adults who take care of them in the institutions. Mental hospitals broaden and intensify programs of work and recreation, open their doors, and shorten patients' stay to prevent the syndrome. The impact has even been felt in the correctional field so that many find it preventive of social breakdown for prisoners to work in the community and return to the prison at night, to spend weekends with their families, and the like.

Too often, social deprivation is considered identical with poverty. Such identification leads easily to a conclusion that only some radical socioeconomic and political revolution can have preventive effect; quite possibly this sort of mistaken logic underlies the frequent political revolutions that are observed over the world today. Actually, the two factors are separate. Poverty leads to social deprivation more easily than does affluence, without doubt, and too much poverty is frustrating to such an extent that chronic social deprivation can occur, but even so there can be poverty and a sufficient amount of social life to support personality development. We may snigger at the politician who points with pride to his financially deprived background, but the fact is that he is often living proof that poverty did not harm his social development or make him a mental case.

The second psychological factor of etiological importance to mental illness is emotional conflict. Emotional conflict as a cause of psychiatric illness has not yielded to investigation as well as has the Social Breakdown Syndrome. It is, however, equally well supported by animal experimentation and by clinical observation. The newer methods of hormonal assay now becoming available may furnish new and useful evidence as to how and under what conditions emotional conflict gives rise to illness. One of my pet theories, that the apathetic depression seen in the army in men who had fought too long and seen too many men killed, was blown up by this type of investigation. I had thought that the "old sergeant's syndrome," as we called it, was somehow related to an exhaustion of the body's ability to react to conflict. But I am told by the best man in that field of biochemistry that he can find no evidence of inability to react because of previous over-reaction, that the underactivity we see appears to be related to successful psychological denial that a conflict exists. The point is that the role of conflict in disorganizing behavior is yielding to research approaches and that speculation may be replaced by fact before too long. It will be a happy day for us psychiatrists who have had to take refuge in hypotheses derived from clinical observation for so long. Animal experimentation in this area, using Pavlovian and other methods, is so well known that it does not require review here, nor do the difficulties introduced by its application to the tremendously complex animal which is man.

Emotional conflict is also a difficult problem as an etiological concept because it requires the introduction of the idea "optimum." No emotional conflict implies the social deprivation just discussed. Too much emotional conflict is also bad. Conflict successfully dealt with probably leaves most personalities stronger; unsuccessfully coped with it often leads to reactions of illness. Preventive psychiatry seeks to find an optimum of conflict for the individual which will develop his ability to cope but not overwhelm him. Furthermore, emotional conflict is not as specific in its effect as is social deprivation so far as we know now. Deprivation leads to "loveless" individuals and retarded individuals. Emotional conflict can, apparently lead to a far wider range of possible reactions, from anxiety neurosis to schizophrenia or to the lowering of the threshold for the appearance of a senile psychosis. The situation is not a happy one, scientifically speaking.

In this situation, prevention can hardly be expected to have many specific characteristics. Many have accepted the platform that all that can be done is to avoid crises of conflict when they are avoidable, to avoid "unnecessary anxieties." As I have put it elsewhere, it is enough stress to have to wash diapers at six months, without adding conflict because of a mistaken idea that the baby should be toilet trained at that age. It is difficult enough to deal with temper tantrums without the feeling that no other child has them and that their appearance means a failure to raise the child properly. Bad as a siege of military service looks to a young man whose career plans are to be interrupted, it will be less if it is first faced as an idea, rather than as an actual experience. This line of thinking has been widely discussed and need not be further labored here. It is nonspecific prevention of psychiatric illness or, perhaps even better, it is the promotion of mental health which makes the personality less vulnerable to mental illnesses. Perhaps because it is so nonspecific, anticipatory thinking about predictable life crises has extremely broad application in preventive health educational services.

The final factor is environmental stress. The theory is, and so far as I know there is no real experimental support except in animals, that every person has a breaking point and that if pushed beyond it, he will show symptoms of psychiatric or other disease. This, too, is so familiar that its theory need not be discussed. Societies appear generally over the world to protect individuals from absolutely overwhelming environmental stress as soon as they are able to. The British have chosen to do it through the medium of the welfare state. The Communist countries do it in another way. In the United States we do it through voluntary sickness insurance, retirement systems, social security, medical care for the aged, and all the other multiple and sometimes duplicating programs our economy can afford. We do it through the provision of public housing and the inspection of other types of housing. We do it through minimum wage laws, workmen's compensation, unemployment insurance. We do it through public health programs that reduce disease. Who can say how many psychotic depressions have been prevented because children no longer die in droves of diphtheria or spouses of typhoid fever or malaria? The exact relationship of such programs to preventive psychiatry, or, some of them, to the profession of medicine, cannot be defined. There can hardly be any doubt, however, that there is a relationship between such programs and the occurrence of mental illnesses. One day, I hope, we shall be able to measure the relationships more exactly, and, perhaps, to find some specifics among the welter of situations to be studied.

In this presentation I have not dealt with the issues of treatment or the rehabilitation of people who have been ill. It is possible without torturing scientific logic too severely to call treatment and rehabilitation secondary and tertiary prevention and these areas are, in psychiatry, at the moment more popular than primary prevention.

Here is a brief summary of the field of preventive psychiatry as it has been developed in this presentation:

First: Every model of pathological process produces diseases that have psychiatric symptoms. Preventive psychiatry is an inevitable component of all disease prevention and every physician has a role as preventor of psychiatric illnesses. Regardless of how narrow his concept of his specialty, he cannot avoid this role.

Second: Social deprivation, emotional conflict and environmental stress are included as models of processes which produce pathological behavior. The first of these, because of successful research in the last two decades, has begun to have increased specificity while the other two remain too much for anyone's satisfaction as influences of a general type leading to various types of ill health. Each of the three offers opportunities for direct preventive action; however, because of their nonspecific character and probably because of time relationships, the evaluation of preventive effect is extremely difficult.

Nevertheless, it can be said that the concept of preventive psychiatry is a little less vague and tenuous than it was a decade ago. The theory is tighter and the opportunity for action is more inviting.

---

42 | Revolutionary Treatment of the Mentally Ill

Chandler Brossard

Two million Americans, according to recent studies, are overtly psychotic, have been diagnosed as such and treated in hospitals. There is no way of telling how many psychotics are being treated privately or how many are wandering around not being treated at all. Some psychiatrists say the total number of psychotics in this country would be about two percent of the population, or about four million men, women and children. A rough estimate on the amount of money being spent on care and research on such seriously ill people—in- and out-patients of hospitals—is $4 billion. Again, the immense amount of money spent by people going to private physicians would be very difficult to estimate, since the figures are not divulged to any central agency.

Psychotics—schizophrenics, paranoids, etc.—have a very wide behavior and image range: They can act like berserk animals, screaming, ripping their clothes, threatening the lives around them; they can sit for days in absolute motionless withdrawal; they can imagine they are gods or loathsome toads. Their fantasies are incredible. Ambulatory psychotics, say, those who hold down jobs and seem to be members of a functioning community, can wreak inestimable damage on the situations and people around them, and often, nobody will know just what it is all about. A manic psychotic schoolchild can, and frequently does, destroy the dynamic balance of his classroom or school.

Treating psychotics, or helping them get better and back into the everyday world, is an extraordinarily difficult job. By and large, they are simply too difficult to reach, too strongly unwilling to face reality. So, in many, many places, the deranged are dismissed by heavy sedation or shock treatments, i.e., not helped. A few places, however, have done remarkable work with the seriously ill, and among them is the Delaware Valley Mental Health Foundation in Doylestown, Pa. The story on these pages is about its work: its daring and imaginative clinical techniques; its dedicated and brilliant young director, Dr. Albert M. Honig; and one patient, a 22-year-old who had spent most of his life in various "institutions" getting nowhere—until he began seeing Dr. Honig. Dr. Honig is an eclectic: That is, he employs a variety of concepts and techniques in his treatment. He uses no drugs or any kind of shock therapy. His two major concepts-methods are direct analysis, which, in a simplified way, is countering psychosis with threats or orders or seemingly assaultive statements, and interpersonal psychiatry, conceived by the late Dr. Harry Stack Sullivan. His method is total participation of doctor and patient. The following text is condensed from tapes made during treatment sessions with Dr. Honig and his patient, and a member of the psychologically oriented family with whom the patient lives at the clinic. This living-in is also a Honig innovation. Dr. Honig is talking and conversing in unconscious talk. That is, he is talking not to the patient's conscious mind, but directly to the patient's unconscious.

The boldface type is Dr. Honig talking; the roman type is the patient. The purpose behind Dr. Honig's method and persistence is to get the patient to connect with reality and stop being psychotic. "Emil" is Emil Ondra; he and his wife Miriam are the patient's substitute family.

Doctor: Go ahead. Talk a little bit.

PATIENT: Dr. Honig? I like the room I'm in. That's right—camping out—charcoal—it's yours, you know—there are so many things of yours you know—the room—that's right—he won't take it.

That's your room, and even if you get well enough, you work around here. You'll have a room here. Don't worry about it.

I will.

You're not going to lose that.

Right. Now, I'm looking forward to getting well. That's right.

All right, now let's talk a little bit.

I think about. . . . May I hold hands with you too?

Not yet. If you get into some of those obsessions, maybe I'll let you hold my hand.

All right, let's start on the room. I know you like your room, and we've been locking you out of that room. What does a room signify to the unconscious?

A room would signify maybe a mother's breast. That's right. Have things of yours there.

What do you feel in your room? Yeah, go ahead.

Now, in a room you sort of feel that if I did have one, that maybe I would get . . . love . . . and forget about things happening in the summer so things can stay out. That's right.

. . . If we give you your own room, it's not for being crazy in.

I understand that.

That room is a place where you can go and be by yourself, and you can think, and you can relax. In that way, it is like a mother's breast.

I understand that.

Be quiet. But I don't want you to do any mannerisms there or to hallucinate or carry on that way.

There will not be none.

If you do, you may lose your room.

Just happy to be there, you know. I like it.

All right. Now, let's hear you talk about an obsession or two. How was he last night?

EMIL: *There are two things I want to bring out. One is that he wanted candy again. Now, this never happens in our place. It's always when we take him somewhere. He goes for candy. And again, swiping it. Secondly, he's starting to rearrange furniture at our place—outside of his room. He has a really crazy way of arranging furniture in his room. Like the drawers will be askew. Now, the dynamics behind that is if I make everything topsy-turvy, it won't be actual. Now, the word "actual" to him is real. It won't be real. Therefore, I'm dreaming. And when I wake up from the dream, I will be with my mother.*

He's setting up his own fantasy, and then, he can wake up from this and enter the fantasy he wants to achieve. Being back with his mother.

I remember something, you know. Like I sort of remember the time a boy could . . . I just came along and tried it once . . . was in our house a little while. That's what I'm trying to think. . . .

Keep talking.

And I often think about things that I do. I was thinking of the party.

That's right. The party.

Will cover what? What will happen? Will be taken out or what?

I don't know if you'll be able to go yet. Just keep talking.

I think. . . .

Your obsession is warding off the anxiety which is related to that which is the mother's breast. Our battle is with your compulsion.

Lot to work on. Think about, you know.

First of all, tell me what thoughts you had of your mother. Don't lie to me.

I will not lie.

Do you know what holiday it is in your religion?

Let me see. Jewish New Years. I'll feel chipper—like see—one holiday, that's right.

Come on. What holiday is it? You know.

That's right.

The festival of lights. What is that?

Hanukkah. For Jewish people.

Well, how do you celebrate Hanukkah in your house?

We think about that, and we light the candles.

Who lights the candles?

We take turns. It's whatever my family says. It's right. I remember. . . .

They'll be lighting it tonight, and you're not there.

I'm here. That's right.

You'd be very upset around this time of the year.

That's right.

Well, I got a call from your mother.

What is it?

She's lighting a *jahrzeit* [memorial] night candle for you.

Well, I have a tendency to think. I think I could get well. I could go to the shop—the workshop. I could put things together. Now, I could sort of make things.

Do you know what a *jahrzeit* night candle is?

When they have to rest and nourish.

You fake. What happens when they light a *jahrzeit* candle?

. . . even though I would not be here, they would still think we'll have a good time. . . .

What are you faking for and lying? Don't you know what it is?

That's for something. . . . They have a relative who got very old.

And what happens to them?

First though, they need a rest. They get tired.

They drop dead. You can't even say it.

I'm not. I have imagination. That's right. It's so much fun that I can know. That's right. Have a bad dream.

Yes, you've got it bad. You're living in a bad dream.

Sometimes they can get tired too. Maybe it was something I think of . . . maybe some kind of bad smell. . . .

Well, c'mon, you'd better talk your way out of it because I'm mad about this.

God . . .God's manners . . . of something I. . . .

Are you telling me about a memory?

About what came into me.

Well, how come you took that candy?

Because I thought. . . .

And stop letting your mouth go like that. I saw that. Where did you put your tongue?
Do it again so everybody can see it. No, you didn't. Stick your tongue out. You were licking your lips. You still taste that candy in your mouth. How many pieces did he take?

EMIL: *He took three.*

He didn't ask for them?

. . . thought . . . could have been welcome too. I knew I still belonged. . . .

The fact is that you don't know that you belong—even belong to the human race.

Interesting to my mind though.

Do you know what autistic means?

Yes, I know.

What?

Like artistic. . . .

Autistic is somebody that stays by themself and eats candy and lives in a dream world, and doesn't want to have anything to do with anybody else.

I know what that means. Maybe there's something that could be. . . .

. . . Let's get him some candy. And I want it right in his room.

Try to be helped.

You want chocolate?

Yes. That's right.

All right. We're going to put ten pieces right in your room, and you'd better not touch one.

I understand that. I will not.

They're going right on your dresser. If one of those is gone. . . . Ho! Ho! Just don't show up the next morning.

. . . that's right . . . the opportunity to make myself sick.

You'd better not touch one of those.

Right. I will not touch it. I will not.

Because you might not be alive.

I will not touch. I'll just leave it. Remains. Sit on the dresser.

What am I telling you?

I will not touch. I'll just leave it. Remains. Sit on the dresser.

Why?

Cause ah-ah-ah-ah it might be. . . .

Stop stuttering so much. Every time you get nervous, you start stuttering.

It might be that other stuff, you know. You never can tell.

These candies are going to come from your mother. Direct. And she's going to put a little of her own brand of stuff in there.

Right.

What?

Like . . . stuff is going to come from my mother . . . put a little brand in there. That's right.

Do you know what I'm talking about?

We're talking about. . . .

It makes people dead. Poison.

I'll remember that so I'll be careful. I'll watch out for it.

We'll have to bury you.

I'll be careful what things are.

Was that to make your mind think better?

Yes.

Well, you'd better do it ten times.
I hate to be so mean to you, but I don't know how else to cure you.

Be cured. I can be careful what I take. . . .

You were made such a mess before you got here.

That's right.

Look how big you are.

Yeah, I'm getting bigger.

Yeah, you're getting bigger, but you're not getting any smarter.
You'd better start thinking. Because when you die. . . . You know, your spirit just doesn't leave. You've got a body too.

Right, I'll be careful of this.

That stuff will taste pretty good—for about a minute, until you start to get the violent bellyaches.

Well. I'll just not do it in the first place. Stay away. That's right.

What's that for?

Maybe I imagine I'd better stay away from it if I don't know what it is.

Because we have to cure you of that. In order for you to be a human being, you have to be able to sit with people and talk with people at a table, which you've never been able to learn.

That's right. In my whole life, I never learned that.

Now, what's on your mind now? Your eyes are a little shifty again. Another obsession?

The things that you are thinking about.

Well, tell me one of the secretive obsessions.

*Wh*up!

What was that? What happened there?

Something fell—got stuck.

What were you doing, checking your penis?

There is something. Something was tangled there, that's right.

You'd better start thinking. I'm not being silly. Maybe that's all you're good for–nothing.

That's right. If I had tools, I could build something. Could do other things.

Now let's hear a secret obsession.

Sometimes I think about things. . . .

I asked you about an obsession, and you started to talk about something.

I think, what comes out of my mind. . . . Like there is something that maybe I want to tell. . . .

Well, say it now.

Like I think about my father, you know, coming for me from different places. That's what I think about.

That your father is coming for you in different places?

Yes. Someplace he could have seen me. That's right.

Now, don't talk a lot of mumbo jumbo. Get right to the point.

That he would have thought that the. . . . I was able to go.

Do you trust your father?

Sure I do.

Do you trust your mother?

I do. I think I'd be careful.

Heh! Heh! Something tells me that underneath you don't.

Maybe something I imagined. That's right. Maybe could wait for it.

What do you mean?

So much of a mess. I remember. I would be able to go.

Can you follow him, Emil? He's trying to tell me something.

EMIL: *Look at his eyes. He looks terrible.*

I don't understand what he's talking about.

That's right.

Can't you express yourself better than that?

I think I can.

I think you're trying to say something, but it is beyond me to find out what it is.

EMIL: *If he doesn't say it right, I think we ought to take the toilet paper away from him that he uses to make those twiddles with.*

You've got to say it right. I think we ought to take it away from him anyway.

I'm just happy to use it. That's right.

Well, if you want to twiddle, you at least have to talk clearly and express yourself.

Oh, we said that. That was why I do that. . . .

You just wanted to say something to me, and I didn't understand you. Try again.

Something of my father, because I remember the time when I would see him.

Why do you talk through your nose all the time?

Talk like this.

No, you don't. Talk. You'll see how you sound.

Now, this is what I want to say.

You don't talk through your mouth.

I would imagine that maybe the talk. . . .

Talk through your mouth. Go ahead.

Ah. I would imagine that. . . .

You see? They never even taught you how to talk. You don't know how to read.

I could draw a picture.

Yeah, but you won't be able to tell me what's on your mind when you draw. You can't express your feelings drawing.

You have to try and remember again. That's right. Catch up.

Yeah, you draw the same thing.

Yes. Maybe I think about those.

It has to do with not getting enough milk.

I know what you mean.

It seems to be all your fantasy life—being with your mother and her breast.

That's right. That's fantasy.

What did you do with Mrs. White? Did you work yesterday—because she's got big breasts too.

He's so bound up, this guy. If we get anxiety, we'll be able to free some of this concretistic thinking, which I think can be done. I'd give a million dollars to see you healthy and happy.

Emil Ondra and his wife Miriam (who work for peanuts because the clinic has so little money) explain their role in M's overall therapy. "Our function as his substitute family works on a broad range," Emil says. "He gets love, attention, emotional support. He gets rewarded, he gets punished. In other words, he gets everything a child would in a normal family setting.

"What happens here with us and M is a sort of feedback. First of all, he feeds back some information, in relating with us, about how he related to his mother and father. We, in turn, take this information and try to reconstruct, reeducate is a better word, him on the basis of a more normal family relationship."

Part of the Ondras' immense job is to help change the patient's behavior. Emil explains it this way. "M has a beautiful defense system. We have found that he works best not under reward, but under anxiety. In M's case, if we reward him, we have found again and again that he will stop working because his world is in the world of fantasy, and reality to him is unpleasurable.

"To follow the logic further, if he constantly wishes to be in the world of fantasy, and you reward him for doing something well in the world of reality, this gives him the incentive to escape."

His wife extends the explanation of their unusual situation. "We are constantly pulling him toward health and reality by whatever means. Sometimes with love and affection; other times, you have to threaten punishment."

"You can't treat a severely sick person, or a psychotic, if you prefer," says Dr. Honig, "with theory only. You've got to give of your entire self."

Dr. Honig discovered his own empathy with psychotics while a general medical practitioner, several years ago, before entering psychiatry. "I saw the way institutions treated these very ill people," he recalls, "and it made me ill and ashamed of the whole medical profession. Animals are treated better. They are given drugs or shock treatments continually, and they become subhuman."

Early in his career, he successfully treated, with "direct analysis" techniques, two women who were regarded as incurable: a catatonic and a girl who seemed to be blind. "This catatonic woman wasn't responding to anyone or anything. She wasn't even responding to normal body-release functions. I went into her ward one day and just sat on the top of her and held her nose and mouth until she finally shook me off and shouted, 'You get off of me!' It was almost like the cure of a vision. This woman started talking after that and behaving like a human being."

The girl who was blind was also giving the doctors a hard time in all kinds of ways. Again using his intuition plus direct "attack" on the illness, Dr. Honig made her see again.

Dr. Honig's other remarkable results besides those he is currently achieving at his Delaware Valley Mental Health clinic (which, incidentally, is being run on a nonprofit, shoestring basis), include the curing of epileptics, a virtually unheard-of phenomenon, since epilepsy has always been considered a brain-damage, or physiological, illness.

In the beginning, about five years ago, when his clinic was set up, the community regarded him with apprehension. "One lady," he remembers, "went so far as to go to the local authorities and complain that she was afraid for her family's safety because we had a lot of nuts wandering around the place." Gradually, however, the community has accepted him and his group.

The greatest thing, to him, is that people from the so-called "uneducated" class have finally come to him for help. "This takes real belief and guts," he says, "because there is still so much shame attached in our society to being mentally sick."

His hope is to get the clinic to become a thorough community operation, with participation in its operation by local teachers, therapists, crafts workers, even nonexperts. "That's the only way a project like this can become a dynamic, living part of the society; otherwise, it becomes meaningless."

He is very concerned with this "symbolic help" idea. "You know, it's like some ancient ritual, like the scapegoat, or willing rain or sunshine. People get together, raise money, build a classy-looking building, hire classy-sounding people, and once in a while, even go down there and play around with putty or basket weaving. All this is to get rid of their guilt. But it doesn't help the sick."

He is quite aware that his daring, inventive setup has alienated conservative members of the psychiatric community at large. "The rigidly constructed people feel actually menaced by new ideas, threatened, and they react just as if a lion had suddenly crossed their path."

Finally, Dr. Honig insists that mental-health projects be totally separated from hospitals. "There is absolutely no connection between the two operations," he asserts. "Hospitals are oriented biologically, we're oriented psychologically."

---

43 | Dr. Berne Plays the Celebrity Game

Jack Langguth

Not long ago, Dr. Eric Berne tried to play games with Frank Sinatra and nearly got his teeth kicked in. Their playground was The Daisy, a private discotèque in Beverly Hills. Dr. Berne is the author of a best-selling volume of pop psychology called *Games People Play.* Mr. Sinatra sings for a living.

To observers untrained in Dr. Berne's method, the exchange seemed surly but simple enough: a 56-year-old psychiatrist and a 50-year-old singer were intently watching a girl in the act of frugging. "Ha, ha!" said Dr. Berne to Mr. Sinatra, "you're as big a lecher as I am."

Two hulking strangers materialized in the night to ask Dr. Berne, "You want your teeth down your throat?" With another pleasantry, the psychiatrist excused himself.

For Dr. Berne, who has shared this version of the episode with his colleagues in Nothern California, his adventure did not involve four men but a full dozen. His theories of behavior are based on the division of every human being into three separate and competing ego states: Child, Adult and Parent.

At The Daisy, Dr. Berne's Child had tried to engage Mr. Sinatra's Child, but reached instead the singer's puritanical Parent. Deeply offended, this Parent decided to punish the obstreperous Child and called on two men retained for that purpose. Within the doctor's framework, only this duo behaved as Adults. If part of their job was to threaten other people's teeth, and if they fulfilled their contract, then their actions were fully rational, with neither their Child nor their Parent showing.

The example does scant justice to Dr. Berne or his theories. In public, he seldom displays his Child. And those theories are being used in therapy groups, prisons and hospitals throughout the country to treat more serious problems than the unexpected appearance of Mr. Sinatra's Parent.

But at least the misunderstanding shows how Dr. Berne's life has changed, not always for the better, in the year since his short, slangy catalogue of neurotic games has become a great success. True, from the proceeds on almost 300,000 hard-cover copies, he's acquired a four-bedroom house in the hills of Carmel and a Maserati 3500 GL convertible, and he's taken a holiday in Hawaii. "At the same time, I've accepted too many speaking engagements," he says fretfully. "I haven't been at my typewriter for six months. That's very hard on me."

Ah, Doctor! Isn't it possible that your Parent fears and resents the popularity that your Child enjoys so thoroughly? And so the Child defends his indulgence by claiming overcommitment?

"That's true," the doctor freely agrees. "I'm probably playing a variation of 'If It Weren't For Them.' "

During his 30 years as an analyst, Dr. Berne has caught patients playing dozens of games. To each of them, he's given a breezy name that makes Freudian practitioners wince and sensitive stylists bite their tongues. The literary circle in Carmel, where Robinson Jeffers spent much of his life, accepts Dr. Berne as a friend but no peer. "His book," was one appraisal, "is silly, cheap and corny."

Yet whatever fault one finds with his taste, Dr. Berne's terms are direct and clear to every patient or reader: "Ain't It Awful," "Let's You and Him Fight," "Now I've Got You, You Son of a Bitch," "Rapo."

A casual reader might skim the *Games* book to locate his own favorite maneuver, or his wife's, and miss the theoretical base Dr. Berne has built to explain human behavior. The doctor calls his system Transactional Analysis, and like most of his writing, that name is literal. Dr. Berne analyzes "the overt manifestations of social intercourse" which he calls "transactions." In a book on the subject published six years ago, "Transactional Analysis in Psychotherapy," he explains that he begins treatment by watching the patients in his therapy groups as they conduct the normal conversations and byplays—the transactions—of everyday life. He widens his inquiry gradually, learning more about complicated relationships at home or on the job, in the present or the past. Then he traces these patterns of behavior back to Greek myths, fairy tales, fantasies. As an example, he pointed to the woman who married one alcoholic after another as someone caught in a rescue fantasy.

A current patient is a troubled 16-year-old boy in San Francisco whose father had divorced his mother years before, moved to St. Louis and married again. The boy is headed for the Midwest this summer to meet for the first time his father's second wife. With him, Dr. Berne probed for a "Hansel and Gretel" fantasy, recalling that in one version of the story the children return from killing the witch to find their father with a new wife. "A better wife," the boy added.

Where Freud probed forces below the conscious level, Dr. Berne deals chiefly with the three "different and inconsistent" selves—or ego states—that he believes alternate in speaking for each person. First there is the ego state which "resembles that of parental figures." The Parent, at its most benevolent, is the confident self that knows which fork to use, which temptations to resist. At worst, the Parent may crush all joyousness in a person or in the people around him.

Second there is the ego state which "is automatically directed toward objective appraisal of reality." This is the Adult, whose rationality should be employed to make those decisions for which the Parent has no precedent.

Third, the ego state which "was fixated in early childhood"—a still-active archaic relic. The Child is the easiest of the three categories to define, since everyone has been a child and can see traces of the childish or childlike in his grown-up behavior. The Child may be charming in its spontaneity or embarrassing in its willful folly.

A healthy man allows the right ego state to function at the right time. If the Child keeps showing up at his office or the Parent is nagging his marriage into divorce court, the man may need a Transactional Analyst to help him program his personality. The methods that analyst will use are fundamentally different from the classical analysis, for Dr. Berne and his adherents do not sit mute for 50 minutes, taking notes and looking shockproof.

A Transactional Analysis session might look, from the dark side of an observation mirror, much the same as several other forms of group therapy now being practiced. But none of the other systems are anchored to the Parent-Adult-Child theory that these analysts now find indispensable. "My patients always understand right away what I'm talking about," a therapist will say when asked why he was attracted to Dr. Berne's system. "It's so clear."

Dr. Berne himself is not eager to get into a fight on every psychoanalytic front. He often says there's much about his theory he must still fill in. He'll remark, diffidently, that "everything in my books I learned from my patients." What they have taught him, however, he's zealous about passing on to others, and he suggests this general summary of the difference between Transactional and other analyses:

"Most psychotherapists, it would appear, are interested in what they can learn from their patients. We're interested in what the patients can learn, and we have no hesitation about teaching them."

In a typical exchange, quoted in Dr. Berne's 1960 text, a woman in a therapy group abruptly said, "I have something to tell you today. I like to fight, too. That's why I fight with my daughter."

Laughing, Dr. Berne answered, "I'm glad that you finally admit that you like to fight."

And the woman volunteered, "I have to fight with somebody to keep interested."

The moment of self-analysis, combined with a resolve to break out of a harmful pattern, may come in an instant, the psychiatrist has found. But preparation for that instant may take months or years. Like most professional healers, Dr. Berne refuses to promise results by a timetable. He speaks of six months as an absolute minimum for effective therapy.

Despite his casual names for transactions, they must meet rigid qualifications before Dr. Berne will accept them as true games. He insists on locating a con, a gimmick and a payoff. If, for example, a woman courts a compliment and receives it gracefully, she has only indulged in a social pastime. But if she has asked for reassurance, received it and then tried to show that the compliment was undeserved, she's played "Yes, But." Her pay-off was not the simple massaging of her vanity but the chance to prove her partner stupid and feel superior at his expense.

In the last few months Dr. Berne has come to believe that games are always harmful because they involve emotional deception—the con. To keep his games theory unmuddled, the doctor would now remove all harmless "games" from his book and label them mere "pastimes." The pastime, like the one he calls "Homely Sage," does not rest on ulterior motives. The sage acquires odd bits of learning during his business career in a big city. When he retires to a small town, he offers this knowledge unassumingly to his new neighbors. In the "Games" book the sage was playing a good game. Now that the doctor has decided that all games, by definition, are destructive, the sage is held to be only passing time.

"Con" and "gimmick," like "shrink" for "analyst," are words instantly adopted by Dr. Berne because they're short. In his guide for group therapists Dr. Berne demands that young shrinks "try to say it in Anglo-Saxon words of no more than two syllables."

He offers this contrast: A Freudian might say, "Oh, yes, another paranoid 30-year-old unmarried woman secretary with no siblings and a strict father." The Transactional Analyst would say, "Oh, yes, a secretive 'Ain't It Awful' player who always looks tearful so that people won't ask her too many questions and who is continually threatening to quit her job."

Or, for another example, the doctor's own life can be quickly outlined in straight biographical prose. Eric Lennard Berne was born in Montreal on May 10, 1910. His father, a medical doctor, died when the boy was 10 years old. Eric and his younger sister were raised by their mother, who wrote for Montreal newspapers to support the family. After completing his medical training at McGill University, Eric Berne migrated to the United States to take up psychiatric residency. He became a U.S. citizen shortly before he was drafted into the Army in 1943. In the Army he got his first chance to practice group therapy on a broad scale.

Divorced twice, he has four children and two stepchildren. In recent years he has split his private practice between Carmel, where he spends weekends, and San Francisco, driving or flying the 70 miles north each Tuesday morning and leaving Thursday nights. Before "Games People Play" he had written a number of more sedate books on psychoanalytic theory.

Besides being dull, that summary insults a man who insists on being trisected. If Dr. Berne is to be analyzed, let it be done transactionally.

Dr. Berne's Parent is firm, fair and rigorous, comforting to his patients and inspiring to younger men who come to study his theories. To his chagrin, his Parent displays almost all of the conventional moral values: moderation, self-control, cleanliness, decency, tireless effort. Throughout his book runs the strong assumption that fame and fortune are automatically good things.

He said lately, "I told my new secretary, who is just finishing college, that her first job for me is to get A's in all her classes." Not to do her best, Doctor? Not to absorb as much as she can? Just to worry about high grades? "It was a joke," Dr. Berne explained. Nevertheless, pretty Pamela Blum is now winning straight A's for the first time in her life.

Miss Blum, who is 23 years old, was less dutiful when Dr. Berne warned her against LSD. She took the drug under the supervision of another psychiatrist and over Dr. Berne's objections that her trip was not necessary. She found the experience well worthwhile, and she does not discuss the drug now with her employer.

Despite a fondness for sporty grammar and backwoods dialect, Dr. Berne's Parent is extremely cautious in the treating of patients. He has experimented a few times with marathon therapy sessions, and he's not at all convinced of their merits. He can't remember when he last referred a patient for shock treatment, and he hasn't used hypnosis for 25 years. As for drugs—"when I prescribe them, as I occasionally do, I feel it's because of my own ignorance."

As the father of a new approach to treating patients, Dr. Berne is properly Parental when he outlines Transactional Analysis, or T.A. Every Tuesday night he opens his second home, a row house in San Francisco, for free seminars with other therapists who want to learn his method. If he thinks a newcomer has come to heckle, Dr. Berne doesn't fret over his failure to appear broadminded or tolerant. "I tell him to stop bugging me, and if he doesn't he can get out. I don't like people bugging me."

As a teacher or therapist however, the doctor is excellent at bugging others. Courteously but relentlessly he probes at those root questions so self-explanatory that they are seldom explained. A psychiatric resident came to him a few weeks ago for advice on setting up a therapy group; the young man spouted case histories and long words. Dr. Berne cut in, "Why do you want this group? What are you personally going to get out of it?"

The resident's baby face fell into a fat grin: "It'll be fun."

That answer did not distress Dr. Berne, who preaches laughter and even practices it. "If I have a concept of God," he has said, "the main thing is that He has a sense of humor."

Like other apostles of joy, notably gag writers and street-walkers, Dr. Berne often seems burdened by his responsibility to make other people happy. "We want patients to hear the birds sing," he can say, making it sound like a duty other people are shirking. "We encourage that kind of childlike awareness. Patients who really do hear the birds and see the trees get very excited."

It was a little boy, back in 1954, who taught Dr. Berne the central truth of Transactional Analysis. Or, more precisely, it was a successful middle-aged lawyer who said during a therapy session, "I'm not really a lawyer. I'm just a little boy."

Rather than preserve an impassive silence, Dr. Berne said, "That's interesting. Tell me more."

From that time on he would ask the patient: "Is that the man talking, or the little boy you told me about?" T.A. was on its way.

Independence has always been one of the frontier values most attractive to Dr. Berne's Parent. "I seem to do better when I'm in charge of things," he said, as he recounted the successes he had with tough Army patients after their whole ward was delivered into his hands. Today the doctor disdains all foundation money or government grants because of the strings attached, no matter how long or loose they may be.

Begun in 1958, the weekly seminars in his home were incorporated last year into the International Transactional Analysis Association, with 500 members in 26 states, Canada, Costa Rica and England. Founder and first president, Dr. Berne now serves as the severe editor of the I.T.A.A. quarterly journal. He's found that only one of his fellow members, an Austrian, can write articles that don't need translation from psychiatric polysyllables into plain English. He also permits no article to run more than two pages because "it looks tidier that way." (He's really very anal," one devotee says of Dr. Berne, "but don't tell him I used a Freudian term.")

Young psychiatrists who employ Dr. Berne's method rarely feel that they are betraying their Freudian training. "T.A. is an offshoot of psychoanalysis," one young man said. "It's a useful method of treatment, but it's thoroughly grounded in Freud."

Dr. Berne's quarrel seems more with his contemporaries than with his predecessors. "I think Freud would consider most analysts today nothing but picture straighteners," he says. "They may be good teachers, but they don't publish enough to share their insights."

His own success as a writer has permitted him to lift his sights as a therapist. Until six months ago he shared with other psychiatrists the desire to help patients get better. Now he ridicules that modest aim. "We don't want patients to make progress," he often says. "We want them to get well. Or, in our lingo, we want to turn frogs into princes. We're not satisfied with making them braver frogs."

Dr. Berne treats about 60 patients a week, usually eight at a time. For a weekly 90 minutes the average patient pays $7.50. With his other consulting work, Dr. Berne was already grossing between $25,000 and $50,000 a year before he became a best-selling writer. Most of the 75-cent royalty he gets from each book goes to the Internal Revenue Service.

Dr. Berne's Child cracked the jokes that helped to push his book to success, but his Parent's mordant wit also deserves some mention. One young woman tells of her first private session with him before joining a therapy group. "I was determined not to hold anything back, although it's very difficult for me to talk about intimate things. Still, I forced myself to sit there and tell him everything I thought he should know about me—my childhood, my marriage, my sex life.

"When I got all done and was really exhausted, he looked up and said, 'Would you take off your dark glasses and tell me that all over again?' "

Inspecting the custom-made sports car of one of his younger colleagues, Dr. Berne observed, "Your patients will start getting well when you get a car with handles that open as easily from the inside as they do from the outside."

The Adult is hard for Dr. Berne to define. In his book on Transactional Analysis he suggests that the Adult is what is left after all Parent and Child aspects have been strained away. More recently he described the Adult as a computer making rational decisions based on realistic alternatives.

When his Adult is in command, Dr. Berne offers this sermon on life: "Life is really very simple. But if people have to face that fact they get very upset. So they invent religions and pastimes and games. These are the same people who then lament how awful it is that life is complicated. But all complications involve decisions, and a person must assess the probabilities and possibilities, make the best decision and then go down the street whistling."

That's Dr. Berne's sensible, logical Adult. But his Adult must always wrestle with the doctor's impish Child. Conducting seminars and therapy groups, his Parent can hold the Child on tight rein. But in social gatherings Dr. Berne's Child wreaks his revenge.

For that reason neighbors in Carmel view Dr. Berne differently from the way his patients or disciples do. They don't understand his contention that a party isn't a real party unless everyone is wiggling to the latest teen-age dances. They are puzzled by his glorification of poker, at which he is an adept, as an existential experience. Some of them find Dr. Berne's jokes juvenile. Others detect a talent for inappropriate remarks that approaches genius.

Ask Dr. Berne's Adult to describe himself and out of the nether reaches comes "I'm a 56-year-old teen-ager" or "I'm sort of a swinger. I like action." If these labels are accurate for Dr. Berne, they are equally apt for George Romney or James Gould Cozzens.

The doctor's Adult fares no better in education. His small study is a shed behind the house in Carmel where his former wife is raising their two adolescent sons. To reach it he goes down the hill from his new four-bedroom bachelor quarters. The study's walls are lined with books on every subject, but Dr. Berne's Adult has little taste for general reading. His Parent has amassed a wide and impressive background to buttress and illustrate his theories. Dr. Berne's Child reads only to dazzle and confound.

The doctor was delighted, for example, when a New York news magazine called to ask what he was currently reading and he could answer "The Kuzzilbash," a three-volume swashbuckler about 18th-century Persia.

When his secretary is working on a college theme, Dr. Berne volunteers obscure references that will intimidate her instructors. The doctor is unabashed about playing Stephen Potter's "One-upmanship." "When we really want to put someone down," he told a visitor as they walked through Carmel, "we call this town Carmel-by-the-Sea." Someday a disciple may trace the rise of Dr. Berne's self-confidence by noting when his books stop listing his residence as Carmel-by-the-Sea.

Dr. Berne's Adult takes little interest, at least for publication, in political affairs. "In 1950," he recalls, "someone burst into my study and said, 'North and South Korea are at war.' I said, 'So what?' A man who has made that kind of gross error in judgment had better not consider himself equipped to discuss public events."

Among friends he makes occasional observations couched in his jargon. ("I saw Nixon on TV and his Child was showing.")

In those personalities which Dr. Berne most admires, the natural and unfettered Child, full of wonder and creativity, is an attractive element. His own Child is something else again.

One of the few poignant moments in the doctor's writing comes when he tells about the failure of a 10-year-old boy named Davy to get other boys to join a club in his basement. By founding the Agamemnon Club, Davy had hoped to become a leader. But the boy, Dr. Berne writes, "had few of the magical or even social attributes of leadership in the eyes of his contemporaries and had only one or two loyal followers."

The boy grew up to be a therapist who treated people in his own home. When pressed, Dr. Berne allows that in the interest of accuracy the "Davy" in his text should have been called "Eric."

That pseudonym is only one of many Dr. Berne has used. As an undergraduate at McGill he wrote comic columns for the student newspaper under the names "Lennard Gandalac" and "Ramsbottom Horsely." Why "Gandalac"?

"Is that a secret I have to tell?" the doctor asks. "Well, the name comes from old French epics. He was a sort of hero. A big man, physically. A giant, I guess."

Later he wrote as "Peter Pinto." And now his association's journal prints short fables about a hillbilly sage named "Cyprian St. Cyr." Even Eric Lennard Berne is something of an invention. His parents had settled for the more conventional "Leonard," but the boy changed the spelling to suit himself. "I don't know why. It just looked better that way."

A word Dr. Berne often uses is "permission." If a man fails in every job, his Parent is not giving him permission to succeed. The therapist must then trace the reasons and help him to see that he has every right to do a job well and reap the rewards. In his own case, whenever Dr. Berne tried to write humor, the result always appeared under a made-up name. But the comic strain was getting progressively wider through his clinical writing until in "Games People Play" he had produced, under his own name, a serious book with jokes, dialogue and an enticing title.

When he finished the "Games" book early in 1962, Dr. Berne sent off the manuscript and then waited more than two years while it was shuffled across editorial desks at Grove Press. He was sure that he'd finally won permission to have a best-seller, but someone in the publisher's office was still blocked. Finally the book appeared in book-stalls during the summer of 1964 and languished there. One copy might be sold to a former patient. Then, in self-defense, the patient's friends would all have to buy copies. Sales were slow, but they never stopped.

After a full year, Grove's teasing advertisements began to ram the book onto best-seller lists and keep it there. No wonder, then, that Dr. Berne has become very friendly with Grove's publicity director but that he can't recall the names of any of the editors.

During his long wait the doctor produced a children's book, "The Happy Valley." It's one of those stories, favored by moralists, in which animals talk like people, only better. When Dr. Berne tires of the Celebrity game he'll turn out a sequel to the "Games" book under another title good enough to keep secret in the meanwhile.

Further in his future, Dr. Berne sees some novels. "I want to creep up on fiction," he explains, "starting with something short and autobiographical." If Carmel's literati are dubious, Dr. Berne has his own reservations about them. "I once met a man in Carmel who wasn't a novelist," he says ironically. His Parent pops up to add, "I have very little sympathy for artists who can't work while they're creating—the ones who let their children starve in order to finish a book."

His Parent is a little tired, too, of hearing people tell him that George and Martha play games in "Who's Afraid of Virginia Woolf?" and that they call their games by even racier titles than his. He's neither seen nor read the play, and he cuts off any discussion by pointing out that it's one thing to have a few insights and another to build them into a consistent theory. To illustrate, he borrows a metaphor from Freud: "Flirting is different from marriage."

So far, Dr. Berne's Parent has vetoed all offers from television producers who want to buy at least his title for a weekly series. But with a shrug of resignation his Parent has permitted Cy Feurer and Ernest Martin to begin turning his book into a musical comedy for Broadway.

Dr. Berne's Adult welcomes the chance to acquaint a new kind of audience with his theories, although the musical won't be a nightly seminar exactly. Art Buchwald is one of the writers working on the book.

But the doctor's Child is delighted with the venture. He relishes the exposure to show business people and the chance to get full credit at last for being funny. Everything is wonderful, and Dr. Berne's Child probably could be happier only if Feuer and Martin would stage the show in his basement.

---

44 | Tracking Down the Causes of Birth Defects

Richard L. Masland, M.D.

Nearly four million babies are born each year in the United States, and usually birth is a happy event for all concerned. But too often it is not: Of every five pregnancies, one fails to produce a living child. About 126,000 mentally retarded children are born each year—one of every 32 babies. One of every 166 live-born infants is afflicted with cerebral palsy. Approximately four million individuals in the United States—one American in 50—have some form of brain damage.

From *Today's Health,* August 1966. Reprinted by permission of the author and *Today's Health,* published by the American Medical Association.

To find the causes of such defects, so that they may be prevented, a vast national study has been under way since 1959. By the end of 1966, it will involve nearly 60,000 women and their 50,000 babies enrolled in one of the most interesting and vital research programs at the National Institutes of Health: the "Collaborative Study on Cerebral Palsy, Mental Retardation, and Other Neurological and Sensory Disorders of Infancy and Childhood."

Some of the mothers and babies under study may live near you, for 14 leading medical centers* in various cities are cooperating with the National Institute of Neurological Diseases and Blindness in the project.

And already the research has uncovered preliminary answers to some of the questions that trouble your physician. What diseases of the mother, for example, harm the unborn baby? What drugs harm the fetus? How can premature births and breech babies be forestalled? What kinds of anesthesia are safest for the infant? If the mother smokes, is the baby harmed? What are the earliest signs of birth defects?

Cerebral palsy, epilepsy, mental retardation, and certain forms of specific learning and perceptual disabilities all may be various manifestations of brain damage, and many different diseases and conditions may be responsible. These causes frequently produce their damage during pregnancy or at the time of birth, but their effects may not become evident until months or years later. For this reason, precise knowledge of the nature of these harmful conditions and the ways in which they affect the unborn child has been difficult to obtain; the Collaborative Perinatal (in the area of birth) Project is an effort to resolve this problem by careful detailed study of a massive sample.

An elaborate program of examination of the mother and child has been developed. For the mother, this includes family history, medical history, prenatal obstetrical and medical examinations, and laboratory examinations. Blood specimens taken during pregnancy are frozen and stored in a vast freezer at Bethesda, Maryland—available for a search for viruses or toxins active during pregnancy. Every delivery is attended by a trained observer—sometimes an Institute scientist—who records in detail every event, thus supplementing the usual nursing and physician's records of this crucial event.

For the child, there has been prepared a series of examination statistics from the moment of birth, when observation of color, respiration, muscle tone, and heart action are recorded. The examinations include pediatric examination at four months of age, a developmental at eight months, a neurological at 12 months, speech and hearing at 36 months, psychological at 48 months, and a broad total evaluation in the early school years, ages seven and eight.

---

* Cooperating institutions are: Boston Lying-In Hospital; Brown University and Associated Hospitals, Providence, Rhode Island; Charity Hospital, New Orleans; Children's Hospital of Buffalo; Children's Hospital of Philadelphia; Children's Medical Center, Boston; Columbia University, New York City; Johns Hopkins University, Baltimore, Maryland; Medical College of Virginia, Richmond; New York Medical College; Pennsylvania Hospital; University of Minnesota; University of Oregon; University of Tennessee.

There are included special laboratory examinations of blood specimens of the mother and child, of the placenta, and of material from infants born prematurely, or dying in infancy. Every effort has been made to develop a series of examinations which will record any deviation of the course of pregnancy, and which detect accurately and at the earliest age any evidences of brain damage or neurological dysfunction in the development of the children.

Today, with registration of Study mothers completed and the last of their infants soon to be born, the Collaborative Perinatal Project is preparing millions of bits of information for the computers which will "mix and match" related facts. Obstetricians, pediatricians, geneticists, neuropathologists, psychologists, biostatisticians, and representatives of many other disciplines will be working together over a period of years to analyze the data. They are seeking to identify new cause-and-effect relationships to devise means of treatment or prevention.

The public-health issues involved are crucial, the pressure for answers great, so although the data are still far from complete, the Project Investigators and their colleagues have already actively involved themselves with some of the most urgent of our contemporary public-health problems—with the epidemic of German measles (rubella), which left thousands of defective babies in its wake; with the sometimes-fearful controversies over the effects of drugs taken by pregnant women on their unborn children; with the contemporary great and hopeful crusade against mental retardation.

When it became apparent in 1963 that the nation was beginning to experience an epidemic of German measles, the Neurology Institute through its Collaborative Perinatal Project was in a most strategic position to conduct what might be called battlefield reconnaissance. In the path of the epidemic stood the 14 collaborating medical centers. Through blood tests of 700 of the Study mothers, Project virologists had established the fact that about one in five of our young women of child-bearing age has no apparent antibody defense against rubella. Previous studies had shown that when one of these women acquired rubella during pregnancy there was a serious danger that this infection might be carried to her unborn baby. When this occurs, such defects as impaired vision, faulty hearing, and brain damage may result.

The Collaborative Project virologists had shared in the first identification of the rubella virus, reported in 1962, and had gone on to work on experimental vaccines. Although crude vaccine materials proved to cause some immune response in prisoner volunteers, unusually difficult problems arose in the development of a safe and effective vaccine. The need was for a potent vaccine, but one which would not possibly harm the unborn child. In 1963, when the epidemic began, such a vaccine had not been developed, although great efforts were made, as they now are, to hasten development.

As cases increased, the Project directors quickly modified the program to meet this emergency, and special additional blood tests of Project women and babies were taken during the 1963–65 period of the epidemic. Meanwhile, the Study virologists developed a more rapid blood test for detecting recent infection by rubella. The Public Health Service's Communicable Disease Center at Atlanta, Georgia, is attempting to make several types of improved rubella tests available to state laboratories so that this procedure developed for research can be used more generally in the management of pregnant women who are exposed to German measles.

A report entitled "Rubella Epidemic, 1964: Effect on 6000 Pregnancies" was published in the American Medical Association's *Journal of Diseases of Children.* This report summarizes the valuable epidemiological information that has been acquired. For example, during an epidemic, from what source do pregnant women contract the infection? The Study shows that exposures at home, from children or others with the disease, were no more likely to cause contagion than were exposures outside of the home. How many exposed women actually become sick with the disease? The Study reports about three percent with obvious disease, but most important, an additional six percent had laboratory evidences of the disease but were unaware that they had been sick. Some of these had defective babies.

Based on data from this Study and related projects, it is estimated that this one epidemic in the United States caused from 5000 to 30,000 babies to be defective. It is hoped that from the experience gained from this epidemic, and through the development of an effective vaccine [one is now being tested—Eds.], a similar tragedy will never need to recur.

Even before this tragic epidemic of German measles had dramatized the problem, the planners of the Study had been aware of the probable importance of maternal infections as a cause of injury of the unborn child. An elaborate program has been established to learn the true role of other infections during pregnancy; two are under particular scrutiny.

Toxoplasmosis is a disease of dogs, cats, sheep, and man caused by a small, malaria-like organism called "Toxoplasma gondi." Analysis of blood specimens from this study revealed that almost one woman in four had demonstrable antibodies suggesting some previous exposure to this germ. When the children of these women exhibiting the most active evidences of infection were examined, a number were found to have visual damage or other neurological disorders due to their also being infected with this organism.

Within this study population, these preliminary data suggest that almost one in each 2000 babies is born with this damaging disease. Efforts are now under way to assess more accurately the full impact of this disease and to determine the means through which it is spread from animals to man. It may well prove to be a more important public-health problem than had been recognized.

Similar studies are also involved in relation to the "salivary-gland virus." This causes another common disease—harmless to the mother, but occasionally producing serious injury to the newborn child. Efforts are being made to determine the condition under which transmission to the baby takes place in this disease.

The recent thalidomide tragedy, in which thousands of babies were born defective because they had been poisoned before birth by a toxic drug taken by their mothers, emphasizes our need to evaluate with the greatest care any drug given to pregnant women. Fortunately, the Food and Drug Administration (FDA) had prevented the release of thalidomide in the United States, and the tragedy was limited here to a few cases where women obtained the medicine elsewhere.

The Collaborative Project is obtaining information to assure us that other drugs do not have some presently unrecognized harmful effect on the unborn child. The records include data on all drugs taken by the women in this study, records which are reviewed and searched for possible effects on the baby. In evaluating these drugs many factors must be considered, including dosage, duration of administration, and time of administration. Analysis is difficult because most drugs are given to treat some complication or maternal disease, and it is often hard to distinguish a harmful effect of the drug from a harmful effect of the disease for which it was given.

Among the drugs taken by Project mothers are antibiotics; various other anti-infectives, including antituberculosis drugs; barbiturates; local anesthetics; narcotics and various types of sedatives; ataractic (tranquilizing) compounds; motion-sickness and antinausea preparations; antihistamines; drugs to control obesity; antihypertensives; analgesic and antirheumatic compounds; hormones; diuretics; and scores of others.

Not long ago, it was comfortably assumed that the mother's placenta—the vascular structure by which the fetus is nourished—formed a barrier effective in protecting the fetus from the passage of drugs and other agents from the maternal circulation to the circulatory system of the unborn child. It is now recognized, however, that many substances can and do filter through the placenta.

The Collaborative Project has set up a computer program to observe results from several hundred different types of medications taken by the Study mothers. Initial results are screened regularly, and the Study scientists, like many other groups, provide information from time to time to the FDA. These clues are provided for immediate consideration but many variables must be taken into account before a cause-and-effect relationship can be established. Precise information and thoughtful analysis are critically important, for many of the drugs under observation are lifesaving in character.

There has been relatively little accumulated experience with many of the drugs being used today. The tendency of many women to use over-the-counter medications without a doctor's prescription, or to be careless in taking more of a drug than has been prescribed, further complicates the problem. A general rule followed by physicians in prescribing for pregnant women is to use new and potent drugs only when there is no good alternative.

In addition to infections and toxins, a variety of other conditions of pregnancy may also be associated with cerebral palsy. About one in 50 of the children of the Collaborative Perinatal Project shows neurological or sensory abnormalities when examined at one year of age. These abnormalities stem from a wide variety of causes. The Study is highlighting the conditions and situations under which there is an increased likelihood of an unfavorable pregnancy outcome. In so doing, it is frequently raising new questions requiring solution.

Premature infants, for example, show a higher percentage of nervous-system defects than do infants of normal birth weight. Is prematurity the cause of, or a result of, the neurological defect; or are both a result of some third factor? By comparing associated factors in a large number of premature births, at least partial answers may evolve.

Breech delivery (rear first) is another condition long known to be associated with high risk of neurological damage. The Study shows, however, that breech babies are often premature. Possibly the prevention of prematurity in breech babies is an important consideration.

Abnormal relaxation of the mouth of the uterus predisposes to premature labor. Among the first 20,000 pregnancies recorded in the Project, 63 cases of this condition (incompetent cervix) were observed. Such premature babies show a high frequency of neurological damage. In a small series of patients in whom the uterus was stitched by surgery early in pregnancy, this unfavorable outcome was reduced. Would this favorable result be confirmed in a larger and more carefully balanced series?

Mothers who smoke show a higher incidence of lightweight (five and one-half pounds or less) babies than do non-smokers. Are these small babies premature or is it that women who smoke have other characteristics that predispose their offspring to prematurity?

Infants born by Caesarian section have a less favorable early outlook than those born by natural delivery. This difference appears to correlate with the type of anesthesia used. Local anesthesia of the mother seems to have less effect on the newborn than general anesthesia. Again, one must wait for more exhaustive analysis to determine whether this difference merely reflects differences in the obstetrical conditions involved, or is a true reflection of the obstetrical procedures used.

Thus, these preliminary analyses are pointing the way toward the more definitive studies still to come.

The Collaborative Project provides an ideal means for precise evaluation of signs and symptoms needed for the early recognition of brain damage in infancy. These thousands of babies have been subjected to close scientific scrutiny at a series of crucial ages. What were the earliest reliable evidences of defect?

Studies of Project children indicate that it may be possible to diagnose neurosensory defects in very early life as the "hallmarks" of damage are more clearly defined.

One psychology group reports that light sensitivity and paroxysms of an infant's eyes a few days after birth may point to nervous-system damage such as mental retardation or epilepsy.

A neurologist has studied postural reflexes of Project infants and others over a period of three years. He has reported that the reflexes are both delayed and distorted in the majority of infants suffering from cerebral palsies, degenerative disease of the central nervous system, or general psychomotor retardation. The study helps establish an average "timetable" of the responses and the earliest or latest age at which a particular response can be stated to be "abnormal."

A Project otologist has published his observations on how early detection of certain ear abnormalities in premature infants can be accomplished employing brilliant white light and an otoscope with a very small speculum. If his observations are borne out in future work, early identification of prematures at risk could lead to preventing later deafness in cases for which methods of prophylaxis are available or can be developed.

Improvements in understanding the infant electroencephalograms (EEG's), so-called fingerprints of the brain, also are being worked out.

In March 1966, the collaborating scientists participated in the Project's Second Scientific Meeting held in Washington, D.C. Some of the reports commented on:

The need to reduce maternal mortality as well as infant defects.

The ability to make more accurate, early predictions of the birthweight of the infant.

A relationship observed between maternal infection with mumps and chickenpox and birth defects.

The correlation of fine-motor dexterity in eight-month-old infants and their higher scores in the four-year psychological examination.

Various factors, such as older age of mother, associated with increase of heart defects in newborn.

Spacing of electroencephalograms to give better pictures of brain development.

The possibility that male youngsters do not respond as well as females to some of the psychological tests may be due to preconditioning at home. Mothers often insist upon more conformity by little girls.

Because the Collaborative Project is limited to the observation of naturally occurring events, many of the questions which it raises cannot be answered within a human population. For answers to such questions, experimentation within an animal population is required. The process of pregnancy and delivery in the monkey closely parallels that of the human. For this reason, the Institute has established in Puerto Rico a Laboratory of Perinatal Physiology to further its search for the causes of cerebral palsy, and to investigate the means through which brain damage can occur and can be prevented.

Utilizing a free-ranging and also a laboratory colony of more than 1000 monkeys, the results of infections, toxins, and other agents are being studied. Various forms of cerebral palsy have been reproduced in these monkeys. Thus monkeys whose breathing was prevented at the time of birth showed irreparable damage, but this could be reduced by prompt treatment to restore normal chemical balance in the blood and tissues. Transitory interception of circulation through the umbilical cord during pregnancy causes other forms of cerebral palsy, excess bile pigment still another. The behavior of these animals, and that of others in whom there is precisely located, surgically produced brain damage, is being compared with that of normal control animals in the caged and free-ranging environment. These studies also are still in their infancy.

Paralleling the results of the observations of human populations in the Collaborative Project, the animal studies also should add much to our knowledge of the many causes of cerebral palsy and point toward means for prevention, early recognition, and management of these disorders.

45 | Children in Conflict

Barbara Culliton

One of every 10 children in the United States has a recognizable emotional problem. Most of these children could be rehabilitated, but only a fraction are. The rest carry their problems with them into adulthood and may eventually be counted among the one million Americans confined in mental hospitals, the three million treated as psychiatric out-patients or among the two million who never receive any help at all.

There are many reasons so few of these children receive counseling and therapy, one of the most important being that their "recognizable emotional problems" are never recognized.

Who is the emotionally disturbed child? What does he look like? Where does he come from? How, in fact, can he be recognized?

He looks like any child. He is not severely retarded or physically handicapped. A neurological examination would reveal no pathology. He is probably of average intelligence or above and often appears to be bright and alert. He can be rich or poor, black or white.

The emotionally disturbed child is more likely to come from the city than the country, and many authorities cite urbanization as a factor contributing to his problem. Too much urbanization seems to work against children in their growing years. It imposes too many rules, too many don'ts, and offers few channels through which they can release their tensions or express their joys.

COUNTRY CHILD CAN RUN

The most natural and emotionally healthy ways of doing this are closed to many city children who have no place to safely run or yell or climb or even sit quietly alone. The country child on the other hand, can escape from his "civilized" family if he wishes and retreat to a field or tree. If he is angry he can run and run and run until his anger is worked out of him or he can throw a stone without danger of getting himself into trouble by breaking mother's knickknacks or the grocery store window.

All this is not to suggest, however, that only country children are emotionally healthy. To say that is as patently false as it is to say that all city children are disturbed. What is important is that avenues of emotional freedom be available to the developing child.

Even though the immediate cause of emotional disturbance may lie in a child's social environment, in a world that is restrictive and frustrating to him in any number of ways, his particular adverse response to his world may well have underlying constitutional causes. That is, his physical and psychological characteristics, determined by a combination of genetic, biochemical and physiological factors, make him more susceptible to emotional illness than are other children. In short, an environment that triggers problems for

---

From *Science News,* **90,** August 1966. Reprinted by permission of *Science News,* weekly summary of current science,

one child might not be a disrupting influence for another, and one could hypothesize that a disturbed child, had he come from a different place or had a different set of parents, might not be disturbed at all.

Although children with problems are by no means a new phenomenon, it is only recently that concentrated efforts have been started to recognize and treat them. In line with these efforts, teachers must be taught to look for signs of trouble, more health facilities must be built or equipped to deal with children in the early stages of illness and thus cure, or at least control, personality disorders that might otherwise grow to monstrous proportions.

SOME ARE LEFT BEHIND

Why is it that some children are brought to clinics and schools while others are left behind? Some come because perceptive parents or teachers recognize their need for help. But many come simply because their pattern of behavior is so disturbing or so atypical that their families or schools cannot stand to have them around, and so they ship them off to someone else to handle. Many are left behind because their illnesses are never recognized, because their problems do not show themselves in obvious or annoying ways. The child who continually smashes everything in his path, or who brazenly and regularly brings chaos to the classroom is far more likely to receive attention than the quiet and withdrawn youngster who is never a source of trouble. A busy working mother or insensitive teacher can easily miss indications of disorder in a child who does not obtrusively demand her attention.

Among those children whose problems are spotted, some are lucky enough to be treated at a comprehensive psychiatric center like the Hillcrest Children's Center in Washington, D.C., where Dr. Nicholas J. Long and a staff of fully trained doctors, psychologists and social workers offer the child and his family a variety of services, including a psychiatric outpatient clinic, a therapeutic nursery school, an elementary school and treatment program, and residential therapy for children who cannot live comfortably at home.

Hillcrest is among the pioneers in the field of comprehensive community agencies providing a range of diagnostic and treatment services under one roof.

BUSINESS IS LEARNING

The business of childhood is learning and Hillcrest offers a therapeutic elementary school program dealing with about 40 children and their families. Five days a week, 11 months a year, classes of about eight children grouped according to their social rather than academic needs meet with two specially trained teachers. They work together at the job of knowing themselves and the world they live in.

At first glance, a class at Hillcrest is like any other small elementary class. Attractive, well-groomed youngsters begin the day seated quietly at their desks.

On one morning when this writer visited the school, a group of 10–13-year-olds, two girls and six boys, were learning about the habits and habitats of wild animals. A student teacher, supervised by two experienced staff members, read to the class and asked them to answer simple questions about what they had heard.

Most answered eagerly, nearly all correctly. But one by one, even within the first few minutes, their attention started to wander. A feeling of restlessness began to take hold. Finally, Sarah, who had been growing more and more tense during the short lesson and who could no longer control herself by clenching her fists or contorting her face, threw a tantrum to the particular delight of at least one of the other children who had been subtly precipitating the crisis. Immediately both children were taken from the class to an adjacent room where a teacher talked with each individually.

Why, one counselor asked, had John deliberately tormented Sarah? "Because I like to see her go 'waa, waa,' " he answered. And so they talked for a while about the reasons John got pleasure from aggravating others and his inability to ever stop himself from inciting Sarah's tantrums.

In another corner of the room a second counselor talked with Sarah and together they thought about why she had been so nervous and excitable that day. She was not sick, she said, or tired. She was afraid to face the second classroom activity of the morning, which was writing a story. She had lots of ideas, she told her teacher, but they left her quickly and since she was given no paper to write on she would have forgotten everything by the time the rest of the class began writing. And so, for a long time she and her counselor talked about her fears and he was able to give her confidence and assurance just at the time she needed it. One of the great advantages of a school with such a high faculty-student ratio is that there is someone available to help cope with problems and crises as they arise, at the very moment when they are most threatening and fearsome to the child.

By 9:30 the class was united again, all members present, and each student did write a short piece about what he expected to see or do on a field trip the class had planned for the following day. Most of them wrote simply that they would go on a bus and then ferry to the Point of Rocks where they would see waterfalls and eat hot dogs. One boy, the most advanced in the group, wrote in full smoothly structured sentences. Another gave his counselors insight into his pathology by writing this story:

"HELP MOTHER"

"Look Ma. Cruty, dirty. No Potomac for me. No No No No No No. Not me. Just ferry for me. Help Mother. I'm on a cliff. Butt, Black Bear, Help."

A disjointed home life with no father and a mother seldom in evidence has made this child feel threatened by any new experience that faces him. His fear of his world is revealed in his brief story, which he finished by announcing to his class, "That's it. I'm not writing any more," and then by scribbling heavy dark lines across the unused portion of his page. In such a situation, the classroom teacher will show the pupil's story to the therapist, who will talk with the child about his anxiety during their next private session.

With stories finished, recess came. At that point, yet another boy, who had behaved beautifully during that first hour, could control himself no more and exploded in a fit of temper and frustration. A private session with a counselor, followed by private period in the art studio where he painted and worked with clay at will, helped him regain his self-control.

In short, what appeared on the surface to be just an ordinary elementary class at 9:00 a.m. had broken down by 9:15 and continued for a typical day during which it would be built up and strengthened, and then disrupted as its members ran out of the stuff that the average child has to hold himself in check or focus his attention. But, gradually, this process of special education, in which no one period lasts very long, and in which study is liberally laced with recess and sports and art, the invisible hurts of emotional illness begin to heal.

IDEAL ENVIRONMENT

The school tries to create, as much as is possible an ideal environment for learning. It tries to maintain a climate that encourages its pupils to examine themselves, to look for the cause of their difficulties internally and not settle for the easy way out.

Although the "real" world may be responsible for a child's inability to cope with himself and others, it is also a justification for his failure. He can always say, in effect, "why should I meet the vague or unreasonable demands of this crumby world?"

This is not an easy question to answer. The psychiatric school tries to create an ideal setting, one that is carefully designed to foster rehabilitation in every possible way. It tries to change its pace often enough to preclude boredom so that students cannot explain away antisocial behavior on the grounds of being bored. It sets limits to behavior which it considers reasonable and comprehensible, and yet maintains a flexibility that would be almost impossible for a public school to offer. And finally, it introduces the disturbed child to well-trained teachers who devote their energies to understanding his needs and who know when to offer love, when authority, when to pay attention and when to ignore.

While the child is enrolled in school, he is assigned to a psychotherapist for at least weekly sessions. His parents receive guidance from the psychiatric social workers. Usually, the combined effect of a strengthened home environment and a specialized school environment, as well as regular psychotherapy, enable the child to return to his public or private school after two years. Supportive therapy will then be offered to him as an outpatient for a year or more, depending on his needs.

WORKS AS PREVENTIVE MEDICINE

More schools and centers like Hillcrest and its counterparts are needed if psychiatry is to be successful as a kind of preventive medicine, reaching the young and rehabilitating them for useful and creative lives. Institutions like Hillcrest are often supported by private donations. The work they do with a limited number of children is itself justification for their existence, but an additional raison d'etre, and an additional reason they deserve community support, is that many are affiliated with local hospitals. Under the medical leadership of Dr. Reginald S. Lourie, Hillcrest, for example, offers training programs in psychiatry, clinical psychology, social work and education to about 25 young men and women yearly from area hospitals and graduate schools—professional people who will move from Hillcrest to other institutions and other areas, taking with them the background and know-how to establish more centers to help more young children and families in trouble.

Unit Ten | DISCUSSION QUESTIONS

41. *Prevention in Psychiatry*
    Discuss some types of programs necessary to prevent the "social breakdown syndrome."
    Discuss preventive psychiatry from the social, emotional, and environmental points of view.
42. *Revolutionary Treatment of the Mentally Ill*
    Why is total participation by the doctor and patient an effective method in aiding the mentally ill?
    Discuss the "eclectic" viewpoint in psychotherapy.
43. *Dr. Berne Plays the Celebrity Game*
    Compare the roles of the child, parent, and adult in Berne's theory with the id, ego, and superego in Freud's theory.
    What does Berne mean by "games people play"?
44. *Tracking Down the Causes of Birth Defects*
    How is the Collaborative Project attempting to cure the causes of birth defects?
    What is being done to prevent such problems as the recent thalidomine tragedy?
45. *Children in Conflict*
    Name three factors contributing to emotional disturbance in children.
    Describe characteristics of an emotionally disturbed child.

Unit Eleven *Self-Understanding and Social Feeling*

From "pop psychiatry" to complex personality theories many viewpoints and interpretations concerning methods for understanding ourselves and others have been introduced. Theories of Sigmund Freud, Carl Jung, Alfred Adler, Eric Fromm, Karen Horney, and Harry Stack Sullivan present ways of viewing the human psyche. These theories and methods have not been the sole province of the behavioral scientist; many have been religious figures, public speakers, and salesmen. Each decade has its own language and methodology. Dale Carnegie in 1936 wrote *How To Win Friends and Influence People.* Two of his most famous maxims are "Believe that you will succeed, and you will" and "Learn to love, respect, and enjoy other people." Norman Vincent Peale believed that one of the main tasks of religion is to help people. Peale wrote several books on this theme, of which *The Power of Positive Thinking* in 1952 gained national popularity. During the 1950's, Bishop Fulton J. Sheen became famous as a television personality for his "Life Is Worth Living" series. The mid-1960's found over 500,000 buyers of psychiatrist Eric Berne's book, *Games People Play.* Recognizing and changing self-defeating attitudes and behavioral patterns of the individual are the objectives of these methods. Standard-bearers of this age are the terms: *basic-encounter groups, sensitivity training, T-groups, intensive-groups,* and *human relations laboratories.*

No one of these past and present theories *is in itself* entirely adequate; each has its own place and as such is of some help. The student who gets the most out of his study of himself and others looks understandingly at the *whole* picture . . . and, having looked, is able to select and integrate the viewpoints or interpretations best suited to his own needs. This kind of understanding enables *you* to decide what will explain *your* living, *your* behavior, and *others* most satisfactorily. In attempting to direct your life pattern, full recognition should be made in accordance with your abilities, interests, and energies.

In *The Will to Meaning,* Viktor E. Frankl is concerned with man's taking into account values that have significance for him beyond self-expression. He emphasizes that a totally conformist and collectivist world renders an individual unable to have personal meaning in his life.

Carl R. Rogers discusses the need for personal fulfillment in a civilized culture in his paper, *Learning To Be Free.* Rogers encourages freedom and spontaneity of the person in the development of creativity and self-responsibility.

Henry Winthrop's *A Humanistic Psychology Is Born* discusses a new direction in psychology, "the third force." Winthrop believes that this new direction would eliminate the narrow views which are presently studied by the behavioral sciences.

The last reading by James F. Brennan, *Self-Understanding and Social Feeling,* is an examination of "self-understanding and social feeling" when viewed by the "individual psychology" theory of Alfred Adler. Brennan explains his definitions with examples and presents therapeutic implications.

---

46 | The Will to Meaning

Viktor E. Frankl

Central to my psychiatric approach known as logotherapy is the principle of the will to meaning. I counterpose it both to the pleasure principle, which is so pervasive in psychoanalytic motivational theories, and to the will to power, the concept which plays such a decisive role in Adlerian psychology. The will to pleasure is a self-defeating principle inasmuch as the more a person really sets out to strive for pleasure the less likely he is to gain it. For pleasure is a by-product or side effect of the fulfillment of our strivings, and it is contravened to the extent that it is made a goal. The more a person directly aims at pleasure, the more he misses it. In my opinion this mechanism underlies most cases of sexual neurosis. Accordingly, a logotherapeutic technique based on this theory of the self-thwarting character of pleasure intention yields remarkable short-term results. Even the psychodynamically oriented therapists on my staff have come to acknowledge the value of logotherapy, and one such staff member has used this technique exclusively in treating sexually neurotic patients.

In the final analysis both the will to pleasure and the will to power are derivatives of the will to meaning. Pleasure is an effect of meaning fulfillment; power is a means to an end. A degree of power—economic power, for instance—is generally a prerequisite of meaning fulfillment. But while the will to pleasure mistakes the effect for the end, the will to power mistakes the means to an end for the end itself.

We are not really justified, however, in speaking of a *will* to pleasure or power in connection with psychodynamically oriented schools of thought, since they assume that man pursues behavior goals unwillingly and unwittingly and that his conscious motivations are not his actual motivations. Thus Erich Fromm in *Beyond the Chains of Illusion* speaks of "the motivating forces which make man act in certain ways, the drives which propel him

---

From *Are You Nobody?* Richmond, Va.: John Knox Press, 1966. Reprinted by permission.

to strive in certain directions." But to me it is inconceivable that man can really be driven to strivings; either he strives or he is driven. To ignore this difference, to sacrifice one phenomenon to another, is a procedure unworthy of a scientist; to do so is to allow one's adherence to hypotheses to blind one to facts.

Freud and his epigones have taught us always to see something behind or beneath human volitions: unconscious motivations, underlying dynamics. Freud never took a human phenomenon at face value; as Gordon W. Allport states in *Personality and Social Encounter,* "Freud was a specialist in precisely those motives that cannot be taken at their face value." But are there no motives at all which should be taken at face value? Such an assumption is comparable to the attitude of the man who, on being shown a stork, said, "I thought the stork didn't exist!" Does the fact that the stork has been misused to hide the facts of life from children in any way deny that bird's reality?

According to Freud, the reality principle is an extension of the pleasure principle and merely serves its purposes. But one could just as well say that the pleasure principle itself is an extension of the homeostasis principle and serves *its* purposes. Ultimately the psychodynamic approach views man as a being basically concerned with maintaining or restoring his inner equilibrium and seeking to do so by gratifying his drives and satisfying his instincts. Even Jungian psychology essentially interprets human motivation thus; the archetypes of Jungian thought are also "mythical beings" (as Freud called the instincts). Both Freud and Jung view man as bent on getting rid of tensions, be they aroused by drives and instincts clamoring for gratification (Freud) or by archetypes urging their materialization (Jung). In either case, reality, the world of beings and meanings, is reduced to instrumentalities for getting rid of unpleasant stimuli. What has been eliminated in this view of man is the fundamental fact that man is a being who encounters other beings, who also reaches out for meanings to fulfill.

This is why I speak of a will to meaning rather than a need for or a drive toward meaning. If man were really driven to meaning he would embark on meaning fulfillment solely to rid himself of this drive in order that homeostasis might be restored; at the same time he would no longer be really concerned with meaning but rather with his own equilibrium and thus with himself.

Nor is the concept of self-actualization or self-realization a sufficient ground for a motivational theory. Self-actualization is another phenomenon which can be realized only as a side effect and which is thwarted precisely to the extent that it is made a matter of direct intention. Self-actualization is of course a desideratum. But man can actualize himself only insofar as he fulfills meaning, in which case self-actualization occurs by itself—automatically, as it were. Like pleasure, self-actualization is contravened when deliberately sought after or more an end in itself.

While lecturing at Melbourne University some years ago I was given a boomerang as a souvenir. In contemplating this gift I concluded that in a sense it symbolized human existence. One generally assumes that a boomerang returns to the thrower; actually it returns only when the thrower has missed his target. Similarly, man returns to himself, to being concerned with his self, only after he has missed his mission, only after he has failed to find meaning in life.

In his doctoral dissertation Ernest Keen, one of my assistants during a teaching period at Harvard's summer session, seeks to demonstrate that the shortcomings of Freudian psychoanalysis are compensated for by Heinz Hartmann's ego psychology, and the deficiencies of ego psychology in turn by Erikson's identity concept. Keen goes on to contend, however, that despite these correctives there is still a missing link in psychotherapy, and that this link is supplied by logotherapy. It is my conviction that man should not, indeed cannot, struggle for identity in a direct way; rather, he finds identity to the extent to which he commits himself to something beyond himself, to a cause greater than himself. No one has put it as cogently as has Karl Jaspers: What man is he ultimately becomes through the cause which he has made his own.

Rolf von Eckartsberg, also a Harvard assistant of mine, has shown the insufficiency of the role-playing concept by pointing out that it avoids the very problem prompting it—that of choice and value. For the question remains: Which role to adopt, which cause to advocate? The same criticism holds for those who insist that man's primary intention and ultimate goal are to develop his potentialities. One recalls the example of Socrates, who confessed that he had within himself the potentiality to become a criminal but nevertheless decided to turn away from such a potentiality.

What is behind all these arguments that man should try to live out his inner potentialities or—as it is sometimes put—to "express himself"? The hidden motive behind such notions is, I believe, to lessen the tension aroused by the gap between what a man is and what he ought to become, between the actual state of affairs and that which he should help secure, between existence and essence, or being and meaning. To say that man need not worry about ideals and values since they are nothing but "self-expressions" and that he should therefore simply embark on the actualization of his own potentialities is to say that he need not reach out for meaning to fulfill or values to realize, that everything is all right as it is. Pindar's injunction, "Become what you are," is thus deprived of its imperative quality and transmuted into an indicative statement, namely, that man has all along been what he should become and hence need not reach for the stars to bring them down to earth, since the earth is itself a star!

The fact remains, however, that the tension between being and meaning is ineradicable in man, is inherent in his humanness. And that is why it is indispensable for mental well-being. Having started from man's meaning orientation, i.e., his will to meaning, we have now arrived at another problem—his meaning confrontation. The first issue refers to what man basically is: oriented toward meaning; the second refers to what he should be: confronted with meaning.

To confront man with values which are interpreted merely as self-expression will not do. Still less valid is the approach which would have him see in values "nothing but defense mechanisms, reaction formations or rationalizations of his instinctual drives"—to use the definition of two outstanding psychoanalytically oriented therapists. Personally I would not be willing to live for the sake of my defense mechanisms, much less to die for the sake of my reaction formations.

To treat a patient in terms of psychodynamic ideas may very well serve the purpose of what I call existential rationalization. If a person is taught that his concern about ultimate meaning is no more than, say, a way of coming to terms with his early childhood Oedipal situation, then his concern can be analyzed away, along with the existential tension aroused by it. The approach of logotherapy is altogether different. Logotherapy does not spare a patient confrontation with the specific meaning which he must act on—and which the therapist should help him find. In his book *Logotherapy and the Christian Faith* Donald F. Tweedie recounts an incident in which an American visitor to Vienna asked me to tell him in one sentence the difference between logotherapy and psychoanalysis—whereupon I invited him first to tell me what he regarded as the essence of psychoanalysis. He replied: "In psychoanalysis the patient must lie down on a couch and tell you things which sometimes are disagreeable to tell." And I quickly responded: "In logotherapy the patient is allowed to sit erect but must hear things which sometimes are disagreeable!"

Erwin Straus has rightly stressed that in existential thinking the otherness of the other should not be attenuated. The same holds true for meaning. The meaning which a person has to fulfill is something beyond himself, never just himself. Only if this meaning retains otherness can it exert upon a person that quality of imperativeness which yields itself to a phenomenological analysis of one's experience of existence. Only a meaning which is not just an expression of the person himself can be a true challenge to him. The Bible tells us that when Israel wandered through the desert God's glory went before in the form of a cloud; only in this way was it possible for Israel to be guided by God. Imagine what would have happened if God had dwelled in the midst of Israel in the form of a cloud: rather than leading the people safely, the cloud would have obscured everything and Israel would have gone astray.

Meaning must not coincide with being; meaning must be ahead of being: meaning sets the pace for being. Existence falters unless lived in terms of transcendence, in terms of something beyond itself. Here we might distinguish between pacemakers and peacemakers: the former confront us with meanings and values, thus supporting our meaning orientation; the latter alleviate the burden of meaning confrontation. In this sense Moses was a pacemaker; he did not soothe man's conscience but rather stirred it up. Moses with his Ten Commandments did not spare his people a confrontation with ideals and values.

There is also the appeaser type of peacemaker who tries to reconcile others with himself. Let's face facts, he says. Why worry about one's shortcomings? Only a few live up to their ideals. So let's attend to peace of mind or soul rather than those existential meanings which only arouse tensions.

What this kind of peacemaker overlooks is the wisdom of Goethe's warning: If we take man as he is, we make him worse; if we take him as he ought to be, we help him become it.

When meaning orientation becomes meaning confrontation, that stage of maturation and development has been reached where freedom becomes responsibleness. An individual is responsible for the fulfillment of the specific meaning of his own life, but he is also responsible *to* something, be it society or humanity or mankind or his own conscience. A significant number of people interpret their own existence not just in terms of being responsible to some*thing* but rather to some*one*—namely, to God. As a secular theory and medical practice logotherapy must restrict itself to such a factual statement, leaving to the patient the decision whether to interpret his own responsibleness in terms of religion or agnosticism. Logotherapy must remain available to everyone; to this I am obliged to adhere, if for no other reason, by my Hippocratic oath. In any case, logotherapy sees in responsibleness the very essence of human existence, and for that reason the patient must himself decide for what and to what, or to whom, he is responsible.

A logotherapist is not entitled consciously to influence the patient's decision as to how to interpret his own responsibleness or as to what to embrace as his personal meaning. The fact that a person's conscience is subject to error does not release him from his obligation to obey it; existence involves the risk of error. He must risk committing himself to a cause not worthy of his commitment. Perhaps my commitment to the cause of logotherapy is erroneous. But I prefer to live in a world in which man has the right to make choices, even if they are wrong choices, rather than one in which no choice at all is left to him. A world in which both fiends and saints are possible is infinitely preferable to a totally conformist, collectivist world in which man is a mere functionary of the party or the state.

---

47 | Learning To Be Free

Carl R. Rogers

To some, it must seem strangely out of tune with the modern world to speak of learning to be free. The growing opinion today is that man is essentially unfree. He is unfree in a cultural sense. He is all too often a pawn of government. He is molded by mass propaganda into being a creature with

From *National Education Journal,* March 1963. Reprinted by permission of the author and publisher.

certain opinions and beliefs, desired and preplanned by the powers that be. He is the product of his class—lower, middle, or upper—and his values and his behavior are shaped to a large extent by the class to which he belongs.

He is unfree in a scientific sense. The behavioral sciences have made great strides in showing that all his actions and thoughts are determined, being simply the result of previous conditioning. Hence it seems increasingly clear that the individual is formed and moved by forces—cultural forces without, and unconscious forces within—which are beyond his control. He is in all these ways unfree.

However, the freedom I want to discuss is essentially an inner thing, something which exists in the living person, quite aside from any of the outward choice of alternatives which we so often think of as constituting freedom. It is the quality of courage which enables a person to step into the uncertainty of the unknown as he chooses himself. It is the burden of being responsible for the self one chooses to be. It is the recognition by the person that he is an emerging process, not a static end product.

The individual who is thus deeply and courageously thinking his own thoughts, becoming his own uniqueness, responsibly choosing himself, may be fortunate in having hundreds of objective outer alternatives from which to choose, or he may be unfortunate in having none, but his freedom exists regardless.

Further, this experience of freedom exists not as a contradiction to the picture of the psychological universe as a sequence of cause and effect but as a complement to such a universe. Freedom, rightly understood, is a fulfillment, by the person, of the ordered sequence of his life.

It is a freedom in which the individual chooses to fulfill himself by playing a responsible and voluntary part in bringing about the destined events of the world he lives in.

It seems at least a possibility that in our schools and colleges, in our professional schools and universities, individuals could learn to be free in this sense. I say this in full recognition of the fact that the current trend in education is away from freedom. There are tremendous pressures today—cultural and political—for conformity, docility, and rigidity. The demand is for technically trained students who can beat the Russians—and none of this nonsense about education which might improve our interpersonal relationships! The demand is for hardheadedness, for training of the intellect only, for scientific proficiency.

For the general public and for many educators, the goal of learning to be free is not an aim they would select. Yet if a civilized culture is to survive and if the individuals in that culture are to be worth saving, it appears to be an essential goal of education.

So I would like to abstract, from various educational experiments and from pertinent research in psychotherapy, those conditions which appear to be essential if we are to inculcate in students this quality of inward freedom. I should like to describe these conditions as I see them.

In the first place, if self-initiated learning is to occur, it seems essential that the individual be faced by a real problem. Success in facilitating such learning often seems directly related to this factor. Professional persons who come together in a workshop because of a concern with common problems are a good example. Almost invariably, when they are given the facilitating climate I will describe, they at first resist the notion of being responsible for their own learning, but then they seize upon this as an opportunity and use it far beyond their expectations.

On the other hand, students in a required course expect to remain passive and may find themselves extremely perplexed and frustrated at being given freedom. "Freedom to do what?" is their quite understandable question.

It is thus necessary for self-initiated learning that the student, of whatever level, be confronted by issues which have meaning and relevance for him. In our culture we tend to try to insulate the student from too many of the actual problems of life, and this constitutes a difficulty. If we desire to have students learn to be free and responsible individuals, we must be willing for them to confront life, to face problems. Whether we are speaking of the inability of the small child to make change or the problem of his older brother in constructing a hi-fi set or the problem of the college student in formulating his views on international policy, some real confrontation by a problem seems necessary for this type of learning.

Thus far I have spoken of the essential conditions which involve the student. I come now to those conditions which only the teacher can provide. Experience indicates that the teacher who would facilitate this type of learning needs, first of all, a profound trust in the human organism. If we distrust the human being, then we *must* cram him with information of our own choosing lest he go his own mistaken way. On the other hand, if we trust the capacity of the human individual for developing his own potentiality, then we can permit him the opportunity to choose his own way in his learning.

Another requisite for the teacher is sincerity—realness, absence of a facade. He is a real person in his relations with his students. Because he accepts his feelings as his own, he has no need to impose them on his students. The teacher can dislike a student product without implying that it is objectively bad or that the student is bad. It is simply true that he, as a person, dislikes the product. Thus he is a *person* to his students, not a faceless embodiment of a curricular requirement or a sterile tube through which knowledge is passed from one generation to the next.

Teachers who have been successful in promoting this type of learning value their students, prize them, feel acceptant of the feelings and opinions of their students. Such a teacher can accept the fear and hesitation the student feels as he approaches a new problem as well as the satisfaction he experiences in resolving it. Such a teacher can accept the student's occasional apathy and his desire to explore byroads of knowledge as well as his disciplined efforts to achieve major goals. He can also accept personal feelings which both disturb and promote learning—rivalry with a sibling, hatred of authority, concern about personal adequacy.

In other words, the teacher is able to accept the whole student—to prize him as an imperfect human being with many feelings, many potentialities. This prizing or acceptance is an operational expression of the teacher's genuine confidence in the capacity of the human organism.

Another essential teacher attribute is the ability to understand the student's reactions from the inside, an empathic awareness of the way the process of education and learning seems to the student. This is a kind of understanding too seldom exhibited in the classroom; yet when the teacher *is* empathic, it adds an extremely potent aspect to the classroom climate.

When a child says, in a discouraged voice, "I can't do this," that teacher is most helpful who naturally and spontaneously responds, "You're afraid that you can never learn it, aren't you?" The usual denial of the child's feeling by the teacher who says, "Oh, but I'm *sure* you can do it" is not nearly so helpful.

In addition to having the essential attitudes decribed above, the teacher who facilitates learning to be free provides many resources. Instead of organizing lesson plans and lectures, such a teacher concentrates on providing all kinds of relevant raw material for use by the students, together with clearly indicated channels by which students can avail themselves of these resources. I am thinking not only of books, workspace, tools, maps, movies, recordings, and the like but also of human resources—persons who might contribute to the students' knowledge.

Most important of these human resources is the teacher himself. He makes himself and his special knowledge and experience clearly available to the students, but he does not impose himself on them.

The teacher thus concentrates on creating a facilitative climate and on providing resources. He may also help to put students in contact with meaningful problems. But he does not set lesson tasks or assign readings. He does not lecture or expound (unless requested to). He does not evaluate and criticize unless the student wishes his judgment on a product. He does not give examinations. He does not set grades.

Such a teacher is not simply giving lip service to a different approach to learning; he is giving his students the opportunity to learn to be responsibly free.

When the teacher establishes an attitudinal climate of the sort I have described, when he makes available resources which are relevant to problems which confront the student, then a typical process ensues.

First, for students who have been taught by more conventional means, there is a period of tension, frustration, disappointment, disbelief. Students turn in such statements as "I felt completely frustrated by the class procedure," "I felt totally inadequate to take part in this kind of thing," "The class seems to be lacking in planning and direction," "I keep wishing the *course* would start."

One mature participant-observer, Samuel Tenenbaum, in my book, *On Becoming a Person* (Houghton Mifflin, 1961), describes the way one group struggled with the prospect of freedom after an initial session in which opportunities and resources had been set forth:

> Thereafter followed four hard, frustrating sessions. During this period, the class didn't seem to get anywhere. Students spoke at random, saying whatever came into their heads. It all seemed chaotic, aimless, a waste of time. A student would bring up some aspect of the subject; and the next student, completely

> disregarding the first, would take the group away in another direction: and a third, disregarding the first two, would start fresh on something else.
>
> At times there were faint efforts at a cohesive discussion, but for the most part the classroom proceedings seemed to lack continuity and direction. The instructor received every contribution with attention and regard. He did not find any student's contribution in order or out of order.
>
> The class was not prepared for such a totally unstructured approach. They did not know how to proceed. In their perplexity and frustration, they demanded that the teacher play the role assigned to him by custom and tradition; that he set forth for us in authoritative language what was right and wrong, what was good and bad.

The statement above is a good description of the bafflement and chaos which is an almost inevitable initial phase of learning to be free.

Gradually, students come to various realizations. It dawns on them that this is not a gimmick; that they are really unfettered; that there is little point in impressing the teacher, since the sudent will evaluate his own work; that they can learn what they please; that they can express, in class, the way they really feel; that issues can be discussed in class which are real to them, not simply the issues set forth in a text. When these elements are recognized, there is a vital and almost awe-inspiring release of energy.

As the learning continues, personal changes take place in the direction of greater freedom and spontaneity. Here is a report given by a student at the end of a course conducted in this way:

> Your way of being with us is a revelation to me. In your class I feel important, mature, and capable of doing things on my own. I want to think for myself and this need cannot be accomplished through textbooks and lectures alone, but through living. I think you see me as a person with real feelings and needs, an individual. What I say and do are significant expressions from me, and you recognize this. You follow no plan, yet I'm learning. Since the term began, I seem to feel more alive, more real to myself. I enjoy being alone as well as with other people. . . .

I believe the story of this kind of classroom experience is incomplete without some mention of the effect upon the instructor when he has been the agent for the release of such self-initiated learning. One such teacher says:

> To say that I am overwhelmed by what happened only faintly reflects my feelings. I have taught for many years but I . . . never have found in the classroom so much of the whole person coming forth, so deeply involved, so deeply stirred. . . . I can only . . . say that I am grateful and I am also humbled by the experience.

Although empirical investigations of the sort of teaching I have described are neither large in number nor noteworthy for their research sophistication, they do indicate that improvement in personal psychological maturity is significantly greater in student-centered classes than in conventional ones. There is also evidence of a greater amount of self-initiated extracurricular learning and of greater creativity and self-responsibility.

As to the factual and curricular learning, this seems roughly equal to that achieved in conventional classes. Some studies report slightly more, others slightly less. The fairest summary seems to be that if we are solely concerned with the teaching of teacher-selected content material, this approach is probably no better or worse than the ordinary class. If we are concerned with the development of the person—with initiative, originality, and responsibility—such an approach produces greater changes.

In closing, I would like to say that it is my opinion that for the most part modern culture—in its two main streams, Western and communist—does not, operationally, want persons to be free, and is extremely fearful and ambivalent of any process which leads to inner freedom. Nevertheless, it is my personal conviction that individual rigidity and constricted learning are the surest roads to world catastrophe.

It seems clear that if we prefer to develop flexible, adaptive, creative individuals, we have a beginning knowledge as to how this may be done. We know how to establish, in an educational situation, the conditions and the psychological climate which initiate a process of learning to be free.

---

48 | A Humanistic Psychology Is Born

Henry Winthrop

Recent years have seen the formation of a group of psychologists who, in a sense, constitute a school to end all schools of psychology. Its members wish to see the vision and the concerns which have permeated the humanistic traditions of the West reflected in those scientific enterprises which are concerned with the study of man. The scholars, scientists and thinkers comprising this group seek to launch a program which they refer to as "a humanistic psychology." They are also frequently referred to as The Third Force in psychology. In a sense it is a misnomer to think of them as comprising a school. This is not so much because they deplore schools of psychology but rather because their professional concerns are eclectic and their interests tend to be truly interdisciplinary. The phrase "The Third Force" has been used by various writers to distinguish heterogeneous groups described in this paper from members of various psychoanalytic schools, on the one hand, and from behavioral and social scientists with an exclusively logico-empirical and behavioristic bent, on the other.

Among members of the Third Force one can find behavioral and social scientists as well as natural scientists, humanists as well as philosophers, and theologians as well as educators. In fact, representatives from any field are

---

welcome when their competencies, interests and holistic efforts make it natural for them to co-operate with members of this group. Perhaps the best way to describe the concerns of the Third Force would be first to state what trends humanistic psychologists are most critical of in the behavioral and social sciences and then to describe, in the positive sense, the types of theoretical and research concerns with which they are preoccupied.

As for some of the faults on the liability side of the ledger, humanistic psychologists are severely critical of what they take to be an excessive faith in the power of a stimulus-response psychology to explain most of the important characteristics of complex human behavior. They likewise see great limitations in the power of psychoanalysis, both in its orthodox and neo-Freudian varieties, to account for vast and important stretches of human behavior, particularly such phenomena as self-transcendence and creativity. A third whipping boy for this group is the widespread idolatry of statistical method in the behavioral and social sciences. Its members abhor the worship of quantitative methods for their own sake. They have little patience with those who esteem the mathematical model when such esteem is unaccompanied by common sense and by a feeling for what Sorokin calls "meaningful-causal analysis." They deplore the ubiquitous tendency upon the part of many behavioral and social scientists to place undue and uncritical reliance on "accidental samples" which are fictitiously assumed to be representative of a certain parent population, and from which samples these scientists draw a large number of unwarranted conclusions. No effort is usually made to achieve what is called simple random sampling. With Lancelot Hogben many members of the Third Force believe that much of the statistical razzle-dazzle in the social and behavioral sciences may have to be junked and that social and behavioral scientists will have to begin to use their brains.

Some members of the Third Force, coming from a background of laboratory research and methodological sophistication, have become a little impatient with professional lack of imagination and professional preoccupation with what they often feel are trivial research problems. They feel that a good many social and behavioral scientists find a sanctuary from the complexities of social reality by needlessly fragmenting it through an obsessive preoccupation with methodology. In doing this there is often a tendency to lose sight of the forest for the trees. To paraphrase a biblical injunction, humanistic psychologists do not believe that "By their numbers ye shall know them."

In order to avoid any misunderstanding, let me emphasize here that the Third Force *does not reject* these three approaches. It agrees that there are contexts of research to which they are centrally relevant. However, its members refuse to use these approaches as Procrustean beds. They reject efforts to cut down to size important problems for which these approaches are not completely adequate. On the other hand they resent their use to amplify the trivial in research and theory by embedding such trivia in a stimulus-response analysis, trying to make it seem important by psychoanalytic theorizing which runs amok, or gracing it with modern forms of number-worship which strain at gnats and swallow camels.

It is on the positive side, however, that the Third Force can be best understood. The positive biases can be made abundantly clear by discussing first the concepts and problems which are central to a humanistic psychology, then its presuppositions and finally its methods. I am referring here to those methods of analysis which members of the Third Force feel must be employed to supplement but not supplant the tried and tested procedures which have been found so successful within the body of inquiries dominated by the logico-empirical tradition.

ITS POSITIVE BIASES

It would, of course, be somewhat unrealistic to try to enumerate all the matters which are of central concern to a humanistic psychology. I shall here discuss only ten of them, it being understood that limitations of space make it impossible to deal with the others.

1. Values and Behaviors. Humanistic psychologists are deeply interested in research studies which make clear the degree to which the individual's value-system determines his behavior.

2. Autonomy. This new group is interested in studies which will reveal the factors that produce "self-starters"—those persons who may be considered to have a vital center, in Schlesinger's phrase, or who are inner-directed, to use Riesman's terminology, and they are interested in describing the variable expressions of autonomous behavior.

3. Ontoanalysis. To a large extent members of the Third Force are concerned with the analysis of Being in the existentialist and phenomenological senses in which this term is currently employed; but when this essentially philosophical concept is translated into psychological terms, this concern becomes a matter of describing and understanding the "unique" in human behavior and personality.

4. The Exploration of the Self. In this area the group of which we speak concentrates on the whole unstructured realm of research which is devoted to the meaning of the concept of "self" (which is somewhat erroneously referred to in current literature as "self-psychology") and in determining experimentally and/or clinically the types of behavior which define such a construct *ostensively*.

5. Agape. Third Force psychologists wish to extend behavioral theory and investigation to the various human manifestations of the non-carnal forms of love—a concern which is completely understandable when one realizes that it is rare to find a textbook of psychology whose subject index contains the term "love" or whose pages deal at all with this phenomenon which many regard as our most distinctively human characteristic.

There are a group of concerns that are somewhat more closely related to individual development than the preceding.

6. Creativity. Many humanistic psychologists are deeply interested in the phenomenon of human creativity, a concern which they of course share with other behavioral and social scientists, and they are especially interested in individual differences and descriptions of the "stream of consciousness" which accompany creative expression.

7. Personal Identity. Devotees of the point of view we are describing feel that the volume of research devoted to the meaning of the quest for personal identity must be considerably increased and that the advantages which accrue to those who achieve it must be studied more carefully, particularly in relation to the improvement of therapy and the reduction of alienation. It is furthermore felt that more work needs to be done on the psychological and sociological processes which aid and abet that achievement.

8. Growth. Humanistic psychologists are obsessed to some extent with the factors which produce or block both psychological and spiritual growth and development—where we are referring not only to the expansion of our intellectual powers but also to the sharpening of our moral, social and aesthetic sensibilities. At the same time they are calling for fuller research and theory concerning the biological, psychological and sociological factors which abort such development.

9. Psychological Health. Members of the Third Force are marked by their determination to increase the fund of human understanding concerning the processes and response repertoires involved in achieving psychological health and wish to arrive at a better understanding of this much abused term. In particular they feel that the psychopathology which results from what Maslow calls pathological normalcy, needs more extended investigation, and that more recognition is needed of the fact that there exist many levels of well-being, a fact which has been ably investigated by Halbert Dunn. With more understanding of the nature of psychological health, the field of mental hygiene will receive a major spurt in development. It will then be more adequately rooted in an understanding of the role which values, and man's orientation towards his own future, play in achieving psychological health. Humanistic psychologists also wish to ascertain what determinants of psychological health are "culture-free" in the biological sense of this term.

10. Self-actualization. This concept is very closely related to the quest for personal identity. It refers to a greater understanding of the processes by which the human organism—equipped with certain "potentialities" in the Aristotelian sense of this term—succeeds in fulfilling these potentialities in different ways in different natural and social contexts. Maslow has done most of the research in this field. He has catalogued the behavioral patterns and personality traits of self-actualizers. Among the leading traits found are the following: clearer perception of reality, more openness to experience, greater personal integration, more spontaneity, a firm identity, detachment and self-transcendence, creativeness, the capacity to fuse the abstract and the concrete, a democratic character structure and the ability to love in the sense of *agape*.

THE PRESUPPOSITIONS

The major presuppositions of a humanistic psychology become obvious enough from the available literature on the subject. Although it cannot be said that every member of the Third Force subscribes to each of the basic postures we are about to mention, in a statistical sense it is probably true that most of them are shared by most humanistic psychologists. Among these presuppositions then are those now to be described.

It is assumed that, although the subjective side of human behavior does not lend itself readily to the intersubjective and public demands of logico-empirical procedures, nevertheless the subjective elements of experience do play a major role in the causation of behavior. While recognizing that it would be impossible to present a complete list of what is meant by the subjective elements of experience which determine human behavior, nevertheless among the more important of these subjective elements would be the following:

1. *Felt* values, in contrast to statements about value asserted as abstractions, account for a great deal of human motivation.

2. Among the budget of causes that produce man's behavior are the *personal frame of reference* which is idiosyncratic and the *cultural frame of reference* which is shared.

3. Much of man's behavior results from the drive for what Allport calls *ego-extension,* that is, the desire to relate to others. These others may be one's contemporaries or they may be individuals who are remote in space or time—the latter referring to either the spirit of the ancients or the spirit described in a projected utopia. All our effort to relate to others generally indicates some desire to share their ways of life and patterns of value.

4. A great deal of human behavior is to be explained by the tendency of the individual, thought of psychologically as a system of ideas, ideals, sentiments, attitudes and levels of aspiration, to preserve himself intact and to select only those stimulus patterns to respond to which guarantee the fulfillment of those potentialities and tendencies already existing in the system. Thus two well-known textbooks of general psychology have been written which in large measure incorporate this principle, namely, *Psychology,* by Ross Stagner and T. F. Karwoski, and *Personality Dynamics and Effective Behavior,* by James C. Coleman. Although none of these writers are actually members of the Third Force, the works do illustrate this particular presupposition which is supported by a substantial number of humanistic psychologists. It is a principle which is central to what is today called General Systems Theory.

5. A deep-lying conviction of this group is that a great deal of human behavior can be understood and predicted in what psychologists call molar terms, that is to say, a great deal of knowledge and understanding of man can be achieved in terms of the meaningful aspects of his gross behavior, without trying to translate that behavior into some form of physiological, neurological or physico-chemical explanation. Translations of this type are said to be reductionistic and, although in principle members of the Third Force accept parallel reductionistic accounts of gross behavior and, in fact, credit their use, they nevertheless believe that much of our behavior can be understood and predicted through the use of molar concepts by themselves.

6. Perhaps the most basic assumption shared by humanistic psychologists is the belief that the most important aspects of human behavior—certainly its more complex varieties—are to be understood only in terms of our values and purposes and of the meanings we try to pour into that flicker between eternities which we call our life. This is to say that we recognize the legislation of the symbolic. As a result of this conviction many Third Force psychologists hold that the importance of these intangibles have also been

grasped by other types of thinkers concerned with the human condition and human behavior. In particular they feel that these intangibles are often grasped within the framework of the greatest works which are our legacy in literature, the humanities, the arts, philosophy and religion.

UNORTHODOX METHODS

The methods on which members of the Third Force lean are no different from those which characterize orthodox, academic research in the social and behavioral sciences. In addition, however, humanistic psychologists also welcome the use of such less orthodox and less well established methods as those of phenomenological and existential analysis. Furthermore they feel that there are certain contexts of inquiry in which those methods may have more to contribute than those traditionally employed in orthodox, scientific inquiry. They also encourage the use of *hermeneusis* or interpretation in its philosophical sense and the methods and techniques of cognitive psychology. Methods of statistical analysis and design are employed with the recognition that explanation frequently has to begin where statistical analysis leaves off.

Humanistic psychologists also place great value upon highly original methods of criticism such as are occasionally found in the humanities. Two good examples of what I mean, which immediately come to mind, would be the works of Kenneth Burke and those of Wyndham Lewis. Then, too, Third Force psychologists are anxious to study individual and social behavior via the methods of philosophical anthropology as demonstrated, for instance, in the work of one of its pioneers, Max Scheler's *Man's Place In Nature,* or as demonstrated in the work of a contemporary like F. S. C. Northrop, particularly in the form in which it appears, for instance, in *Philosophical Anthropology and Practical Politics.*

Humanistic psychologists are also open to the methods of the different psychoanalytic schools, where these are used critically and are subject to check either experimentally, by clinical observation or the field survey. Psychoanalytic methods, however, are looked at askance when they are used slavishly and uncritically, by being imposed on one's materials as a sort of *rite de passage* by certain cultists of various types. Third Force psychologists are also critical of psychoanalytical methods when they are employed to the exclusion of all other theoretical postures and methodological *Weltanschauungen.*

ALLIED AREAS AND PIONEERS

Certain interdisciplinary fields which have experienced their major development in recent decades share a great part of the outlook of a humanistic psychology. A few of them should be mentioned here. They include, but without limitation, existential psychiatry and psychology, philosophical anthropology, cognitive psychology, phenomenological psychology and philosophical psychology. This latter discipline now has a separate section in The American Psychological Association. In addition to the preceding, but somewhat less known to the professional public, are certain newer disciplines which I shall have to merely mention without furnishing any definition or explanation of their purposes here. These bear such labels as onto-analysis, orthopsychiatry and studies which can only be classified properly under the rubric of "metapsychology." To these it would be just to add the kinds of studies which Kenneth Boulding has referred to as *eiconics* in his interesting little volume *The Image*. Eiconics is a neonate field, interdisciplinary in scope, which boasts only scattered contributions at present and therefore still awaits systematization.

The growth of a humanistic psychology and its cognate areas has been somewhat phenomenal. This is indicated, I believe, by some of the professional journals of relatively recent vintage. Some of the currently better known of these journals are: The *Journal of Humanistic Psychology*, the *Review of Existential Psychiatry and Psychology* and the *Journal of Existential Psychiatry*. Although more than a decade older than these, nevertheless the *Journal of Individual Psychology* should be included in this group.

Certain prominent American scientists and scholars have pioneered either in humanistic psychology or in one of its allied areas. In the area of humanistic psychology proper, the leading figure has been Abraham M. Maslow. Dr. Maslow has spent a great deal of research effort on the characteristics and behavior of self-actualizing persons, on growth and its relationship to motivation, cognition, love, creativeness and values. Clark Moustakas has been active on some of the major problems in the sphere of self-psychology and the effects of loneliness on behavior. Charlotte Buhler has been active on a variety of problems related to the concerns of psychotherapy and particularly the role of values in psychotherapy. Other well known scientists and scholars who are, for instance, on the editorial board of the *Journal of Humanistic Psychology* are Hadley Cantril, Kurt Goldstein, Carl Rogers and Ernest G. Schachtel. Third Force psychologists now possess a professional organization of their own, the *American Association for Humanistic Psychology*, and a brief history of the movement which led to the formation of this organization is given in the first issue of its journal (Spring 1961) mentioned above.

In the field of existential psychiatry and psychology there is an equally distinguished coterie of original thinkers. Among them is Rollo May who has been one of several figures who have pioneered in introducing American psychiatrists and psychologists to the fields of existential psychiatry and psychology. He will be remembered as the author of two well received volumes, *The Meaning of Anxiety* and *Man's Search for Himself*. Outstanding leadership and some unusually important papers have come from Dr. Adrian van Kaam, the editor of the *Review of Existential Psychiatry and Psychology*. Other well-known names on the editorial board of this journal are Gordon Allport, Viktor Frankl, Paul Tillich and John Wild.

Outstanding contributions to existential psychiatry also appear in the pages of the *Journal of Existential Psychiatry*. Major work on the concept of the self in schizophrenia has been done by the editor of that journal, Dr. Jordan M. Scher, M.D., of the faculty of the Department of Neurology and Psychiatry at Northwestern University, who is also Director of the Chicago Psychiatric Foundation and Ontoanalytic Institute. He is responsible for the editing of the very impressive recent volume entitled *Theories of the Mind*, a 748-page volume featuring contributions from psychologists, philosophers, physiologists, psychiatrists and theologians, all seeking to answer the question "What is mind?" Associated with the editorial board of this journal are some national and international figures of first-rate distinction. Two of its United States editors are, for instance, Iago Galdston and Eugen Kahn. Among its international editors are such well thought of figures as Medard Boss, M.D., of Zurich, and Eugene Minkowski, M.D., of Paris. Perhaps one of the best ways of illustrating the postures of existential psychiatry and its interdisciplinary emphases is to quote in full the "Prolegomena" or opening editorial statement which described the journal's philosophy in its first issue:

> Man is more than mere mechanism or statistical abstraction. Toward this conclusion evidence and opinion have been mounting. Resolving old discrepancies has only made new ones visible. Problems, not solutions, have become apparent in the search for a knowledge of man, of how he functions, and where he is going. Obviously, many observers of man-in-action have felt an unrest with theoretical frameworks that confine, rather than define. Too consistently overlooked has been the fact that the human organism is relatively open to new experience and evinces at every moment the plasticity of a growing, creative, newly-confronting agent. Man is not merely the prisoner of mental mechanisms, diagnostic categories, primitive urges, or repetitions. He is capable of the unexpected as well as the expected. It is this order of thinking we must employ in attempting to understand, much less treat, the individual patient.
>
> Contributions toward such an understanding will come from many convergent sources. Psychiatrists, psychologists, phenomenologists, sociologists, religionists, philosophers, ethologists, anthropologists, behaviorists, biochemists, physiologists, and others, will participate in this effort. In his approach to the demands of individual disciplines, each will be able to help shape the picture of an organism at once mechanical and random, statistical and individual, limited and free.

THE PROSPECTS FOR A HUMANISTIC PSYCHOLOGY

Although fundamental disagreements still exist among psychologists and workers in allied areas, these disagreements today are not of the type which result in a conflict of schools. The differences are a matter of emphasis rather than a matter of the one true faith. When stimulus-response psychologists, Gestaltists, psychoanalysts, phenomenological psychologists and cybernetically oriented psychologists approach a problem today, the differences which are likely to emerge occur as a result of prevailing interests in different aspects of a given problem, process or phenomenon. The conflict of ideologies in psychology is now somewhat "old hat." This can be most forcefully seen, for instance, in the six recent volumes—actually a compendium—edited by Sigmund Koch which bear the series title *Psychology: A Study of a Science.* The conflicts which remain in psychology now reflect more of a difference in personal philosophies and value, more of a difference with respect to how eclectic one should be in methodology in the behavioral and social sciences and more of a difference in the breadth of the cultural interests of the protagonists.

It is differences such as these which are now the dominant ones rather than conflicts among ideologies, which were so characteristic two and three decades ago. Almost all of these differences have now merged into a well-known polarization of attitude found among many psychologists. This polarization refers to a tendency among psychologists to bifurcate themselves into either idiographic psychologists or nomothetic psychologists, while recognizing that perhaps most psychologists maintain ambivalent positions which lie between both these poles. Those who cluster around the idiographic pole are said to function in terms of the Leibnitzian tradition while those who cluster around the nomothetic pole are said to function in terms of the Lockean tradition. The latter tradition is essentially that of logical empiricism.

Among those who cluster around the latter pole are stimulus-response psychologists and partisans of the conviction that learning theory should be central to the study of behavior. Other types of psychological theorizers, of course, are also found around this pole. Among those who may be said to cluster around the former pole are Gestalt psychologists, cognitive psychologists, psychoanalysts, various brands of clinical psychology, proponents of various, semi-philosophical positions in psychology, organismic and holistic psychologists and advocates of a variety of different theoretical positions in psychiatry. In addition, we would find not too far from this pole personalistic psychologists, champions of psychological field theories, psychologies which emphasize the social and interactional determinants of behavior, self-psychologies, individual psychologies and biosocial positions in psychology. It is the Lockeans, however, who are dominant in academic psychology today. However, that dominance is being somewhat loosened. Actually, as Jerome Bruner has put it in a series of charming essays which appear in a volume entitled *On Knowing: Essays for the Left Hand,* the imbalance between the nomothetic and idiographic tendencies—an imbalance which is presently in favor of tough-minded, nomothetic, logical empiricists in psychology—is changing slowly in the reverse direction, but it definitely is changing. Bruner puts it this way:

> The decade in psychology and its allied fields has been energizing: the lock step of "learning theory" in this country has been broken, though it is still the standard village dance. It is apparent to many of us that the so-called associative connecting of physical stimuli and muscular responses cannot provide the major part of the explanation for how men learn to generate sentences never before spoken, or how they learn to obey the laws of the sonnet while producing lines never before imagined. Indeed, all behavior has its grammatical consistency; all of it has its consistency of style.

Humanistic psychology and the fields allied with it are simply the latest entrants into the Leibnitzian pastures. The Leibnitzian tradition in American academic life is represented by a small minority but a minority which is perhaps needed to restore a better balance between the nomothetic and idiographic approaches in psychology. It is only through a better balance that needed perspective can be retained on so complex a matter as human behavior. Encouragement needs to be given to eclecticism in the choice of both problems and methods. Psychologists should be willing to promote a pluralism in both outlook and purpose. Only in this way can we eliminate "tunnel vision" in the behavioral and social sciences. Humanistic psychology, together with the areas presently cognate to it, are all needed to emphasize precisely those types of concern which, by and large, are neglected by partisans of the more tough-minded approaches.

The price which often has to be paid by a tough-minded psychology resolutely committed to imitating the hard methodologies of the physical sciences, is the frequent sacrifice of the significant in both individual and social behavior. In orienting themselves to behavioral and social problems of larger scope and perhaps of greater personal and social significance, humanistic psychologists may succeed in introducing a much needed eclecticism in cultural breadth and a much needed interdisciplinary emphasis in the behavioral and social sciences. Their hope is certainly to supplement the roster of tough-minded methodologies by methods which give room and scope for interpretation and for restoring the recognition, sadly overdue, of the importance of the subjective and the unique in human behavior.

For the time being tough-minded, brass-instrument psychologists tend to regard a humanistic psychology as an example of a professional failure of scientific nerve. Any decision as to the value of a humanistic psychology and the quality of its achievements will actually depend upon what the Third Force succeeds in accomplishing in the next decade or two. In the meantime the upstart has made a moderately good beginning; judgment concerning the prospects for a healthy development should be reserved until it has grown a little older.

REFERENCES

ALLPORT, G. *Becoming: Basic Considerations for a Science of Personality.* New Haven: Yale University Press, 1955.

BOULDING, K. *The Image.* Ann Arbor: The University of Michigan Press, 1956.

BRUNER, J. *On Knowing: Essays for the Left Hand.* Cambridge: The Belknap Press of Harvard University Press, 1962.

BUHLER, C. *Values In Psychotherapy.* Glencoe, Illinois: The Free Press, 1962.

BURKE, K. *A Grammar of Motives and a Rhetoric of Motives.* Cleveland and New York: The World Publishing Company, 1962.

CANTRIL, H., and BUMSTEAD, C. H. *Reflections on the Human Venture.* New York: New York University Press, 1960.

COLEMAN, J. C. *Personality Dynamics and Effective Behavior.* Chicago: Scott, Foresman, 1960.

DUNN, H. L. *High Level Wellness.* Arlington, Virginia: R. W. Beatty, 1961.

FRANKL, V. E. *From Death-Camp to Existentialism.* Boston: Beacon Press, 1959.

GOLDSTEIN, K. *The Organism.* Boston: Beacon Press, 1963.

HOGBEN, L. *Statistical Theory.* New York: Norton, 1957.

KOCH, S. (Editor). *Psychology: A Study of a Science;* 7 vols. New York: McGraw-Hill, 1959 to date.

LEWIS, W. *Time and Western Man.* Boston: Beacon Press, 1957.

MASLOW, A. H. (Editor). *New Knowledge In Human Values.* New York: Harper, 1959.

MASLOW, A. H. *Motivation and Personality.* New York: Harper, 1954.

MAY, R. *The Meaning of Anxiety.* New York: Ronald Press, 1950.

MAY, R. *Man's Search for Himself.* New York: Norton, 1953.

MOUSTAKAS, C. E. *Loneliness.* Englewood Cliffs, New Jersey: Prentice-Hall, 1961.

NORTHROP, F. S. C. *Philosophical Anthropology and Practical Politics.* New York: Macmillan, 1960.

RIESMAN, D., et al. *The Lonely Crowd.* New York: Doubleday, 1953.

ROGERS, C. *On Becoming a Person.* Boston: Houghton Mifflin, 1961.

SCHACHTEL, E. *Metamorphosis: On the Development of Affect, Perception, Attention and Memory.* New York: Basic Books, 1959.

SCHELER, M. *Man's Place In Nature.* Boston: Beacon Press, 1961.

SCHER, J. (Editor). *Theories of the Mind.* New York: The Free Press of Glencoe, 1962.

SCHLESINGER, A. M., JR. *The Vital Center.* New York: Houghton Mifflin, 1962.

SOROKIN, P. A. *Fads and Foibles In Modern Sociology.* Chicago: Henry Regnery, 1956.

STAGNER, R., and KARWOSKI, T. F. *Psychology.* New York: McGraw-Hill, 1952.

TILLICH, P. *The Courage To Be.* New Haven: Yale University Press, 1952.

WILD, J. *The Challenge of Existentialism.* Bloomington: Indiana University Press, 1959.

---

49 | Self-Understanding and Social Feeling

James F. Brennan

I discover that I am everybody, and that I discover myself in discovering my fellow man, and vice versa. —ERICH FROMM [6, p. 186]

For the psychologist the rule is never to worry about his own success; if he does so, he forfeits it. The psychotherapist must lose all thought of himself. —ALFRED ADLER [2, p. 341]

Adler's concept of social feeling offers the psychologist a means by which he is better able to comprehend the process of self-understanding, and most important, articulate his comprehension of the process to others. This statement implies that at present many psychologists are unclear as to the nature of self-understanding and consequently refrain from discussing it, specially as an issue in itself. It is the author's contention that the nature of self-understanding as process is a problem for therapeutic psychology. It is simple enough to say that mental health is to know thyself, but precisely how one goes about knowing thyself remains an enigma.

From *Journal of Individual Psychology,* **23,** 1, May 1967, pp. 53–57. Reprinted by permission.

(*U.S. Army Photograph*)

Emotion and Understanding. A grief-stricken American infantryman whose buddy has been killed in action is comforted by another soldier.

The purpose of this paper is to examine self-understanding as a problem, study this problem in terms of the Adlerian notion of social feeling, formulate a definition of self-understanding, illuminate this definition with examples, and present its therapeutic implication through a case study.

SELF-UNDERSTANDING AS A PROBLEM

"Know thyself." This utterance has been handed down through the ages as the criterion of wisdom and peace of mind until our present day where it is transformed through psychological sophistication from a religious-philosophical notion into a slogan of mental health or the central theme of an academic course in mental hygiene. Today it is assumed that one gets to know himself by learning about man in the abstract, i.e., man as a social, psychological, biological, economic, and religious being. Consequently, the "knowledgeable person" ends up knowing about a fictive man constructed from a web of ideas, not the man who lives and breathes, nor the one to whom the personal pronouns "I" and "me" apply.

Then how does one "know thyself"? This slogan or academic theme implies that one does not ordinarily come to know himself; that is why it is conceived as a goal to be attained or a lesson to be learned. Then knowledge of one's self is not the exclusive goal of amnesiacs; rather, insight into self is understanding why we behave as we do. For instance a person may still not understand the reason why he yells at his wife in certain situations, although he knows his socio-economic status, genealogical decent, IQ score, level of academic achievement, physiological make-up, and religious heritage. Clearly, such information is not wisdom, nor does it bring about peace of mind, nor does mental hygiene commence and mental health prevail because of it. Instead, self-understanding appears to be particularized knowledge involving one's unique individuality which is constantly situated with and implicating others. How then does one come to understand himself as a unique individual always situated and involved with others?

DEFINITION OF SOCIAL FEELING

Adler's concept of social feeling offers us a powerful conceptual tool which we may bring to bear upon the thorny question of self-understanding.

What does social feeling mean? Basically, it is a notion which refers to a person's ability to empathize with another: to see, hear, and feel with him [2, p. 135]. Buchheimer's analysis of the original German term *Gemeinschaftsgefühl* is helpful here: *Gemeinschaft* means specifically community with general aspects implicating also the universe; *Gefühl* signifies a person's attitude and action tendency [5, p. 242]. The English translation of *Gemeinschaftsgefühl* as social feeling or interest loses merely the implication of one's relation to the universe. What is interesting and rather paradoxical is that Adler combined the idea of social, an objective referent of commonality, with feeling or interest, a subjective referent of personality. The former implicates common meaning; the latter indicates private experience and desire. The synthesis of the objective "social" with the subjective "feeling" or "interest" seems to indicate a triumph over the dichotomous relationship of common meaning and private meaning, a bridge between "you" and "me." Now let us be more specific.

Ansbacher states that Adler considered social feeling to be "an innate cognitive aptitude" [3, p. 50], an aptitude, the author believes, which allows one to transcend his private meanings and feelings by focusing his interest on the other's words and behaviors in terms of what they mean to the other, a feeling with the other. This point can be seen in the way Adler sums up the notion of social interest: "The capacity for identification, which alone makes us capable of friendship, love of mankind, sympathy, occupation, and love, is the basis of social interest and can be practiced and exercised only in conjunction with others" [2, p. 136].

Such identification is a self-transcendence, a going beyond the limited horizons of one's private motives and thoughts to an understanding or sharing of another's aims and desires. In the context of this paper, the nature of social feeling is seen as an aptitude to understand one's self through the understanding of others. At this point it is possible to make more definitive statements concerning the nature of self-understanding conceived as social feeling.

DEFINITION OF SELF-UNDERSTANDING

Self-understanding is, paradoxically, self-transcendence, i.e., focusing one's interest and feeling upon the other in order to discover what his words, gestures, and postures mean to him. It is becoming less involved with one's own hopes, fears, shame, and doubt in order to become more concerned about how the other sees and experiences the world and others. Self-understanding conceived as social feeling means to see one's self (insight) by participating with another, sharing mutual concern, or more succinctly, being an "I" for a "thou" as Buber [4] would say. It is precisely in such an "I-thou" relation that one is able to establish the necessary distance between himself as figure and his self-seeking pragmatic involvement as ground, for self-understanding to come about. Schutz, the late social philosopher of common sense life, comes to a similar conclusion through a phenomenology of face-to-face relations: "I experience myself through you, and you experience yourself through me" [7, p. 30].

THE PRACTICE OF SOCIAL FEELING: SELF-UNDERSTANDING

How can one practice social feeling and thereby understand himself? This question is not easily answered, for we lack adequate descriptive-explanatory concepts with which to exemplify social feeling in action. Here I ask you to imagine along with me. Suppose, for the purpose of exemplification, that you finish eating supper and sit down in the easy-chair and begin to read the newspaper. Your wife enters and begins to nag you about never doing anything around the house and calls you "lazy."

You can respond in different ways. You can mimic her actions as she scolds you, thereby causing her to break into tears. Or, you can not listen to her words, and slip into your own thoughts of self-pity, or think of some ideal love who is always affectionate to you. Or, you can try to understand her point of view, i.e., what her words mean in terms of herself. You actively direct your interest toward how she must feel in making such remarks. All of your knowledge, past experience, and emotional sensitivity is summoned in order to understand why she behaves in such a manner. At this point you are not self-conscious (ashamed, embarrassed, enraged, threatened, etc.), but totally directed toward understanding her point of view. This self-transcending movement achieves distance from self and affords you the possibility of understanding her and hence yourself. For instance, you may realize that she acts as though she is inadequate to the task of being a homemaker, leading you to see that she needs some encouragement and help in doing household chores. It then impresses you that the reason for not helping her in the past springs from an inflated idea of manliness which you unknowingly harbored. On the other hand, you may suddenly see that she is afraid to be affectionate and feels that only harsh words bring results. This understanding also brings with it insight, for you realize that you have been treating her abruptly due to your own mistrust of affection. Let us now pursue what psychotherapeutic implication the reciprocal aspect of self-understanding has in terms of a case study.

THERAPEUTIC IMPLICATION OF A CASE STUDY

In the analysis of an apparently paranoid woman with a persecution complex, Adler [1, pp. 183–185] revealed how lack of social feeling can make wrong spring from right. It so happened that Adler's patient was actually being disparaged by her supposed friend who in truth depreciated others behind their backs. At first not even the patient's husband and friends believed the patient's accusation: that the apparently kind lady was prone to assassinate a person's good name, and had already done so in the patient's case. In the end the hostile side of the accused woman was revealed for all to see. However, in the interim, the patient suffered alienation from her husband and friends, became hostile and anxiety-ridden even though she was right. The point Adler makes is that his patient failed to understand her two-faced friend; instead, she became so hurt and insulted that she risked her own sanity to prove herself right and the other wrong.

Adler's patient responded to the other's depreciating remarks in terms of her injured self-esteem; she depreciated her deceptive friend in the name of truth instead of understanding what the depreciatory tendency meant to this two-faced woman. If the patient had practiced social feeling she would have become aware of this same tendency within herself and everyone else and thereby been able to see that everybody has faults. Despite the fact that this patient was right in what she said, her behavior was not adaptive; she failed to understand the other and to understand herself. Reciprocal understanding of self and others transcends the argumentative mode of being with others, i.e., being interested in being right and proving the other wrong.

SUMMARY

Self-understanding is only attained through understanding others. Understanding others is a function of social feeling. Social feeling implies self-transcendence. The self-transcending movement of social feeling overcomes self-centeredness and leads to greater reciprocity between self and others. Fostering social feeling in psychotherapy allows the patient to transcend the struggle between right and wrong through a reciprocal understanding of self and others.

REFERENCES

1. Adler, A. *Social interest: a challenge to mankind* (1933). New York: Capricorn Books, 1964.
2. Adler, A. *The Individual Psychology of Alfred Adler.* New York: Basic Books, 1956.
3. Ansbacher, H. L. Sensus privatus versus sensus communis. *J. Indiv. Psychol.,* 1965, 21, 48–50.
4. Buber, M. *I and thou.* New York: Scribner, 1958.

5. Buchheimer, A. From group to "Gemeinschaft." In K. A. Adler and Danica Deutsch (Eds.), *Essays in Individual Psychology*. New York: Grove Press, 1959. Pp. 242–247.

6. Fromm, E. *Beyond the chains of illusion*. New York: Pocket Books, 1962.

7. Schutz, A. *Collected papers*. Vol. 2. The Hague: Martinus Nyhoff, 1964.

Unit Eleven | DISCUSSION QUESTIONS

46. *The Will to Meaning*

Define and discuss "logotherapy."
Distinguish between "pacemakers" and "peacemakers."

47. *Learning To Be Free*

How does the student-centered class promote individual growth and freedom?
If society depends in part on conformity for stability, what is the value of a "free" individual?

48. *A Humanist Psychology Is Born*

What is meant by the phrase, "The Third Force?"
What are the methods and goals of Humanist Psychology?

49. *Self-Understanding and Social Feeling*

Describe a situation in your personal experience in which you can apply the concepts of "self-understanding and social feeling."
What therapeutic methods are mentioned by the author in developing "self-understanding and social feeling?"

Unit Twelve *College and Occupational Success*

College life, for many students, marks the beginning of independence, self-direction, and goal-setting. As a result, students all over the nation are in the process of evaluating themselves in terms of the future. While there are intrinsic values to be gained in seeking a higher education, many students also view going to college as the best method to ensure later occupational success. This viewpoint gains support when a cursory glance in the local newspaper's "Jobs Offered" column reveals that many of today's jobs call for a college education. A recent job announcement for a janitor at a major western university stated that some college was preferred! A national committee for Economic Development recently stated that a man with a grade school education earns an average of $152,000 in a lifetime. A high school graduate earns $252,000, while college graduates average $452,000.

Further, look at your college catalog and notice the training programs geared toward degrees that a decade ago were unheard of. Culinary Arts, Ornamental Horticulture, Home Furnishings Merchandising, Real Estate, Sales Management, Technical Writing, Diesel Technology, Fire and Police Science are but a few of the endless list of new college programs. San Diego Mesa College recently became the first community college to offer an Airline Pilot training program in cooperation with a major airline. Today's college student faces a unique college curriculum.

Evening division college classes are rapidly becoming filled with part-time students who are realizing the importance of college training. The majority of major industries are encouraging and even financing their employees to receive advance training through the local colleges. The complex nature of our society demands this kind of training. Jobs that yesterday called for muscle and brawn are steadily being converted to mechanization. Manpower needs in 1975 are illustrated in *Tomorrow's Jobs—Where the Best Will Be.* The staff of Changing Times points out the scope and breadth of the vast occupational needs for tomorrow's wage earner. In the second reading, *Time to Kill: Automation, Leisure and Jobs* by Eric Larrabee, presents the challenge offered by automation, and the problems that must be answered in order to cope with the mechanized society.

The staff of American Education presents interesting views regarding the purposes of a college education in *What People Think About College.* This article is the result of a national survey of people from all walks of life.

Adjustment to the differing demands of college life is one of vital importance. *Dear Freshman . . . If You Want Our Advice . . .* is an appeal written by college students to other college students that offers sound advice about studying, courses and professors, extracurricular activity, and making the most of college.

Finally M. Olin Cook's *College Students Change Majors* is a statistical inquiry into the growing difficulty young people have in selecting a field of study while attending college.

---

50 | Tomorrow's Jobs—Where the Best Will Be

For people who are young today, unexampled opportunity lies ahead in an America growing bigger, more intricate, more affluent by the hour.

Opportunity . . . for all?

No, not for everybody.

While new techniques, new needs, new knowledge open doors to many, others will see skills and specialties once highly prized fall into disuse, no longer wanted.

The big rewards are marked "reserved." They will go to those who look ahead and aim for the businesses and professions that are bound to flourish.

And which careers—specifically—are on the upgrade? Which declining?

Naming names in answer to this question is the sole object of a hefty, helpful 862-page government tome the Superintendent of Documents is releasing this month.

This prescient volume, the Labor Department's 1966–67 *Occupational Outlook Handbook,* assesses prospects for over 700 different occupations and tells how each will fare in coming years, into the mid-1970's.

Behind its forecasts for individual occupations lie these big-picture conclusions.

• Opportunity will expand fastest for those with the most training and education. In many fields, those with only bachelors' degrees will find competition far fiercer than it now is.

• Really top jobs, particularly in the sciences, will go to those who acquire advanced degrees. Specialization will increasingly offer special rewards, too.

• Overspecialization, on the other hand, can be risky. The job that is a narrow specialty today could be made obsolete by an unforeseen development tomorrow.

• Although those with the least training, the least education, will find pickings ever slimmer, in an expanding economy the actual number of jobs for the unskilled and semiskilled may not decrease.

• Nor do the facts indicate that good jobs will go to degree holders only. Lots of worthwhile careers will be open to those who don't attend four-year colleges.

A BRIGHT WHITE-COLLAR FUTURE

Say that jobs in a given line will increase 10%, even 15%, in the decade ahead and it sounds good. But it isn't. The total number of jobs of all kinds is expected to increase 25% by 1975. Bear that benchmark figure in mind.

The fastest-growing occupational group of all is labeled "professional, technical, managerial." In that white-collar classification, openings are expected to multiply by a bumper 40%.

Why? Two reasons: Sciences and technologies will continue to expand, although somewhat slower than in the past. Recall that fields virtually unheard of ten years ago—bionics, cryogenics, ultrasonics, microelectronics, laser dynamics—employ thousands today. Then, too, increasing federal and local involvement in many aspects of social and economic betterment will spark demand for experts in health, education and urban problems.

Not all areas will grow equally rapidly, of course, and even among those with the fastest growth rates, the actual number of job openings may be relatively small. Here's a closer look at what's ahead, job by job.

Managers, officials, proprietors. Growth outlook, average. The downtrend in number of self-employed that set in after World War II is expected to level off.

Accountants. Growth prospects, very good as size and complexity of industry increases and as small and medium-sized firms increasingly require their services. Average current starting salaries: about $6,400.

Advertising, public relations, market research. Moderate to rapid expansion. Best prospects in big-city agencies, chiefly New York, Chicago, Los Angeles, Washington. New products, need for more accurate, more sophisticated research will spur most growth. Salaries begin at $3,100 to $7,800 in advertising; about $5,000 for public relations; $6,300 in market research.

Personnel. Outlook generally good. Better for college graduates and specialists (psychology, labor relations, training, safety, etc.). Generalists will face stiffening competition. Prospects best in large industrial centers of East, Midwest and West Coast. Starting pay averages $5,000 in government; $6,600 in industry.

Purchasing agents. Good prospects, but trend favors those with college background in business. Those with science and engineering savvy will be most in demand. Government salaries start at about $5,000; $6,200 in industry.

Clergy. Persistent shortages continue, especially among denominations requiring years of study, as churches increase and become more involved in society outside the church door.

Counselors. Supply of well-trained school, vocational and rehabilitation counselors is short and will grow shorter. Outlook excellent. Beginning pay about $5,000.

Engineers. Prospects vary. Strong demand in electrical equipment, aircraft, machinery, ordnance, instruments, and primary and fabricated metals. Graduate students in some newer fields (ceramics, metallurgy) will be particularly sought.

Less growth (but many openings) in aerospace, chemicals, agriculture. Mining and civil engineering will grow moderately. A potential bright spot for mining engineers: undersea mining.

Caution: About one-fourth of all engineers are in defense and defense-related work, potentially precarious for job security. As far as can be seen, though, defense spending will continue at about current levels.

Health services. New laws plus expanding older and younger age groups provide excellent prospects, particularly for dentists, dental hygienists, dietitians, doctors, hospital administrators, occupational and physical therapists, osteopaths, registered nurses.

Moderate growth expected for dental lab technicians, podiatrists, veterinarians and sanitarians. Slowest relative growth for chiropractors, optometrists and pharmacists.

Some typical starting salaries: Dental hygienists, $6,000; dietitian interns, $4,700–$5,500; hospital administrators, $7,500; optometrists, $6,000–$6,500; pharmacists with big drug companies, $6,000–$7,000; registered nurses average $86.50 a week in big cities.

Mathematicians, statisticians, actuaries. Growth outlook bright over-all, brightest for mathematicians and particularly those adept with computers. Demand increasing, too, for math teachers. Starting pay: $7,000 (bachelor's degree) to $16,000 (Ph.D.) in private firms.

Statisticians, needed for market and production analyses, sales forecasts and the like, start at about $5,500. Actuarial workers average $6,000 to start.

Scientists. Continued rapid expansion generally, but not quite so fast as in the past. Employment prospects excellent for those with advanced degrees.

Physical scientists will fare best as demand swells for new plastics, metals, synthetic fibers, drugs, fertilizers, exotic fuels. Physicists' starting pay ranges from $6,200 to better than $15,000, depending on their education and specialty.

Biological scientists, too, have a very good future as disease research grows. For those who lack advanced degrees, heavy demand as research and lab assistants. Salaries start at $5,000.

Earth sciences will grow only moderately. Two comparatively small "frontier" disciplines, oceanography and meteorology, will grow rapidly as government and industry probe unsolved mysteries of seas and weather.

Long-run prospects for earth scientists will brighten, however, as undeveloped nations begin to tap natural resources.

The arts. Chronically overcrowded. Prospects generally bleak except for those exceptionally talented, lucky, or both. A few bright spots: industrial design, commercial art, interior design and decoration, technical writing.

Social sciences. Fairly rapid expansion as college teaching positions increase and the war on poverty escalates.

Economists, political scientists, sociologists, psychologists (especially those with advanced degrees) will find employment opportunities best. Less growth ahead for anthropologists, geographers, historians.

Social workers. Growth outlook excellent, for all types—family, medical, school, psychiatric, rehabilitative, and probation and parole officers. Average starting salary for social case workers is about $4,700.

Lawyers. A heavy demand will continue for graduates of top law schools. Graduates of lesser institutions will find stiff competition. Best places to begin practices: small towns, expanding suburbs.

Teaching. Prospects excellent at all levels; the nation's teaching staff will have to grow by one-third by 1975.

Teachers with Ph.D.'s will find prospects excellent at most colleges and universities; those with masters' will be in increasing demand at junior and community colleges. At junior highs and high schools, demand will be especially high for science teachers.

Librarians. Excellent field, with continuing shortages and continuing growth of specialized libraries. Biggest need: elementary school librarians.

Technicians. Rapid expansion as industry research and development grow. Best chances for growth: electrical equipment, machinery, chemicals, aerospace. Salaries begin around $4,000 in government, slightly higher in industry.

Job Futures . . . Industry by Industry

Here is a career-minded appraisal of how things look for the decade ahead, industry by industry.

You expect opportunity in expanding industries, where opportunity multiplies. But remember that there will be jobs by the thousands in stable, nonexpanding industries, and even in those where total employment is contracting, good openings are being created constantly by turnover, retirement and other normal attrition.

Aircraft, missiles, space. Heavy concentration in California, New York, Connecticut, Massachusetts, Florida, Texas, Washington, Alabama. Missilery expected to shrink somewhat, aircraft to level off and stabilize. Spacecraft, moderate increase.

Apparel. Moderate growth, mostly in design and sewing. Most jobs will result from attrition.

Atomic energy. Excellent promise but little actual growth until well into the 70's, when research into medicine, food preservation, power and propellant systems begins to pay off.

Baking. Slight decline, with some expansion for routemen as suburbs sprawl.

Banking. Rapid growth as banks multiply and expand services. Most openings will be clerical, but demand for bank officers will also rise sharply.

Aviation (civil). Business flying will require 15,000 pilots within ten years with another 15,000 needed for air-taxi service. Mechanics in constant demand. More moderate growth for airline jobs, crop dusters, instructors, air-survey fliers.

Electric power. Growth in output, not jobs.

Electronics manufacturing. Rapid growth ahead. Industry is on threshold of vast new fields ranging from electronic highways and ultrasonic dishwashers to color television. Heavy demand for scientists, engineers, technicians, salesmen, mathematicians, physicists, specialists in fields such as quantum mechanics and solid-state circuitry.

Metals foundries. Growth in output, not jobs.

Hotels. Rapid job expansion, particularly in new hotels, urban motels and resort hotels.

Industrial chemicals. Rapid future expansion in prospect and ultimate growth not yet in sight. Best prospects for professional, administrative jobs. Also very good for maintenance workers, machinists, instrument repairmen, pipefitters, electricians.

Insurance. Moderate job expansion, chiefly clerical, sales.

Iron & Steel. Job openings will decline while production increases. White-collar workers, from technicians to plant management personnel, will find the picture brightest.

Automotive. Continuing strong demand for professional and skilled technical personnel. Semi-skilled and unskilled will find jobs becoming increasingly scarce.

Petroleum & natural gas. Employment decline will continue, despite increased output.

Pulp, paper & allied products. Moderate growth foreseen, particularly in South and West. Most openings will be for engineers, scientists, technicians and skilled workers, clerical and administrative workers.

Radio & television. Fierce competition for available openings. Educational TV expansion is a bright possibility.

Railroads. Job decline expected to continue, but slower.

Telephones. Technical improvements will keep employment stable. Thousands of jobs will be available, however, as craftsmen hired in the 1920's reach retirement.

Agriculture. Jobs down nearly 42% since 1947 and will drop another 20% by 1975, with fewer farms, more mechanization, improved materials and methods.

Government. Growingest growth industry of all, with big expansion in education, health services, hospitals, sanitation, police. Local governments—cities, counties, states, school districts—will account for most of the job increase; no appreciable expansion seen in federal manpower requirements.

SERVICE, CLERICAL, SALES

On the whole, service occupations will expand almost as fast as professional-technical-managerial jobs.

Demand will rise sharply for protective service workers—firemen, policemen, guards—and in hospitals and other institutions, public and private, the need will be as acute as ever for practical nurses, attendants and aides.

Expanding food services will create more jobs for waiters, waitresses, cooks, counter and fountain workers, charwomen, janitors. Need for household workers will rise, too, slowed only by the advent of new products and new equipment to lighten household chores.

In some service areas, however, opprtunities will shrink: theater ushers, elevator operators, porters, pinboys, boot-blacks.

For clerical and similar jobs, prospects will be bright as expanding industry and government create new mountains of paperwork.

Opportunities will be best for those who master the newer business machines and for those with a flair for meeting the public. No letup in the shortage of topnotch secretaries and stenographers.

Automation will make more inroads on routine tasks such as inventory and payroll clerking, billing and check sorting.

For sales jobs, average prospects. Expansion will come chiefly in real estate, insurance, manufacturers' sales and wholesale trade. At retail, the spread of vending machines and self-service stores will dampen growth.

THOSE WHO WORK BY HAND

Manual workers, the mechanics, repairmen, building craftsmen and others who form about a third of the labor force, may expect a favorable job future —if they are skilled or semi-skilled. The unskilled haulers, hoisters, diggers, loaders and unloaders will see their livelihoods hit hard by further automation.

Here is how some of these fields will fare.

Mechanics and repairmen. Excellent growth potential, especially for those trained to service vending and business machines. Outlook good, too, for auto mechanics, instrument repairers, and specialists in air conditioning, refrigeration and household appliances.

Building trades. Although growth prospects are only moderate, heavy demand ahead for glaziers; structural metal workers; excavating, grading and road machinery operators; lathers; cement masons; sheet metal workers; electricians; plumbers and pipefitters.

Driving. Many openings in jobs from local delivery routes to long-haul tractor-trailer operations. Best prospects: long-distance and local trucking.

WHAT'S THE MESSAGE?

There's a moral in all the job outlook facts reported on these pages. It's a simple point: "Stay in school."

Why? Because it may mean the difference between having a job and going on relief. Statistics show that young workers with less than eight years of school have an unemployment rate seven times that of college graduates. And the least skilled worker is seven times more likely to be unemployed than people in the professions.

Not that college is mandatory. Hundreds of thousands of jobs will await high school graduates with post high school vocational training. Many of these jobs pay very well, too, especially in some fast-growing industries.

But to reach top pay, the more book learning you have, the better your chances. Remember, too, that your first job won't be your last. A 20-year-old will change jobs six or seven times before he retires. And that means, increasingly, that young people must have enough educational background to switch from one job to another, perhaps as technological progress takes one job away—and proffers a half dozen others.

51 | Time to Kill

Automation, Leisure and Jobs

Eric Larrabee

The parable of automation and leisure is that of the sorcerer's apprentice. Half-educated man, lured by the prospect of relief from toil, mechanizes and eliminates his work. The chores get done, idleness is achieved, but the would-be wizard finds that he is drawn into a nightmare where the machines will not stop and his fate is to be their victim.

Man of his nature is a tool-using animal, but a machine—as Lewis Mumford was pointing out thirty years ago, in *Technics and Civilization*—is something different from a tool. It is a tool which can function independently of its operator's skill or expended energy. The difference, Mumford wrote, "lies primarily in the degree of automatism. . . ." Mechanization implies automation, and all self-controlling mechanisms are to some extent uncanny. The dancing brooms and mops of the sorcerer's workshop are only the extreme case; all machines hold possibilities for awe and terror.

Mumford's argument, in his pioneering book, was that humanity had to mechanize itself before it was ready for the machine. People had to be willing to constrict their lives, to adapt themselves to regularity and repetitiveness, before the machine would unloose its power on their behalf. For Mumford the turning point was the introduction of the mechanical clock into Western Europe about the 13th century, since the clock is the type case of automatized precision and order, and since no other machine so permeates and controls our daily lives. The history of mechanization, as Mumford, Siegfried Giedion, and others have told it, is one in which man increasingly makes himself the machine's servant, and fears his master.

Automation is the currently fashionable object of that recurrent fear. In the past fifteen years, with the application of electronic computers to commercial and industrial tasks, true automation—or what some writers, following Donald N. Michael, prefer to call cybernation—has become a reality. Vast domains of hitherto human handicraft in farm, factory, office and even executive suite can now be invaded and occupied by machines. While the depth and meaning of this invasion are still in dispute, the fears which it arouses are many and natural, most of them deriving from a fundamental fear of being dehumanized: being deprived of identity, deprived of function, deprived of meaning—that is, the fears of bureaucracy, of unemployment, and of empty leisure.

The fear of losing identity is the most individual and immediate. One is vividly made aware of becoming a punched card and a number by one's inability to communicate with institutions except through a screen of coded responses, often inappropriate and always impersonal. Though every number is in fact unique, the sense of being treated as a number is one of being reduced to a common denominator. A mechanized economy, on the face of

---

Reprinted by permission of *The Nation,* **201,** 8 (Sept. 20, 1965), p. 198.

it, seems to produce nothing but interchangeable objects and demand nothing but interchangeable men and women to operate it. The characteristic posture of youthful revolt, in an incipient age of automation, is understandably one of revulsion and flight from the prospect of stereotyped lives: identical jobs, identical cars and consumer goods, identical houses, and virtually identical spouses and children—like a row of little boxes, in the words of the modern folk song, all made out of ticky-tacky and looking just the same.

The fear of unemployment is the most general and traditional. It is general in that a threat of vanishing jobs produces the only organized response to automation, that of organized labor, whether in defiant resistance to all change or in grudging accommodation to the inevitable. It is traditional in that the arrival of automatic machinery in the textile industries of Germany, Holland, and England caused riots and brought on prohibitory edicts as early as the 17th century, and eventually reached a symbolic climax in Yorkshire with the Luddite riots of 1812, which have given their name to an attitude of hatred for machines and the desire to smash them. So deeply does this history permeate the world of learning that C. P. Snow, in his *Two Cultures and the Scientific Revolution,* was constrained to describe all humanistic intellectuals as "natural Luddites."

The fear of leisure participates in these other fears, but it is neither so impingent nor specific. It is, by comparison, a fear one feels on behalf of others. Leisure is a recent arrival on the agenda of officially defined "problems"; as long as there was not enough of it to go round, it could be regarded as an undoubted good, as indeed the rare but indispensable ingredient of art and high culture. Leisure in this context is not merely inactivity or time free from labor, like the unoccupied but unusable time of the prisoner or the peon sleeping in the sun. It is disposable time, time paid for by work, whether your own or someone else's. Leisure is the luxury and the burden of conscious choice; it compels a statement of what you would do if left to your own devices—a definition, for yourself and others, of who and what you are. The machine has democratized this type of leisure, making gifts of it to many who never before possessed it, until one can now legitimately speak of Mass Leisure, an unprecedented phenomenon in which enormous numbers of people have not only free time but the resources to do with it what they will.

The fear of leisure is at base the fear of boredom, of what the medieval monks called *acedia* or what Robert M. MacIver has called "the great emptiness," the restlessness that comes upon us when we have time and nothing to do with it, or when we look inward and find nothing there. Modern experiments in sensory deprivation (in which the subject spends as much time as he can tolerate at rest in a sightless, soundless cubicle) have emphasized the obvious: that if you force a man to do literally nothing he will eventually go mad. Deprived of variety, the mind begins to oscillate and empty itself until a new message, whether in brainwashing or a mystical conversion, comes to it radiant with ineffable truth. Multiply individual boredom by the millions and you have all the unattractive attributes of mass culture: the worst of the mass media and the ever present possibility of mass hysteria. "When men and women find nothing within themselves but emptiness," in the words of the *Report of the Commission on the Humanities* last year, "they turn to trivial and narcotic amusements, and the society of which they are a part becomes socially delinquent and politically unstable."

When leisure was limited to a minority class the burden of it could be borne, so to speak, vicariously. What Veblen called conspicuous consumption by that minority had to be conspicuous in order to allow the majority to watch, to derive that paradoxical pleasure the employed multitudes have always seemed to get from the spectacle of the idle rich being ostentatiously unemployed. Envy is not eliminated, to be sure, so that people at any given level of social stratification—given the chance—tend to adopt the leisure styles of the strata immediately above them, with the regrettable consequence that the 20th century middle class exhausts itself (and strains the available facilities) trying to behave like the landed aristocracy of the 19th. Also, it is a question whether vacations for recreation (which is to say, recovery from work) can properly be defined as leisure at all, and the frantic exhaustion which characterizes them is a telling weapon in the debating armory of those to whom mass leisure is a contradiction in terms.

Old-fashioned optimism about the indolent paradise which automation will bring, as you might expect, is more likely to flourish today in the Soviet Union than in the United States. Mihajlo Mihajlov, a Yugoslav teacher of literature who published in the Belgrade monthly *Delo* an account of his visit to Moscow during the summer of 1964 (reprinted in translation in *The New Leader*), tells of how surprised he was to find even a Westernized intellectual like Ilya Ehrenburg completely doctrinaire and inflexible about the coming future in which machines will liberate mankind from work and "people will read a lot, listen to music, conduct intelligent conversations. . . ." The American experience with a declining work week (from sixty-six hours in the mid-19th century down nearly to forty by the mid-20th) has already been extensive enough to induce profound doubts and, where an even shorter work week has been tried for any length of time—in Akron, Ohio, for example, as described for THE NATION by Harvey Swados in 1958—the most notable result is moonlighting, an increase in the number of men who hold two jobs at once. Perhaps the only reasonable balance between naïve hope and premature despair is the point so clearly and forehandedly made by the Canadians E. W. Leaver and J. J. Brown in their *Fortune* article "Machines Without Men" in 1946, one of the earliest announcements of automation's imminent arrival. "The new machines," they wrote, "will force the issue, force society to find better use for men than to make them the mechanical operators of machines."

But what are the alternatives? The potentiality of leisure for self-cultivation is one that, historically, no more than a minority has been allowed to exploit. Though no evidence exists that this limitation is ordained by natural law, since lifting it has not been tried, writers of an elitist persuasion have traditionally maintained that it was—that culture of necessity had to be supported by a few, and those happy few supported by the rest. "On inequality," as Clive Bell bluntly put it in his little book *Civilization* (1928), "all civilizations have stood." Now that such outright snobbery is no longer respectable this view is less often heard, but similar reservations about mass leisure are entertained by those to whom true leisure seems unattainable in a society organized around work, as ours still is. Leisure in a civilized sense is a form of inner equilibrium and grace which cannot simply be ordered up as part of a three-week holiday package. As long as people define themselves in terms of their work, in work will their deepest satisfactions lie; and the image of unlimited leisure will be inseparable from a threat of self-deprivation and loss. "What we require," as Michael Harrington has said, "and this is particularly difficult for English-speaking countries, is an end to the Protestant Ethic that a man establishes his worth in the eyes of his neighbor and his God, and works out his eternal salvation, by doing drudgery and engaging in saving."

It is no accident, if the phrase may be used, that Michael Harrington is the author of an influential book on contemporary American poverty and that he spoke these words (over the Chicago radio station WFMT) as a member of the Ad Hoc Committee on the Triple Revolution, a private group which is trying to generate public concern over automation (along with civil rights and thermonuclear war) as part of an interlocked crisis for our times. Members of the committee vary in the emphasis they put on one aspect or another, but in outline they hold that automation is coming on a great deal faster than any preparations being made to meet it, and that a major social disaster is implicit in the efforts of the dispossessed minorities, especially the Negroes, to move upward into those very jobs which automation will destroy just before they get there. The economist Robert Theobald, one of the committee members, took the extreme position on the same radio program that within the present decade "most of the new factories, the new public works, will employ machines rather than men and that it will be absolutely impossible to give everybody a job."

The consequences would be so far-reaching, if this conclusion were accepted as a base for public policy, that the conclusion itself is naturally being challenged. Charles E. Silberman, in a *Fortune* magazine series on "Technology and the Labor Market," has said of the Ad Hoc Committee's predictions that "nothing of the sort is happening," that no fully automated process for any major product exists anywhere in the United States, and that employment of manufacturing production workers has actually increased by one million in the past three and a half years. At a national conference on automation in March, 1965, sponsored by the American Bankers Association, the popular viewpoint seemed to be that no one really knew how many jobs had been destroyed by automation, since those industries which had automated the most had also been expanding the most in employment. Yet Charles Silberman himself willingly agrees with his adversaries about the long-term trend. "Sooner or later," he writes, "of course we will have the technical capability to substitute machines for men in most of the functions men now perform"—a confession which carries weight, coming from this quarter, even if it seems to imply that the future is clearer than the present.

The conclusion Robert Theobald draws from this minimal possibility, and from the economy which secular increases in productivity have already brought about, is that we must immediately start reconciling ourselves to the inevitability of paying people merely to exist. Theobald's latest book, *Free Men and Free Markets,* ends with a ringing demand for what he calls "an absolute constitutional right to an income." This concept, he says, "would guarantee to every citizen of the United States, and to every person who has resided within the United States for a period of five consecutive years, the right to an income from the federal government sufficient to enable him to live with dignity."

Theobald's proposal has the qualities of clarity and excess. As Leaver and Brown said of automation, it forces the issue; there could hardly be a more concrete reduction to cases of what it means to substitute a Keynesian doctrine of consumption for the Protestant Ethic. Anyone who wants to argue with Theobald has got to propose some better solution of what to do with economically no-longer-necessary people, or else propound some competitive morality to the mild humanitarianism which has shaped the present, almost worldwide welfare state. One can take the position that humanity is simply not ready yet to stop working, that it has not yet found anything remotely suitable as a substitute. As William Faulkner told an interviewer from the *Paris Review* in 1956, "One of the saddest things is that the only thing a man can do eight hours a day, day after day, is work. You can't eat eight hours a day nor drink for eight hours a day nor make love for eight hours—all you can do for eight hours is work. Which is the reason why man makes himself and everybody else so miserable and unhappy." But to differ with Theobald one has to be as categorical, if perhaps not so ironic, as Faulkner.

To be sure, when Faulkner spoke of work he spoke as an artist, knowing full well that what he did as an artist for eight hours a day was in fact hard work. In principle, there is no reason why the challenge and satisfaction he derived from the craft of novelist could not be found by the multitudes in similarly uneconomic activities, from the arts as such to the more mundane and less honorific arts of daily living. For the individual's well-being it is the struggle rather than the goal which matters, provided only the goal is defined as admirable by one's own standard and that of one's peers. Theoretically, again, we can conceive of a society superficially not too different from our own in which self-respect could be based on personal achievement of a purely aesthetic or even spiritual kind, but the word "achievement" itself is a booby trap packed explosively tight with traditional Western assumptions about virtue and individuality. A truly Keynesian aesthetic would be built around the ephemeral experience, since this is the only thing we can all consume indefinitely, and it would therefore put as high a value on a dew-tipped blade of grass as on Beethoven's Ninth. There is just not room enough, either physically or psychologically, for everyone to be Beethoven all at once; we would have to be seeking fulfillment in self-expression while denying ourselves permanence, and to say as much is to ask for a reversal of inherited criteria in art as wrenching to individual ego and integrity as the economic idea of becoming a permanently de-pauperized ward of the government.

The consequences of denying mankind the one thing it can do eight hours a day are not likely to be manifest immediately, since they are so various and interrelated as to resemble a generalized psychic malnutrition of the body social rather than the onslaught of any single disease. But certainly it requires no tight certainty about cause and effect to observe that industrial democracy needs a number of incentives spread through the population in order to function properly, and that it functions very poorly without them. For one thing, the whole machinery of upgrading deprived social classes, such as the immigrants to America, has called for ambition and discipline on their part which today's deprived, for good and evident reasons, no longer share. Character is hard enough to come by even in the awareness that it generally profits a white, upper-middle-class male to apply himself and behave decently; take away that awareness and a decay of morale sets in, spreading inescapably into education and the formation of coming generations. The sense of hopelessness which pervades the New York Public School system, as Martin Mayer has described it in the *New York Times Magazine,* is but the mirror image of hopelessness in its pupils' future. "We have just got to accept the fact," a junior high school principal told Mayer, gesturing at an assembly of nine hundred Negro and Puerto Rican students, "that half of these children will never hold a job in their lives."

Their misfortune is to have been born into an overdeveloped society engaged in the headlong pursuit of economic goals it has long since left behind; all of its habits are organized around the struggle for material sufficiency and it doesn't know how to break them. These several hundred children are not useless by any objective measure; they are merely classified as useless by contrast with the energy and sophistication of a world metropolis. In any other surroundings there would be plenty for them to do. Remove them to a South Sea island or Siberia and they would reveal all the motivations and resources which New York City has bred in them but will presently deny them the scope to exercise. They learn as victims what it means to belong to an insufficiently utopian society. The fault is not in Manhattan Island's dynamism but in the failure of its aspirations to keep up with its capabilities, so that surplus human energies are left unengaged—surplus, that is, in the sense of being the most convenient to disregard. In an equal race for a previously awarded prize most of the contestants are superfluous, and the vulnerable minorities—in pain, in public disgrace, and mainly in ignorance—have but the honor of being first to make the discovery.

For it is absurd to suppose, given the amount of ugliness and suffering the world still affords, that we have run out of work; what we have run out of is a set of organized connections between purposes crying out to be achieved and people crying out for purpose. Utopianism is one of the names for a connection between aims and efforts. It has to be a serious fantasy in that means must exist for pursuing it, but it must nonetheless remain fantastic to the extent of picturing a future worth extravagant risks to win. Automation is not the villain of this parable but only the occasion for it; there is so far no disequilibrium caused by increased productivity which could not be restored to balance by raising social goals. Automation forces the issue, as Leaver and Brown might have said, by compelling a given society to decide what its goals are going to be. It is a weapon put in man's hand like the dagger of the Gurkha: once drawn, it must be used.

If a reversal of the Protestant Ethic seems too much to ask, or an America given over to culture and contemplation is unrecognizable, then the reader should at least remember that utopianism is a national habit of long standing, and that the nation was in part created by men who expected sound institutions to nourish prosperity, and prosperity in turn to nourish art. "I must study politics and war," wrote one of them, "that my sons may have liberty to study mathematics and philosophy. My sons ought to study mathematics and philosophy, geography, natural history and naval architecture, navigation, commerce, and agriculture, in order to give their children a right to study painting, poetry, music, architecture. . . ." The prophecy was John Adams's, and the last portion of it has yet to be realized.

---

52 | What People Think About College

Americans believe wholeheartedly in higher education. Many, in fact, believe that a college education is practically the birthright of every American boy and girl. Presumably the public will support added expenditures for higher education if it feels that college training is worth what it costs. But not all people are willing to accept the tax hikes that would probably accompany more support of *public* higher education.

Opinion? Guesswork? Not at all, but statements of fact based on information from a recent national survey of public attitudes toward higher education conducted by the Survey Research Center of the University of Michigan's Institute of Social Research. The project received partial financial support from the U.S. Office of Education's cooperative research program.

To obtain a national sample, we interviewed 1,310 persons from nearly all parts of the country (Alaska and Hawaii were the only exceptions), in all walks of life. We have grouped responses according to the respondent's income, education, age, religion, political affiliation, organizational leadership, race, region, location, and extent of State support for education in the region. Respondents had been selected from a sample that had been developed by the Center.

The problems of getting a higher education have different degrees of meaning for different people, we soon discovered. Age makes a difference and, of course, education and income. But almost to a man the respondents believed that a college education is a good and desirable thing. In fact, most thought that even two years of college are better than no college training. About 90 percent would have advised a young man who could finance only two years of college but who had a good job offer to pass up the job and pursue the education. A young man with a 12th-grade education expressed what seemed to be the feeling of most respondents: "Go to college. The job he gets won't last the rest of his life, and he can't have too much education." Another young man who had had some college training spoke from his own experience: "Definitely go for two years," he said. "That would be

---

From *American Education,* 1, 30–32, February 1965.

a stepping-stone to more education. After that he could take night school. The more education the better."

Education for young women also received a vote of support from the respondents, though only 77 percent would have told a young woman to choose education over a job. Apparently some people believe that higher education, as one man with a trade school education put it, "isn't as important for a girl because she's not actually stuck with supporting a family as a man is." This type of response came most often from persons in the low-income brackets or from those with little education. There was, however, a notable exception to this pattern of response: Negroes, who are certainly among the poorest people in the United States and among the least educated, were inclined to believe that higher education is as important for a young woman as for a young man.

Why do Americans consider a college education desirable? The number one reason, judging from the responses we obtained, seems to be the job training it offers. Our responses correspond to the findings of earlier research—that Americans think of higher education in terms of income. Newspaper stories and magazine articles from time to time remind the public that every year of education adds so many dollars to income, and it is easy to see that the college graduate has an advantage in the job market. Our respondents overwhelmingly indicated that they were aware of the financial advantages of higher education and listed it as the best reason for going to college. The artistic and cultural values of developing an interest in music, art, and literature received only a small response as the major reason for going to college.

But, we hasten to add, so did the opportunity to participate in athletics, which got an even lower rating.

The only group that gave substantial support to any reason other than job training was the group with the highest income and the most education. About 48 percent of the respondents in this group said that the most important reason for a young person to obtain a college education is "to increase his understanding of the world and himself."

The respondents believed that the worth of a college education for a young woman is about the same as for a young man: education means a better paying job. Highly educated and well-to-do respondents placed less emphasis than other respondents on job training. And nearly all groups included a few people who thought the most important reason for young women to go to college is to develop socially, a reason almost no one gave for young men.

About 42 percent of the respondents found some disadvantages in going to college. Dissatisfaction took the form of criticism of college graduates. The critics said that college graduates tend to become condescending and snobbish. This complaint came most often from the people who had gone on to nonacademic training after completing high school.

Obviously, Americans see clearly the economic value to the individual of a college education. But many people have no conception of how education can benefit the Nation as a whole. Over half of the respondents were unable to think in terms of public benefits accruing from higher education.

When asked why they favored higher education for reasons other than personal job advantage, about half could provide no answer but a restatement of the same reason. Some replied in general terms. A high school graduate said, "We would be better off if more went to college. Anyone with a college education has a better chance of being someone, doing things that are better for the country." A college graduate was hardly more specific. He said, "This is a good thing. We would be more progressive and our people would have a better standard of living if more were educated."

The respondents who did have some idea of the broader value of education thought mostly in domestic terms. They recognized, in varying degrees, the importance of an informed citizenry and of having a supply of trained men and women to meet the demands of the technological age. They could see that a lack of education is partly responsible for unemployment and dependency. But only a few respondents had any idea of the possible international effects of higher education in the United States. One in ten thought that education would help the Nation keep up with the international competition in space and in trade. One middle-aged woman with less than high school education said that "the more understanding students get from books and school the better off the world is because they will get to understand what the world is all about."

In order to bring the evaluation of the importance of a college education from the hypothetical to the concrete, we asked respondents with children of precollege age whether they expected their children to go to college. In line with the high value placed on a college education, respondents expressed high aspirations for their children. A high school diploma was considered minimum attainment by most respondents. The majority expected their children to attend college. Of parents with children five years of age, about 70 percent expected sons and 62 percent expected daughters to go to college. The percentage dropped as the age of the children rose. Only about half of the parents with sons and 42 percent with daughters 16 or 17 years old expected them to go to college. These differences may represent an adjustment to the realities of financing an education, or they may have sprung from the differences in age and education among respondents. The parents of young children tend to be younger and better educated than the parents of older children, and each generation has higher aspirations for its children than the preceding. Parents who did not go beyond grammar school said they expected one out of three of their children to go to college. Parents who had graduated from college expected all of their children to go to college. Negro parents were not so hopeful as white parents, but racial differences were not nearly so large as the differences between parents of contrasting income and occupation. Protestant and Catholic parents differed very little in the expectations they held for their children.

It seems to us that the most important observation to be made about the aspiration of the parents of young children is that they far outrun the present or expected capacity of our colleges. Great as the country's education system is, we are approaching a period when the ability of our colleges and universities to accommodate the qualified young people seeking higher education will not be adequate to the demand. How aware is the public of the problem?

Half of the respondents said they thought it a serious problem that colleges are having to turn down high school graduates because of inadequate space. Another 25 percent thought the problem "somewhat serious." Those who considered the problem serious based their response on the belief that "education is a good thing; every young person who wants education should have it. There should be equal opportunity for all." Half the respondents thought the problem would get worse in the next few years. A quarter thought the problem would get better; another quarter simply didn't know. Those saying the problem would get worse were aware that the population is increasing and that this means more young people knocking at the college door.

In general, those who thought the situation would get better said that taxes would probably go up and that more facilities would be provided with tax money. Recognition of the seriousness of the problem increased with the education, income, and social level of the respondent; it decreased with the age.

At times the respondents did produce surprises for us. For instance, although respondents with more than average education were generally more concerned with the lack of space in colleges and universities than others, one-fifth of the college graduates in the sample did not consider the shortage as serious. Since they were probably well informed, we have come to the conclusion that their reply stemmed from the fact that they were aware of the availability of places in the less known colleges and of the efforts being made to find openings for applicants who have been turned down by the popular institutions.

Since the average American citizen will ultimately have to provide the financial support, how does he propose to go about it? Most of our respondents were convinced of the personal advantage of a college education, and without considering the cost or ways of financing higher education they were highly in favor of expanding college facilities. But when they were faced with the reality of raising money, some respondents showed less generosity. We found that few respondents had a realistic comprehension of the financial demands which an expanding program of higher education would make on the Nation. We presented respondents with three courses to choose from for financing higher education: Control of college costs by the college itself, restriction of enrollment, and increased taxes or increased student support. The majority responded to the suggestions by proposing a continuation of the present system of State support and individual tuition or frankly said they didn't know the best way to meet rising costs.

The prospect of paying "a little more in taxes" to support State universities got a mixed reception from our respondents. Nearly two in three were willing to pay a little more taxes, if necessary. But one in three flatly rejected a tax increase, even though many of them had earlier expressed a strong belief in higher education. Resistance to taxes was highest among people with the smallest income ($3,000 a year or less). It was also high among older people and people over 45 who had no direct responsibility for children.

About a third of the respondents would not give an opinion on the question of whether their States were doing enough for higher education. About half the respondents said that they were satisfied with their State programs. About one-fourth were dissatisfied, complaining of crowded conditions, high tuition, and lack of action of the part of the State to cope with increased enrollments.

Satisfaction with State programs, we found, differed by regions. In the West, where appropriations for higher education are high, three out of four persons believed their States were doing a good job. Only half the respondents in the Northeast, where appropriations are relatively low, were satisfied. But, in the South, where appropriations are the lowest in the country, satisfaction was higher than in the Northeast.

Only a minority—one in five—felt that financial pressures on colleges could be reduced by cutting costs. The majority of respondents (60 percent) had no opinion on this question. Those who thought colleges could cut costs suggested that the institutions do away with such "frills" as basket-weaving, use educational television, accelerate programs, and enlarge classes.

As to the suggestion that the college meet its financing problem by curtailing enrollments, the respondents were firmly against it. We had expected this resistance in view of the strong support for higher education for all qualified students. Response to our question as to whether we should build more colleges or curtail enrollments was without a doubt in favor of college construction.

Only about eight percent of the respondents thought that only the brightest students should be admitted to our colleges. Most people simply believe that education should be available to students who want it. A young doctor said, "There should be more colleges for all to go to. More general education will help any student. The average student as a rule turns out to be the best asset to his country and his community. All should go to college." An elderly woman with little formal education reiterated his words, "Everyone should have a chance to go. You don't know when they are bright or not."

The policy of our State institutions has been for the State to bear most of the expense of education and the student to make minimal contribution. But public institutions as well as private have been forced to raise tuition and fees. Our respondents, faced with the question of whether the State or the student should pay more, or whether to maintain the present balance, had divided opinions or no opinion at all: 31 percent said the present arrangement should remain in effect, 24 percent thought the State should pay more and the student less, and 13 percent thought the student should pay more and the State less. Those advocating the status quo felt that there was already a reasonable balance between the State and the student. Those wanting the State to pay more were concerned that deserving young people might not obtain higher education unless the State increased its support. Some of those who wanted the student to pay more were against subsidized education in general. But in all groups some respondents felt that the student should pay more "if he is able."

In all our inquiring we took for granted that the present system of support—which calls for the student's paying at least part of his expenses—will remain in effect. We closed our interview by asking the parents who had said they expected their children to go to college what provisions they were making to finance it. "How much," we asked, "do you think it will cost to send your child to college for a year, counting board and room, tuition, fees, books, clothes, travel, and everything else?" We did not specify the year. The average answer was $1,947, a realistic figure. The American Council on Education says that in 1960 the average student in a private college spent $1,671.

Despite the fact that most parents knew what they would have to pay, only a little over half had saved anything toward a college fund. The average yearly savings for all parents who were planning to send at least one child to college was $162. Of course, the largest savings had been made by the higher income groups. But reports of savings are rough approximations at best since most families do not handle a budget with an accountant's precision.

Our description of public attitudes toward higher education is not likely to remain valid long. The crisis developing in our colleges will compel both State and national government agencies to act, and public opinion will influence and be influenced by government action. Social and economic changes now taking place will also acect the value the public puts on higher education and the aspirations it has for its children. The study we conducted points out where the public stood in the spring of 1963; it also provides a benchmark which should help everyone interested in higher education to understand the trends in public attitudes and the changes the future may bring.

---

53 | Dear Freshman . . . If You Want Our Advice About . . .

STUDYING . . .

You've got to get organized! College life is so different from high school. I had to get used to a whole new way of life. By the end of my freshman year, I'm just getting used to it enough to be able to budget my time effectively. What do I mean by a new way of life? Well, all the little decisions which have to be made—when to eat, when to go to bed, how to take care of the laundry—used to be made for me. Now I have to decide them all by myself. Since they were new, I got carried away with them at first and found that I wasn't studying enough. Or, I would get so engrossed in studying that I'd wake up at 10 p.m. to the fact that I'd forgotten to eat supper or that every suit of clothes I owned was stacked in a laundry bag ready for me to take it to the cleaners day before yesterday!

Study hard the first week, the first month, the first semester, and you'll have a large part of the battle won. There's probably no better advice than to

---

From the September 1959 issue of *The Intercollegian.* Reprinted by permission of the National Student Council YMCA and the National Student YWCA, New York.

start off on the right foot in your studies. Concentration is much more important than the time spent studying. And it takes conscious effort on your part to learn to concentrate.

Try to find some interest in each subject. There are no limits, actually, to how easy and pleasant studying can be made, if only you are able to develop some interest (or else imagine some interest) in the subject matter. *The attitude of interest is probably the most essential factor in efficient studying.*

Have a definite time to study and avoid disturbances. Don't flop down on your bunk with the physics book, with the radio blaring forth the ten top tunes, and expect to get any return for your investment of time. If studying is drudgery for you, pleasant accompaniment with music is not likely to mitigate this feeling. It is better to pretend to have an interest in the subject and for short periods of time sacrifice everything else for the sake of this interest. Frequently a genuine interest will then develop as you study.

It's not the hours spent studying that takes the time. It's the hours you waste getting ready to study!

Do your studying, and then fool around! Not vice versa. And for goodness sake, do go to bed!

Don't wait 'till after that date! Start studying early in the evening when you are fresh. If you have any extra time, you can spend it at leisure.

It can't be done in one night! Tests in college are not like those in high school. Not only are they harder; they also cover more material. Nightly studying of a subject may prove impossible, but at least start preparing for a big quiz days ahead of time.

COURSES AND PROFESSORS . . .

Understanding a subject, not just memorizing it is the important thing in studying in college. *Try to get what is back of it all, rather than just the facts.* The same sort of thing goes in a lecture. Ask yourself, what is it the teacher is driving at? If you don't know, if you are lost in the outline and the subpoints, then brother, you've missed the whole point!

Don't take for granted that you've got a course made! Many freshmen I know made the same mistake I did first semester. They assumed that they could easily pass the courses connected with their major subject. I spent my time on the peripheral courses, or the ones in which I was less interested. Come to find out, I made my lowest grades in the courses which counted the most toward my major!

Don't rely on the textbook! In college the student has to combine what he reads in the textbook, what he hears in lectures, and his own research. To pass an exam, you have to be able to combine all three, with your own ideas on the subject as well!

Students are to be heard, not just seen! Looks do not persuade a college professor. He rates intelligence by ideas. A corollary to this fact is that college classrooms are used more often for lectures and discussion than for recitations. You are expected to raise questions, share ideas, comment critically and reflectively.

Let your professor know you are alive! Even in a big university, it is possible to talk over your academic problems with professors during their office hours or after classes. Usually, a professor is human, too, and he will treat you as human if you take the time to consult him about your problems *before* you flunk his quizzes!

Regard professors as people. Consider that they have feelings, and that they experience many of the same frustrations as you. Give them the courtesy of listening to what they have to say, weighing this carefully against your total experience thus far. Don't reject a professor because you don't agree with his ideas or his methods. Don't forget that he can be of tremendous help to you as you seek to gain new understanding.

It's a mistake to settle for shooting at a B or C. Aim at an A. Even if you don't make it, you'll end up with something respectable.

Don't cut classes! This is one thing I can say with authority and without reservation. Don't cut just because it's a pretty day outside, or you are a bit tired, or you really aren't prepared for class. If you do, you may hear a professor say, as I did, "One more cut, and you're out!" Stick with it!

It is easy to keep up, or to catch up, but it is impossible to do both at the same time. Don't get behind. And don't rely on holidays to catch up—it just doesn't work!

EXTRA-CURRICULARS . . .

You learn by doing, as well as studying! Get into action fast as a good citizen of your University or college community. In student government, student Unions, the Y and religious foundations, you have a chance to put ideas into practice. Some students are "gung-ho" activities. If you are going to get swamped by them, make sure you are in ones that contribute to your education. But my advice is to take on extra-curriculars responsibly. Make sure you can handle one effectively before you take on another. Better to do a good job in one than a mediocre job in all!

College is not so difficult—it's just that there are so many things to do! All in one evening, I find myself torn between a lecture on atomic science, a required sorority meeting, a Y meeting I want to attend, and to top it off, a night lab. So much to do. *And you have to choose!*

For students who live at home: Many students who enter college these days are lucky to have a college or university in their home town. There are many advantages in living at home while you go to school, as I have found out, but there are also many disadvantages. The chief disadvantage is in not having as good a chance to meet and to get to know other students than your high school gang. The best remedy for this is to spend some of your time at a dorm or fraternity house. A chance to spend a weekend in a dorm, visiting acquaintances and making new friends, offers many rewards to the student who lives at home. Commuting and part time jobs often make it difficult to find time for campus organizations. Your college experience will be enriched and *you* will benefit as a person if you plan to participate in the Y, student religious foundations, student government, student Union, and other extra-curricular activities.

Be sure to take advantage of the cultural activities and facilities available to you on the campus. This includes choral concerts, symphonic music, art shows, drama, and the like. Becoming an educated person means much more than just cramming your head full of information or joining organizations.

Don't be afraid to accept responsibility. You may not have much self-confidence, here; but your freshman year is a good time to get your feet wet and to gain some valuable experience. By the time you are a senior, if not before, you might be a top-flight leader on the campus and contributing valuable services to the campus community.

MAKING THE MOST OF COLLEGE . . .

Have an aim in college, but don't make it too inflexible. Don't be like the sightseer who drives through a national park with no goal in mind, nor like the one who drives through it with his eyes on a speedometer pointing to 60.

Be open minded. At least give views which oppose or differ from yours a hearing, then try to see how your ideas really stack up as objectively as you can. You'll be surprised at how much you can learn very quickly.

College does not mean that we all leave the campus convinced in the same direction, holding identical theories, nor evincing the same approaches to life. It is a good rule that if you cannot stand to listen to people with views which differ from you[rs], even radically, you'd better try to understand why.

Expect the unexpected. Don't be knocked off balance by every little frustration or every little plan which does not go off as you thought it should. Learn to be flexible so that you can bounce back quickly from personal disappointments.

Expect your faith to change. College will challenge not only your beliefs but also many of your basic presuppositions. Here an attitude of open-mindedness might be suggested: Don't hold tenaciously to your tradition, denouncing all criticism, but, on the other hand, don't be too quick to abandon your heritage and to lose your roots.

54 | College Students Change Majors

M. Olin Cook

The percentage of high school graduates who attend college has increased immensely over the past three decades. During this time, occupations which were available to American youth have become more numerous and complex. Accordingly, college students today have more difficulty in selecting their field of study when they enroll in college than students of past years.

The following study sought to find some of the reasons students had for changing their majors after they had enrolled at Auburn (Ala.) University, some of the trends established in changing, and some of the effects these transfers had on the students. Of the total students who entered Auburn University in the summer and fall of 1959, about 32% had changed their major one or more times by the fall of 1962, which was the beginning of their senior year.

The percentage of students who changed majors at Auburn University did not appear to be an exception. Gamble reported that nearly 43% of the Pennsylvania State University students who enrolled in the fall of 1957 made at least one change in major before graduation from college.* MacIntosh found that 30% of the students in his study conducted at Pennsylvania State University changed their major during their first year in college.†

All students included in the study were enrolled as beginning freshmen at Auburn University either the summer or fall quarter, 1959, and took all their college work at Auburn. The students also changed majors one or more times after enrolling in college. Finally, they were enrolled in the fall quarter, 1962. The sample included 102 students who met the requirements listed above. A control group of 102 students was selected at random from the same entering freshman class which was utilized in the comparison of grades between those students who had and those who had not changed their majors.

Of the 1,995 students who entered Auburn University in the summer and fall quarters of 1959, 632, or 32%, had changed majors at least once during the period from summer, 1959, to fall, 1962. The mean number of changes made was 1.2. Only 46% of the total group still was enrolled at Auburn University during the fall quarter, 1962.

The basic data for this study were collected by interviewing 102 Auburn University students, studying students' records in the registrar's office and

---

From *School and Society,* May 1, 1965. Reprinted by permission of the author and *School and Society,* published by The Society for the Advancement of Education, Inc.

* Glenn C. Gamble, "Pre-College Experiences and Curriculum Changes by College Students," *Personnel and Guidance Journal,* **40**:562, February, 1962.

† Archibald MacIntosh, "A Study of Factors Associated with the Stability of Vocational Goals in College Students" (unpublished doctor's dissertation, University of Pennsylvania, 1953).

the Student Counseling Center, and reviewing various articles and books which reported related studies.

Sample selection involved the drawing of subjects randomly from a pool of qualified students' names. A total of 110 students was selected. Of this number, 102 agreed to participate in the study.

After a tentative interview guide was prepared, 20 Auburn University students who had changed their major were scheduled for interviews. These interviews were conducted for the purpose of standardizing the interview guide. After this preliminary study, a semi-standardized interview was regarded to be the best for the situation.

All interviews were held in the same room during the fall quarter, 1962. The range of time for interviews was from 30 to 70 minutes and the average length was 45 minutes. The interview guide was followed in every case and notes were taken during the conference. Assessment of interview error reflected agreement to be from 80% to 100%.

Changing majors could take place in one of two ways: first, the transfer might have changed the student's major within the same school; or second, the students might have transferred to another school on the Auburn University campus. Of the 632 who made at least one change, 126 made all their transfers within the same school. This number is about 20% of the total number of students who made at least one change. Of this group, many students made more than one change within the same school. In a number of cases, the second or third change carried them back to their initial choice of major.

Considering each change in major that a student made, the School of Science and Literature received more students than any other school on campus. Of the 573 total changes made to schools other than that which the student entered as a freshman, 240, or 42%, were made to the School of Science and Literature. The next highest in number and percentage was the School of Education, which had 163 transfers, or 28% of the total transfers made to other Auburn University schools. The School of Engineering enrolled more freshmen than any other school. Therefore, with respect to enrollment, the School of Engineering received fewer students who changed their majors than any other school on campus.

The 506 students made the 558 changes outside their original school. The School of Engineering led all others in the total number of changes made from one school to another. The total number made from the School of Engineering was 197, or 35% of the total changes made from the different schools on the Auburn University campus. The Schools of Science and Literature and of Architecture and Arts followed with 20% and 16% of the total transfers, respectively.

Science and Literature had the highest percentage of transfers to enter that school and had the second highest number to transfer out. Thus, it can be inferred that the School of Science and Literature over the three-year period gained a higher percentage of students who changed their majors than it lost.

The School of Engineering, which led in the number of freshmen who chose a major within that school, suffered more loss than any other school on campus and did not pick up many through the process of students from other schools transferring to engineering. A reversal in stability was reported by the data from the Schools of Education and of Chemistry. The School of Education received a number of transfers from other schools on campus but lost few of its students to other schools. Chemistry appeared to gain few but lost a number of students. Much the same picture was shown for the School of Architecture and Arts. The School of Agriculture, except for the difference in number enrolled, reflected much the same stability as Home Economics and Pharmacy.

Students gave a wide variety of reasons for transfer. Primary categories of reasons included the influence of parents, relatives, and friends; vocational interests; and personal desires and social interest.

Regardless of the change made or the reason for the transfer, a student usually realized some effects. As a result of changing majors, some students lost credit hours.

The mean number of quarter hours lost by the 102 students as a result of change in majors was 5.2, while 61 were able to transfer all of their credits to their new program of study. Considering only those students who lost hours, the mean was 12.9.

The standard deviation for hours lost was 12, which means that two-thirds of the students fell within the range of losing from zero to 29.2 hours.

The requirements for graduation with a bachelor's degree could be completed in 12 quarters in most courses of study, assuming that the student took an average load each quarter and passed all his work. More than 12 quarters were required in several majors at the time the students, included in this study, enrolled at Auburn.

From student responses it was found that the range of quarters required for graduation was from 12 to 17. The mean number of quarters required was 13.3, with a standard deviation of 2.6.

The 81 students from the sample who were required to attend college for additional quarters, or quarters above the minimum number required in their curriculum for graduation, made an estimate of the extra cost involved. Since the students who were interviewed had not graduated, it was

Number and Percentage of Changes in Majors Made by Auburn University Students to and from Schools on Campus Other than the One in Which They Were Previously Enrolled

School	Number of transfers to the school	Percentage of the total transfers	Number of transfers from the school	Percentage of the total transfers
Agriculture	35	6	55	9
Architecture and Arts	63	11	87	16
Chemistry	15	3	56	10
Education	163	28	37	7
Engineering	35	6	197	35
Home Economics	6	1	11	2
Pharmacy	16	3	6	1
Science and Literature	240	42	109	20
Total	573	100	558	100

necessary to arrive at the additional cost on the basis of average expenses in the past.

The range in the amount of extra money required was from zero to $1,075. Considering the 78 students who were required to spend extra money for their degree, the mean was $206.27 and the standard deviation $151.

When all the students were considered, the mean for the amount of extra money required for graduation was $157.74 and the standard deviation was $135. This mean figure was slightly above the amount required for tuition alone for a period of two quarters.

Besides loss of hours, requirement of extra quarters for graduation, or extra money needed, grades of students possibly could be affected by the change in major. In order to determine whether the over-all grade-point average of the students in the sample was affected by transfer, a control group of 102 students was selected randomly from the same 1959 class. The only difference between the sample and the control groups was that the control group had remained in their original major throughout the three-year period covered by the study.

The students who changed their majors one or more times also expressed some change in attitudes. Of the 33 different attitudes expressed, 79% were positive. As many as 45 students stated that there were no shifts in their attitudes about the university as a result of the change in major. The following positive attitudes were expressed: the change was for their personal benefit and welfare; the feeling of better adjustment to college; the new majors were more difficult than the old ones; but this was desirable; more electives were allowed; the new major offered them an advisor, which was very appealing; they took school more seriously and enjoyed studying; their grades would improve; and the change would result in more money, job possibilities, and security in the future.

Feelings which were categorized as negative were expressed by 21%. All of these attitudes were related to courses or staff in their "old" school. Around half of the students did not change their feelings about Auburn University as a result of change in major.

Although students who had changed their majors from the time they entered Auburn University had a slightly better grade-point average, there was no significant difference between the averages of the two groups. This would suggest that grades were not significantly affected by changing majors. Attitudes concerning their future at the university and after graduation and possibilities of success seemed to be more positive than negative as a result of changing majors.

This study suggests that colleges should concentrate more in helping students find an area of study which is appropriate to their desires, interests, and abilities. Guidance-minded college personnel are faced with helping students find their places in a college setting.

Unit Twelve | DISCUSSION QUESTIONS

50. *Tomorrow's Jobs—Where the Best Will Be*
What are the fastest-growing occupation groups? What are the reasons for growth?
What are your occupational goals? Discuss the outlook in terms of hiring, qualifications, and salary.

51. *Time to Kill: Automation, Leisure, and Jobs*
List and discuss five current fears concerning automation.
Discuss possible solutions that will be needed in the age of automation.

52. *What People Think About College*
How do you explain the recent growth of the community college?
What are the purposes of the community college?
According to this article, what reasons are given for attending college?

53. *Dear Freshman . . . If You Want Our Advice . . .*
What problems are most frequently encountered by college freshmen? List in order of importance.
What recommendations would you offer to a prospective college student to alleviate adjustment problems?

54. *College Students Change Majors*
What are the reasons college students change majors?
Should freshmen declare a major field of study? What are the advantages and disadvantages?

Unit Thirteen *Courtship and Marriage*

Each stage of life requires particular kinds of roles. The "developmental task" theory of Robert Havighurst holds that the role for the 18–35-year-old group includes: (1) selecting a mate, (2) learning to live with a marriage partner, (3) starting a family, (4) rearing a family, and (5) managing a home. Most colleges and universities enjoy large enrollments in classes that are specifically designed to cover these topics. Discussions in several other courses find themselves centered around these subjects. Magazines, books, motion pictures, forums, and social gatherings draw upon this audience. Television programs, such as "The Dating Game" and "The Newlywed Game," are further examples of the attention focused on young people during courtship and marriage. It is of no surprise that many college students are clamoring at the chance to let computers choose agreeable dating companions for them. The vast majority of those who have tried this method have not given the machines very high ratings. It seems that the successful dates occurred at about the same significance as chance expectation. Nevertheless, the dating-by-computer companies continue to profit, and more and more companies appear on the dating scene. It has been estimated that a quarter-of-a-million Americans participate in lonely-hearts clubs that range from letter writing to so-called scientific endeavors.

Regardless of the methods used, the selection of a mate is by far the most significant decision confronting a person. The basic foundation of our society is centered around the successful home and family. No one clear method for marriage partner selection exists; however, sociologists have recognized certain factors that are found in successful marriages, e.g., similarity of attitudes, interests, and values. The recognition and adherence to these factors will undoubtedly increase the possibility of a happy union. In the first reading of this unit, *Marriage Is Not a Personal Matter,* J. F. Scott presents a concise discussion of the problems of electronic match-making and the various criteria of love and marriage.

Initial Adjustment Processes in Young Married Couples by Beverly R. Cutler and William G. Dyer examines marital adjustment in young couples. It discusses seven frequent areas of marriage adjustment in terms of discovering which ones were violated by whom and the responses made toward adjustment: (1) verbal expressions of affection; (2) frequency of sexual intimacy; (3) spending time at home; (4) sharing ideas; (5) care of the home; (6) personal neatness and appearance; and (7) spending family income.

The third paper by the Staff of Changing Times explores the question of marital happiness and disharmony. *The Unsolved Mystery of Marriage* questions why seemingly perfect matches fail and why the unlikely ones last for years.

This year, it is estimated that close to 400,000 American couples will be divorced. The last article by Hugh Carter, *Eight Myths About Divorce,* discusses inaccurate beliefs that are shared today concerning the problem of divorce.

---

55 | Marriage Is Not a Personal Matter

Who Marries Whom and Why

John Finley Scott

The newest wrinkle in the old game of courtship is match-making by computer. It goes something like this: a young man lists in a "data bank" what he most desires in a prospective female companion and supplies information about his own characteristics. The computer compares the qualities and interests desired against those of a (presumably vast) inventory of candidates who have also put themselves on file. After some adjustment and compromise, our young man is presented with the name, address and telephone number of a "Miss Just-Right-and-very-nice-too." Since electronic match-making is not quite yet an exact science, he may also be informed of a few alternates (who are also very nice) in case something goes wrong and he doesn't quite hit it off with Miss Just-Right.

The fact that many "computerized introduction services" are pretty much fly-by-night operations does not mean that computer match-making is unworkable in principle. If marital felicity can be accurately defined, then it would seem that a compatible marriage partner would more likely be found among the thousands of candidates to which a computer could refer than among the handful that any one person could ever meet face to face.

But the problem is identifying "marital felicity"; what on earth *is* a successful marriage? Can any kind of successful matching be based on the verbal responses of the largely adolescent segment of the population that is on the verge of matrimony? Any programmer will tell you that a computer is no better than the information put into it. In many respects, the verbal professions of persons facing marriage are the last things on which to base predictions about the future condition of the families thus formed. That a number of marriages—a minority, to be sure, but a substantial one—will terminate in divorce within three years will hardly be revealed through polling the expectations of brides-to-be.

Part of the problem with the sort of individualistic mate-selection that computer match-making proposes derives from the fact that marriage, though

---

often regarded as an intensely personal affair, is one of the least individualistic of all social institutions. The family—which is, by the way, surprisingly invariant among societies in its basic features—has evolved not because it satisfies individual preferences but because it is socially useful. It combines the functions of reproduction, child care, sexual gratification and economic cooperation with an over-all efficiency that no alternative arrangement has so far been able to match. Since marriage is such a good thing from the society's point of view, it is convenient to make young people want to get married by teaching them that marriage satisfies their *own* needs, and to soft-pedal the demands of the larger society. This is why marriage (like the

For Women

1. *In which of the following situations would you feel most comfortable?*
   1) exploring Vesuvius and the ruins of Pompeii
   2) sipping cappucino on the Via Veneto (Rome)
   3) boating off the island of Mykonos (Greece)
   4) conversing with peasants in Skoplje (Yugoslavia)
   5) visiting the Uffizi galleries (Florence)
2. *Of the following, which would you prefer?*
   1) loving a man who did not love you
   2) being loved by a man you could not love
   3) neither loving nor being loved until the feeling was mutual, regardless of how long it took to come about
3. *How well can you cook?*
   1) expertly, exotic dishes and proper wines
   2) quite well, but nothing fancy
   3) hit or miss
   4) TV dinners and canned soup
   5) can-openers are for picture-hanging
4. *Which of the following fields are you most closely associated with or interested in?*
   1) nursing
   2) secretarial
   3) modeling or fashion
   4) sales or purchasing
   5) fine arts or design
   6) education
   7) business administration
5. *Your date has spent his money on an electronic fish-finder, but you had wanted him to escort you to a concert. You would most likely:*
   1) pay your own way
   2) lend him money
   3) find another date and let him go fishing
   4) treat him
   5) go fishing with him
6. *You are with your friends when an argument develops about the evening's activity. You would:*
   1) remain silent
   2) compromise
   3) go along with the majority
   4) insist upon your choice
   5) go off alone
7. *Which of the following date ideas most appeals to you?*
   1) dining and dancing
   2) horseback riding
   3) a picnic in the country
   4) watching TV
   5) attending a concert
8. *How important is it that your match own and drive a car?*
   1) very important
   2) moderately important
   3) he can borrow mine

armed forces) is easier to enter than to leave. Young people are recruited to matrimony, but at the same time their hopes come to depend on frequently unrealistic aspirations and their ability to predict what lies ahead becomes limited.

Here lies the problem with any scheme of match-making that relies solely on the expressed preferences of the young people involved. This is hardly anything new: many parents, and most professional matchmakers—from Japanese villages to American suburbs—have known it for years. It would be interesting to see what kind of matches a computer would arrange if it interviewed parents as well as their eligible children.

We live in a society where unprecedented numbers of young people, aided by rapid social change, higher education, urbanization and widespread

---

For Men

1. *Which of the following activities most appeals to you?*
   1) skindiving in Montego Bay
   2) touring the Rijksmuseum in Amsterdam
   3) watching a bullfight in Seville
   4) mountain climbing in Lausanne
   5) eating leberkase and drinking dark beer in a brauhaus in Munich
2. *With which of the following cars can you most readily identify?*
   1) Rolls Royce
   2) Mustang
   3) Cadillac
   4) Jaguar XKE
   5) Maxwell (vintage)
   6) Volkswagen
3. *You are at a party where you don't know anyone. You would very likely:*
   1) leave early
   2) find a comfortable chair in a corner
   3) join a conversation about sports
   4) introduce yourself to the women
   5) introduce yourself to the men
4. *Which of the following fields are you most closely associated with or interested in?*
   1) medicine and research
   2) law
   3) education
   4) social services
   5) advertising-public relations
   6) science and technology
   7) military service
   8) sales
   9) finance and industry
5. *Your fiancee informs you that she has had relations with another man. You would probably:*
   1) break the engagement
   2) marry her despite grave misgivings
   3) tell her it doesn't matter
   4) tell her of your own amorous adventures
   5) feel that her experience would make for a more successful marriage
6. *Which of the following would probably give you the greatest personal satisfaction?*
   1) working for the welfare of others
   2) traveling extensively
   3) being elected to public office
   4) earning a fortune
   5) raising a family
7. *You've taken her out to dinner three or four times, but when you ask her to prepare the next meal herself, she informs you that she can't cook. You would most likely feel:*
   1) angry
   2) dejected
   3) relieved
   4) indifferent
   5) hungry

---

geographical and social mobility, negotiate marriages on their own, without the help of kith and kin. But the notion that the process as a whole is primarily an individual matter is a myth. When two people date who did not know each other beforehand, it is called a "blind date"—a name which stresses the fact that most dates are not blind. Wherever dating customs are studied closely—from church socials to Army barracks—intermediaries and "fixer-uppers" are found busily at work, pairing off the boys and girls in roughly the same way as the new computers. Considering the cost involved, it is economical for persons who date to rely on some outside help. For a young man, expected to take the initiative, dating is one of the most ruthless and unprotected forms of competition in which he can engage. He must put himself up for acceptance or rejection, and rejection can produce severe psychic wounds.

For a young woman, masculine attention in dating and courtship is the greatest social reward she will ever receive, and she therefore desires it to an extreme degree. But for her to accept dates indiscriminately is to run a variety of risks from boredom to sexual assault. The services of intermediaries, who present young men with invitations already accepted and young women with escorts already screened, are therefore greatly appreciated and widely practiced. But intermediaries bring their own interests into the transaction as well as those of the boy and girl whom they introduce. And since the dating career of any person is likely to make use of several intermediaries over time, dating and courtship thus become a thoroughly social process, affected by prevailing norms of mate selection even when the dating partners are not themselves committed to them. When young people today talk in all sincerity about their freedom to date anybody they please, they simply are not describing the entire process, of whose many controls they are often artfully kept unaware.

One very general answer can be given to the question of who marries whom: Most people marry someone pretty much like themselves. (If opposites do attract it has yet to show up in the statistics.) But scientific and garden-variety curiosity alike concentrate on the unexpected and unlikely combinations. It is rather like asking the question in a college classroom: "Which girls are going to get pregnant this semester?" Our curiosity runs so much to the irregular, the exotic and the immoral that we usually overlook the one obvious answer that covers almost all cases: "The ones who are married."

Unexpected marriages, like unexpected pregnancies, catch our attention when they deviate from social norms. The salient thing about marriage in this society—indeed, in any society with an organized system of kinship—is that it is regulated by the kinship-based groups which it affects. On the one hand, rules against incest drive young adults out of their own families; yet everywhere these young adults are expected to marry someone from a quite similar family. The anthropologist A. R. Radcliffe-Brown put the matter well when he referred to marriage as a "crisis."

Norms of mate selection—as sociologists rather coarsely phrase it—can be looked at as a classification of social groups in some of which marriage is to be preferred and in others is to be avoided. The practice of marriage within a group is called endogamy. All large groups formed by inheritance

—what we call "ethnic groups"—will prefer endogamy to some degree. Since two parents who share the same ethnic traditions can pass them on more consistently than two whose backgrounds differ, endogamy makes a good deal of sense if one wishes to preserve traditions. And the more traditions are cherished, the stronger is the urge toward endogamy. American Jews, for example, voice great concern over the extent of Jewish exogamy—the opposite of endogamy—although, from a comparative point of view, it is amazingly small—probably less than 10 per cent of all marriages involving a Jew. But it seems that the only way for Jewish traditions to survive is through lifelong training of persons born into the group. (A Yiddish aphorism puts it: "A converted Jew is no Jew and no gentile.") Jewish control of endogamy is therefore remarkably strong, and the democracy and indulgence that seem characteristic of Jewish family life usually end abruptly when the prospect of intermarriage looms. Similar rules can be found among American Oriental population groups, the Mormons and, in weaker form, Roman Catholics (who more willingly accept converts).

One of the strictest rules of endogamy applies to "Negro-white" intermarriage. It is an essential part of the caste-like status of the black man and the innumerable rigid, two-class distinctions that derive from it. If, for a few generations, there had been practiced in America a degree of intermarriage amounting to 10 per cent of all marriages involving blacks, with the wife assuming the status of the husband and the children combining the genetic and social characteristics passed on by their parents, the contemporary racial situation would be profoundly different. "Black" and "white" would not be two discrete categories of color and (more important) of status, but a widely dispersed continuum, and the two-color caste system, with all its social consequences, would have crumbled in the face of the multiplicity of distinctions that in practice would have to be made. So patterns of marriage have historical consequences.

Predicting whether a certain proportion of marriages will be endogamous or exogamous actually depends on a few rather obvious variables. The relative numbers of the two sexes—the "sex ratio"—is one of the most obvious. It is historically important because men are more likely to migrate than women. This is largely why America, as a land of migrants, has been as much of a melting pot as it has. Many immigrant men who felt strongly about "marrying a nice (Jewish-Polish-Irish-Armenian, etc.) girl" found there wasn't enough of the kind they wanted to go around. Faced with the choices of marrying out or not marrying at all, many of them married out. The same thing goes on inside America today because men migrate to one place and women to another (there are usually more unmarried women than men in big cities, for example), so that rules for some sort of endogamous marriage get slighted in the competition for anyone to marry at all.

Another factor is the degree of parental control. This is important because it is the older generation that most respects the traditional rules of endogamy, while young people are easily swayed by personal attractions. Here residence is important. A young lady who lives at home and receives her suitors there cannot easily entertain young men of whom her parents strongly disapprove. Even when she is given much freedom, the elders can still influence her choice. Daughters can hardly fall in love with unsuitable men they never meet, and the chances of their not meeting them are greatly increased if the parents happen to have moved (for the children's sake, of course) to a class-homogeneous suburb. When a girl becomes infatuated with a boy beneath her station, parents can use the old strategem of inviting him to a rather formal dinner, the better that his incorrigible unfitness for symbolically important occasions will be forced on the daughter's attention.

Today, however, parental control faces the peculiar threat of college education. When children live at home, parents can keep track daily of whom they are dating. But college often requires "dependent" and "irresponsible" children to live away from home. To be sure, a few young people have been going away to college for generations. But three trends combine to make college today a major threat to endogamy: (1) More persons of college age are in college (currently about 40 per cent); (2) An increasing proportion of students are women; and (3) The average age at marriage has dropped (especially for women) to a point where it falls for many in the traditional undergraduate years.

College and matrimony thus combine to render the campus the most active marriage market of modern times. Even when children live at home while attending college (a growing trend as new campuses and junior colleges are built) the dating situation on the campus is hard for parents to control. Student bodies tend to be large and heterogeneous, and almost any of the many campus activities can be used for making contacts and thus beginning the process of dating and courtship. Not that parents have not fought back. College fraternities, and especially sororities, embody many ingenious arrangements whereby the courtship of young persons is kept in line with the desires of an older generation. Yet it is safe to predict that an increasing number of American marriages will be between persons who meet in college, and they are likely to meet under conditions largely indifferent to older rules of endogamy.

A third factor affecting the maintenance of endogamy is social mobility —the process by which members of a generation achieve a higher class position than that into which they were born. In America this movement is intimately related to higher education, for we widely believe that upward mobility is a good thing and that higher education contributes to it. But to the extent that young people start moving up before they are married, and that boys move up in different ways, or at different rates, than girls, then the traditional ways of pairing them off endogamously no longer work.

The most basic difference here is that a man gains his status mainly through his job, whereas a woman's status is mainly conferred on her by her husband. We often speak as if occupational success were equally important for both sexes, but actually it is much less important for women. Women *can* gain a tolerable status through work, but a better one can usually be gained more easily through marriage. Where men move up most directly by competing for good jobs, women move up mainly by marrying men who move up. Marriage thus becomes the means of mobility for women. Insofar as she responds to the American dream of upward mobility, every unmarried American girl has a bit of the gold-digger in her.

Consider the situation of American Catholics. Catholic girls are expected to marry Catholic boys, but they also want to marry successful men. And it just so happens that, for most of the country, Protestant men on the average hold higher-ranked positions than do Catholic men. If the Catholic girl marries up, she is likely to marry out. And evidently this does occur, because more Catholic women marry outside their faith than do Catholic men. Among Jews, however, the situation is reversed. Men in this group are eminently successful and are "good catches" for girls of any faith who want to marry up. Evidently they do get caught, for many more Jewish boys marry gentiles than do Jewish girls.

The pressure for marrying up among women produces a kind of imbalance in marital bargaining, to the advantage of high-status men and low-status women and the disadvantage of low-status men and high-status women. A low-status man has little wealth or prestige to offer a wife. In addition, he must compete for a wife not only with others in his own station but with higher-ranked men as well.

A well-born woman, if she is to maintain through marriage the status conferred on her by her parents, must marry a man at least equally well-born —but for such men she faces a deadly competition from lower-status female rivals who also regard them as desirable husbands. As a result, low-status men are more likely to remain bachelors, and high-status women are more likely to remain spinsters. This is the "Brahmin problem," so named because it reached its most extreme form among the high castes of Hindu India (but it can be observed among Boston Brahmins as well).

If a sociologist is so artlessly blunt as to ask young women whether they marry for money or for love, he will be lucky to escape with his questionnaire forms. Love, the girls indignantly tell us, conquers all. Lovable personal qualities eclipse Philistine wealth. But this is too simple by far.

On the one hand, there is a strong statistical tendency for women to marry up. If our hypothetical sociologist returns, suitably chastened, with a subtler set of questions on what makes men lovable, he will receive a list of characteristics of which many—urbane good manners, sensitivity, sophisticated good taste, interesting conversation, and so on—depend on expensive education and are thus associated with wealth. Money, in short, tends to be despised only in the abstract: in concrete form, enjoyed by the unmarried scions of a rich family, it is highly admired.

On the other hand, there probably never has been a society in which all lovable attributes were monopolized by one class. Love thus becomes a potentially random factor in marriage, one contrary to all rules of endogamy. In societies with stronger rules of endogamy than our own, love is not unknown, but it is strongly controlled and is regarded as irrelevant in the choice of marital partners.

The emotions of love are strong, but they are also ambiguous and volatile, and are therefore subject to deception and fraud. This places an emphasis on sincerity, but sincerity in love is very hard to assess. Young women are besieged with professions of love which they suspect are voiced simply to facilitate a quick seduction—and this is not what "love" means to most of them.

Especially where courtship tends to be individualistic, so that suitors cannot be effectively held to account for their promises, young women tend to measure the love of a young man not simply by what he says, but also by what he invests in the relationship. Often this is his money, but more often it is his time. Because any marriage market involves a wide age range of men competing for the smaller range of women in the years when they are young and pretty, the investment required in courtship gets bid up to a high level. Feminine nubility, thus rewarded, becomes a veritable institution in its own right. The extravagance of attention that young girls expect, however, paradoxically limits their chances for marrying well. Regardless of his income, the *time* of a successful man is always dear, while the adult male who is "still finding himself" is the one with the leisure to invest in courtship.

This applies also at the college level, where the pre-professional student who is going places occupationally has little time for dating and leaves most of the social life to the less ambitious campus playboys. This means that women who expect their suitors to spend a great deal of time in dating are likely to marry men of modest achievements in other areas.

Now: How can all this be put in a matchmaking computer? It would be easy to specify the information that would be required, but awfully hard to find any way of digging it up. Getting it by simple interrogation—which is what the computers use now—would make the money-or-love question look like a masterpiece of diplomacy.

The problem, of course, is that the factors that do explain who is likely to marry whom are systematically obscured for the young people directly involved, the better to inspire them to get married in the first place. And if the parties involved *do* take a calculating attitude toward the bargaining and exchange that is part of any system of marriage, they are likely to practice fraud and deception, systematically misrepresenting their age, income, background and other assets and liabilities, just as in face-to-face contact they tell tall tales and white lies and wear elevator shoes and falsies.

The marriage practices of human society embody both ancient traditions and novel responses to changing times. The broad patterns of marriage—movement across class lines, the age at which it occurs, its impact on education and work—can be pretty well predicted, and in fact are predicted by sociologists, demographers and insurance actuaries. But the narrow practical questions—"Will he marry her?" or "Will they be happy together?"—are likely to remain inexplicable, at least to the people involved. And the mystery is what gives these questions their abiding appeal. Successful computer matching—unlikely, anyway—would only spoil the fun.

56 | Initial Adjustment Processes in Young Married Couples

Beverly R. Cutler and William G. Dyer

The matter of "adjustment" in marriage is an area of discussion in almost every marriage textbook and class. A number of years ago, Kirkpatrick stated, "The investigation of marital adjustment is still almost a virgin field for sociological research. There is a need for checking of previous research, for contributing additional fragments of evidence, and for a piecing together of the results of isolated studies into a meaningful whole" [1]. This condition still appears to exist.

ADJUSTMENT AS PROCESS OR GOAL

In the literature on marital adjustment, two different approaches are often taken and sometimes intermingled indiscriminately. Some writers refer to adjustment as a state of marriage to be achieved [2], while other writers refer to adjustment primarily as a process of interaction [3].

Bowerman feels that both conditions are important. He says:

> In addition to measures of overall evaluation of the marriage, there would seem to be considerable use, in both research and counseling, for measures of the *degree of adjustment* in the various aspects of the relationship, such as adjustment about financial matters, recreation, homemaking duties, etc. In studying the *processes of adjustment* in marriage, it is necessary to take into account the relationship between different kinds of adjustment which must be made, how these types of adjustment are differentially affected by the various forces affecting the marriage, and how each contributes to the evaluation of the marriage as a whole[4].

When seen as a goal, marital adjustment is commonly equated with such conditions as marital success, marital satisfaction, and marital happiness. It would seem that these terms are all referring to the same end condition which is arrived at through some interactive process. Research-wise it is much easier to develop a measure of marital adjustment or success and then relate a series of independent variables to this dependent condition and discover which variables are most highly related to the condition of adjustment, than it is to investigate the processes couples go through to arrive at the end condition. This paper is an attempt to add "an additional fragment of evidence" to the matter of adjustment as a process. Very little research actually shows the process married couples go through to achieve adjustment.

The focus of this research report is centered on the question, "When a young married person finds that his spouse engages in behavior that violates his expectations, what kinds of actions does he engage in to deal with this disturbance in the relationship?" Adjustment, generally speaking, is the process used in successfully reducing disturbance in a relationship.

From *Social Forces,* **44,** 195–201, December 1965. Reprinted by permission of University of North Carolina Press.

ADJUSTMENT POSSIBILITIES USING ROLE THEORY

In a previous paper, a theoretical analysis of marital adjustment using role theory was presented [5]. This formulation is the basis for the following analysis.

Adjustment is defined as the bringing into agreement the behavior of one person with the expectation of another accompanied by a feeling of acceptance of the modified behavior by the one making the adjustment.

From the point of view of role behavior, when conflict in marriage occurs because one person has violated the expectations of his spouse the possible adjustments are:

1. The husband (or wife) can change his role performance completely to meet the role expectations of his partner.

2. The husband (or wife) can change his role expectations, completely, to coincide with the role performance of the partner.

3. There can be a mutual adjustment, each partner altering some. The husband (or wife) can alter his role to a degree and the partner alters his role expectations to a similar degree so that role performance and role expectations are compatible. In each of the above cases the end result is an agreement between role performance and role expectations.

4. There is also another type of adjustment possible. In some cases the couple might recognize a disparity between role performance and role expectations or between norms and also acknowledge that change is difficult or impossible and could "agree to disagree." In such cases the one partner recognizes and respects the position of the other without accepting or adjusting to it. This pattern of "agreeing to disagree" is not adjustment in the same sense as the others listed above. The "adjustment" comes from both partners agreeing that a certain area is "out of bounds" as far as the application of sanctions are concerned. There is no change in behavior but some change in expectations in that each now expects certain areas not to be raised as issues and that no sanctions will be applied over these "out of bound" issues [6].

This study focuses on the following problems:

1. Are the initial reactions of young married partners to violations of role expectations (in the sense described above) adjustive or non-adjustive?

2. Do husbands and wives differ in their adjustment processes?

3. Do couples use different adjustments in different areas of marriage?

METHODOLOGY

Following an initial pilot study of depth interviews with ten couples, an extensive questionnaire on marital adjustment was administered to a random sample of young married couples at Brigham Young University during the fall and winter of the 1962–63 school year. Couples were selected on the basis of the husband's enrollment in the University. Since the study was aimed at the adjustment in young married couples, only those couples were selected where the husband was under 23 years of age. There were 75 couples in the sample. Fifteen couples were eliminated for various reasons leaving 60 couples in the study. Participants were asked to fill out the questionnaire separately and privately and not consult the marital partner.

DESCRIPTION OF THE SAMPLE

Eighty-five percent of the couples had been married less than three years. Fifty-five percent had no children while 35 percent had one child. All of the couples were members of the L.D.S. (Mormon) church. Seventy-four percent of the couples had known each other for more than one year prior to marriage. Only 13 percent of the husbands and 18 percent of the wives were reared in communities over 100,000. While all of the husbands were in college, 30 percent of the wives had not attended college.

The following areas of marriage were examined in the questionnaire:

1. Verbal expressions of affection
2. Frequency of sexual intimacy
3. Spending time at home
4. Sharing ideas
5. Care of the home
6. Personal neatness and appearance
7. Spending family income

From the pilot study, it was indicated that the above represented the primary areas within which couples were making adjustments to each other. The questionnaire was constructed to determine the following:

1. The expectations of husbands and wives towards each other in the areas listed above.
2. The ways these expectations are violated by husbands and wives.
3. The responses by the marriage partner when the spouse has violated one's expectations.
4. The reaction of the spouse to the initial responses of the marriage partner.
5. The current feelings of the couple about the area of marriage following the initial adjustment responses and reactions.

For each of the seven areas of marriage examined in the study, the following questions were asked concerning responses to the violation of expectations: (1) In what ways has your spouse failed to live up to your expectations? What has he (she) done to violate your expectations you held for him (her) concerning this aspect of your marriage relationship? (2) If your spouse did not meet your expectations, what did you do? (3) When you responded as indicated in the previous question, what did your spouse do in return?

Initial responses and subsequent reactions were judged either adjustive, non-adjustive, or non-action. An adjustive response is one that brings behavior and expectations closer together and reduces the degree of negative sanction. A non-adjustive response is one that either does not reduce the disparity or sanction or may actually intensify the difference. A third type of response was noted in the pilot study, namely non-action. The problem is recognized but no action is taken in hopes that the problem will resolve itself through the passing of time. One might conclude that non-action is a non-adjustive response, but the non-adjustive response actually represents a behavioral strategy that was being attempted in some type of behavior. There was no behavior strategy being attempted in non-action, only the hopes were that it would be adjustive in the long run, hence, the decision to make this a special category.

In addition to being adjustive or non-adjustive, responses and reactions to responses were categorized in terms of two dimensions: sharing and valence. This gave the following possible responses in the coding guide:

1. Adjustive Response

A. *Shared positive response.* This is a response that is shared with the marriage partner and positive in the sense that it appears to be directed toward achieving adjustment.

B. *Non-shared positive.* This is a non-shared response but also adjustively centered.

2. Non-Adjustive Response

A. *Shared negative.* This is a shared response but apparently not given with the idea of facilitating adjustment, hence, a negative valence.

B. *Non-shared negative.* A non-shared response not geared toward facilitating adjustment.

3. Non-Action

A non-shared response with suspended valence.

Following are examples of the various possible responses: Respondents would check these categories in response to the question "If your spouse did not meet your expectations, what did you do?"

A. *Shared positive response:* "Talked it over rather openly and calmly."

B. *Non-shared positive:* "Didn't say anything at all; just accepted the situation as it was—didn't let it bother me."

C. *Shared negative:* "Got upset and argued, quarreled, pouted or sulked with spouse."

D. *Non-shared negative:* "Got upset, worried about it, cried, or felt sorry for myself; but didn't say anything to my spouse."

E. *Non-action:* "Didn't say anything at first; just waited to see if things would work out."

DISCUSSION OF FINDINGS

A. Initial Reactions to Expectation Violations

1. *Husbands*

From Table 1, the totals indicate that the generally most prevalent strategy adopted by husbands when they felt their wives had violated their expectations was a non-action response. The husbands indicated they initially took a "wait and see" stance but these data do not tell us how the wives perceived these same responses.

The next most prevalent response of the husbands, as perceived by themselves, was an open talking about the problem in a calm manner. These shared, adjustive type responses were followed numerically by non-shared adjustive responses. These two adjustive type responses account for 51 percent of all responses made by husbands. Husbands felt that only five percent of their initial responses were of a non-adjustive type.

For each of the areas taken separately, some differences appear. The non-action strategy is most apparent in *Area 2* which is frequency of sexual intimacy. There were more violations of expectations in this area than any of the others, yet this is the one area where no husband checked a non-shared adjustive response—that is, "didn't say anything at all; just accepted the situation as it was—didn't let it bother me." While non-adjustive responses were rarely indicated at all, this area, more than any other, was one where some husbands admitted making some non-adjustive responses.

Area 1 (Verbal Expressions of Affection) appears to be the area most easily accepted by the husbands without talking it over with his wife. Eight out of 19 husbands with non-met expectations in this area indicated that they accepted this situation as it was—didn't let it bother them.

Area 7 (Spending Family Income) appears to be the area most easily talked about openly and calmly. Seven of 11 violations were met in this manner.

Area 3 (Spending Time at Home) was the area of least violations. Apparently most of these new husbands were satisfied with the amount of time the wife was spending in the home. Such is not the case, however, with the wives.

2. *Wives*

While 44 percent of the husbands' initial reactions were of the non-action variety, only 31 percent of the responses of the wives were in this category. Wives indicated they responded initially with more shared, adjustive type responses than their husbands and also with more non-adjustive type responses than were admitted by their spouses. Again it should be remembered, this is how the wives perceived their initial responses—not how the spouse experienced it.

Rather consistently, the pattern for the wives in most areas was one of more open sharing in contrast to the non-action strategy which characterized many areas for the husbands. This is especially true in the area of frequency of sexual intimacy. Husbands indicated they generally took a "wait and see" approach, while the wives initial response was to talk about the problem. Interestingly enough this sensitive area resulted in only two admitted non-adjustive type initial responses. Like the husbands, this was one area where no wife adopted a non-shared adjustive response.

As with the husbands, *Area 1* (Verbal Expressions of Affection) was the area where more wives adjusted internally without talking about this with their spouses.

Areas 1 and *5* had the highest number of violations marked. These are Verbal Expressions of Affection and Care of the Home, respectively. *Area 5* is also the area with more non-adjustive reactions than any other. It should

Table 1. Initial Responses of Husbands and Wives to Violations of Expectations

Type of Response	Verbal Expression of Affection	Frequency of Sexual Intimacy	Spending time at home	Sharing ideas	Care of home	Personal neatness, appearance	Spending family income	Total
Husband	*1*	2	*3*	*4*	*5*	*6*	*7*	
S+	3	5	2	6	6	4	7	33
NS+	8	0	1	3	1	1	1	15
Non-Action	8	14	0	5	9	3	2	41
S–	0	1	0	1	0	0	1	3
NS–	0	2	0	0	0	0	0	2
Total	19	22	3	15	16	8	11	94
Wife	*1*	2	*3*	*4*	*5*	*6*	*7*	
S+	8	12	6	6	10	9	6	57
NS+	5	0	2	2	4	0	1	14
Non-Action	9	6	6	8	5	2	5	41
S–	1	0	4	2	5	0	2	14
NS–	2	2	1	1	1	0	1	8
Total	25	20	19	19	25	11	15	134

Table 2. Subsequent Reaction to Initial Responses

	Verbal Expressions of Affection	Frequency of Sexual Intimacy	Spending time at home	Sharing ideas	Care of home	Personal neatness and appearance	Spending income of family	
Wives Reaction to Husband (as perceived by husband)								
	1	*2*	*3*	*4*	*5*	*6*	*7*	Total
Adj.	14	10		6	9		5	44
No Action	2	5		2	1		2	12
Non Adj.	5	7		7	6		3	28
Total	21	22		15	16		10	84
Husbands Reaction to Wife (as perceived by wife)								
	1	*2*	*3*	*4*	*5*	*6*	*7*	Total
Adj.	14	13	10	12	19	6	7	81
No Action	2	2	4	4	0	0	0	12
Non Adj.	5	5	4	2	5	5	6	32
Total	21	20	18	18	24	11	13	125

* Too few responses to be tabulated.

be remembered that this does not indicate which of the areas was the most important to the couple, only which areas showed the most number of violations of expectations. Care of the Home had the most non-adjustive type reactions on the part of the wife. This may indicate not that she felt strongest about this, but that she felt freer to express her negative feelings about this than any other area.

The area with the fewest expressed violations of expectations was number *Area 6* (Personal Neatness and Appearance). This was followed by *Area 7* (Spending the Family Income).

As indicated above, the biggest area of disparity in terms of numbers of violations in the areas was in *Area 3* (Spending Time at Home). Wives checked violations in this area six times as often as did the husbands. The other areas were relatively similar with some noticeable difference occurring in *Area 5* (Care of the Home), where the wives had more non-met expectations than did the husbands at a ratio of 25 to 16.

B. Subsequent Reactions to Initial Responses

Table 2 shows the subsequent reactions to the initial responses as perceived by the spouse making the initial response. Both husbands and wives felt that the majority of their spouse's reactions to them were of an adjustive nature. In the questionnaire subjects were asked, "When you responded as indicated in the previous question, what did your spouse do in return?" Adjustive responses were the following:

1. "Made a real attempt to change and meet my expectations."
2. "We agreed that we differed, but we have tried to accept this difference."
3. "Said he (she) was sorry and would try to do better, but didn't really change."

This last response was considered to be an adjustive type response even though the spouse with the non-met expectations felt the other had not "really changed." The initial part of adjustment had begun—the spouse knew of the violation, had expressed regret for this and indicated a willingness to "do better." Final adjustment does not come until expectation and behavior are in agreement, but this response indicates that perhaps adjustment has started.

Subjects were also asked to list other responses. Considered as adjustive were such responses as: "He is patient with me and tries to be understanding." "Made a genuine effort to change every now and then." "Got professional doctor's help and counseling."

It is interesting to note that while 44 percent of the husbands responses and 31 percent of the wives initial responses were of the non-action type, there were very few subsequent non-action responses. One would normally think that a non-action response would be followed by non-action. This may indicate that when one's expectations are violated, one really does give off certain cues about his feelings to which the spouse subsequently responses. A non-action response to the initial reaction was: "(Spouse did) Nothing, since he (she) didn't know how I felt."

Thirty-three percent of the wives' subsequent reactions were felt by the husbands to be non-adjustive, while 26 percent of the husband's reactions to the wife were seen by the wife as non-adjustive. Non-adjustive responses were as follows:

1. "Got upset and argued, complained, or grumbled back."
2. "Suggested that I accept him (her) as he (she) was."
3. "I told him (her) but nothing happened—we just dropped it."

Considered as non-adjustive were written in comments such as: "We quarrel occasionally about it." "He thought it was funny and persisted more strongly."

Some interesting patterns are indicated when we examine the non-adjustive responses and the behavior that elicits a non-adjustive pattern. Nearly half of the non-adjustive responses for both husbands and wives came as a result of an initial shared adjustive reaction. This immediately raises the question—why should a shared adjustive initial reaction result in non-adjustive responses? There are at least these possibilities:

1. While the one reacting initially thinks he is reacting in an open, adjustive way, the marriage partner may not experience this in the way the first intended. The partner may see the initial reaction as critical and punitive while the reacting party thinks he is just talking it over "openly and calmly."
2. The initial reaction may be an open, calm sharing of one's feelings about a problem situation but an adjustive response from the mate presumes such conditions as an adequate level of maturity of the mate, proper timing and suitable circumstances for sharing sensitive information, and a non-threatening method of presenting the information.
3. The shared information may be presented calmly and openly but the information may be a hard blow to the self-image of the partner and the response may be immediately defensive and not adjustive.
4. Sharing sensitive information may be a violation of the expectations of the other partner. He or she may not expect such things to be talked about and when this is done, non-adjustive type responses result.

Seven non-adjustive responses for both husbands and wives came as a result of initial "non-action." This is another apparent contradiction. How can a non-response result in any type of reaction? The problem here may be in the weakness of the questionnaire in carefully sorting out the sequence of reactions. (Or it may be, as indicated above, that cues as to how the person feels are given off even though he feels there was no response made). There are indications in examining the data that a person filling out the questionnaire coming to the question, "What was your initial response?" marked a non-action category. The next question asked, "What did your spouse do in return?" It appears that a number of subjects jumped the time sequence and checked what may have been a response later in time. Thus, it appears that a non-adjustive reaction followed a non-action response. This same condition may account for non-shared reactions eliciting non-adjustive responses.

Percentage-wise, the biggest number of non-adjustive responses came as a result of initial negative type reactions for both husbands and wives. There were five negative reactions listed by husbands and these resulted in three non-adjustive reactions. In fact, all three shared negative initial reactions resulted in non-adjustive responses.

Wives indicated 22 negative type reactions initially and these resulted in 11 non-adjustive type subsequent responses from the spouse.

One would tend to predict that a negative reaction would result in further negative type reactions. The data from the husbands in this study are too limited in this area to allow for any support of this generalization. For the wives, it shows from a limited number of responses, that about 50 percent of the time negative responses on their part resulted in non-adjustment on the part of the other. The data here do not tell us how the other partner feels about making an adjustment to a negative reaction by his spouse. It would seem that adjustments that came from shared positive type responses would be made out of a more positive feeling than adjustment that resulted from negative reactions.

SUMMARY

This study was designed to investigate the initial adjustment processes in young, married couples attending college. Adjustment was conceptualized in terms of role expectations, response to expectation violations and the subsequent reaction to the initial response. The data indicate the following trends in these couples:

1. Husbands, more than wives, appear to adopt a "wait and see" strategy when their wives violate their expectations, according to their self-perceptions. Wives say they more often meet a violation of expectation with an open sharing or talking about the situation or reacting negatively.

2. When difficulties occur, the several areas of marriage appear to be handled differently by married couples. Husbands say they talk openly about violations of expectations in the area of finance but not in the area of frequency of sexual intimacy.

3. Wives and husbands differ in the number of expectation violations in certain areas of marriage. In the area of spending time at home, wives checked a violation of expectations in this area six times more frequently than did husbands. Wives also had more non-met expectations in the area of care of the home.

4. While a considerable number of both husbands and wives reacted to an initial violation of expectations with a non-action response—a "wait and see" strategy—subsequent reactions to the spouse's initial response were very infrequently found in this category. Husbands more than wives felt their spouses reactions to them were non-adjustive in nature.

5. The data of this study indicate that nearly half of the non-adjustive responses for both husbands and wives came as a result of an open sharing of the feelings about the violation of expectations. Contrary to what might be expected, an open talking about the violation of expectations does not always lead to an adjustment.

6. The data, especially for wives, also show that in a large percentage of times, a negative reaction on the part of one partner does result in an adjustive response by the other. Negative reactions are apparently not always followed by reciprocal negative reactions.

REFERENCES

1. CLIFFORD KIRKPATRICK, "Factors in Marital Adjustment," *American Journal of Sociology,* 43 (November 1957), p. 270.
2. JUDSON T. LANDIS, "Length of Time Required to Achieve Adjustment in Marriage," *American Sociological Review,* 11 (December 1946), pp. 666–677.
3. CLIFFORD KIRKPATRICK, "Marriage as a Process," *The Family* (New York: Ronald Press, 1955), pp. 443–448.
4. CLARK BOWERMAN, "Adjustment in Marriage, Overall and in Specific Areas," *Sociology and Social Research,* 41 (March-April 1957), pp. 257–263.
5. WILLIAM G. DYER, "Analyzing Marital Adjustment Using Role Theory," *Marriage and Family Living,* 24 (November 1962).
6. *Ibid.,* p. 374.

---

57 | The Unsolved Mystery of Marriage

Francine has almost decided to leave Jack, after three years of marriage. The trouble seemed to begin when she told him she wanted to quit her job and have children. He was against it. Although he had a promising future, he was not yet earning enough to maintain their household as it was. They could wait a few more years before starting a family, he argued; they were still young enough.

For a while they quarreled on and off. Then an uneasy truce set in. Now they rarely speak to each other for any length of time. And they avoid topics that might touch off a fight.

Jack often brings work home from the office and volunteers for out-of-town sales assignments. Francine recently started feeling attracted to a man at her office and allowed him to take her out for a drink. He wants to take her out again. She feels guilty about her desire to see him and would like to "confess" to Jack. But she knows he won't understand.

Tonight Jack is away. While watching television alone, Francine suddenly begins sobbing. Their marriage seems so joyless . . . a trap. Wouldn't it be better to get out now?

THE ROAD TO SEPARATION

At work or at a social gathering, Francine and Jack seem to be a contented pair. Behind appearances are two anguished people who have lost faith in each other.

If they do break up, they will be one of more than 400,000 couples to be divorced or have their marriages annulled this year. For every four couples who vow to stay together until death, one couple decides not to wait that long.

All sorts of people get divorces. Most, though, are under 35, and about half of the childless couples have been married five years or less. The divorced share other characteristics, too. Sociologist William J. Goode says these conditions indicate a "greater proneness" to divorce:

- Urban background.
- Marriage at 15 to 19 (the teen-age divorce rate is about three times the general rate).
- Short acquaintanceship before marriage.
- Parents had unhappy marriages.
- Nonattendance at church.
- Mixed faith.
- Disapproval of the marriage by relatives and friends.
- Dissimilarity in social and economic status.
- Differing ideas between husband and wife as to their marital obligations.

Naturally, not every couple whose marriage happens to include some—or even most—of these factors is doomed to divorce. If they were, there would be few marriages left. It's still normal for a couple to marry and stay married. Yet staying married is far from being a measure of married happiness.

For each marriage that ends in divorce, says Dr. Nathan W. Ackerman, a psychiatrist who specializes in treating families, there are many in which the partners stay together but are emotionally alienated from one another.

"They stay joined not out of reasons of love, but out of economic need, duty to children, personal dependency, fear of loneliness, or simply because there is no place else to go. The family unit remains together physically, but there is, in effect, an emotional divorce." Others have called those unions "empty shell" marriages.

The longer a couple stays married, the less likely they are to get divorced. However, one study of couples married from two to twenty-one years indicates that the longer a marriage endures, the less satisfaction the partners find in it, another suggestion that a marriage is not necessarily good just because it lasts. The real problem is not so much that a couple may separate as it is that they might not achieve happiness together.

WHERE HARMONY BEGINS

Why is nonhappiness so prevalent? What makes one couple happy, another unhappy? Where does the trouble begin?

Probably many more marriages start off "right" than "wrong." Young men and women don't pick mates at random. The process seems haphazard, but in practice their field of choice is usually confined to people much like themselves. They tend to marry someone from the same area, race, religion, ethnic background and social and economic class. Young men who have never been married tend to marry women who have never been married. Divorced people tend to marry other divorced people. Widows tend to marry men who have been married.

People from like groups have like attitudes toward many aspects of life, and this agreement is a bond.

But with hundreds of possible mates from their own or outside groups to choose from, how do people narrow the choice to one person?

Many experts believe love springs from a meshing of basic needs. Each person wants people to act in a certain way toward him; he also wants to be able to act in a certain way toward others. When a person finds someone who helps him function in accord with his underlying motivations, love develops. Thus a man who likes to dominate is inclined to seek out a submissive woman, a submissive woman will be attracted to a dominating man.

Selecting a mate with complementary needs is not a conscious, deliberate procedure, for a person may not be aware of his own needs, let alone those of a prospective spouse. Ask what he sees in her and he will cite some ill-defined attribute: "She's kind and gentle." She finds him irresistible because he's "so gay and happy." A probing psychiatrist may discover that the man really wants to be mothered and perceives a mothering disposition in the woman's solicitous attitude. She may in fact be a mothering type who sees in his high spirits a little boy who has to be taken care of.

Naturally, a man and woman can't interlock psychologically on every point. Nor do their needs always have to be opposite. Both may have needs that run in the same direction but are present in one to such a small degree that they do not cause conflict during courtship.

A study of college students who were engaged or seriously considering marriage suggests that similar background and attitudes and complementary needs may act like a series of filters, to sort out appropriate partners. In the early stages of courtship, likeness of social status and ideas brings couples together. Later on, complementary needs move toward a permanent union.

IT'S AN IMPERFECT SYSTEM

With all the forces at work to bring together men and women suited to one another, it seems strange that so many marriages turn out wrong.

One reason is that the like-to-like attraction is at best a rough way of matching people. And it doesn't operate effectively for everyone. Many couples never get a chance—or take the opportunity—to find out much about each other.

Moreover, the courtship itself is not an infallible method of matching young people for marriage. The boy is more interested in the girl's feminine charm than in, say, whether she is likely to comfort him or berate him if he should lose a job. The girl is often more concerned with his outward displays of masculinity than in whether he's mature enough to accept responsibility for a family. Each is inclined to idealize the other. The person that emerges after marriage can be shockingly different.

A man and woman from dissimilar backgrounds can enter marriage with sharply conflicting expectations and values. But that happens among people with similar backgrounds, too, for there is diversity within any group. The husband, for example, may have been brought up to expect women to do all the household chores, the wife brought up to expect the men to help out. He may end up washing dishes—and resenting it.

Some people carry neuroses into marriage that are bound to cause trouble. Take the acquiescent, deferential man married to an aggressive woman. In a sense, they fit together. She runs things, makes the important decisions. He defers to her because he sees himself as unworthy and helpless. Yet he resents his inferior position and may rebel occasionally by exploding with rage, perhaps on an irrelevant or inconsequential issue. Neuroses do not necessarily destroy a marriage, though. On the contrary, psychiatrists have found that some neurotics make good partners and good parents.

Even well-conceived marriages may falter under the impact of a crisis. The arrival of the first child, for example, can be a crucial turning point. Often an occasion of great personal fulfillment, this is also a time of stress for both husband and wife. A study of first-time parents showed that all had experienced some degree of shock, and 25% of the couples interviewed said they had gone through a "severe" crisis. Mothers feared they were neglecting their husbands, doubted their ability to be good mothers and had trouble adjusting to being tied down and having to give up outside interests. Fathers were disturbed by the disruption of the old household routines and the prospect of supporting a larger family.

WHAT THEY FIGHT ABOUT

One problem in identifying the causes of marital unhappiness lies in the fact that all couples do fight at times, and about much the same things.

University of Pennsylvania researchers interviewed 300 couples to determine why and how often they quarreled. Two hundred were chosen from families that had at one time sought family counseling help. The others were from a group of couples who considered their marriages sufficiently successful to compete in a nationwide contest for "representative families" from each state. The husbands and wives were given a list of possible points of disagreement and asked to indicate (independently of each other) what they fought about and how often. The 300 couples rated their problems in this order, going from the points of most conflict to those of least conflict:

finances
household management
personality disagreements
sexual adjustment
sharing household tasks
children
recreation
husband's mother
personal habits
jealousy
husband's work
wife's mother
other relatives
wife's working
husband's father
religious matters
infidelity
health
wife's father
social background
education

When the answers of the two groups—the 200 and the 100—were tabulated separately, it was found that the couples who had had marital trouble ranked the problems in about the same order as those who considered themselves happily married. The difference was not in the nature of the issues but in the extent of disagreement. Ironically, the one thing husbands and wives in both groups tended to agree on was which issues they disagreed about.

The young man and woman who start marriage believing that they love each other too much ever to quarrel are sure to be disillusioned before long. In fact, their chances of achieving a stable marriage probably are better if they anticipate spats and learn how to cope with them. Sometimes an argument helps clear the air and starts a couple toward reconciliation. Part of the trouble between the couple described at the beginning of the article is that they have bottled up their anger and lost contact with each other.

Although happily married couples do fight occasionally, they manage to preserve an appreciation of their mates.

Dr. Eleanore B. Luckey of the University of Connecticut has discovered that in successful marriages each spouse tends to agree with the other's estimation of his or her own qualities. The husband, for example, will think of himself as considerate and helpful, and the wife rates him the same way—or as even stronger and more loving than he sees himself.

Among less satisfied couples, there was significantly less agreement. The wives thought of their husbands as colder than the men considered themselves. The husbands saw their wives as considerably more bossy than the wives were in their own view.

THE MOST PRECIOUS GIFTS

A good marriage, then, seems to be a fairly harmonious union in which a little conflict is tempered by a great deal of mutual respect. But what makes it that way?

Psychiatrist Joseph Barnett suggests that perhaps the most important quality a man and woman can contribute to a marriage is a sense of "esteem" for one's self and other people. The two usually go together. A person with an inner sense of his own worth does not have to make unreasonable demands on his partner. Nor does he have to win an argument or disparage someone else in order to protect his prestige.

In a happy marriage, the partners can act as friends as well as mates. And that kind of rapport appears to be more treasured than other values commonly associated with marital compatibility. When some 400 couples were asked to rank what they considered conducive to a satisfying marriage, their first choice was companionship. Being in love was second, followed by being needed, having children, calmness, financial security, sexual relationships, developing personal interests, an orderly home, and intellectual stimulation. Last on the list, incidentally, was good food.

58 | Eight Myths About Divorce

Hugh Carter

This year, close to 400,000 couples will be divorced in the United States. The figure is one that many people find alarming, but much of the talk about the divorce problem in America seems to be based on misunderstandings or fallacies. Here are some of the most frequently encountered myths about divorce:

1. *The divorce rate is going up rapidly.*

The figures do not support this. For more than 20 years nothing drastic has happened to the divorce rate except for a brief, sharp increase caused by the war, followed by a decline. In 1946—when many war marriages ended—the rate was 4.3 per 1,000 of the population, an all-time high. In that year, more than 600,000 couples were divorced. For the next five years the rate fell, reaching 2.5 in 1951. In 1960 the rate was 2.2 per 1,000 of the population, identical with the 1941 rate. Provisional figures point to no drastic change in the rate through 1963. It *is* true that the rate is higher now than it was 40 years ago; it stood at 1.5 in 1923.

2. *The divorce rate is about the same in all parts of the United States.*

Actually, the rate in the Western states is 3.4 per 1,000 of population—almost four times as high as the rate in the Northeastern states of 0.9. The remainder of the country is in an intermediate position, the rate being 2.1 in the North Central states and 2.8 in the south.

It is true that the rates are affected to some extent by migratory divorce—establishing residence in a state in order to obtain a divorce. Then, too, since most divorcing persons are young adults, the divorce rate depends, in part, on the age distribution of the population. Where there is a heavy concentration of young adults, the divorce rate tends to increase. There are also marked differences in divorce laws and in the strictness with which judicial authorities interpret the laws. However, the differences among the four regions are greater than could be explained by these factors.

There is a good deal of speculation that because the West is a new region its people have a relaxed attitude toward divorce. On the other hand, the South, which has the second highest rate, cannot be considered a new region. The truth is that we really do not know the reason for the regional differences in divorce rates.

3. *Most divorces are granted in Reno and similar places.*

The evidence indicates that migratory divorces are only a small fraction of the total. *All* Nevada divorces equal less than 3 per cent of the national total.

The figures probably seem high because of the great amount of publicity attending them. The majority of divorcing persons cannot afford to establish residence in another state to obtain a divorce. This seems to be true also of divorces for American citizens in Mexico and other foreign countries. From time to time there is a great deal of publicity about divorce mills, but the number of cases involved is small compared with the national total.

4. *The third year of marriage is the hardest.*

A first glance at divorce statistics may seem to support this myth. In some divorce tables the largest number of divorces is shown after three years of marriage. (In other tables the peak comes after two years, or after one year).

However, the facts are more complicated than appears at first glance. Frequently, because of marital discord, a couple separates, but without serious thought of divorce. Months, or even years, may pass before the beginning of legal action.

After a decision is made for divorce, the plaintiff, usually the wife, consults a lawyer. He, in turn, must inquire into the pertinent facts. If the grounds appear adequate, he prepares the case and has it entered on the appropriate court docket. In due time, the case is heard and the decree granted. All these steps require time—from several months to several years.

An analysis of the statistics and related facts leads one to conclude that the first year of marriage is the hardest, even though the peak in divorces may come after three (or two) years. It also appears from the statistics that each year of marriage is less likely to end in divorce than the immediately preceding year.

5. *Having children will prevent divorce.*

Latest published statistics show that more than one-half of divorcing couples have children.

Two opposing views are sometimes presented on marital stability and children. On the one hand, children are said to provide a common interest and a focus for family life. On the other hand, children may serve to intensify an existing conflict. In any event, in recent years the proportion of divorcing couples with children has been rising. Whether the number of divorces would have been larger or smaller if there had been more or fewer couples with children is unknown.

6. *The wealthy and the highly educated have a higher divorce rate than the poor and those of limited education.*

Although comprehensive national statistics are not available on this point, a number of excellent research publications indicate that the higher professional and business groups have the lowest divorce rates, while the highest divorce rate is found among working-class families. The great publicity attending divorce actions of wealthy and prominent persons may account for the popular myth that these groups have the highest divorce rate.

7. *Because of the high divorce rate, there are enormous numbers of divorced persons in the population.*

Census figures do not support this view. A 1962 sample survey indicated about 3 million divorced persons—that is, about one divorced person in the population to every 29 married persons.

Remarriage, of course, is the main reason for the relatively small number of divorced persons. In the same survey, the Census Bureau reported more than 14 million persons who had been married more than once. Some had been widowed, but the majority had been divorced.

8. *Divorced persons are less likely to remarry than are the widowed.*

Just the opposite is true: About three out of four remarriages involve a divorced person. The reason is the early age of most couples at the time of divorce. Age at widowhood has been advancing in recent years and the likelihood of marriage declines with age. Most remarriages of persons past 55 years of age are of the widowed; however, the majority of remarriages occur at younger ages and involve divorced persons.

While it is easy to point out some of the obvious misinformation about divorce—the myths—it is not easy to obtain the comprehensive facts the importance of the subject warrants. An insurance actuary estimates the risk of death from a study of death statistics. Excellent divorce statistics would make it possible to calculate the risk of divorce from such facts as age at marriage, differences between ages of husband and wife, number of previous marriages and whether they were dissolved by divorce or death.

Unfortunately, persons interested in the stability of family life cannot get the needed facts from official sources. With considerable chagrin, after years of working to improve them, I must make it clear that the United States is far behind most countries of Western Europe in the accuracy of its divorce statistics.

Why is this true? For one thing, the vital statistics (including divorce statistics) of the United States are different from the national censuses of population. The latter are provided for in the Constitution as a responsibility of the Federal Government. Vital statistics are a responsibility of the states.

Early in this century births and deaths were not fully reported. That they are now is the result of a campaign led by public-health specialists and leading physicians. Similarly, the American Bar Association has urged its members to support the central registration of divorces. Leading social scientists in the 28 states not now participating in the Divorce Registration Area program are actively urging their states to join. It can be hoped that it will not be long until all 50 states are cooperating. Then there will be fewer myths and more solid facts about divorce.

Unit Thirteen | DISCUSSION QUESTIONS

55. *Marriage Is Not a Personal Matter*
How do you explain the success of dating-by-computer companies?
What characteristics are important in the selection of a marriage partner? List in order of importance.

56. *Initial Adjustment Processes in Young Married Couples*
List six possible adjustment problems in young married couples. Give a brief description of each.
What approaches would you recommend to reduce adjustment problems in marriage?

57. *The Unsolved Mystery of Marriage*
Why do some unlikely marriages manage to survive while some so-called "perfect marriages" fall apart?
What are some of the qualities of a happy marriage. . .not one that just endures?

58. *Eight Myths About Divorce*
Why is the divorce rate higher in the western states than in other regions?
In general, do children help or hinder a marriage? Discuss.

Unit Fourteen *Applied Behavioral Sciences*

Application of the behavioral sciences to the daily tasks of living is apparent; no field of endeavor dealing with life is unaffected by it. During our age in which man investigates the most distant galaxies and explores depths of the ocean floor, a full understanding of behavior and its requirements is necessary. Whatever the structure of tomorrow's world, the contributions of behavioral scientists will play a vital role.

This unit presents a few other interesting areas of applied behavioral sciences: human engineering, consumer psychology, and communication.

Since World War I, the armed forces have played a significant part in the growth of psychology. Using results from psychological testing to human engineering, the military psychologist has been involved in increasing the efficiency of servicemen. Psychologists have made valuable contributions to space exploration, in the fields of astronaut selection, equipment design, and training methods. In *Psychology and the Space Frontier,* Walter F. Grether discusses the different roles that psychologists performed in Project Mercury, man's first attempt to explore outer space.

Consumer psychology investigates the characteristics and needs of individual buying behavior. Its focus is twofold: the design of products and the economic behavior of individuals. Its chief methods of investigation are surveys and opinion polls. Advertisement is the vehicle by which it projects its results to the public. It is interesting to note that the first newspapers of the seventeenth century contained advertisements. Radio and television are among the dominant methods of today's promotional campaigns. *The Impact of TV Advertisement: Learning Without Involvement* by Herbert E. Krugman investigates the efficacy of this form of consumer psychology. Krugman discusses content, message, and the persuasive ability of radio and TV advertisement.

Man's unique ability to handle symbols and think abstractly differentiates him from all other living organisms. It is this uniqueness that Robert Oliver discusses in *Mind and Language.* This interesting essay on language and human behavior illustrates the growing concern to understand man and his environment.

59 | Psychology and the Space Frontier

Walter F. Grether

In the history of our world, few, if any, previous events have had an impact on science equal to the successful launching of vehicles into space. For many centuries, people have looked up at the heavenly bodies and dreamed of the time when men could leave the earth and explore the universe. While, as yet, only the most simple beginnings have been made in terms of manned trips into space, the gravitational ice has been broken; manned flights to the moon and the planets now appear within man's grasp. The achievement of this age-old dream of flight into space had to wait until our technology, particularly the physical and engineering sciences, had prepared the necessary foundation of scientific knowledge. Many further advances in science and technology must be made before the major objectives of manned space flight become possible. So dependent is space flight on science that the people of all nations around our globe measure the scientific capability of our country and the USSR by our successes in space. That this is a valid measure we, as psychologists, might disagree, but it is used nevertheless.

While the impact of space flight on many areas of physical science and engineering are quite obvious, what has been the effect on psychology and how has psychology been contributing to the national space flight efforts?

My purpose in this paper is to examine some of the activities of psychologists who have been most directly involved in space flight work, to see what the nature of their contribution has been, and to look at some of the future problems that space flight poses for psychology.

In a program as complex as that of Project Mercury, combining the efforts of many thousands of individuals, it is difficult to isolate the contributions of particular scientists. There are, however, quite a number of psychologists who have made important direct contributions to the Mercury Program and many more who contributed in ways which are less apparent, but, nevertheless, important. I will try to show some significant psychological contributions which I can identify.

No discussion of psychological contributions to Project Mercury would be complete without some mention of the selection program whereby the seven astronauts were chosen. Quite a large number of psychological tests were used in this selection program. Besides Robert Voas, the psychologists who played important roles in planning and carrying out the selection program were David Trites, of the Air Force Personnel Laboratory, and William O'Connor, of the Naval School of Aviation Medicine. Since the Mercury astronaut selection program has already been well publicized, I will not go into it further here, but go on to discuss some of the vehicle design, training, and human performance aspects.

In the early planning of Project Mercury, it was generally thought that the extreme environmental stresses and the compressed time scale at the

From Walter F. Grether, "Psychology and the Space Frontier," *American Psychologist,* 17, 1962, pp. 92–101. Reprinted by permission of the author and American Psychological Association.

high speeds would make the pilot quite useless as a controller. Thus, it was thought that all vehicle functions must be automatically controlled just as in an unmanned satellite. The role of the astronaut was considered to be that of a passive passenger or a biological specimen with little, if any, control of the vehicle entrusted to him.

As the Mercury Program advanced, the planned role of the astronaut became more and more like that of an aircraft pilot with some of the direct control of the vehicle in his hands. For many other functions that were automatically programed and controlled, the astronaut was provided with emergency controls as back-ups to the automatic systems. Thus, the astronaut could contribute much to the potential success of the mission and to his own safety.

Before reviewing the specific contributions of psychology to Project Mercury, let us first look at some of the pertinent data (Shepard, 1961; Voas, Van Bockel, Zedekar, and Backer, 1961).

Figure 1 shows the major events in the first Mercury (MR-3) flight by Alan Shepard on May 5, 1961. Along the outside of the parabolic curve, representing the ballistic flight path, the major flight events are indicated. Under the curve is shown the time of the event in minutes after launch. Of particular interest to us here is that part of the flight from booster separation to the beginning of re-entry. This constituted the weightless portion of the flight. But, more important, I think, is the fact that during most of this period Shepard had manual control of the attitude of his capsule.

. . . Shepard was engaged in communication with the ground. Of particular interest is the time during which he actually controlled attitude of the vehicle.

From the motion picture records obtained during the flight, Voas and his staff were able to plot the eye movements in terms of the area of the capsule being observed. . . . The time period covered Shepard's first attempts to control attitude. . . . The attitude indicator, the periscope, the clock, and the manual fuel handles were occupying most of his attention.

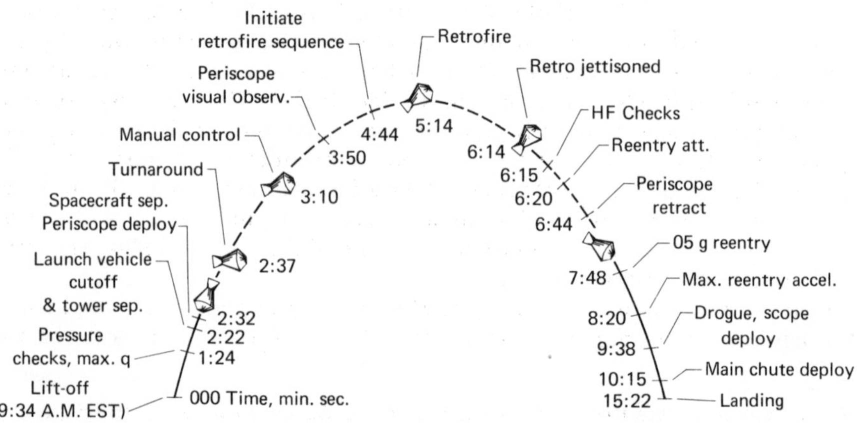

Fig. 1. Major events during Mercury MR-3 flight. (From Shepard, 1961.)

Probably the most interesting psychological data from Shepard's flight is that relating to his *manual control** of vehicle attitude. The control of attitude was a rather difficult tracking task. Control was accomplished with pairs of small rocket jets for each rotational axis. Thus it constituted an acceleration tracking task, about three axes. This task had been thoroughly practiced by Shepard and the other astronauts on various training simulators. One of these was a so-called procedures trainer, resembling a fixed-base aircraft flight simulator. Separate records for attitude control in pitch, yaw, and roll were made. . . . They show that performance in actual flight was equal to that on the trainer. Certainly there is no evidence that the performance was degraded by weightlessness.

In obtaining these data on astronaut performance as well as in guiding the training of the Mercury pilots, Voas played a dominant role as a member of the Project Mercury team. I would like to cover briefly the work of several other psychologists who worked closely with Project Mercury and made significant contributions to the program.

As one of the major subcontractors to the McDonnell Aircraft Corporation, the Minneapolis-Honeywell Regulator Company developed much of the complex control equipment in the Mercury vehicle. At the initiation of this development, there were important questions about *how much control a human pilot could be expected to exercise under the stresses and speeds of space flight,** and how to design the control system and related equipment to be used by the pilot. John Senders and his associates at Minneapolis-Honeywell made a thorough analysis of pilot's work load during Mercury flights, assuming different modes of operation and possible flight emergencies. This analysis used several engineering psychology techniques, including task simulation using analog computers, human transfer function analysis, and work-load (or task) analysis. This analysis demonstrated that the probable work load would be manageable by the pilot and that the pilot could manually control attitude of the vehicle during most phases of the Mercury mission.

One of the more specific inputs to the Mercury vehicle by John Senders and the group at Minneapolis-Honeywell relates to the attitude indicator. The attitude indicator is quite different from conventional aircraft attitude indicators in that the pitch and bank indications are on separate dials. Also novel is the manner of showing rate information at the center of the instrument. It appears to me that this novel integration of attitude and attitude rate information is excellently suited to the Mercury vehicle and mission. Without wishing to detract from the accomplishment of the Minneapolis-Honeywell group, it is of interest that earlier versions of this instrument have been studied for possible aircraft use both at our laboratory and in England.

Other major contributions to the design of the Mercury vehicle were made by Edward Jones and his associates at the McDonnell Aircraft Corporation where the Mercury capsule was designed and built. To use Jones' own term, we can describe the work of his group as "man's integration into the Mercury capsule." In other words, they did the human engineering of the

* Editor's italics.

system. One of the more interesting activities of the McDonnell group was their Failure Task Analysis. This consisted of an analysis of possible equipment failures that could occur during flight, a determination of the symptoms which the pilot or ground crew would have of the failure, the appropriate actions to take, and the consequences to be expected. It is easy to see the value of such a failure analysis for making improvements in the design, and for crew training. Much of the astronauts' training was based on this failure analysis. Although some type of failure analysis in design of complex systems is not new, I believe the McDonnell analysis was considerably more complete and detailed than any previously done, in terms of the cues to the pilot and the actions he could take. I fully expect that this technique will set a pattern for human engineering of future manned space vehicles.

Other important efforts of Jones and his group dealt with the visual problems of the astronaut, both inside and outside the Mercury capsule, and with the design of the procedures trainer (or simulator) to which I have already referred. In commenting on the training for his flight, Astronaut Shepard (1961) attached high value to two training devices, one of which was this procedures trainer.

The other trainer that Shepard felt was of great value was the *Navy human centrifuge** at Johnsville, Pennsylvania. On this centrifuge, operating through a computer, the astronauts were able to experience the accelerations of flight as well as effects of their own control of the capsule. In the work with the Johnsville centrifuge, we again find psychologists playing an important role, in this case working very closely with navy physiologists and medical personnel. John L. Brown (1960) and, more recently, Randall Chambers have obtained performance measures of X-15 pilots and Mercury astronauts on the Johnsville centrifuge. Their experiments demonstrated that with properly designed hand controls the pilots could maintain quite good tracking performance while exposed to high acceleration forces. Their experiments included the type of accelerations required to place a manned satellite into an earth orbit and bring it back into the atmosphere. These studies, plus the training which the astronauts obtained on the Johnsville centrifuge, contributed greatly to the Mercury Program.

Besides the problem of high accelerative forces during launch and reentry, there has been the long-standing question of how men will be affected by the weightlessness that becomes the normal state of affairs in space. For psychologists, the primary question has been, how will the pilot or astronaut's work performance be affected by lack of gravitational force? The only satisfactory way of producing weightlessness without actually going out into space has been by flying an aircraft in a parabolic path so that gravity is exactly counter-balanced by centrifugal force. The first significant experiments on human performance as affected by weightlessness were done by Gerathewohl, Strughold, and Stallings (1957) in fighter-type aircraft at the Air Force School of Aviation Medicine. Later, experiments were conducted by Brown and others at our laboratory with subjects tied down as well as free floating in a cargo-type airplane. These experiments (Loftus and Hammer, 1961) proved that human performance would not be disrupted or even

* Editor's italics.

General Dynamics Corporation/Astronautics

Human Engineering. Psychology and psychologists have made important contributions in our nation's space efforts.

significantly affected for subjects strapped in their seats, as planned for Project Mercury. Thus another of the potential obstacles to space flight had been dispelled.

Just as kings of old protected themselves against the hazards of eating by having food tasters precede them, so the modern astronaut likes to have animals precede him to sample the hazards of space flight. Before Shepard's Mercury flight on May 5, 1961, a *chimpanzee, Ham,** was put through an approximate duplicate of the flight on January 31, 1961. Ham's successful return to earth verified not only the physiological safety of such a flight, but it also verified that voluntary manual performance could be carried out during the stresses and strains of a rocket launching, weightlessness, and re-entry. The credit for Ham's performance goes to two psychologists, Fred Rohles and Marvin Grunzke, at the Air Force Aeromedical Field Laboratory at Holloman Air Force Base. They had trained Ham to operate a lever in response to a light signal to avoid an electric shock. Ham had been trained to continue his task even while exposed to some of the environmental stresses of space flight. During his pioneering flight in a Mercury capsule, Ham continued faithfully at his task with only a few lapses during the most stressful periods.

From the foregoing samples, we can see that psychology and psychologists have made important contributions, along with many other sciences and scientists, in the early phases of our nation's space efforts. *These contri-*

* Editor's italics.

*butions have been generally in the selection of astronauts, the determination of astronaut capabilities and design of the work station to match these, and the design of training equipment and methods for astronaut training.** These are the traditional areas of psychological contribution to personnel selection, human engineering, and training.

What has already been accomplished is only a small beginning by comparison with the work needed to meet the challenges of the future. Looking ahead a decade or two, let us examine some of the activities we can reasonably expect human beings to perform, or attempt to perform, in space.

The following are some of the jobs now foreseen for future astronauts:

1. Work and live in a relatively small space vehicle for weeks or months.
2. Rendezvous and join up with another space vehicle in an earth orbit.
3. Move about the interior and exterior of a space vehicle and transfer from one vehicle to another.
4. Assemble or construct space platforms in an earth orbit.
5. Land a space vehicle on the moon, explore the surrounding surface, and return to earth.

All of these activities, of course, must be carried out under the handicap of an extremely hostile environment, including weightlessness (except on the moon), lack of atmosphere, extremes of temperature, and radiation. Even a superficial analysis tells us that here are many challenging problems for psychological research. Let us review a few of the problems and see how some psychologists are already subjecting them to vigorous attack. To keep it within manageable proportions, I have chosen to restrict this review to work either carried out or sponsored by our Behavioral Sciences Laboratory at Wright-Patterson Air Force Base.

In discussing contributions to Project Mercury, I have already mentioned research studies on human performance under weightless conditions, as obtained for brief periods in aircraft. From these aircraft studies and the brief flights of Shepard and Grissom, we are assured that the performance of a man strapped in his seat will not be impaired significantly by weightlessness.

The situation is quite different, however, if the man must move about and do work inside or outside his vehicle. For him the lack of gravity is a great inconvenience. Fiction writers have long ago solved the weightless man's problems by giving him magnetic shoes with which to walk on the walls and ceilings and a personal rocket gun with which to propel himself from place to place. These ideas of the fiction writers have been tested in our zero-g airplane by Brown, Simons, Gardner, and others (Loftus and Hammer, 1961; Simons, 1959; Simons and Gardner, 1960). Unfortunately, the problems are not so easily overcome as thought by the fiction writers.

For purposes of walking, magnetic shoes, suction cups, and other means of gluing the feet to a surface, have so far proved to be unsatisfactory substitutes for gravity. They hold only when touching the surface and lose their hold or pull when separated from the walking surface. Whereas the mag-

* Editor's italics.

netic shoes and other adhesion methods fail to replace gravity for purposes of walking, they seem to be a good gravity substitute for human perception of the vertical. For all of our subjects who have tried the magnetic shoes, the ceiling of the airplane has immediately become the floor, or downward direction. Evidently, for the standing man under weightless conditions, down is always the direction where his feet are attached.

The fiction writer's personal rocket gun, for the weightless astronaut to use in moving from place to place, also turns out to have many weaknesses. Unless this thrust can be directed precisely at the center of mass, the subject's body will be thrown into a spin instead of being propelled in the desired direction. Unfortunately, men are not endowed with a sense organ to tell them the location of the center of mass. To make the personal rocket gun useful, therefore, will require some elaborations and improvements on the basic idea. Several of these are now being studied.

That men will ever propel themselves in open space with hand-held rocket guns seems somewhat doubtful. It is more likely that they will move from one vehicle to another within a small capsule with suitable rocket propulsion. Certainly, we can expect men to be guiding a spaceship so as to *rendezvous with another ship** in approximately the same orbit. But the execution of such a rendezvous presents rather formidable problems in guidance and control. Any change in velocity of an orbiting object will cause it to seek a new orbit. Suppose a man in an orbiting capsule were to increase his speed to rendezvous with another satellite ahead of him in the same orbit. Because of the increased speed, his capsule would move out to an orbit of greater radius, but with a longer time per orbit. Thus, his capsule would move above and then drop behind the target satellite. Similarly, if the man were to decrease the speed of his capsule, it would drop to a lower but faster orbit. For executing a rendezvous, therefore, we truly have a case where the shortest distance is not a straight line, but an arc. This arc will end at the target satellite only if the amount and direction of thrust have been properly chosen.

Besides having complex control problems in executing a rendezvous with another spaceship, an astronaut faces rather difficult *problems of visual perception.** Usually his visual target, the other ship, will be seen against a background of black sky, punctuated only by stars. Usually part of the other vehicle will be brightly illuminated by direct sunlight, part of it by earth reflection, and part of it will be completely dark. The earth may or may not be visible. Thus, orientation cues for direction may be lacking. Here is a fertile field for visual perceptual research, which Baker and Steedman, in our laboratory, have begun to explore in a specially prepared dark room. Their research has been directed toward obtaining thresholds for the kind of target movements which an astronaut would be required to judge in visually controlling a rendezvous in space. . . . Thresholds were determined for target motion toward and away from the observer, using targets of different angular sizes. Note that for the largest target size the direction of movement can be judged correctly (90 per cent threshold) in less than 5 per cent of the observer-to-target distance. The curves have a break at about

* Editor's italics.

twelve minutes of visual angle. At the smaller visual angles, it appears that the target motion is judged not by size change but by a change in brightness much as in Ricco's Law. At the larger visual angles, the subject judges the target motion by the change in stimulus area.

A study of the human problems of performing assembly and construction operations in space has led several people in our laboratory to return to a traditional psychophysical technique that is almost as old as experimental psychology. This is the measurement of thresholds for lifted weights, but with a space-age twist. In space, objects have no weight, but their mass remains unchanged. Thus, it is of interest to know how the thresholds for mass alone compare with the thresholds for both weight and mass. Furthermore, we expect that in space many operations will have to be performed by remote manipulators such as those used in nuclear laboratories. . . . The thresholds for mass alone were obtained on a frictionless (air-bearing) table. Some measurements were also made under true weightless conditions in our zero-g airplane, which verified the validity of the results obtained on the frictionless table.

A final human problem of space flight which I will discuss is the problem of *long-term work and confinement in a very small vehicle.** Once placed in orbit, an earth satellite can keep going almost indefinitely without the application of additional thrust. If such a vehicle is manned, the limiting time that it can remain aloft is most likely to be the tolerance or endurance of the human crew. If the flight time exceeds about 24 hours, we must provide additional men for crew relief. Thus, we have the problems of how large a relief crew must be added and how the duty and rest periods should be scheduled. The situation is somewhat similar to that on a submarine that may remain submerged for weeks or months, except for, at least, one important difference. Unlike the submarine, the spaceship has a severe weight problem. To place each pound in orbit requires several hundred pounds of rocket thrust. Thus, to save weight, it is of the utmost importance that the total number of crew members be an absolute minimum; and these crew members must live and work in a very confined space.

Research on the problems of long-term confinement and work-rest cycles has been conducted for our laboratory by Adams and his colleagues at the Lockheed Aircraft Corporation at Marietta, Georgia. Chiles has monitored this program for our laboratory. The Lockheed research has been conducted in a crew station mockup with duty stations for up to five crew members and a small additional area for sleeping and eating. At each duty station is a work panel providing the subjects with the following tasks: probability monitoring, auditory vigilance, reaction time to warnings, and arithmetic computation. On all of these tasks, performance is continually recorded and there is provision for some recording of physiological measures.

A major experiment (Adams and Chiles, in preparation) conducted in the Lockheed mockup used two B-52 crews supplied by the Strategic Air Command. Each crew spent 15 days in the mockup on a work-rest cycle of 4 hours work and 2 hours rest for the entire 15 days. . . . Through the 15-day period there is only a moderate decline in performance in spite of the rather

* Editor's italics.

severe work-rest cycle of 4 hours work and 2 hours rest. The other significant finding is the diurnal cycle in the performance level with the low point during the morning of each day. This cycle persisted throughout the 15-day period in spite of the subjects having been removed from the usual day-night routine and environmental changes. . . . All of the performance tests showed evidence of a diurnal cycle and only a moderate decline in performance during the 15 days. On the pattern discrimination, task performance improved during the confinement period, almost certainly because of learning effects. The daily cycle appeared also in the physiological measurements taken during the fifteen-day study. . . .

From the results just shown, added to the verbal reports of the subjects in the 15-day study, we believe that well-motivated men can be expected to live and work in a confined space or other vehicle for up to 15 days on a schedule of 4 hours work and 2 hours rest. This means, of course, that the number of crew members over and above the duty stations to be manned need be only 50 per cent. Or, put another way, only three men could operate two duty stations on a continuous basis provided the three men are cross-trained on both duty stations.

There is, of course, much additional work by which psychologists are contributing to our nation's current and future space efforts that I have not attempted to cover in this review. There is, for example, the important and interesting work of Brant Clark and others at the Navy School of Aviation Medicine on the effects of slow rotation on human performance. Such rotation of a space vehicle offers a substitute for gravity in space. There have been many studies involving water immersion, isolation, and other techniques for simulating some of the changes in the sensory and social environment of space. Also, there are many psychologists working in government laboratories and in the guarded interiors of our major aircraft and other corporations, helping to shape the designs of our spaceships of the future.

In *concluding this review** of psychology and the space frontier, I would like to restate several points made earlier:

1. Psychology as a science has a vital role to play in the conquest of space.
2. Psychologists have responded with vigor and imagination to the challenging problems of space flight.
3. The space flight challenge brings with it the stimulation of new ideas and opens opportunities for new types of research on human behavior.
4. Psychology has much to gain in the form of new knowledge, and, also, in status as a science, from its participation in the push into space.

Implications

This review of the psychologists' contribution to our nation's space effort shows the importance of psychologists working as a team. Many separate human problems were the object of studies, the results of which all con-

* Editor's italics.

tributed to the final task of space flight. Which of the problems interested you most, and what, in brief, were the findings in respect to them? Can you think of an aspect of general psychology, such as motivation, perception, learning, emotion, adjustment, and individual differences, that was not involved in the studies reviewed here?

---

60 | The Impact of Television Advertising: Learning Without Involvement

Herbert E. Krugman

Among the wonders of the twentieth century has been the ability of the mass media repeatedly to expose audiences numbered in millions to campaigns of coordinated messages. In the post-World War I years it was assumed that exposure equaled persuasion and that media content therefore was the all-important object of study or censure. Now we believe that the powers of the mass media are limited. No one has done more to bring about a counterbalancing perspective than ex-AAPOR president Joseph Klapper, with his well-known book *The Effects of Mass Media* [1], and the new AAPOR president Raymond Bauer, with such articles as "The Limits of Persuasion" [2].

It has been acknowledged, however, that this more carefully delimited view of mass media influence is based upon analysis of largely noncommercial cases and data. We have all wondered how many of these limitations apply also to the world of commerce, specifically advertising. These limitations will be discussed here as they apply to television advertising only, since the other media include stimuli and responses of a different psychological nature, which play a perhaps different role in the steps leading to a purchasing decision.

The tendency is to say that the accepted limitations of mass media do apply, that advertising's use of the television medium has limited impact. We tend to feel this way, I think, because (1) we rarely feel converted or greatly persuaded by a particular TV campaign, and (2) so much of TV advertising content is trivial and sometimes even silly. Nevertheless, trivia have their own special qualities, and some of these may be important to our understanding of the commercial *or* the noncommercial use and impact of mass media.

To begin, let us go back to Neil Borden's classic Harvard Business School evaluation of the economic effects of advertising [3]. Published in

---

From *The Public Opinion Quarterly,* **29**, 3, 1965, pp. 349–356. Reprinted by permission.

1942, it concluded that advertising (1) accelerates growing demand or retards falling demand, i.e. it quickens the pulse of the market, and (2) encourages price rigidity but increases quality and choice of products. The study warned, however, that companies had been led to overlook price strategies and the elasticity of consumer demand. This was borne out after World War II by the rise of the discounters!

The end of World War II also brought mass television and an increased barrage of advertising messages. How much could the public take? Not only were early TV commercials often irritating, but one wondered whether all the competition would not end in a great big buzzing confusion. Apparently not! Trend studies of advertising penetration have shown that the public is able to "hold in memory," as we would say of a computer, a very large number of TV campaign themes correctly related to brands. The fact that huge sums and energies were expended to achieve retention of these many little bits of information should not deter us from acknowledging the success of the over-all effort.

It is true that in some categories of products the sharpness of brand differentiation is slipping, as advertising themes and appeals grow more similar. Here the data look, as one colleague put it, "mushy." In such categories the product is well on its way toward becoming a commodity; even while brand advertising continues, the real competition is more and more one of price and distribution. But prices, too, are advertised, although in different media, and recalled.

What is lacking in the required "evaluation" of TV advertising is any significant body of research specifically relating advertising to attitudes, and these in turn to purchasing behavior or sales. That is, we have had in mind a model of the correct and effective influence process which has not yet been verified. This is the bugaboo that has been the hope and the despair of research people within the industry. Always there looms that famous pie in the sky: If the client will put up enough money, if he will be understanding enough to cooperate in blacking out certain cities or areas to permit a controlled experiment, if the cities or areas under study will be correctly matched, if the panels of consumers to be studied will not melt away in later not-at-homes, refusals, or changes of residence, if the sales data will be "clean" enough to serve as adequate criteria—*then surely* one can truly assess the impact of a particular ad campaign! Some advertisers, too, are learning to ask about this type of evaluation, while the advertising agencies are ambivalent and unsure of their strength.

This seems to be where we are today. The economic impact of TV advertising is substantial and documented. Its messages have been learned by the public. Only the lack of specific case histories relating advertising to attitudes to sales keeps researchers from concluding that the commercial use of the medium is a success. We are faced then with the odd situation of knowing that advertising works but being unable to say much about why.

Perhaps our model of the influence process is wrong. Perhaps it is incompletely understood. Back in 1959 Herbert Zielske, in "The Remembering and Forgetting of Advertising," demonstrated that advertising will be quickly forgotten if not continuously exposed [4]. Why such need for constant reinforcement? Why so easy-in and easy-out of short-term memory? One answer is that much of advertising content is learned as meaningless nonsense material. Therefore, let us ask about the nature of such learning.

An important distinction between the learning of sense and nonsense was laid down by Ebbinghaus in 1902 when he identified the greater effects of order of presentation of stimuli on the learning of nonsense material. He demonstrated a U curve of recall, with first and last items in a series best remembered, thus giving rise also to the principles of primacy and recency [5].

In 1957, many years later, Carl Hovland reported that in studying persuasion he found the effects of primacy and recency greater when dealing with material of lesser ego-involvement. He wrote, "Order of presentation is a more significant factor in influencing opinions for subjects with relatively weak desires for understanding, than for those with high 'cognitive needs' " [6]. It seems, therefore, that the nonsensical à la Ebbinghaus and the unimportant à la Hovland work alike.

At the 1962 AAPOR meetings I had the pleasure of reading a paper on some applications of learning theory to copy testing. Here it was reported that the spontaneous recall of TV commercials presented four in a row formed a distinct U curve. In the same paper a re-analysis of increment scores of fifty-seven commercials tested in a three-position series by the Schwerin television testing method also showed a distinct U curve, despite the earlier contentions of the Schwerin organization. That real advertising materials presented in so short a series could produce distinct U curves seemed to confirm that the learning of advertising was similar to the learning of the nonsensical or the unimportant [7].

What is common to the learning of the nonsensical and the unimportant is lack of involvement. We seem to be saying, then, that much of the impact of television advertising is in the form of learning without involvement, or what Hartley calls "un-anchored learning."* If this is so, is it a source of weakness or of strength to the advertising industry? Is it good or bad for our society? What are the implications for research on advertising effectiveness?

Let us consider some qualities of sensory perception with and without involvement. Last October I participated along with Ray Bauer, Elihu Katz, and Nat Maccoby in a Gould House seminar sponsored by the Foundation for Research on Human Behavior. Nat reported some studies conducted with Leon Festinger in which fraternity members learned a TV message better when hearing the audio and watching unrelated video than when they watched the speaker giving them the message directly, i.e. video *and* audio together [8]. Apparently, the distraction of watching something unrelated to the audio message lowered whatever resistance there might have been to the message.

As Nat put it, "Comprehension equals persuasion": Any disagreement ("Oh no! That can't be true!") with any message must come after some real

---

* This is the title of a working manuscript distributed privately by E. L. Hartley in 1964, which concerns his experimentation with new methods of health education in the Philippine Islands.

interval, however minute. Ray asked Nat if he would accept a statement of this point as "Perception precedes perceptual defense," and Nat agreed. The initial development of this view goes back before World War II to the psychologist W. E. Guthrie [9]. It receives more recent support from British research on perception and communication, specifically that of D. E. Broadbent, who has noted the usefulness of defining perception as "immediate memory" [10].

The historical importance of the Maccoby view, however, is that it takes us almost all the way back to our older view of the potent propaganda content of World War I, that exposure to mass media content is persuasive per se! What is implied here is that in cases of involvement with mass media content perceptual defense is very briefly postponed, while in cases of non-involvement perceptual defense may be absent.

Does this suggest that if television bombards us with enough trivia about a product we may be persuaded to believe it? On the contrary, it suggests that persuasion as such, i.e. overcoming a resistant attitude, is not involved at all and that it is a mistake to look for it in our personal lives as a test of television's advertising impact. Instead, as trivia are repeatedly learned and repeatedly forgotten and then repeatedly learned a little more, it is probable that two things will happen: (1) more simply, that so-called "overlearning" will move some information out of short-term and into long-term memory systems, and (2) more complexly, that we will permit significant alterations in the *structure* of our perception of a brand or product, but in ways which may fall short of persuasion or of attitude change. One way we may do this is by shifting the relative salience of attributes suggested to us by advertising as we organize our perception of brands and products.

Thanks to Sherif we have long used the term "frame of reference," and Osgood in particular has impressed us with the fact that the meaning of an object may be perceived along many separate dimensions. Let us say that a number of frames of reference are available as the primary anchor for the percept in question. We may then alter the psychological salience of these frames or dimensions and shift a product seen primarily as "reliable" to one seen primarily as "modern."* The product is still seen as reliable and perhaps no *less* reliable than before, but this quality no longer provides the primary perceptual emphasis. Similarly, the product was perhaps previously seen as modern, and perhaps no *more* modern now—yet exposure to new or repeated messages may give modernity the primary role in the organization of the percept.

There is no reason to believe that such shifts are completely limited to trivia. In fact, when Hartley first introduced the concept of psychological salience, he illustrated it with a suggestion that Hitler did not so much increase anti-Semitic attitudes in Germany as bring already existing anti-Semitic attitudes into more prominent use for defining the everyday world.† This, of course, increased the probability of anti-Semitic behavior. While

---

* Psychological salience was first discussed in this manner by E. L. Hartley, *Problems in Prejudice,* New York, Kings Crown Press, 1946, pp. 107–115.

† *Ibid.,* p. 97.

the shift in salience does not tell the whole story, it seems to be one of the dynamics operating in response to massive repetition. Although a rather simple dynamic, it may be a major one when there is no cause for resistance, or when uninvolved consumers do not provide their own perceptual emphases or anchors.

It may be painful to reject as incomplete a model of the influence process of television advertising that requires changes in attitude *prior to* changes in behavior. It may be difficult to see how the viewer of television can go from perceptual impact directly to behavioral impact, unless *the full perceptual impact is delayed.* This would not mean going into unexplored areas. Sociologists have met "sleeper effects" before, and some psychologists have long asserted that the effects of "latent" learning are only or most noticeable at the point of reward. In this case, it would be at the behavioral level involved in product purchases rather than at some intervening point along the way. That is, the purchase situation is the catalyst that reassembles or brings out all the potentials for shifts in salience that have accumulated up to that point. The product or package is then suddenly seen in a new, "somehow different" light although nothing verbalizable may have changed *up to that point.* What we ordinarily call "change of attitude" may then occur after some real interval, however minute. Such change of attitude after product purchase is *not,* as has sometimes been said, in "rationalization" of the purchase but is an emergent response aspect of the previously changed perception. We would perhaps see it more often if products always lived up to expectations and did not sometimes create negative interference with the emerging response.

I have tried to say that the public lets down its guard to the repetitive commercial use of the television medium and that it easily changes its ways of perceiving products and brands and its purchasing behavior without thinking very much about it at the time of TV exposure or at any time prior to purchase, and without up to then changing verbalized attitudes. This adds up, I think, to an understandable success story for advertising's use of the television medium. Furthermore, this success seems to be based on a left-handed kind of public trust that sees no great importance in the matter.

But now I wonder about those so-called "limits of effectiveness" of the noncommercial use of the mass media. I wonder if we were not overusing attitudes and attitude changes as our primary criterion of effectiveness? In looking for behavioral changes, did we sometimes despair too soon simply because we did not find earlier attitude changes? I wonder if we projected our own attitudes and values too much onto the audiences studied and assumed that they, too, would treat information about such matters as the United Nations as serious and involving? I wonder also how many of those public-spirited campaigns ever asked their audiences to *do* something, i.e asked for the kind of concrete behavior that at some point triggers whatever real potentials may have developed for an attitude change to begin or perhaps to complete its work.

I would like to suggest, therefore, that the distinction between the commercial and the noncommercial use of the mass media, as well as the distinction between "commercial" and "academic" research, has blinded us to the existence of two entirely different ways of experiencing and being influenced by mass media. One way is characterized by lack of personal involvement, which, while perhaps more common in response to commercial subject matter, is by no means limited to it. The second is characterized by a high degree of personal involvement. By this we do *not* mean attention, interest, or excitement but the number of conscious "bridging experiences," connections, or personal references per minute that the viewer makes between his own life and the stimulus. This may vary from none to many.

The significance of conditions of low or high involvement is not that one is better than the other, but that the processes of communication impact are different. That is, there is a difference in the change processes that are at work. Thus, with low involvement one might look for gradual shifts in perceptual structure, aided by repetition, activated by behavioral-choice situations, and *followed* at some time by attitude change. With high involvement one would look for the classic, more dramatic, and more familiar conflict of ideas at the level of conscious opinion and attitude that precedes changes in overt behavior.

I think now we can appreciate again why Madison Avenue may be of little use in the Cold War or even in a medium-hot presidential campaign. The more common skills of Madison Avenue concern the change processes associated with low involvement, while the very different skills required for high-involvement campaigns are usually found elsewhere. However, although Madison Avenue generally seems to know its limitations, the advertising researchers tend to be less clear about theirs. For example, from New York to Los Angeles researchers in television advertising are daily exacting "attitude change" or "persuasion" scores from captive audiences, these scores based on questionnaires and methods which, though plausible, have no demonstrated predictive validity. The plausibility of these methods rests on the presence of a more or less explicit model of communication effectiveness. Unfortunately, the model in use is the familiar one that assumes high involvement. Perhaps it is the questionnaires and the research procedures themselves that are responsible for creating what high involvement is present, which would not otherwise exist. The wiser or more cautious researchers meanwhile retreat to the possibilities of impersonal exactness in controlled field experiments and behavioral criteria. What has been left out, unfortunately, is the development of a low-involvement model, and the pretest measures based on such a model. The further development of this model is an important next step, not only for the perhaps trivial world of television advertising but for the better understanding of all those areas of public opinion and education which, socially important as they may be, may simply not be very involving to significant segments of the audience.

In time we may come to understand the effectiveness of mass media primarily in terms of the *consistency* with which a given campaign, commercial or noncommercial, employs talent and research sensitively attuned to the real level of audience involvement. In time, also, we may come to understand that behavior, that is, verbal behavior and overt behavior, is always consistent provided we do not impose premature and narrowly conceived rules as to which must precede, or where, when, and how it must be measured.*

REFERENCES

1. Joseph Klapper, *The Effects of Mass Media,* Glencoe, Ill., Free Press, 1960.
2. Raymond Bauer, "The Limits of Persuasion," *Harvard Business Review,* September-October, 1958, pp. 105–110.
3. Neil Borden, *The Economic Effects of Advertising,* Chicago, Irwin, 1942.
4. H. A. Zielske, "The Remembering and Forgetting of Advertising," *Journal of Marketing,* January 1959, pp. 239–243.
5. H. Ebbinghaus, *Grundzuge der Psychologie,* Leipzig, Germany, Veit, 1902.
6. C. T. Hovland *et al., The Order of Presentation in Persuasion,* New Haven, Yale University Press, 1957, p. 136.
7. H. E. Krugman, "An Application of Learning Theory to TV Copy Testing," *Public Opinion Quarterly,* Vol. 26, 1962, pp. 626–634.
8. L. Festinger and N. Maccoby, "On Resistance to Persuasive Communications," *Journal of Abnormal and Social Psychology,* Vol. 68, No. 4, 1964, pp. 359–366.
9. E. R. Guthrie, *The Psychology of Learning,* New York, Harper, 1935, p. 26.
10. D. E. Broadbent, *Perception and Communication,* London, Pergamon Press, 1958, Chap. 9.

---

* The consistency of verbal and overt behavior has also been reasserted by Hovland, who attributes pseudo-differences to those *research designs* which carelessly compare results of laboratory experiments with results of field surveys (C. I. Hovland, "Reconciling Conflicting Results Derived from Experimental and Survey Studies of Attitude Change," *American Psychologist,* Vol. 14, 1959, pp. 8–17); by Campbell, who attributes pseudo-differences to the fact that verbal and overt behaviors have different situational thresholds (D. T. Campbell, "Social Attitudes and Other Acquired Behavioral Dispositions," in S. Koch, ed., *Psychology: A Study of a Science,* Vol. 6, McGraw-Hill, 1963, pp. 94–172); and by Rokeach, who attributes pseudo-differences to the fact that overt behavior is the result of interaction between *two* sets of attitudes, one toward the object and one toward the situation, and that most research leaves one of the two attitudes unstudied (M. Rokeach, "Attitude Change and Behavior Change," paper presented at the annual conference of the World Association for Public Opinion Research, Dublin, Ireland, Sept. 9, 1965).

61 | Mind and Language

What it Means to be a Thinking, Languagized Mammal

Robert T. Oliver

Everyone who works with language—and this of course includes our profession of speech—has often had occasion to ponder on some very profound and difficult problems. Among these are: 1. The nature of mind; 2. Relation of mind and body; and 3. Relation of mind (or reason) and feeling for (emotions). These are a problem I propose to discuss.

The human mind is one of nature's most fascinating and mysterious productions. Equally wonderful and almost as mysterious is human language. There is no real doubt that the two are so closely related as to be inseparable. Without language as we know it there could be no mind as we know it. And without our human mind, language could not exceed the fifteen or twenty "signs" which comprise the largest sub-human vocabulary.

The manner in which mind and language are related has intrigued human curiosity at least as far back as the beginnings of recorded history—and still we do not know the answer with any certainty. Is all our thinking grammar-bound and limited to the extent of our vocabulary? Do we think in words? Does an individual increase his general mental powers as he improves and extends his mastery of language? The precise nature of the relationship is speculative; but the fact that there is a relationship is unquestionable.

Max Muller, in his *Lectures on the Science of Language,* says flatly; "To think is to speak low. To speak is to think aloud." Edward Sapir, in *Language,* declares that "thought is nothing but language denuded of its outward garb." Charleton Laird, in his *Miracle of Language,* defines man as "a languagized mammal," and concludes that "when we study language, we are, to a remarkable degree, studying human nature." A. D. Ritchie, in *The Natural History of Mind,* writes: "As far as thought is concerned, and at all levels of thought, it is a symbolic process. . . . The essential act of thought is symbolic." Susanne Langer, author of *Philosophy in a New Key,* believes that the discovery or invention of language marked "a whole day of creation" between men and lower animals and was "the real beginning of mentality."

One of the most striking contributions to the theory that mind and language are absolutely inter-dependent, if not, indeed, identical, was made by Benjamin Lee Whorf. In an article on "Science and Linguistics," published in *Technological Review* for April, 1940, he wrote: "We dissect nature along lines laid down by our native languages. . . . We cut nature up, organize it into concepts, and ascribe significances as we do, largely because we are parties to an agreement to organize it in this way—an agreement that holds throughout our speech community and is codified in the patterns of our language." The biological psychologist N. J. Berrill rephrased this Whorfian view in his popular book, *Man's Emerging Mind,* as the "inability to see or think except along the lines that our kind of language imposes upon

---

Speech delivered to the annual convention, The Texas Speech Association, Houston, October 2, 1964. Reprinted by permission of the author.

us." A Russian linguist, L. S. Vygotsky, in his book, *Thought and Language,* insists that unspoken and internalized thought is vague, dim, undifferentiated, and mistily unreal. It is only when this amorphous mixture of understanding and feeling must be communicated that it is transmuted into meaningful and distinct words. "Thought undergoes many changes as it turns into speech," he says. But the changes are to make precise what, while it is internal, is at best vague.

Artists in the use of words agree, on the whole, with the Vygotskian view that words give meaningful form to the relatively formless unspoken thoughts. James Stephens, the Irish poet and short story writer, declared: "A thought is a real thing, and words are only its raiment, but a thought is as shy as a virgin: unless it is fittingly appareled, we may not look on its shadowy nakedness; it will fly from us and only return again in the darkness, crying in a thin, childish voice which we may not comprehend until, with aching minds listening and divining, we at last fashion for it those symbols which are its protection and its banner." Rudyard Kipling, in a lecture to the Royal College of Surgeons, said: "I am by calling a dealer in words, and words are, of course, the most powerful drug used by mankind. Not only do words infect, egotize, narcotize, and paralyze, but they enter into and color the minutest cells of the brain very much as madder mixed with a stag's food at the zoo colors the growth of the animal's antlers." The poet, O. Mandelstam, wrote: "I have forgotten the word I intended to say, and my thought, unembodied, returns to the realm of shadows."

MIND, LANGUAGE AND HUMAN NATURE

Animals live without either thought or language, but depend upon *instincts,* which are precise and impressive guides to specific forms of behavior. A baby robin grows up knowing how to build a nest (a very complicated procedure) without being taught. Beavers know how to build dams and houses with underwater entrances. Migratory birds can navigate through thousands of miles of unknown territory. Bees and ants amaze us with the complexity of their social organization, their skill in gathering and preserving food, and their intricately engineered colonies. Many animals seem better fitted to their environment than do people; but they cannot invent, they cannot adapt to changing conditions. Progress is impossible for them. They lack the minds and they lack the language which together make variable adjustments possible.

Su-Tzu, a Chinese philosopher of the Sixth Century B. C., observed that words are like pieces of glass: they obscure everything that they do not clarify. We human beings who speak (and think) words are either helped or hurt by them. Stuart Chase, in *The Tyranny of Words,* pointed out that animals make a "realistic appraisal of the environment." They live in the here-and-now, unconcerned about the mistakes of yesterday or the problems of tomorrow. But people live in the *pseudo-environment* created by their own linguistic mentality. They imagine a vast complexity beyond the tight little universe of their own immediate sensory experience. "Language," Chase points out, "is no more than crudely acquired before children begin to suffer from it, and to misinterpret the world by reason of it."

The reason for both our superiority to other animal creatures and our greater tendency to get into far more complex troubles than they are capable of is the way in which our human nature is affected by our linguistic mentality. Words, for us, are not merely labels-of-identification, or *signs* of a direct and invariable relationship (as are the grunts and squeaks of animals), but they assume a power of their own. In addition to naming things, our words become *invested* with the power of the thing itself. Thus, when we can we avoid speaking of death and instead have developed hundreds of synonyms designed to lessen its fearfulness, such as "passed on," "gone to eternal rest," "sleeping," "departed," "relieved of pain," and the like. We feel that "nasty" words are almost as objectionable as "nasty" things. Words, indeed, tend to become substitutes which are even more powerful than the fact-item they are supposed to identify. For example, if a man is called a "conservative," even a wide pattern of "liberal" behavior will be ignored or interpreted as somehow being a form of conservatism. Say of a man that he is "too ambitious," or "egotistical," or a "drudge," and his associates color their reactions to him in accordance with such terms.

Words, as Kipling said, are powerful drugs, both in our solitary thinking and in our communication with one another. Sometimes they clarify our understanding, sometimes they obscure it. They lead us into kindliness and also into hostility. Our minds, our language, and our human nature are so inextricably intertwined that it is impossible to separate them.

Is mind the peculiar ability, apparently unique to human beings, of "associating" facts and factors of very different types and of "interpreting" from this association "new" meanings that had to be invented? For example, is it mind that permits (or perhaps requires) human beings to draw conclusions from the mutual behavior of a mother and child to which we give the name *love* and then to apply this quality, or something like it, to relations between friends, or between husband and wife? Is it mind that leads us to further elaborations, deducing that similar relationships constitute what we call loyalty, friendship, unselfishness, cooperation, and sacrifice?

Is mind wholly or even especially a kind of "reasoning process"; or does it also include such "emotions" as liking, disliking, fear, contentment, and the exaltation of spirit which we name happiness? Is our sense of beauty a function of mind—and, if so, to what degree is it rational and to what degree emotional?

If mind is located basically in the cerebral cortex, and if it is a practical synonym for intelligence, then what is the "muscular sense" which enables us to gain skill in playing golf, or in carving wood, or playing the piano, or painting a picture? What is the relationship of mind to *empathy*—the "sizing up" of a situation through muscular responses? What is the relationship of mind to *intuition*—the "sixth sense" that may warn us of danger when we don't actually perceive anything dangerous, or that may attract us to or repel us from a person whom we meet for the first time and about whom we know very little? Why is it that some people appear to have keen *insight* into character and personality, yet may not excel in other forms of intellectual capacity?

Obviously, what we refer to as *mind* is actually a mysterious and broadly inclusive quality. But so is language. We may have a large vocabulary or a small one. We may use words with a high degree of grammatical precision or string them together quite loosely. We use and respect dictionaries which define words with precise finality; yet we may say affectionately of a friend that he is a "no-good scoundrel" (men especially talk this way to one another), meaning quite the opposite of the defined meaning. Similarly, we agree on grammatical forms (such as that two negatives make a positive), yet when we violate them there is seldom any question of our meaning. For example, if we hear, "I don't have no time free," we are certain it means the speaker is busy, even though grammatical rules assure us he has actually said there is no time at which he is occupied. Meanwhile, and not at all incidentally, we also conclude that the speaker is uneducated and may go further and consider him crude or even unintelligent. The words we use and the way in which we use them always are important, though not necessarily in the way we might expect.

Thus far we have been concerned more with problems than with solutions, with questions more than with answers. Final answers to the questions remain elusive. But there is much we can do to improve both the quality of our thinking and our use of language. These are *personal problems* which to a helpful degree can be *solved.*

THE NATURE OF MIND

When we seek to understand the nature of mind, it is helpful to compare it with non-human minds and observe the differences. Wolfgang Kohler, author of *The Mentality of Apes,* observes that among simians, "out of sight is out of mind." If a chimpanzee or a monkey is killed or wounded and left among its fellows, they mourn for it and pay considerable attention to it; but if the dead or wounded animal is removed, the others appear quickly to forget all about it. On the contrary, people spend much of their time thinking about sons away in the armed forces, daughters off to college, or events and situations that are distant in time and space.

If some deer are feeding in a meadow and something disturbs them, white tails will flash up as they warn one another of danger before leaping off to seek individual safety. Deer, like many other sub-human creatures, do communicate. They do cooperate. They help one another, as some stand guard while others feed. They call one another to a newly discovered source of feed. All this is impressive—until we realize how quickly and definitely the limits of their cerebration and communication are reached, and how far short they fall of what even stupid or uneducated human beings do as a matter of course.

A classic demonstration of the vast gulf between the "minds" of chimpanzees (the most humanoid of all sub-human forms of life) and of men is the behavior of a chimpanzee in a cage when a banana is outside the bars, beyond its reach. If a stick is placed midway between the chimp and the banana, close enough so the animal can reach it, he will very quickly seize upon the "idea" of using the stick as a tool to draw the banana within reach. This is a very impressive display of original thinking and of the invention of a tool. But when the banana is placed outside the cage on one side, and the stick is placed outside the opposite side of the cage, so that the chimpanzee cannot see the two of them simultaneously, he *never* will get the idea of using the stick to get the banana. Unless he can see the two objects together he cannot put them together in his mind. "What monkey cannot see, monkey cannot do." Contrast this with the behavior of a child playing outside his house, who remembers his mother's spoons and runs to the kitchen to get one to use in building a clay castle.

What we human beings do easily and indeed almost constantly is to "pick up" external reality into our brains, in the form of symbols, there to recast them into all sorts of new combinations. We "try out" experiments or experiences in our minds before we do with our hands. Moreover, we remember something we saw, heard, or read about at some previous time and adapt or invent a new use for this remembered fact in terms of our present interests. And we invent new ideas. If we wish to blow soap bubbles to amuse the baby, we recall the corncob pipe that father bought as a joke and stuck away in his desk drawer; and we "imagine" that if we filled its bowl with soapy water and blew out through the stem (instead of drawing the air in through it, as father did when he smoked) we might get a series of bubbles. To us this kind of thinking is commonplace and ridiculously matter-of-course. But no creatures other than human beings can do it.

By *mind* we mean the *manipulation of symbols*: of words, mathematical formulae, pictures, or images. A symbol is something which stands for or means something which it is not. Our ears have learned to identify a certain combination of sounds as *standing for* or meaning our own name, or the command, "Come here." Our eye has learned to interpret these marks on paper (letters) as *meaning* the ideas which we readily assimilate from the page. A symbol is a substitute form of meaning which can be picked up and removed from the external world and taken in to the brain, where it may be stored, interpreted, or combined with other symbols to produce an additional meaning.

The process is extraordinarily complex and our mastery of it places us in a sphere far removed from all other animals. For example, "Come here" may be heard by a child as its mother's voice and he knows it has the formal meaning of a summons. However, he combines this hearing with memories of other times when the phrase served the general function of a reminder that "Mother is attentive, so don't wander too far away." The child readily understands the conventional meaning, but he also realizes that now his mother does not intend to be issuing a summons. When she actually does want him to come to her, her voice will rise to a higher key and the phrase will be uttered with a forceful downward inflection that to the listening child will carry the additional message: "This time I really do want you to come."

Minds operate internally and in conjunction with one another by means of symbols; and the symbols are far more complex in their nature, and are susceptible to far more subtlety of interpretation, than is readily apparent.

One basic fact, then, about mind is that it is symbolization in action. Other vital questions are how *mind* relates to *body,* and how *intellect* relates to *emotions.*

"The problem of the relation between body and mind . . . has been named the central problem of all philosophy, fundamental alike in the theory of knowledge, in ethics, and in religion." So wrote James L. McIntyre, in "Body and Mind," an article in the *Encyclopedia of Religion and Ethics.* Human beings have puzzled for countless centuries over the relation between mind and body. Are the two separate? Are they different types of being? How are they related?

Leslie A. White, in *The Science of Culture,* suggests a plausible solution: "Mind is minding; it is the behaving, reacting, of a living organism as a whole, as a unit." This definition, if we accept it, will lead us far from the usual view of mind as it has traditionally been considered by philosophers and psychologists of the Western world. It is more akin to the ancient Oriental interpretation, which has become popularized in the West through Freudian psychiatry and through Existential philosophy.

We have confused ourselves about the true nature of mind, Professor White believes, by thinking of it as a noun, as a thing-in-itself. The difficulties largely disappear when we think of mind as a *verb,* as a process, as something happening rather than as something being.

Major advantages of this view are that it avoids the great difficulties of trying to separate "body" from "mind" and also "thinking" from "feeling." We know that many of our ills and also much of our enthusiasm, happiness, and energy are psycho-physical. When our bodies are genuinely healthy, our minds tend to be more exuberant, energetic, and effective. A feeling of general lassitude, and even specific bodily pain, appears to be largely "imaginary." Where should the line be drawn between body and mind? Perhaps the answer is that there is no line or barrier. It is simpler to conceive of mind as a form of *behavior* of the body.

Moreover, we cannot avoid awareness of the close relations between what we call "thoughts" and what we call "feelings." "I don't *know* it's so; but I *feel* it is," we may say, perhaps with the uncomfortable awareness that we are unable to explain or to justify logically why we distrust a proposal or like the particular way of doing something. On another occasion, we may ridicule a suggestion we hear from a friend on the ground that it is emotional, not logical. But we know very well that we ourself do not always act or think logically. We value logic (when it serves our purpose); but it is no secret that a great deal of our behavior is emotionally motivated. We all accept, in action if not in words, the observation which Woodrow Wilson wrote into his book, *The American College*: "We speak of this as an age in which mind is monarch, but I take it for granted that, if this is true, mind is one of those modern monarchs who reigns but does not govern. As a matter of fact, the world is governed in every generation by a great House of Commons made up of the passions; and we can only be careful to see to it that the handsome passions are in the majority." We accept Wilson's meaning; but we can solve our problems only when we reject his words. By "mind" he obviously meant "reason" and he also obviously thought of reason as being quite distinct and separate from the emotions. *Minding,* however, the internalized, symbolic behavior of human beings, is far from being narrowly logical or intellectual. It is surely a combination of reasoning and feeling, of logic and emotion.

The Oriental philosophers have never been in doubt on this point. Daisetz T. Suzuki, the famous Japanese interpreter of the Oriental mode of thinking, in his latest book, *The Essentials of Zen Buddhism,* offers some trenchant observations that help solve the difficulty. "Logic has so intimidated us," he wrote, "that we shrink and shiver whenever its name is mentioned." Nevertheless, "The intellect is peripheral and dichotomous"—which is to say, the logical faculty deals only with the surface of life and does that by slicing it up into segments or categories. "For all we can say of it," he believes, "the intellect is after all a spectator, and when it does some work it is as a hireling for better or for worse." Another Oriental, Jawaharlal Nehru, India's late Prime Minister, in his *Discovery of India,* pleads with us: "Let us not, therefore, rule out intuition."

Whether we turn for guidance to Western scientific methods or to the mysticism of the Orient, or to a combination of the two, whenever we seek to *test* the workings of our mind, we do so operationally. That is, we do not, finally, care very much whether a given mental process is logical or emotional, whether it is based on reason or on intuition. What we do care is whether it *works,* whether it corresponds to reality as we experience it, whether it serves as a dependable guide to helpful actions.

So long as we think of mind as *minding,* as a verb rather than as a noun, we are unconcerned with whether it is labelled as reason, or as feeling, or as a mingling of the two. Our interest, rather, is in finding out whether the symbolic internal "trying out" of a situation does or does not serve as a dependable guide for "acting out" that same situation externally.

The interpretation of mind which has thus far been presented can be summarized as follows: (1) the human mind is a unique phenomenon of nature; (2) it is a process of manipulating symbols; (3) it is a functioning of bodily processes; (4) it is a unitary operation which is neither "logical" nor "emotional," but a totality of response that includes muscular, glandular and neurological reactions; (5) it is the means by which we maintain contact with the world outside ourselves and internalize an interpretation of that world; and (6) it is a mode of "living" an idea or an experience within our bodies before (and often after) engaging in it as an overt activity.

Most of these conclusions differ in some degree from the ordinary or "common sense" view of the nature of mind. It follows that, if these conclusions are sound, we ought to be using our minds and reacting to the thinking of other people differently than we habitually do. How differently I will briefly consider in the following sections.

WHAT LANGUAGE DOES TO AND FOR US

If mind is a process of manipulating symbols, and language is by all means the most useful and meaningful of all our symbol systems, we shall learn a good deal about the nature of our minds and the ways in which we use them by inquiring into our use of language.

Attention needs to be directed not only to what we do with language but also to what it does to us. A mistake commonly made is to regard words as tools, which we use with more or less refinement to accomplish the communication of our thoughts. Much less understood is the fact that language is the primary channel through which culture, tradition, and the immediate environment operate dynamically to shape our individual minds. If language is a tool, it is a sort of universal Frankenstein, with a tremendous facility for dominating the individuals who are immersed in it. What language does to us is at least as important as what we do with it.

Susanne Langer has popularized the phrase, "symbolic transformation," to depict the link between our minds and the exterior world. All that lies outside our immediate consciousness must be *transformed* into symbols before it becomes possible for us to take it into our minds. Furthermore, everything that is present in our consciousness is also symbolic. If you place your hand on a hot stove, you know immediately through sensory experience the meaning of "hot" and "pain." But you have almost identical feelings if you place your hand upon an extremely cold object. Interpretation of the meaning of experiences requires the naming of them.

The process is something like digesting food before it can be assimilated into the bloodstream and used to nourish our bodily tissues. The meat and potatoes that lie upon our plate have little resemblance to the soluble particles of food that have been broken down chemically by the digestive acids. We can no more put a *chair* or an *act of courage* into our minds than we could put a potato or a slice of ham into our bloodstream. There has to be a positive *transformation* of the fact-item into a symbol which the mind is capable of receiving.

The analogy can fruitfully be extended. Any chemist can assure you that the food particles in the final processes of digestion are not co-equal to the potato. A great deal has been *added to* them, in the form of acids; a great deal has been *taken away* from them, in the form of roughage and wastes that are flushed on out of the system; and, finally, their structure, form, and *meaning* are all quite different from the potato.

One of the most important things to recognize about language is that these same three types of change also take place when any fact-item is transformed into a symbol fit for entry into the mind. A great deal of its meaning is *omitted*—for it is observed only from the point of view of the observer, and even then merely selectively, in terms of his present interest. Meanwhile, a great deal is *added,* in the form of memories, and present needs, and self-interested interpretations. Finally, the whole form and meaning are *changed,* as "chair" (in the exterior world a family heirloom, covered with faded brocade) becomes a symbol intellectually attached to some train of ideas and emotionally laved in whatever feelings the mind is entertaining about it.

Words are labels which name or identify fact-items; and they do this well enough so that we can use them to communicate with a generally approximate degree of mutual understanding—so long as the message is simple. When Henry says, "The candy is good," Susan understands that she may expect a rather pleasant taste-sensation from eating it. But under many circumstances words are inadequate as labels. Their labeling function breaks down whenever there is a language barrier (as from French to English, or from chemical formulae to layman's terms); or when there is an expertness barrier (as when a physician says "duodenal ulcer" and the patient understands "cancer"); or a discriminative barrier (as when a professor says "political privilege" and his students interpret "graft").

The label function also miscarries when the individual encounters words for which he has not had experiences (as in reading a book that is too "deep" or too "technical"); or when he encounters experiences for which he has not learned definitive words (as when an adolescent wrestles with half-understood feelings of resentment and rebellion against his parents' behavior, attitudes, and beliefs). Words progressively lose their labeling value as we apply them to fact-items which are broadly generalized or abstract (as when we seek a meeting of minds—or a clarification of our own—about "public opinion" or "mysticism").

Words are always inadequate as labels for a very simple additional reason: namely, the world of realities is infinite; whereas, all languages are finite. It would be impossible to have a word for every fact-item in the whole time-space universe. Hence, words at best have to serve as "approximate labels," one word serving to dominate a large array of similar but distinct concepts.

One enormously suggestive fact about language is that the 2,500 or so different languages now in use in the world vary greatly in size. The English and Chinese languages each include about 650,000 words. This is more than twice the size of the French, German, Italian, Spanish, Russian, or Portuguese languages. The Australian aborigines had a language of only about 350 words. Some American Indian languages had total vocabularies of only about 2,000 words. Yet cultural anthropologists believe that every language is adequate to serve the needs of its users.

Obviously, the larger a language is, the larger the number of topics its users can think and discourse about, and the more refined and discriminative their thoughts can be. If limited languages are adequate to serve their users' needs, it can only be because those peoples have developed only a narrow range of needs. If their experience is limited to a narrow environment, narrowly conceived, they need few words with which to think and communicate about it. This is true for nations; and it is true also for individuals. Indeed, one of the leading intelligence testers, Professor David Wechsler, insists that "the size of a man's vocabulary is not only an index of his schooling, but also an excellent measure of his general intelligence. Its excellence as a test of intelligence is seemingly derived from the fact that the number of words a man knows is at once a measure of his learning ability, his fund of verbal information and of the general range of ideas."

The labelling function of words, however, is only a part of their service and of their influence. What language does to us and what we can do with it extends far beyond the simple process of identifying objects by naming them.

Words are also *incitements;* they are stimulants. Words are used much as a red flag is used to arouse the anger of bulls or as bait is used to attract fish. In the heat of a presidential campaign, the words "Democrat" and "Republican" are used less as labels than as inducements to loyalty or to enhance antagonism. "I love you" is not only a label for an emotion but also an invitation to reciprocity. "Communist" and "Nazi" are words used to arouse dislike; "patriotism" and "duty" are used to stir up loyal devotion. Much of our use of words is aimed less to define meanings than to create or magnify attitudes. And attitudes are not attributes of fact-items as they exist in the exterior world but are personal preferences. They assume forms and serve functions determined by the mind rather than prescribed by the fact-items to which they refer.

Words also have a *fixative* function. They seize upon transitory items in the flux of experience and give permanency to them. Often we have a vague feeling about an individual or an event which would soon pass and be forgotten *unless we give it a name.* When we do this, the label, sticks in our mind and becomes a lasting element in our thinking about the person or the occasion. Social experimenters have found that feelings which have not been publicly stated are readily changed; but when the *feeling* has been put into words and heard or read by others, it assumes the status of an *opinion* which is to be defended. Both in solitary thinking and in communicating, we give fixity to a sensation by labelling it.

Another way in which this fixative function operates is that a person often does not know what he himself thinks or feels about a subject until he speaks or writes about it. When he sees or hears his own words, he knows for the first time what was previously but half-formulated in his own semi-consciousness. On the whole, we tend to be what Dr. Wendell Johnson has termed "our own most enchanted listeners." No one else is as attentive as we are to our own utterances. We are the most susceptible recipients of our own persuasion. We create our own version of the world by expressing it.

CONCLUSION

As we sum up what we have said about the nature of mind, it will be useful to remind ourselves of the cardinal contribution of one of the greatest of European philosophers, Rene Descartes. He was much concerned, as we are, to understand *what is,* and what we can do about it. He concluded that he heard what was not rightly there to hear; he saw things differently than they really are; and so with the senses of taste, touch, and smell. But he finally concluded that his very doubt must mean that at least there was a doubter. Hence, he formulated his famous aphorism: "I think (doubt); therefore, I am." Man exists, and so, for him, there also exists the world as he perceives it. The final resting place for certainty, in Descartes' philosophy, was the unquestionable existence of mind. All Western philosophy since then has combatted scepticism, or utter doubt, on this basis.

The view of mind which I have presented, however, is far from Cartesian. I have described mind as a type of behavior of the whole body: a minding, a manipulation of symbols, whereby reality may be internalized. In this view there is no priority given to "reason," for it is evident that the logical capacity blends with the other bodily reaction possibilities. All the perceiving, interpreting, and creating abilities of the human organism are treated in this chapter as a form of "minding" or as behaving in a manner that brings the human being into his own kind of relation with the exterior world. There is, in this concept, no conflict between emotionalism and rationality; no need for shame because some things are "felt" while others are "known." The important consideration is less *how* than *whether* the individual manages to achieve a symbolic transformation which, when tested operationally, or through experience, proves to be sound.

If a label is required for this mode of explanation of mind, it may be called Oriental rather than Western. For it is Zen Buddhism, a synthesis of Taoism and Buddhism, that most clearly makes the point that analytical reason *by itself* is like a dissecting table, on which reality is cut into pieces, but by means of which it cannot be understood in its intrinsic nature. On the contrary, as Lin Yutang says, the Oriental way is "to size up things at a glance and thus preserve a better sense of their totality." As Suzuki phrases the same idea, Zen teaches "that there is a certain transcendental statement that cannot be attained by mere intellectual cleverness." None of this is in any way a denial of the value of reason when reason is treated as an appropriate component of a wholeness of apprehension. All we wish to say is that *minding* is a process of coming to terms with reality by all available means: muscular, emotional, and intellectual.

The function of language in the operations of minding have been shown to be central, for better *and* for worse. Once again, Suzuki has phrased the essential point so well that we borrow his words: "Without language we cannot live even for a day, but at the same time language is a curse to human life. Just because we have given a name to something, we think the name is the thing itself and forget that it is a mere sign, devised for the sake of convenience. . . . Language is like a map. . . . But the real earth is the one we tread upon."

Language enables us, symbolically, to take the world outside into our own consciousness, as we could not otherwise do. But in the process of symbolic transformation, many changes occur. The world within which we live is our own symbol universe—demonstrably not the true universe, but the nearest we get to it. As we strive to eliminate or control the various diseases of language, and as we keep in mind that language not only labels fact-items but also serves to incite feelings and to fix impressions, we should be able to think and to communicate more in accord with reality and in better consonance with one another. The sharper our command of language is, and the better we understand its nature, its values, and its limitations, the better we can find our way more comfortably about in this world.

Without language, we should be like the beasts of the field; with language we transcend them in many ways, and in other ways we suffer as they do not. It is through language that, in Milton's words, "We make a Hell of Heav'n, a Heaven of Hell." Through improving our use of words, we can improve our minds and thereby enhance the value of our lives. It is a goal worthy of our quest.

Unit Fourteen | DISCUSSION QUESTIONS

59. *Psychology and the Space Frontier*
Discuss three human problems encountered in space flight.
Name two methods of investigation psychologists have used in solving these problems.

60. *The Impact of TV Advertisement: Learning Without Involvement*
Does television advertising produce significant sales by "changing attitudes"?
Select your favorite TV advertisement and discuss the reasons for its appeal.

61. *Mind and Language*
How does the author define "mind"?
What is the relationship between mind and empathy? Between mind and intuition?

COLOR ILLUSTRATIONS ON BACK COVER: *Progress of a Disease* . . . A famous series of paintings by Louis Wain, a London illustrator who succumbed to schizophrenia in middle age, reflects the artist's mental deterioration. At first realistic, the cats become progressively stylized and fragmented. Wain died in 1939.